Nonfinancial Defined Contribution Pension Schemes in a Changing Pension World

Nonfinancial Defined Contribution Pension Schemes in a Changing Pension World

VOLUME 1
PROGRESS, LESSONS, AND IMPLEMENTATION

Robert Holzmann, Edward Palmer,
and David Robalino, editors

THE WORLD BANK
Washington, D.C.

Contents

Figures

Tables

Foreword

It takes time to discern the impact of reforms, especially those of a pioneering nature. Sweden was one of a handful of countries that developed and implemented a nonfinancial defined contribution (NDC) public pension scheme in the 1990s along with Italy, Latvia, and Poland.

One fundamental principle of our pension reform in Sweden was to honor the long-term commitment to Swedish pensioners and savers that the pension promise entails. With this in mind, we believed that small or gradual reforms would risk exacerbating the weaknesses of the system that was in place at the time. Sweden therefore launched on a political journey entailing a significant systemic change to the pension system and the launching of a NDC scheme. The philosophy underpinning the reform was that the system should be financially stable in a changing demographic and economic climate and should, at the same time, create fairness between generations and income groups by diversifying economic, financial, and demographic risks.

Does this sound like a tall order? Yes, it was. But the systemic shift to a NDC system allowed us to embed these philosophies into the design of the Swedish pension system. We have a public, universal, and compulsory system that is based on the fundamental principles of socioeconomic fairness. A system where pensions are based on life-time earnings and correspond to the contributions paid into the system. The direct link between contributions and pensions has also created incentives to work, which are augmented by the actuarial structure of the system, which has an annuity divisor based on remaining life expectancy at retirement. These features have, in hindsight, also been designed so as to create a structural gender balance, even if there is still a lot left to do to equalize the actual pension outcomes of men and women. The Swedish NDC system also allows for increased transparency, especially into the finances of the system. We have seen that this type of system puts greater decision-making demands on beneficiaries. As a consequence of this, policy makers and pension providers have a responsibility to provide understandable and comprehensive information to the public if the incentives and structures of the system are to work adequately.

Pension reforms are once again being triggered by the strained economic situation around the world. The economic crisis has highlighted weaknesses in pension systems across Europe and reform has heavily influenced pension policy making over the past five years. Initially, the reforms in the wake of the crisis have been more reactionary and usually a part of government budget consolidation or stimulus packages. We now see a trend toward more structural reforms in order to ensure the long-term adequacy of pensions despite economic and demographic pressures.

Some other countries, such as Norway and Egypt, have chosen to implement NDC systems. The Swedish pension reform was implemented in 1999 and has, on the whole, been able to weather the stormy economic climate during the past 15 years. We do, however, recognize the need to review our pension reform in order to ensure that the structural shift we made is having the desired effects given changing labor market behavior and conditions, especially for women.

For this reason, the Swedish government was happy to co-fund a conference in Stockholm in 2009 jointly organized by the World Bank and the Swedish Social Insurance Agency. This meeting brought together a constellation of international experts who have examined the pros and cons of the designs of different NDC systems. We have been able to draw policy lessons from other nations and revisit the founding ideas around our reforms and establish areas for further improvement. Those of us unable to attend the conference can still partake of the knowledge that was gathered then and is documented in this publication.

I would like to thank participating officials and experts from around the world for sharing their experiences and knowledge on this important subject as well as our colleagues at the World Bank and the Swedish Social Insurance Agency for their efforts in realizing a successful conference and this subsequent publication. I believe that due to these efforts we now have a good ground to review our reforms and pave the way for other countries interested in introducing NDC characteristics within their own pension policies.

Ulf Kristersson
Minister for Social Security
Stockholm, Sweden

Preface

Pensions and social insurance programs are an integral part of any social protection system. Their dual objectives are to prevent a sharp decline in income and protect against poverty resulting from old age, disability, or death. The critical role of pensions for protection, prevention, and promotion was reiterated and expanded in the new World Bank 2012–2022 Social Protection Strategy. This new strategy reviews the success and challenges of the past decade or more, during which time the World Bank became a main player in the area of pensions. But more importantly, the strategy takes the three key objectives for pensions under the World Bank's conceptual framework—coverage, adequacy, and sustainability—and asks how these objectives and the inevitable difficult balance between them can best be achieved. The ongoing focus on closing the coverage gap with social pensions and the new outreach to explore the role of matching contributions to address coverage and/or adequacy is part of this strategy.

This comprehensive anthology on nonfinancial defined contribution (NDC) pension schemes is part and parcel of the effort to explore and document the working of this new system or reform option and its ability to balance these three key objectives. This innovative, unfunded individual accounts scheme provides a promising option at a time when the world seems locked into a stalemate between piecemeal reform of ailing traditional defined benefit plans or their replacement with prefunded financial account schemes. The current financial crisis, with its focus on sovereign debt, has enhanced the attraction of NDC as a pension scheme that aims for intra- and intergenerational fairness, offers a transparent framework to distribute economic and demographic risks, and, if well designed, promises long-term financial stability. Supplemented with a basic minimum pension guarantee, explicit noncontributory rights, and a funded pillar, the NDC approach provides an efficient framework for addressing poverty and risk diversification concerns.

This anthology is the product of a joint venture between the World Bank and the Swedish Social Insurance Agency, emanating from a conference on nonfinancial (notional) defined pension schemes held in Stockholm in 2009. This was the second conference and publication sponsored jointly by Sweden and the World Bank. We are thankful to the Swedish government for their financial and intellectual support and proud about the outcome as it shows development cooperation as its best: analyzing the working of a policy innovation in developed economies, investigating the conceptual and design challenges still to be resolved, and exploring the application of the approach for developing countries.

Tamar Manuelyan Atinc   Arup Banerji   Robert Palacios
Vice President   Sector Director   Team Leader
Human Development Network   Social Protection and Labor   Pensions

The World Bank
Washington, DC

Acknowledgments

The joint Swedish Social Insurance Agency–World Bank Conference on "Non-Financial Defined Contribution (NDC) Pension Systems: Progress and New Frontiers in a Changing Pension World" (Stockholm, December 2–4, 2009) and the resulting two-volume anthology is the work of many people and institutions. Starting with the latter, we would like to express our immense gratitude to the Swedish government, specifically the Swedish Ministry for Social Security, not only for their financial support of both the conference and the publication but also for the encouragement to have a special look at the gender dimension of NDC. All this has proven critical to make the event and anthology possible and stimulating. The World Bank has offered us a great convening venue and intellectual playground to toss and turn ideas and receive feedback and guidance from many colleagues across all sectors. It enabled us to stay busy during evenings, weekends, and holidays.

The 24 chapters plus comments were only possible through the commitment and patience of 58 engaged experts throughout the world and whom we kept busy for some 3 years since the inception of the project. We convinced and pestered, motivated and cajoled—as needed, and they were willing to endure this with only the nonmonetary compensation of being part of a fascinating project. As the chapters and comments reveal, not all the contributors are hard core *aficionados* of NDCs. On the contrary, we all tried to keep a critical distance; the reader will have to be the judge of our success. But it seems safe to say that all the contributors are fascinated by the NDC approach and its potential and wanted to contribute to exploring its strengths and weaknesses. We are deeply indebted to them for their time, effort, and engagement.

Last but not least, ideas need to be managed, transformed, and appropriately formatted before presented to the reader. We are very fortunate to have the superb support from the World Bank's Office of the Publisher, with Paola Scalabrin as acquisitions editor and Mark Ingebretsen as production editor. Their commitment and professionalism was simply outstanding. We have also been blessed with two great copy editors who have been critical and have contributed greatly toward putting the ideas and writing into proper and intelligible English: Nancy Levine and Linda Stringer. We are deeply thankful for their caring, professional touch. Of course, without strong administrative support, none of this effort would have been possible, and for this we would like to express our gratitude to Shams ur Rehman and Amira Nikolas (Washington, DC) and Paula Abboud and Kerstin Carlsson (Stockholm).

Robert Holzman, Edward Palmer, and David Robalino, editors

Abbreviations

ACFTU	All-China Federation of Trade Unions
AFP	collectively agreed early retirement scheme (Norway)
AFP	administrator of pension funds (administradora de fondos de pensiones) (Chile)
ARMA	autoregressive moving average
CEPAL	Comisión Económica para América Latina y el Caribe
CPI	consumer price index
DB	defined benefit
DC	defined contribution
DSI	disability and survivorship insurance
EC	European Commission
ECB	European Central Bank
ECLAC	Economic Commission for Latin America and the Caribbean
EGAD	Egyptian Government Actuarial Department
EMU	European Monetary Union
EU	European Union
FDC	financial defined contribution
GARCH	generalized autoregressive conditional heteroskedasticity
GDP	gross domestic product
GSIF	Government Social Insurance Fund (Egypt, Arab Rep.)
HPA	affiliates' pension histories (historias previsionales administrativas) (Chile)
IKA	Social Insurance Organization (Greece)
IMF	International Monetary Fund
INE	National Statistical Agency (Instituto Nacional de Estadísticas) (Chile)
INP	Instituto de Normalización Previsional (Chile)
INPS	National Social Security Institute (Italy)
IT	information technology
MDC	matching defined contribution
MHRSS	Ministry of Human Resources and Social Security (China)
MPG	minimum pension guarantee
NDB	nonfinancial defined benefit
NDC	nonfinancial (notional) defined contribution

NIB	National Investment Bank (Egypt, Arab Rep.)
NOSI	National Organization for Social Insurance (Egypt, Arab Rep.)
OECD	Organisation for Economic Co-operation and Development
PASIS	assistance pensions (pensiones asistenciales) (Chile)
PAYG	pay as you go
PSIF	Public and Private Social Insurance Fund (Egypt, Arab Rep.)
PSS&UT	public service sector and public undertakings (China)
SAR	special administrative region
SP	Pensions Supervisor (Superintendencia de Pensiones) (Chile)
SSIA	Swedish Social Insurance Agency
ZUS	Social Insurance Institution (Poland)

PART I

Taking Stock of Lessons and Issues

CHAPTER 1

NDC in the Teens: Lessons and Issues

Robert Holzmann and Edward Palmer

In this introductory chapter, we set forth the motivations and background for this two-volume collection of studies on nonfinancial (notional) defined (NDC) contribution schemes. We survey the brief history of countries' experience with the adoption of NDC models, summarize the contents of the two volumes, and offer policy conclusions and suggestions for a policy research agenda. The principal conclusions are as follows:

- NDC schemes work well, as shown by the experiences of Italy, Latvia, Poland, and Sweden, but there is room to make them work even better.
- Go for an immediate transition, to avoid future problems.
- Identify and finance the transition costs in an explicit manner as they emerge—you will have to face them sooner or later.
- Adopt an explicit stabilizing mechanism to guarantee solvency.
- Establish a reserve fund to guarantee liquidity.
- Develop an explicit mechanism for sharing systemic longevity risk.
- Identify, analyze, and address the gender implications of NDC schemes.

The suggested priority policy research agenda focuses on four tasks:

- Assessing the outcomes of NDC schemes in view of the primary goals of pension systems and in comparison with alternative scheme designs
- Developing better measurements of pension assets and liabilities to guide the introduction, adjustment, and sustainability of NDC schemes
- Clarifying the interaction of NDC (as a central consumption-smoothing pillar) with other pillars and benefits
- Addressing the design and implementation issues of NDC schemes in low- and middle-income countries

NDC schemes are now in their teens. The concept was born in the early 1990s and has been put into practice in a number of countries, beginning in the mid-1990s. To date,

Robert Holzmann is professor of economics and director of the RH Institute for Economic Policy Analysis, Vienna, and holds the Old Age Financial Protection Chair at the University of Malaya, Kuala Lumpur. He also serves as a senior adviser (consultant) to the World Bank. Edward Palmer is professor emeritus of social insurance economics at Uppsala University, research fellow at the Uppsala Center for Labor Studies, and senior advisor at the Swedish Social Insurance Agency.

the most complete implementation has been in Italy, Latvia, Poland, and Sweden, but key components of NDC schemes have recently been introduced elsewhere. This innovative unfunded individual account approach aroused high hopes at a time when the world seemed to be locked in a stalemate between piecemeal reforms of ailing traditional defined benefit systems and the introduction of prefunded financial account schemes.

We reviewed the childhood of NDC in an earlier anthology (Holzmann and Palmer 2006). Six years later, the time has come to examine the lessons of NDC in its adolescence and to take stock of the issues that need to be addressed to ensure a successful adulthood.

The first book was the product of a conference, held on the island of Sandhamn outside Stockholm in September 2003, that was designed to inform a worldwide audience about the innovative NDC pension scheme model. The aim of the conference was to scrutinize this new idea, and the ensuing volume documented the content of that conversation among leading experts in the field.

The present collection emerged from a second NDC conference, held in Stockholm in December 2009 under the sponsorship of the World Bank and the Swedish Social Insurance Agency. The aims of the second conference, and of this anthology, are to offer a deeper and more comprehensive review of the experience of countries where NDC schemes have been in place for a decade or more; to take stock of the recent discussions of the place of NDCs in the world of pension reform; and to address in detail important issues related to design and implementation to which the first anthology gave little or no attention.

The importance of solvent pension systems was highlighted during the financial crisis of 2008–09 and the ensuing economic recession in much of the world. The fiscal dilemma of Greece, Portugal, Spain, some Eastern and Central European countries, and, potentially, other highly indebted countries has demonstrated the adverse repercussions that financially unsustainable pension systems can have. What we are now seeing is the market's judgment on the creditworthiness of sovereign states, in cases where a large percentage of future commitments is the pension debt. Financial markets are likely to react increasingly to uncertainty about pension liabilities and to the resultant question of solvency. Public finance consolidation is unlikely to succeed without pension reform, particularly in those developed economies in which population aging is most advanced and the survival rates of the retired population are rising rapidly.

Developed countries are not alone in this picture. There are also fiscal concerns in middle- and low-income countries for which United Nations demographic projections for the coming half century show considerable population aging. Many of these countries, despite their short pension histories, are already burdened by financially unsustainable pension systems. Others need to learn from the now considerable international experience in building national pension systems.

A further challenge in middle- and low-income countries is the fragmentation and low coverage of current pension systems. In addition, badly designed defined benefit (DB) schemes often operate in parallel, and weak provisions for the portability of benefits affect labor mobility and can create inequalities. On average, less than 30 percent of the workforce in middle- and low-income countries is covered by mandatory pensions, but it is proving difficult to increase coverage under the pension regimes currently in place. Even where coverage is relatively high and is expanding, there may be no hope for long-term fiscal sustainability without systemic change.

It is against this background that an NDC reform becomes attractive, even in low- and middle-income countries. It brings to the table a pension scheme with fully transparent liabilities and a built-in approach toward ensuring solvency and financial sustainability. NDC is neutral vis-à-vis individual labor supply decisions and has exactly the same potential to promote formality as financial (or prefunded) defined contribution (FDC) schemes, in contrast to typical DB pay-as-you-go (PAYG) plans (NDB). In addition, the design of NDC opens the door to integration or at least harmonization of parallel schemes and facilitates the portability of benefits. NDCs can also become a building block for designing alternative arrangements to expand pension coverage to workers in the informal sector.

Another reason that countries are taking an even closer look at NDC is that confidence in what many economists had considered the preferred alternative for a national pension scheme, FDC, has been shaken by the repeated and severe financial crises of the first decade of the 21st century. After this past decade of financial crises, FDC may now be less attractive for many. In addition, quite a few experts now expect the financial market to deliver lower rates of return in the future as populations age and move into the dissaving stage of their life cycles, with continued extreme fluctuations associated with phenomena other than economic fundamentals.

On top of this, fiscal capacity and willingness to pay for the transition costs for prefunding schemes are likely to be reduced in view of a higher explicit public debt in many countries. Downplaying transition costs and ignoring the fiscal impacts of large economic shocks has proved deadly for reformed pension systems in a number of countries in Latin America and Central and Eastern Europe. Against these constraints, an NDC reform offers an attractive alternative for emerging economies. Even where the ultimate goal is to have a fully funded pension system, NDCs can prepare the ground by establishing an individual account system that is solvent but is only partially funded by financial assets. As enabling conditions improve, the level of funding of the system can increase.

The purpose of the 2003 NDC conference and the subsequent 2006 book was to bring to the world's attention a new and promising approach toward reform of traditional and nonfinancial (or "unfunded") defined benefit (NDB) schemes. The participants' contributions described and discussed the microeconomic and macroeconomic foundations of the NDC concept, the approaches used by the initial reformers in moving from NDB to NDC, the early lessons from the experience, and the principal remaining issues, as then perceived. The publication had a significant impact, as witnessed by the inroads of its findings and messages into the deliberations of pension reform commissions around the globe, the adoption of NDC in some countries, and the translation of the volume into Chinese, German, and Spanish.

This 2012 publication is in two volumes, owing to the number of contributions and our unwillingness to omit any of the presentations. Volume 1, "Progress, Lessons, and Implementation," includes a detailed analysis of experience and lessons in four pilot countries, Italy, Latvia, Poland, and Sweden; a discussion of new pilots in the Arab Republic of Egypt and in Norway that follow the NDC approach; and general thoughts concerning the implementation of NDCs in other countries, including Chile (retrospectively), China, and Greece. One chapter discusses whether certain NDC features can be emulated in the context of NDB scheme reforms, as illustrated by experience in several member countries of the Organisation for Economic Co-operation and Development (OECD). Volume 2, "Gender, Politics, and Financial Stability," includes new and deeper analyses of issues that received little or no attention in the 2006 publication. The gender perspective is the focus of five chapters that contain perhaps the most complete discussion available in the field to date. Issues related to financial stability are addressed in six chapters covering critical micro-economic and macroeconomic aspects of NDC, such as the balancing mechanism and the possible role of an NDC bond, the use of a reserve fund, the handling of legacy costs, and technicalities related to the management of longevity risk when designing annuities.

Although the two volumes address numerous issues, and in considerable depth, new questions nevertheless arise for which good answers are still not readily available. We return to these in the closing sections of this chapter.

The next section surveys the structure of the twin volumes and their 24 chapters. Subsequently, key policy lessons are identified, a future research agenda is outlined, and conclusions are drawn.

Overview of the Contributions

The contents of this collection are grouped under six headings. In volume 1, part I takes stock of country lessons and issues, and part II presents reforms that are being implemented or considered. Part I in volume 2 addresses the gender dimension of pension reforms that incorporate NDC schemes; part II discusses issues of political economy; part III investigates issues related to the solvency, liquidity, and stability of NDCs; and part IV contains reflections on four additional topics by a panel of researchers and practitioners.

VOLUME 1, PART I: TAKING STOCK OF LESSONS AND ISSUES

Chapter 1. "NDC in the Teens: Lessons and Issues" states the objectives of the anthology, introduces the issues treated in the two volumes, and outlines general conclusions and recommendations.

Chapter 2. In "The First Wave of NDC Reforms: The Experiences of Italy, Latvia, Poland, and Sweden," Agnieszka Chłoń-Domińczak, Daniele Franco, and Edward Palmer offer a comprehensive overview and assessment of NDC schemes in four early adopters of NDC schemes. The authors describe and analyze the various paths to reform, the design of the reforms, the course of implementation, and the outcomes. Italy, Latvia, and Poland immediately had to deal with the questions of how to "cash in" legacy benefits and privi-leges and how to increase the pension age, especially for women. Sweden avoided these particular problems: its existing public pension system was already truly universal, and the normal pension age at the time of the reform was already 65 for both men and women. In all four countries, a full career worker with average earnings can expect a gross earnings replacement rate of about 65 percent.

All four countries lack rules for redistributing rights between partners in a couple. That shortcoming and others, such as early retirement for women and insufficient credit for time out of the formal labor force in conjunction with childbirth, increase the likeli-hood of relative poverty among women who survive their partners in old age.

The sine qua non of NDC is the maintenance of financial stability, which is, in principle, ensured by the design of the scheme. The study examines the responses of Italy and Sweden to a permanent decline in labor productivity, higher life expectancies for retirees, and a permanent decrease in the size of the youngest cohort. Sweden's balancing mechanism safeguards financial stability, albeit sometimes with a lag, whereas the Italian design does not provide an automatic gyroscope to steer the system toward financial stability following a negative economic or demographic shock. The study shows that negative shocks lead to deficits over long periods of time. Because pensions in payment are only price-indexed in Latvia and Poland, the schemes will be in surplus in periods with positive real wage-sum growth (even without a reserve fund) and will run a deficit in periods when nominal wage-sum growth falls below the rate of inflation.

In 2011, Italy responded to the emergence of increasingly higher market rates on sovereign borrowing by accelerating the transition toward the NDC regime through tightening seniority rules for all workers and creating NDC accounts for all contributors as of 2012. In addition, the statutory pension age will be raised to 66 for all workers from 2012 (2018 for women in the private sector), and from 2013 onward the statutory pension age (as well as the minimum number of contribution years required for seniority pensions) will be automatically indexed to increases in life expectancy. While Italy (like Poland and Latvia) is still missing an explicit mechanism to deal with surpluses and deficits, the accelerated NDC transition puts it in line with other pilot countries, and the indexing of pension age is a unique feature.

A final observation is that the economic crisis of 2008–10 stimulated public debate in Latvia, Poland, and Sweden but that NDC survived this wave of public scrutiny a decade or more after implementation.

Chapter 3. Edward Whitehouse, in "Parallel Lines: NDC Pensions and the Direction of Pension Reform in Developed Countries," investigates the extent to which recent reforms in OECD countries have incorporated important elements of NDC system design. To this end, the author compares notional accounts with two alternative designs for public, earnings-related pension schemes: points systems and defined benefit plans. He examines in detail four economic advantages of notional accounts that enable them to deliver retirement incomes in an equitable and economically efficient manner:

- Benefits are based on lifetime average earnings, rather than on a subset of "best" or "final" years of pay.
- An extra year's contribution brings about an increase in the replacement rate.
- Benefits are reduced to reflect the longer expected duration of payment for people who retire early and are increased for people who delay retirement.
- Benefits are reduced as life expectancy increases, again to reflect the longer duration for which benefits would be paid.

Whitehouse concludes that during recent years, many OECD countries have achieved many of the objectives innate to NDC schemes without explicitly adopting notional accounts. Not everybody will share this assessment.

Yet the clear message of this chapter is that the rules governing pension entitlements for the calculation of defined benefits in OECD countries are slowly but surely converging with the basic NDC structure. This is one part of the NDC picture. The other part of the picture—not surveyed in this chapter—is the use of indexation as a stabilizing mechanism to steer the scheme toward a fixed contribution rate and the specification of transparent rules for introducing and financing desirable distributional features and for maintaining long-term financial solvency.

VOLUME 1, PART II: REFORMS LEGISLATED OR PROPOSED

Following the implementation of NDC reforms in a few European countries, the approach has been touted for replication elsewhere. Part II offers studies of two recently legislated NDC reforms, in Egypt and Norway, and of proposals for NDC-type reforms in China and Greece. China is the subject of two papers, in view of the country's interest in NDC models and the prominent place of the NDC approach in independent country advice (see, e.g., Barr and Diamond 2008). The chapter on Chile draws on historical data on contribution densities, wages, and rates of return on investment to examine how that country would have fared if, back in 1981, it had implemented an NDC scheme instead of an FDC reform.

Chapter 4. "Pension Reform in Norway: Combining an NDC Approach and Distributional Goals," by Arne Magnus Christensen, Dennis Fredriksen, Ole Christian Lien, and Nils Martin Stølen, surveys the recent Norwegian pension reform and its most important elements. The reform incorporates many but not all of the components of a complete NDC scheme. The main elements of the reform are as follows:

- Accumulation of entitlements based on an imputed contribution rate on lifetime earnings that are the basis of individual accounts
- Contribution credits for periods of child care, unemployment, sickness, and military conscription
- A means-tested guaranteed pension as a basic safety net, and a ceiling on annual earnings for the accrual of pension entitlements
- Flexible retirement from age 62 to age 75, from 2011 on, and benefits that are based on account values at retirement, cohort life expectancy at retirement, and a front-loading factor of 0.75 percent
- Indexation of workers' accounts and pensioners' benefits by average wage growth

New retirees born between 1954 and 1962 will receive benefits based on a combination of their benefit according to the old and new rules, with an increasing share of pension entitlements from the new scheme for successively younger cohorts. The entire benefit is based on the new rules for people born in 1963 and later. The new indexation formula for pensions has nevertheless been implemented already in 2011. From 2011, all pensions in payment are indexed by average wage growth minus the 0.75 percent, which is the frontloading factor in the new NDC lookalike Norwegian formula for defining entitlements and for calculating the annuity. Frontloading shifts a portion of future wage growth into the initial annuity value, a feature also found in the Italian and Swedish NDC schemes.

Compared with the prereform system, the new model for accumulating pension entitlements tightens the link between individuals' labor income and their pension benefits and thereby improves incentives to work. These incentives, however, are modified by redistributive elements such as the means-tested guaranteed pension, credit for unpaid child care, and the ceiling on annual earnings. More important for labor supply and sustainability is the incentive that benefits based on account values and cohort life expectancy give for individuals to postpone retirement, counteracting the effect of higher life expectancy on pension expenditures. The authors estimate replacement rates for typical cases, using a microsimulation model to compare the old and reformed pension systems, and document the sustainability and distributional effects of the reform.

Norway's NDC look-alike pension system remains in the general government budget; there is no attempt to make the scheme autonomous from the budget, as in Sweden. Although increasing life expectancy is counteracted in the formulation of the annuity, there is no balancing mechanism to deal with unexpected demographic events—notably, a declining labor force, but also underestimated life expectancy projections. If such events occur, the financial deficit created will be absorbed in the general government finances. It is then up to politicians to decide how taxes and government expenditures should be adjusted to balance overall public finances in the long run. Thus, in the Norwegian model the general budget covers the demographic labor force risks. Because of the present low number of old-age pensioners compared with the size of the labor force, the actual contribution rate needed to cover payments is currently much lower than the rate of 18.1 percent that creates NDC pension entitlements. Larger cohorts of pensioners will necessitate an increase in the required contribution rate, which is estimated to stabilize around 2040 at a rate consistent with that for NDC account entitlements.

Chapter 5. In "Egypt's New Social Insurance System: An NDC Reform in an Emerging Economy," Mohamed Maait and Gustavo Demarco outline the genesis and structure of the NDC reform, legislated in June 2010, that was scheduled for implementation prior to the Arab Spring of 2011. The implementation date has now been postponed to July 2013. The reform has been driven by projections of chronically increasing financial deficits. The aim of the reform is to create a pension scheme that addresses problems of financial sustainability in response to future demographic trends, makes redistribution explicit and better targeted to respond to current social demands, improves incentives to contribute, and provides complete and affordable guaranteed income coverage for the entire population age 65 and older.

The scope of the new system will gradually become universal, reaching populations not previously covered, such as casual and seasonal workers, farmers, unskilled and skilled workers in the construction industry, and many others. The new system also eliminates the special privileges accorded to certain groups, treating all plan members equally. The core of the reform is a mandatory transition from an unfunded (DB) system to a combined NDC and FDC system for new entrants and for persons with no previous coverage record, and a voluntary shift for persons with a previous contribution history at the time of the introduction of these schemes. The overall contribution rate for the NDC and FDC schemes will be 19.5 percent. Reform plans call for 20 to 40 percent of total contributions to be directed to the FDC component, which will be centrally managed with outsourcing of portfolio management. In addition to the combined NDC–FDC contribution-based schemes, there will be a universal basic pension, to be financed by the Egyptian Treasury, that will amount to 18 percent of the after-tax national average wage. The general design of the NDC component has been completed, but implementation and institutional capacity building will demand increasing efforts in the near future.

Chapter 6. "China: An Innovative Hybrid Pension Design Proposal," by Zheng Bingwen, presents ideas for a comprehensive pension reform in China that has at its core an NDC–FDC approach. The author proposes the merger of the current flat-rate pension ("social pooling") and the individual accounts—introduced as funded pensions in 1997 but only implemented in a few provinces—into a single individual account that is split between notional and full prefunding. Zheng illustrates with model calculations the financial sustainability of the proposal, for different total contribution rates and funding splits. According to the author, this policy proposal takes account of the specific Chinese institutional and cultural context, and it represents an innovation in pension design, differing both from the Swedish NDC model and from the present pension system, which lacks a direct link between contributions and benefits. Zheng asserts that the reform will address the main challenges of the current system: it will (a) enable the unification of fragmented programs at the county level, which will improve redistribution, the portability of benefits, and labor mobility; (b) increase the level of funding for the current system; (c) address the problem of financial sustainability; (d) improve transparency and the incentives that individuals have to enroll and contribute; and (e) create the conditions for expanding the coverage of pensions to the entire labor force.

Chapter 7. In "China: Pension Reform for an Aging Economy," Heikki Oksanen analyzes options for reforming the fragmented Chinese pension system, which covers only 55 percent of urban employees and only a few percent of the rural population, and argues for an NDC-type reform. After briefly outlining the history of pension provision in China, Oksanen discusses principles of pension reform and examines recent reform proposals, giving particular attention to the need to reduce contribution rates with a view toward improving compliance and increasing coverage. The Chinese population is aging rapidly, and Oksanen argues that a transition to an NDC system is an efficient way to introduce pension rules that ensure financial sustainability in a context of increasing longevity.

Oksanen notes that a move toward transforming accrued pension rights into NDC accounts and applying the new NDC-inspired rules on indexation is not necessarily a jump into the unknown for the Chinese pension system; rather, it could be a useful and long-awaited clarification of present rules and a means of progressing toward a more uniform system nationwide. With the help of a simulation model using Chinese data, Oksanen produces scenarios for a range of possible reform designs and assesses their social and fiscal impacts. To address incentive and coverage issues, the scenarios for introducing an NDC scheme assume contribution rates of 20 and 16 percent, rather than the high current rate of about 28 percent. In the simulated three-tier scheme (flat-rate, NDC, and funded pensions), average replacement rates for the 20 and 16 percent contribution levels would be only 40 and 30 percent, respectively. This is the consequence of accelerated population aging during the next decade, which leaves as options only a more rapid increase in the retirement age (beyond the already assumed age 64 for women and age 67 for men) or a much higher contribution rate.

Chapter 8. "Greece: The NDC Paradigm as a Framework for a Sustainable Pension System," by Milton Nektarios, presents a vision of an NDC-type pension reform against the background of the country's current financial and economic crisis and the ad hoc pension reform implemented in the summer of 2010. Prior to 2010, Greece was one of the few countries in the European Union (EU) that had not undertaken a full and effective reform of its pension system. The pre-2010 pension system was a representative outgrowth of the "Mediterranean welfare state," characterized by extensive segmentation, very high payroll tax rates, and, despite the high contribution rates, inadequate pension benefits. Nektarios examines this paradox, describes the successive attempts to reform the system (mainly through inadequate parametric measures), and quantifies the long-term financial imbalance of the system. He discusses how the imposed and rushed pension reform of 2010 constituted yet another missed opportunity to improve financial sustainability, intergenerational equity, and transparency. He argues that a paradigm shift to the framework of a combined NDC-FDC model could restore the confidence of the Greek people in the nation's long-term pension commitment by openly addressing the issues of financial sustainability and intergenerational equity while creating a transparent structure that can improve desirable behavioral incentives. At the micro level his proposal would increase awareness of an individual's own role in lifetime consumption smoothing. At the macro level the proposal would increase the degree of formality, making it possible to lower the presently very high contribution rate. The latter also increases the perception of fairness among those who already fully comply.

Chapter 9. In "Assessing Fiscal Costs and Pension Distribution in Transitions to Defined Contribution Systems: A Retrospective Analysis for Chile," Eduardo Fajnzylber and David A. Robalino examine what might have happened if, instead of its FDC reform in 1981, Chile had introduced an NDC scheme. The discussion is relevant for countries that are considering structural pension reforms to address problems of financial sustainability and improve economic incentives and that are consequently weighing the pros and cons of a move to an FDC or an NDC plan. Usually, comparisons regarding the performance of the two systems in terms of the pensions provided, transition costs, and so on are based on prospective actuarial modeling, since it is impossible to perform an experiment in which both systems are tested in a particular economic and historical environment. This study takes advantage of the unique opportunity to draw on data accumulated during the FDC era to simulate what would have happened under an NDC reform.

Three results stand out. First, and not surprisingly, the transition costs under an FDC scheme are considerably higher than under NDC—in the Chilean context, by about 50 percent of gross domestic product (GDP) for the first 45 years. Under either scheme, however, the inherited legacy costs are high, owing to the reduction in the contribution rate from that of the unreformed system. Second, the cost of the (pre-2008) minimum pension guarantee would have been higher under an NDC scheme that pays a benefit indexed to the growth rate of the covered wage bill. This is because during the first 20 years after the reform, the rate of return on financial assets was higher than the growth rate of wages. The analysis suggests, however, that this outcome does not always have to be the case. Finally—depending on the assumptions regarding the stochastic process that drives the dynamics of the rate of return paid by the FDC system relative to the NDC economic rate of return—the expected replacement rates under the NDC are not necessarily lower.

VOLUME 2, PART I: THE GENDER DIMENSION OF PENSION REFORM WITH NDC

Gender considerations continue to receive only limited attention in the pension reform discourse around the world. For this reason, with the encouragement and support of the Swedish conference sponsor, the second NDC conference included five papers dedicated specifically to the gender dimension of NDC reforms. The studies cover a broad range of issues, and the results bring to the forefront the importance of gender issues in pension reform. Without the contributions on this topic, the collection would have missed a critical dimension of pension policy making.

Chapter 10. "Gender in the (Nonfinancial) Defined Contribution World: Issues and Options," by Estelle James, opens with an overview of concepts and gender issues in pension reform. James focuses on key choices that must be made in NDC plans and that have gender implications: decisions about retirement age, safety net provisions, payout terms, and arrangements for survivors and the very old. Except for the earlier retirement age for women in Poland, practically no gender-specific provisions remain in NDC countries, but many provisions still have subtly different impacts on men and women. The same policies affect the two genders differently because of the more limited labor force attachment of women, their lower earnings when they work, their higher life expectancy, and the likelihood that they will eventually become widows and live alone in very old age.

Because women live longer than men, they face a greater risk of running out of money in their later years. Rules regarding annuitization, indexation, survivors' benefits, and joint pensions therefore shape their standard of living over time. Compulsory annuitization and the required use of unisex tables in the NDC pillar, buttressed by minimum pensions in the safety net, have implicit distributional effects that favor women. However, the likely absence of an increase in real value of NDC pensions over the retirement period, the move toward price indexation of the safety net benefit, the shift from pure to clawed-back flat pensions, and cutbacks in survivors' benefits have negative consequences for women (and men). An earlier legal retirement age for women may appear to be a privilege, but in reality, in defined contribution (DC) plans women (and men) receive lower yearly pension payments due to the combination of fewer contribution years and longer life expectancy from an earlier retirement age if they take this offer, as many do.

For each design feature, James lays out general analytical points and then describes the empirical situation to distinguish between choices in NDC plans that are inherent and those that are discretionary (and therefore amenable to fine tuning). Two discretionary effects are worth particular attention: the remnants of work disincentives for women stemming from the high implicit tax on contributory work for persons who may not accumulate high enough entitlements to earn a pension above the minimum pension, defined-benefit and survivors benefits schemes that provide a sure outcome regardless of the woman's own formal contribution history. The author points out that the position of very old women in some NDC countries is probably deteriorating, owing to the absence of provisions, whether mandatory or voluntary, on sharing of pension rights or on joint annuities, together with price indexation rather than wage indexation of benefits.

Chapter 11. "To Share or Not to Share: That Is the Question," by Anna Klerby, Bo Larsson, and Edward Palmer, addresses the thorny question of whether and to what extent individual NDC accounts should be shared among couples or partners. The chapter begins by exploring in a global perspective the structural reasons why women generally have lower pensions than men. In addition to the structural determinants of earnings differences, the authors emphasize that in all cultures, including those that have made the greatest progress toward gender equality, women spend a larger portion of their time than men in informal work, caring for children and relatives. This leads to differences in the distribution of pension rights that become especially blatant in defined contribution schemes.

Even if there were absolute gender equality in the labor market in terms of participation and earnings, and even if the earnings and pensions of spouses were exactly the same, the surviving partner in a couple will nevertheless be forced to live on half of the joint income—yet something like 60 percent of that income might be needed to maintain the same per capita standard of living, owing to the loss of economies of scale derived from joint consumption. The authors examine data for Sweden to determine what would happen if Swedes were mandated to contract joint annuities. (Today, there is not even the option to contract a joint NDC annuity.) They show that, using the same utility function for both genders, a joint annuity mandate increases utility for women by more than it decreases it for men. Given the construction of the Swedish guarantee and tax system, such a provision would reduce the government's tax revenues because some men fall into a lower tax bracket after the redistribution and the loss is not compensated for by an increase in taxes on women. It would, however, also reduce the government's payments of guaranteed benefits because after the redistribution of partner benefits within partnerships, women's benefits after the death of their partners are higher, and they qualify to a lesser extent for a guaranteed supplement to their NDC benefit.

Chapter 12. Anna Cristina D'Addio, in "Pension Entitlements of Women with Children: The Role of Credits within Pension Systems in OECD and EU Countries," surveys and analyzes, from the point of view of gender policy, the roles of the minimum pension age and of noncontributory rights for women. Women who spend periods of time out of the labor market caring for children or other relatives typically earn lower pension entitlements, but most OECD countries award credits in the pension system for time spent outside paid employment to care for children or sick relatives. D'Addio takes a detailed look at how credits granted to mothers who interrupt their careers to care for their children affect their pension entitlements. In doing so, she explores to what extent caregiving credits offset the difference in pension outcomes in OECD and selected European Union countries between someone with an interrupted career and someone with a full work history. She also reviews other aspects of pension systems that affect the pension entitlements of mothers with interrupted careers.

The results demonstrate that many of the countries analyzed grant favorable treatment to women who leave the active workforce to raise children. Although the compensation mechanisms and their impacts vary with the rules of the pension scheme, funding sources, and objectives, D'Addio finds that child-care credit systems do boost the pension entitlements of mothers but that the additional benefit does not fill the gaps caused by career breaks. She concludes that the child-care credit is and will remain a valuable tool for supplementing the low pension entitlements of women with children and in the long run contributes to reducing poverty rates among older female pensioners.

Chapter 13. "Gender Policy and Pensions in Chile," by Eduardo Fajnzylber, addresses the same topic as does D'Addio in chapter 12, but in the form of a case study of Chile. The author analyzes the different ways through which the design of DC systems can affect pension entitlements for women in middle-income countries. To do so, he uses the labor and contribution histories of Chilean women to simulate the effect of alternative arrangements on women's pensions and on the pension gender gap. The use of Chilean data is interesting for at least three reasons. First, Chile is the country with the longest history of a pension system based mostly on a financial DC scheme. Second, it is a middle-income developing country with a medium-size informal sector—the latter being a factor often overlooked in analyses of developed countries. Third, in 2008, Chile implemented the most significant reform of its pension scheme since the 1980s. The reform included a number of initiatives specifically aimed at reducing the gender gap in pension benefits such as child credits for mothers and a new social pension.

Fajnzylber includes these recent improvements in his simulations, together with the minimum pension in the contributory scheme and the increase in the minimum retirement age for women from age 60 to age 65. The results suggest that the introduction of a per-child credit can significantly raise pensions for women in the lower part of the pension income distribution. The new social pension (the solidarity pillar) introduced in 2008 will have a tremendous impact on individuals with small pensions, especially women, who are more likely to be eligible for these benefits. Finally, raising the retirement age for women to 65 would have an important benefit effect (an increase of 9 percent, on average), especially among women who are not eligible for the new solidarity pillar. By contrast, because of restrictive eligibility criteria, the minimum pension within the main financial DC scheme has a limited effect on raising women's pensions or lowering the pension income gender gap.

Chapter 14. Alvaro Forteza and Ianina Rossi, in "NDC versus NDB for Infrequent Contributors," investigate the effect of an NDC system on income replacement rates when contribution densities are sparse owing to the sporadic formal employment that is typical for women. The analysis is based on actual employment history data for Uruguay. The authors' findings contradict the usually accepted view that pure (N)DC schemes are not adequate for protecting individuals with sparse contribution histories against the risk of poverty in old age because they do not incorporate any within-scheme redistribution. They show that, in fact, sparse contribution histories and weak social protection (for example, lack of child-care credits) can be more serious issues in an NDB scheme than in an NDC scheme. To do this, they simulate labor income, contributions, and the pension rights of the cohort born in 1995, assuming that historical patterns remain unchanged in the future. They characterize the distribution of pension rights and calculate the pension cost for two regimes: the current NDB–FDC regime and a simulated NDC–FDC regime. They also consider a pure NDC scheme supplemented with a minimum pension and an NDC scheme supplemented with government contributions for child-care credits. The authors find that an NDC scheme would provide better social protection than an NDB system, even without a minimum pension guarantee. This is because an improvement in the actuarial fairness of the scheme leads to an improvement in the welfare of low-income workers.

VOLUME 2, PART II: THE POLITICAL ECONOMY OF NDCS

Although the NDC approach has promising and attractive features for reform of unsustainable and unfunded DB schemes, it does not automatically follow that political support for its application and implementation will be easy to come by. Three chapters address the political-economy issues of NDC reform from different angles, delivering cautions as well as supporting arguments.

Chapter 15. In "Is Social Security Secure with NDC?," Tito Boeri and Vincenzo Galasso explore the political stability of NDC schemes in four pilot countries with respect to the alarming increase in the age of entrance of youths into the labor market. The introduction of NDC public pension schemes in Italy, Latvia, Poland, and Sweden in the 1990s was motivated, among other reasons, by the need to (a) ensure the long-term financial sustainability of the public pension system by linking pension returns to a proxy of the internal rate of return; (b) reduce the existing distortions in the labor market caused by the strong incentives for early retirement in the existing systems; (c) increase the intergenerational equity of the system, which was jeopardized by the different returns across generations in the old systems; and (d) reduce the systematic political interference in public pension systems and address fiscal problems related to aging by introducing a sequence of automatic, nondiscretionary adjustments to key parameters.

More than 10 years after their introduction, the pilot NDC schemes have performed reasonably well in achieving their original objectives, in the authors' estimation. However, some degree of political interference with the operations of the systems has continued (as in Italy), and new concerns have emerged. In particular, the combination of a pension system that strongly bases the benefit calculation on contributions (and thus on labor market participation) and a dual labor market in which young workers work for years in jobs that do not give them access to pension rights creates a new and potentially serious challenge to NDC schemes. The authors' simulations of future pension benefits for the current generation of young workers with discontinuous working histories in Italy and Sweden suggest that replacement rates will be low unless these cohorts work significantly longer than earlier generations. In the absence of significant labor market reforms, this effect may ultimately jeopardize the political sustainability of NDC systems. The authors discuss the effects on future generations of retirees in Italy and Sweden of a current labor market reform—the introduction of a unique labor market contract aimed at reducing the dualism between temporary and permanent workers.

Chapter 16. András Bodor and Michal Rutkowski, in "NDC as a Pathway toward Politically Feasible Pension Reform," probe the power of the key features of NDCs relative to NDBs in constructing messages that policy makers can use to motivate and facilitate pension reform. The authors first review the theoretical literature on the political economy of pension reforms. They challenge the present paradigm because it assumes agent rationality and suggests that reforms driven by deteriorating demographic dependency ratios are equally (un)feasible through either NDB parametric reforms or NDC ("paradigmatic") reforms. The authors argue that the more appropriate analytical paradigm is one that focuses on the role of "stories" and abandons the rationality assumption. This paradigm follows the pathbreaking writings of Kahneman (Kahneman and Tversky 1979; Kahneman 2003a, 2003b) and the more recent work of Akerlof and Shiller (2009). It suggests that the right "stories" can be driving forces in shaping behavior under bounded rationality and can make technically desirable reforms politically feasible, as well.

As an illustration of this general argument, the authors develop the theme of the emergence of NDC pension schemes as the result of "collective intelligence"; that is, of constructive thinking generated at the national-actor level, which becomes collective as the actors interact. Using the specific example of the Polish NDC reform, they describe the process of collective thinking, in which the actors apply both their explicit and their tacit knowledge—the latter being knowledge coming from daily experience that does not originate from a particular thought formula (i.e., a theoretical concept). They argue that the paradigm of NDC framed in the country context can give rise to politically relevant "stories" that convert reform losers—for example, groups with special privileges—into supporters. In fact, the power of the "stories" model may even win over the median voters who swing the balance in the reigning rationality model.

Chapter 17. "The Challenge of Reaching Participants with the Message of NDC," by Annika Sundén, explores the information issues that emerge when reaching out to contributors and beneficiaries to explain pension schemes and pension reforms. The focus is on the experience in Sweden following the introduction of an NDC plan and funded individual accounts. The DC plan redefines the benefit promise and puts more of the risk and responsibility in planning for retirement on participants, who need to have access to reliable projections of expected benefits and an understanding of how benefits change with retirement age. The broad investment choice in the funded individual account requires that participants be familiar with the general principles of investing. Therefore, an instrumental component of the reform has been information, and a large effort has been put into the development of the annual account statement, the Orange Envelope. The information efforts have paid off; almost everyone knows about the Orange Envelope. Self-reported comprehension of the pension system has increased since the envelope was introduced, and in 2009, 44 percent of respondents reported that they had a good understanding of the system.

VOLUME 2, PART III: SOLVENCY, LIQUIDITY, AND STABILITY OF NDC SCHEMES

A core promise of the NDC scheme is to deliver financial sustainability; the rate of return that it yields must be consistent with the fundamentals of an individual account scheme financed on a PAYG basis within a country-specific context. In practice, the achievement of this result encounters many obstacles. One is the existence of prior and inherited commitments that have to be acknowledged and accounted for in the reform design—something that is easily neglected and, even if not neglected, presents computational difficulties. Another is the construction of annuities that are able to withstand the uncertainties associated with the systemic risk of underestimating longevity. Yet another is the calculation of NDC assets or the estimation of the levels of reserves needed to manage temporary macroeconomic shocks or demographic bulges without abrupt changes in the notional rate of return on contributions. Even if all this could be done with ease, the mechanisms for making the appropriate adjustments and provisions in an uncertain world still have to be put in place. The six papers in this section address these challenges conceptually and empirically.

Chapter 18. Robert Holzmann and Alain Jousten, in "Addressing the Legacy Costs in an NDC Reform: Conceptualization, Measurement, Financing," provide a policy framework for managing the legacy costs that need to be addressed when moving from an NDB to an NDC scheme. As the new contribution rate is fixed and, perhaps, reduced, "overhang" of accrued-to-date liabilities not directly covered by the creation of commensurate assets in the NDC scheme leaves a financing gap. It is important to identify this gap and to assign a source of financing to it.

The authors conclude as follows:

- For an NDC reform to be credible and fully effective in its desired results, the legacy costs of the reformed system must be determined, no matter how these costs will be financed.

- For a shift from an NDB scheme to a full NDC scheme with a fixed and long-term-sustainable contribution rate, the legacy costs simply amount to the actuarial deficit (or financing gap) at the time of reform and are finite.

- Different sources of the legacy deficit may be differentiated—in particular, inherited legacy costs reflecting prior reforms and benefits above the steady state under the old scheme and reform-induced new legacy costs resulting from the shift toward a lower sustainable contribution rate.

- In estimating legacy costs, actuarial- and macroeconomic-based projection models have advantages over pure actuarial studies because they are less dependent on mere technical parameter assumptions that may not be consistent with general equilibrium considerations.

- Distributive effects emerge at both the intergenerational and intragenerational levels because the benefits and costs of the reform are borne unequally by different subgroups of the current and future population.

- In the developing world, a promising way to finance the legacy costs is to rely on the expansion of coverage that would increase the value of future PAYG assets.

- For developed countries, theoretical models show that tax financing, in particular via indirect taxes such as a value added tax (VAT), is an interesting tool, but empirical limitations that are particularly relevant for developing countries make assessment of its real-world usefulness difficult.

Chapter 19. In "Generic NDC: Equilibrium, Valuation, and Risk Sharing with and without NDC Bonds," Edward Palmer presents the properties of generic NDC systems. Because NDC is a recent innovation, the generic features of NDC have not been previously explored in a cohesive and coherent way, as is done in this chapter. The chapter derives and analyzes the demographic, economic, and distributional properties of NDC schemes. The residual (systemic) longevity error arising in the computation of annuities leaves a risk to be covered either by the overall NDC insurance collective (through the solvency adjustment mechanism), the older survivors (through variable annuities), or the government (through general taxes). The chapter argues for creating an NDC bond, which then becomes the asset that closes the system financially, transferring the residual longevity error in a *fixed* annuity and other residual risk to the government (taxpayers). The *unissued* NDC bond is thus tantamount to a nonmarketed financial longevity bond, where the rate of return is set equal to the covered wage sum. The author argues that this may be considered by many to be preferable to distributing the risk more narrowly within the NDC scheme collective (which is what the solvency ratio approach does) because the government's general tax base comes closer to reflecting the ability-to-pay principle.

Chapter 20. In "The Economics of Reserve Funds in NDC Schemes: Role, Means, and Size to Manage Shocks," Robert Holzmann, Edward Palmer, and David A. Robalino investigate the economic rationale for a reserve fund when implementing an NDC reform and discuss its potential size. An NDC scheme promises to deliver solvency even under adverse circumstances, but it cannot promise liquidity when it is most needed. To avoid shock-related, revenue-dependent fluctuations of benefits, such a scheme requires a predictable and transparent liquidity mechanism that guarantees a preannounced indexation rule consistent with long-term solvency. The unattractive alternatives are ad hoc mechanisms such as government transfers or unexpected benefit adjustments that risk damaging the credibility of the NDC scheme and reform. The authors review the liquidity policy options (borrowing, NDC bonds, and reserve funds), the issues involved, and the size of reserve funds needed for addressing macroeconomic and demographic shocks. They conclude that V-type macroeconomic shocks can and should be handled through a reserve fund but that large and protracted economic and demographic shocks will require additional adjustments in account and benefit indexation for economic and political reasons. They stress that country circumstances matter for the determination of size and use of reserve funds.

Chapter 21. In "A Decade of Actuarial Accounting for the NDC Scheme in Sweden: Quantifying Change in the Financial Position of a PAYG Pension Plan," Ole Settergren presents a critical but not undisputed innovation in PAYG accounting. As part of the Swedish 1994–98 NDC reform, special accounting rules were introduced that had been developed to secure full and automatic financial balancing of the new scheme. The accounting method that was developed is a legislated form of evaluation of the scheme's ability to finance the accrued pension liability through a point measure of the ability of the flow of contributions to finance (amortize) the pension liability. Traditional actuarial evaluations of public PAYG pension schemes evaluate the scheme's ability to finance both accrued and estimated future pension liabilities by projecting future flows of benefits and contributions.

Settergren explains the accounting method used in the Swedish NDC pension system and illustrates it with the actual evolution of the scheme's income statement and balance sheet for the nine years between 2002 and 2010. The accounting results determine a solvency ratio for the NDC scheme. According to the Swedish NDC legislation, if the solvency ratio falls below unity, indexation is triggered that reduces the growth of liabilities (rights) until balance is restored. This indexation came into effect in the wake of the 2008–09 economic recession and the fall in equity prices. The author describes the adjustment process and the policy responses to the ensuing negative impact on pension benefits in 2010 and 2011. The bottom line is that Sweden's balancing mechanism withstood its first political stress test, with only minor alterations.

Chapter 22. Juha Alho, Jorge Bravo, and Edward Palmer, in "Annuities and Life Expectancy in NDC," investigate the efficacy of current state-of-the-art life expectancy modeling in projecting life expectancy at "the" pension age—that is, the age at which a life annuity must be granted according to current practice in NDC (and FDC) schemes. The authors provide an overview of current modeling philosophy and of the genre of projection models inspired by the work of Ronald Lee and Lawrence Carter (1992). They demonstrate that models of this type, which essentially distribute an aggregate trend among the birth cohorts covered, will systematically underestimate life expectancy in an environment characterized by declining rates of mortality—which is a rather typical scenario. This has certainly happened in Japan, but also in countries such as Finland, Norway, and Sweden. The authors provide suggestions for better modeling under these circumstances but acknowledge that, regardless of the proficiency in modeling, systematic errors may continue to be part of the landscape for many decades.

Consequently, Alho, Bravo, and Palmer ask whether it is possible to devise annuity models that fairly distribute the residual risk between the insured and the insurer. Simple variable annuity models, in which the annuity is reestimated at yearly and five-year intervals on the basis of continuously revised life expectancy estimates, are examined for the Scandinavian countries. The variable annuity reduces the risk for the insurer—other cohorts in a mutual insurance setting, or the government (taxpayers)—but at the relative expense of older members of the birth cohort. This is clearly not a fair outcome and suggests that we need to learn more about other models of distributing the systematic error in estimating longevity and that a more palatable safeguard is to transfer the systematic estimation error to the government (taxpayers) through an NDC bond, as discussed by Palmer in chapter 19.

Chapter 23. In "The Actuarial Balance of the PAYG Pension System: The Swedish NDC Model versus the U.S. DB Model," María del Carmen Boado-Penas and Carlos Vidal-Meliá explore the arguments for computing and keeping track of an actuarial balance in NDC and NDB pension schemes to improve their transparency, credibility, and solvency. The chapter focuses on the two main methods used by government social security departments to construct an actuarial balance for nonfinancial pension schemes; these are the methods used by Sweden and the United States. The authors discuss methodological and actuarial issues and compare the two approaches. In addition, they briefly examine the Japanese NDB model, which includes certain features of both methods. Three main suggestions emerge from the investigation: (a) countries that have not yet done so are well advised to estimate and report actuarial balances because they improve transparency, motivate responses to address financial imbalances, and thus strengthen the credibility of the PAYG system; (b) countries that already have elements of an actuarial balance should formalize and enhance the frequency of the exercise and establish an independent expert panel to provide or approve assumptions and procedures; and (c) social security institutions and researchers should investigate key questions regarding the estimation of the actuarial balance, in particular, the applicability of market-based evaluation methods and issues specific to old-age, survivors', and disability benefits.

VOLUME 2, PART IV: PANEL DISCUSSION

Chapter 24. The final chapter, "Reflections on Aspects of NDC Schemes," reports on the closing panel discussion that brought together representatives from academia, politics, and research.

David Blake, in his contribution "NDC versus FDC: Pros, Cons, and Replication," examines the advantages and disadvantages of NDC pension schemes compared with FDC schemes. He defines an NDC pension plan as a PAYG pension plan with greater intergenerational and intragenerational equity than a standard PAYG plan. The rate of return to plan members is linked to the wage growth of the particular economy and to the realized postretirement lifetimes of each cohort of members. NDC plans, he cautions, cannot be considered as offering a well-diversified investment. Furthermore, given the long-run dynamic efficiency of economies, NDC plans, in Blake's view, fail the Aaron test (they do not offer a higher rate of return than a funded scheme) and so will generate lower average pensions compared with FDC plans.

Blake asserts that NDC outcomes could be replicated using an FDC framework if the government were to issue wage-indexed or GDP-indexed bonds for the accumulation phase and index-linked longevity bonds for the decumulation phase. These bonds would help overcome the poor international portability of NDC plans but would not address the issue of poor international diversification of investment risks or the failure of NDC plans to pass the Aaron test.

Lans Bovenberg, in "NDC Schemes: Strengths and Weaknesses," highlights the strong and weak sides of the NDC approach from a pure economic-analytical level, abstracting, for the most part, from any implementation issues. The strong aspects of NDC schemes emerge largely from a comparison with traditional unfunded DB schemes. The weak sides are measured against individual features that may be economically desirable with respect to welfare but not against any alternative pension system that has been fully conceptualized, much less implemented.

Bovenberg notes, in particular, that the NDC approach improves labor market incentives by making the retirement decision actuarially fairer and by linking the accumulation of new pension rights to contributions over the entire life cycle. Moreover, computing annuities on the basis of life expectancy contributes to the financial stability of the pension system, and the provision of wage-related pension benefits helps share wage risk between generations. Nevertheless, the author asserts, all of these benefits can, in principle, be reaped from other pension schemes, and NDC schemes fail to address all the problems associated with PAYG systems. Specifically, there is room for better design in terms of covering intergenerational risk sharing and intertemporal consumption smoothing. Indeed, the NDC system can be seen as a transitional arrangement on the way to better pension arrangements that optimally distribute financial market and human capital risks across generations in countries with advanced financial markets and well-functioning private and public institutions. However, there is presently no model of how to achieve such a result based on ex ante information.

Harry Flam, in "NDC Reserve Funds: The Swedish Reserve Funds after 10 Years," looks at the issue of the efficiency of having more than one reserve fund in an NDC scheme, drawing on an analysis of the experience of Sweden, which from the outset has had four separate funds to manage reserves. His conclusion is that having a single reserve fund is better than having many concurrent reserve funds.

To begin with, he notes that the primary reason for introducing four funds in Sweden was to reduce administrative costs through competition. To date, all four funds have been managed actively to maximize their returns. Yet the analysis shows that the cost of active management of the four funds outweighs what would have been the cost of a single passive (benchmark) fund managing all the assets and that this extra cost is not counterbalanced by the small marginal difference in the return compared with an external benchmark index. In addition, the political fear that these funds, which together constitute the 20th-largest pension fund in the world, would dominate the Swedish market was unfounded, partly because of the size of the Swedish equity market but also because of the large international investment component in the funds' portfolios. Flam notes that portfolio management in Sweden has remained independent from political intervention of any kind.

Mohamed Ahmed Maait, in "Reflections on Introducing NDC in the Arab Republic of Egypt and Other Emerging Economies," traces the reasons for and the structure of Egypt's legislated multipillar reform of 2010, which was part of a broader social security reform. The new system consists of a zero pillar, an NDC pillar, and an FDC pillar. Maait stresses that the Egyptian government was motivated to embrace an NDC pillar because of the three qualities promised from the reform: solvency, transparency, and incentive compatibility.

Citing the deliberative process around the NDC pension reform, the development of a homegrown multipillar structure, and the current struggle to move from legislation to implementation, he offers three important lessons for other emerging economies. First, an NDC plus FDC approach, as the core of the mandated consumption-smoothing pillars, not only is feasible but is also advantageous for emerging economies if the enabling conditions are met. Second, however great, appropriate, and homegrown the reform concept is, it needs broad political support beyond a parliament majority, and it needs a process for obtaining this support. Third—a lesson from the unfinished implementation process—his advice to reformers is to start to think about implementation as early as possible, give it much more attention than you think is needed, be prepared for delays, and implement only when you are ready.

Key Policy Lessons

The chapters in the two volumes offer many policy lessons derived from the reviews of country experience, the discussions of progress in conceptual and empirical work, and the analyses of so-far underscrutinized topics. The seven main lessons identified at the beginning of this chapter are discussed in more detail here.

NDC SCHEMES WORK WELL, BUT THERE IS ROOM TO MAKE THEM EVEN BETTER

The operation of the NDC schemes in Italy, Latvia, Poland, and Sweden over the first 10-plus years is going well. Although these countries adopted different approaches toward design and implementation during the transition period and in the steady state, the approaches share key features: the direct link between contributions and benefits; the use of notional interest for indexing liabilities; and the determination of the initial pension on the basis of remaining life expectancy. In all these countries, the NDC pension scheme weathered the 2008–09 financial crisis and the ensuing recession. However, both Latvia and Poland, with their large prereform commitments, retrenched as the transition costs of NDC and FDC proved to be too heavy a strain on the public budget. The lesson of over-extension stemming from the transition costs is a clear lesson for other countries.

The available data suggest that the outcomes—the increases in the retirement age and the level of replacement rates—are generally in line with expectations. Further data collection and analysis are needed, however. Although the schemes have been generally successful, the reviews of country experiences and conceptual considerations indicate that there is room for and need for improvement.

GO FOR AN IMMEDIATE TRANSITION TO AVOID FUTURE PROBLEMS

When moving from a conventional PAYG defined benefit scheme to an NDC scheme, multiple options for coverage during the transition are available. There are three basic cases: only new entrants are required to join the new scheme; only individuals with fewer than x years in the old scheme are required to join; or all are required to join the scheme from the first day. In the third case, acquired rights under the old scheme are translated into initial capital in the NDC system and are credited to the individual's personal account.

Only one country, Latvia, adopted the full, immediate transition. At the other extreme, in Italy, only workers with fewer than 18 years of contributions were mandated to join the new scheme. Poland and Sweden fall somewhere in the middle.

In addition to its long transition period, Italy was for very long reluctant to eliminate early retirement mechanisms from the previous defined benefit regimes. What is more, Italy's choice of indexation does not guarantee financial stability. The soft transition came back to haunt Italy in 2011, more than a decade and a half after its move to NDC, when financial markets lost faith in the country's capacity to manage its long-term liabilities. It required the financial crisis and the threat of state bankruptcy and forced exit from the Euro for the Monti government to be able to tackle some the scheme's key weakness, in particular the transition to NDC rules for all. Both country experiences and conceptual insights strongly suggest that new reforms should follow Latvia's example and opt for a cold-turkey changeover, which can be achieved technically and offers many advantages for the performance and credibility of the scheme. On day one of such a move, all workers become subject to the same rules and incentives, and politically difficult comparisons between the old and new schemes are avoided. This approach does not necessarily make the workers with acquired rights worse off; their rights are transformed into individual capital and hence into future benefits, the value of which will depend on the internal rate of return in the NDC scheme. Of course, an unsustainable internal rate of return under an unreformed NDB scheme, which is, in essence, the reason for reform to begin with, cannot be replicated.

IDENTIFY AND FINANCE THE TRANSITION COSTS IN AN EXPLICIT MANNER AS THEY EMERGE—YOU WILL HAVE TO FACE THEM SOONER OR LATER

A major advantage of choosing an NDC rather than an FDC scheme is that not all the liabilities accrued to date will become explicit and in need of financing. Nevertheless, the move toward a scheme with a fixed contribution rate that is less than what would have been needed to finance benefits under the old system requires explicit decisions about the financing of rights already acquired. These are inherited legacy costs that would have had to be financed anyway under the old scheme.

So far, the reforming countries have shied away from clearly identifying the legacy costs and the way they are to be financed. Instead, they have opted for nontransparent mechanisms such as contribution financing (with the idea of decreasing the rate as the legacy costs are repaid), curtailed notional rates of return to build up cash surpluses, and setting the parameters of the reformed scheme-based optimistic growth path that excludes any hint of significant future shocks. The financial crisis of 2008–09 exposed the problem with this approach, as evidenced in Latvia and Poland (which had adopted an NDC–FDC approach) and in Hungary, which combined NDB and FDC schemes. In all three countries, the economic crisis and falling revenues, beginning in 2008, led to downsizing of the relatively large FDC schemes—something that more realistic assessment and political acceptance of the legacy could have avoided.

ESTABLISH AN EXPLICIT STABILIZING MECHANISM TO GUARANTEE SOLVENCY

The cornerstone of NDC is the fixed contribution rate. The approach for achieving solvency under a fixed contribution rate involves the choice of the notional interest rate, which is the mechanism that links the permissible growth of liabilities to the expected growth in contribution assets. Conceptually, there are various mechanisms that would include one or more of the following steps: employing a correct measure of the level and growth of the contribution base or PAYG asset to which the notional interest rate is linked (i.e., allowing for possible adjustments because of coverage expansion and the like); choosing a good proxy for the notional interest rate; determining the overall NDC assets and liabilities, establishing a solvency ratio of assets to liabilities, and identifying criteria that trigger an adjustment in the notional interest rate toward solvency in case of deviation (i.e., a balancing mechanism); having the government issue NDC bonds with a return equal to the relevant rate of change in the covered wage base (the country's wage sum); and accepting all other residual risk—specifically, the longevity risk inherent in the creation of annuities based on life expectancy estimates. All these potential stabilization mechanisms are, for the time being, essentially works in progress. There is a big step from the theoretical drawing board to practical implementation, and to date there has been no long-term experience with either the comparative political or the technical viability of these approaches.

As yet, only Sweden has established a balancing mechanism. The Swedish mechanism does not distribute surpluses, except as needed to return liabilities, following a downward adjustment, to the initial indexation path that would have existed in the absence of balancing. Ideally, a balancing mechanism should be symmetric. The economic crisis also led to questions about the valuation of the Swedish NDC scheme's substantial reserve funds and the smoothing method employed to construct the indexes used in practice. The Swedish method can result in potentially strong upward adjustments of pensions as a consequence of previous strong economic growth, even though contributions drop as the economy turns into recession, and to downward adjustments of pensions as the economy once again gains growth momentum.

The NDC schemes in Latvia and Poland rely on indexation features that had been expected to create surpluses in the transition to a state with balanced FDC and NDC schemes. Wage indexation of benefits, which is technically affordable within the framework of NDC, is still an unimplemented goal for these countries. Italy's scheme still has unbalancing features, implying a faith that the government will pick up the bill or change the laws when the selected internal rate of return proves unsustainable. These "unfinished" approaches are not conducive to fostering confidence and building credibility.

ESTABLISH A RESERVE FUND TO CUSHION TEMPORARY SHOCKS

Although an NDC system with a good stabilization mechanism can guarantee solvency, it cannot ensure that resources will always be there to pay the promised benefits; the system can have liquidity problems. Because an NDC scheme remains unfunded, with current contributions used to pay current benefits, a downward shock to revenues caused by a temporary decline in the number of contributors relative to the number of retirees, or by a fall in wages (both of which characterize recessions), requires adjustments on the benefit side, borrowing, or government transfers. All three ad hoc measures can be avoided by keeping a reserve fund that can be used to address (unpredictable) short-term macroeconomic shocks and (predictable) transitory demographic stress. A reserve-financed mechanism to smooth consumption at the individual level by avoiding cuts in benefits can claim to have welfare-enhancing effects for the individual, constitute an automatic stabilizer at the macroeconomic level, and increase the scheme's credibility and the public's confidence in it.

To date, none of the NDC countries has built up either a reserve to cushion the effect on pension payments of temporary declines in contributions or a specific demographic reserve fund to smooth fertility bulges. Sweden does has a large reserve fund that was inherited from the NDB scheme which preceded the NDC. This fund had been built up from 1960, with contributions from the baby-boom generation of the 1940s and 1950s. The retention of part of the then-existing fund in the transition to NDC was an explicit measure to cover the legacy cost of the baby-boom generation's pensions. Nevertheless, the need for a short-term contingency reserve became apparent when the solvency ratio fell below unity as a result of the economic recession of 2008–09. These events triggered the Swedish "brake" on indexation, leading to a reduction in workers' account values and pensions in payment.

The principle of a reserve fund is to provide a cushion against the need to reduce pensions in recessionary times by setting aside earmarked funds during strong growth years. It is important to note that similar (but ad hoc) brakes on benefit levels were introduced in other NDC (and NDB) countries to cope with the drop in revenues, increases in expenditures, and overall deterioration in the fiscal situation. What distinguished, for example, Sweden's NDC scheme from models adopted in other countries was the automatic response through the internal rate of return, in contrast to ad hoc crisis measures.

DEVELOP AN EXPLICIT MECHANISM FOR SHARING SYSTEMIC LONGEVITY RISK

The second main mechanism, after the correct choice of the notional interest rate, for ensuring the solvency of an NDC scheme involves the application of the correct (future) remaining cohort life expectancy to the individual account value at the time of retirement and the calculation of the initial pension. Doing this requires the existence of a statistical model that takes proper account of the uncertainty in the evolution of survival rates—but such a model is not at hand. All known approaches underestimate the decline of mortality rates, in particular, as the decline in mortality accelerates in older ages and across countries.

One can imagine various ways of approaching the problem, but all imply different risk-sharing features between and across generations and hence are subject to various political views and objections. For example, one approach would consist of overestimating the improvement in life expectancy (to be on the safe side), and this would mean that the benefits paid out would be too low. Another method would have already-retired cohorts bear the risk, which would require the adjustment of pensions in payment if life expectancy increased by more than the gain used to compute the annuity. Yet another approach would correct for underestimation of life expectancy through a balancing mechanism that distributes the correction to pensioners and workers; implicitly, a downward adjustment in the notional interest rate triggered by the need to balance would tax the active generation. A more novel and more equitable alternative would be to have the government (all taxpayers across generations) bear the residual risk through the issuance of an NDC bond, which would be linked to changes in longevity.

At present, no NDC country has an explicit mechanism for addressing the longevity risk. Some countries, such as Italy, postponed the political decision to periodically update life expectancy for the calculation of initial pensions, despite provisions in the law. There is a clear need of broader analysis and political discussion about the different risk-sharing options, and perhaps attention should be paid to how to better insulate selected mechanisms from ad hoc political intervention.

ADDRESS THE GENDER IMPLICATIONS OF NDC SCHEMES THROUGH ANALYSIS AND POLITICAL DISCOURSE

The gender implications of NDC reforms have so far not been at the forefront of analytical work and have remained on the sidelines of the political debate. The gender issues inherent in NDC models are also present in FDC schemes, as well as in financial and nonfinancial defined benefit schemes. What makes NDC schemes a bit different from NDB schemes is that gender issues and their redistributive implications can be more easily identified and the options more clearly spelled out.

The key elements of discussion concern the application of uniform mortality rates, differences in minimum retirement ages, the design of survivors' pensions, splitting of pension rights in case of divorce, and individual versus joint annuities. It is too early to put forward well-informed policy proposals that, in any case, will need to be adapted to the cultural norms within each country. Too little research, as well as too little discussion, has hitherto taken place. But what can be advocated as of now is to change the status quo and spend more resources on better understanding the challenges and identifying potential solutions.

The Policy Research Agenda

The two volumes of this anthology offer important insights into the operation of NDC schemes, as well as into the conceptual and empirical issues surrounding their rationale, design, and implementation. They also highlight areas in which more research is needed for better understanding the construction and outcomes of NDCs to improve the design and operation of schemes. In our view, the priority policy research agenda should focus on four areas, which are discussed in greater detail below: (a) the outcome of NDC schemes compared with the primary goals of pension systems and with alternative scheme designs—in particular, NDB and FDC, but also schemes with matching defined contribution (MDC) components; (b) further work on measurement of assets and liabilities to facilitate the introduction, adjustment, and sustainability of NDC schemes; (c) the interaction of NDC (as a central consumption-smoothing pillar for old age) with other pillars and benefits; and (d) application and implementation issues with NDC schemes in low- and middle-income countries.

ASSESSMENT OF THE OUTCOMES OF NDC SCHEMES

The attraction of an NDC scheme designed by the rule book is its promise to deliver on the primary goals of public pension schemes in a consistent and integrated manner. A pension system should, in the first place, be able to ensure adequate, affordable, sustainable, and robust income in old age (see Holzmann and Hinz 2005).

Conceptually, NDC schemes are able to meet these criteria by virtue of their design characteristics. At the design level, the primary goals are secured, in the first instance, through the tight relationship between the contribution rate and benefit levels. A country begins by fixing the contribution rate at an affordable level, which makes the benefit level an endogenous variable. In determining the level of the contribution rate, the policy maker must evaluate the resultant average benefit, given this rate; the expected notional interest rate; the expected (or targeted) number of years of work and contributions; and the number of years of retirement. Given this calibration, the adequacy of benefit levels is determined by work history and the individual's choice of retirement timing, after a publicly fixed minimum retirement age, which can be made dependent on individually available resources. By indexing the individual account value with the sustainable internal rate of return and linking the initial pension to cohort life expectancy at retirement, solvency is guaranteed. The operation of a well-thought-through and sufficient reserve fund provides liquidity and imparts robustness in the face of major economic and demographic shocks.

A critical assumption concerns the ability of individuals to make sound decisions about their labor supply and the capability of the economy to offer jobs. If individuals are willing and able to adjust their labor supply and retirement age according to assumed intertemporal welfare optimization, all the pieces will fall into place. But is this happening, and are the primary goals being achieved? We do not really know yet because the few NDC schemes in operation have not been in place long enough to offer full empirical support. The performance of NDCs in Italy, Latvia, Poland, and Sweden, which is assessed in chapter 2 of this volume, is broadly consistent with the goals but does not constitute proof. Generally, a major task over the next years should be to develop a comprehensive results framework for pension reforms of all kinds. This should be a primary focus of pension research in general and of research on NDC, specifically. The World Bank and other international organizations can play an important role here by gathering, organizing, and analyzing country data.

Relevant research can and should be undertaken by the international research community, as well. A priority area is the response of individual labor supply to NDC design characteristics, including the pseudo-actuarial decrements and increments for earlier or later retirement and the calculation of the initial pension on the basis of remaining cohort life expectancy. Are individuals reacting as expected to these design features? Is individual behavior responsive to the communication and information strategy employed by NDC countries? Are individuals capable of applying the information, and will they do so in line with what is needed for individual welfare optimization? Since experimental design is impractical, how can one model and analyze labor supply reactions to the introduction of NDC? It is easy to construct an even longer list of questions.

MEASUREMENT OF NDC ASSETS AND LIABILITIES

Critical for the introduction, balancing, sustainability, and liquidity of NDC schemes is the correct measurement of assets and liabilities of both the new scheme and the inherited one. This may seem a relatively easy and perhaps already solved task, but as several chapters in this volume document, there is still much territory to explore. The chapters dealing with the issues of legacy costs, the reserve fund, intergenerational equity, actuarial balance, and generic NDC indicate the difficulty of the task, which involves the design of an approach that is not only conceptually clean but also operationally feasible.

A few of the research challenges are highlighted here.

Liabilities. The liabilities in an NDC scheme should be largely, if not completely, known, depending on how meticulous a country is in gathering and documenting information. These liabilities are the account values of the insured population, and this information would be sufficient for steady-state considerations. If, however, a former NDB system is folded into an NDC scheme, the legacy costs of the folded NDB scheme will need to be identified because separate financing will be required. What the best method of identifying and measuring such costs is remains an open question. In fact, it will vary from situation to situation.

Liabilities in an NDC scheme depend in part on the present value of benefits in disbursement, which depend critically on remaining life expectancy. The determination of this last variable necessitates the correct projection and application of the remaining life expectancy of the retirement cohort at the time of the pension calculation. How best to do this is unclear, both technically and politically. The result is likely to be approximate, given current technology.

Assets. In principle, the assets of an NDC scheme consist of future contributions; in addition, there may also be a reserve fund. At the moment, there are only two alternatives on the table that estimate assets in terms of a discrete snapshot in time, and each has issues of its own. The Swedish approach was fine under more or less steady-state conditions but showed its limitations under the economic shock of 2008–09. The proposed theoretical alternative (Robalino and Bodor 2009) may read convincingly on paper, but model simulations may not reflect operational reality.

These approaches define the value of assets in discrete time, using the structure of current contributions (new liabilities) and pension payments. Palmer (vol. 2, chapter 19) shows that such methods do not yield a unique definition of assets for a given steady-state flow of contributions. Because of this deficiency, Palmer proposes introducing an NDC bond as the NDC "asset," with the internal rate of the asset based on the rate of growth of the covered wage base. The proposed asset is a government longevity bond under which the government covers the residual longevity risk and bears the cost of other small design deficiencies that inevitably arise in practical applications.

In view of the challenging research agenda on measuring assets and liabilities for an NDC reform, one may be inclined to think that traditional NDB reforms may actually be a better, or at least easier, choice. The reality is that these alternative schemes or reform approaches are fraught with much the same, or worse, conceptual and operational problems with respect to solvency and liquidity. The questions just do not emerge as clearly because NDB schemes are much less transparent and hence tend to be much more deceptive.

THE INTERACTION OF NDC SCHEMES WITH OTHER PENSION BENEFITS AND PILLARS

The key objective of an NDC scheme is to provide adequate consumption smoothing for most but not all of the population in old age. The policy maker who is interested in mixing the pension portfolio between components with economic and financially based returns will cap the coverage of the NDC scheme at a desired level to include an FDC component. In addition, for the lowest-income groups, which will consist of persons with short and substantially interrupted earnings histories, special measures will be required to support their consumption smoothing and to avoid poverty. Furthermore, the schemes are focused on old-age income, which raises the question of how the old-age schemes interact with disability pensions and how survivors' benefits should enter into the picture. For some of these interactions, no good answers are yet on hand. Two research issues are flagged.

How should low income in old age be addressed? Some participants in NDC schemes will have a low contribution density throughout their active lives, perhaps aggravated by low wages, and, as a result, will receive low benefits even if they delay retirement. Others may never have contributed to formal pension schemes. Should both groups have access to some minimum retirement income—say, in the form of a social pension that is means tested against pensions, income, or assets? Or would it be better to replace, at least partially, these ex post transfers with ex ante transfers and matching contributions for low-wage participants (see Palacios and Robalino 2009; Holzmann et al. forthcoming)? This option may reduce government outlays in present-value terms by providing more of an incentive for formal participation than would otherwise have been the case. But how should such matching contributions be financed? Fully externally, by budgetary resources, or within the system, by allocating some number of percentage points of the average contribution base to all accounts? What are the objectives of the adjustment, and how should the results be estimated?

How should disability benefits be provided in an NDC world? In traditional NDB schemes, old-age and disability benefits are closely linked historically, and the old-age pension was initially a kind of generalized disability pension that few lived to receive. With increasing life expectancy, the relevant risks for both disability and old age became separated and for efficiency reasons could and should be independently established and priced. Such separation was not a feature of NDB schemes, but it has been pursued with success in a few new FDC schemes, such as Chile's. An NDC scheme offers the same opening, but it has not yet been used, except in Sweden, and we lack the comprehensive conceptual and empirical guidance for how best to do it.

NDC SCHEMES IN MIDDLE- AND LOW-INCOME COUNTRIES

For the time being, the implementation of NDC schemes has been limited to high-income countries. A few middle-income countries (such as Azerbaijan, the Kyrgyz Republic, Mongolia, and the Russian Federation) have adopted some NDC features, but system information and assessment of the outcomes has been scanty. Implementing an NDC scheme in the environment of a middle-income country is bound to raise a number of new conceptual and operational issues about which we currently have very limited understanding and even less sound knowledge. Once we have progressed on this knowledge agenda, we will be able to make a first assessment of whether and how the approach can be pursued in a low-income country.

A critical element for implementation is bound to be administrative capacity, which is essential for the efficient collection and registration of contributions and the creation of individual accounts. Data issues will emerge for the estimation of life expectancy that is carried out at retirement to calculate the initial pension. Most middle-income countries do not have reliable data on which to base such important calculations. And conceptual design issues will emerge in the identification of the sustainable notional interest rate in settings with decade-long coverage expansion and wage growth per capita in excess of the financial interest rate.

In view of these and many other policy research questions, enjoy this collection of studies on NDC, and stay tuned for the next one!

Note

Many thanks are due to our coeditor David A. Robalino for his thorough review and numerous useful suggestions.

References

Akerlof, George A., and Robert J. Shiller. 2009. *Animal Spirits. How Human Psychology Drives the Economy, and Why It Matters for Global Capitalism.* Princeton, NJ: Princeton University Press.

Barr, Nicholas, and Peter Diamond. 2008. *Reforming Pensions: Principles and Policy Choices.* Oxford: Oxford University Press.

Holzmann, Robert, and Richard Hinz. 2005. *Old Age Income Support in the 21st Century: An International Perspective on Pension Systems and Reform.* Washington, DC: World Bank.

Holzmann, Robert, Richard Hinz, Noriuko Takayama, and David Tuesta. Forthcoming. *Matching Defined Contributions (MDC) Schemes: Role and Limits to Increase Coverage in Low- and Middle-Income Countries.* Washington, DC: World Bank.

Holzmann, Robert, and Edward Palmer, eds. 2006. *Pension Reform: Issues and Prospects for Non-Financial Defined Contribution (NDC) Schemes.* Washington, DC: World Bank.

Kahneman, Daniel. 2003a. "Maps of Bounded Rationality: Psychology for Behavioral Economics." *American Economic Review* 93 (5): 1449–75.

———. 2003b. "A Psychological Perspective on Economics." *American Economic Review*, 93 (2): 162–68.

Kahneman, Daniel, and Amos Tversky. 1979. "Prospect Theory: An Analysis of Decision under Risk." *Econometrica*, 47: 263–91.

Lee, Ronald D., and Lawrence R. Carter. 1992. "Modeling and Forecasting the Time Series of U.S. Mortality." *Journal of the American Statistical Association* 87 (September): 659–71.

Palacios, Robert, and David A. Robalino. 2009. "Matching Defined Contributions: A Way to Increase Pension Coverage." In *Closing the Coverage Gap: The Role of Social Pensions and Other Retirement Income Transfers*, ed. Robert Holzmann, David A. Robalino, and Noriyuki Takayama, 187–202. Washington, DC: World Bank.

Robalino, David A., and András Bodor. 2009. "On the Financial Sustainability of the Pay-as-You-Go Systems and the Role of Government Indexed Bonds." *Journal of Pension Economics and Finance* 8 (2): 153–87.

The First Wave of NDC Reforms: The Experiences of Italy, Latvia, Poland, and Sweden

Agnieszka Chłoń-Domińczak, Daniele Franco, and Edward Palmer

This chapter surveys the design and implementation of nonfinancial (notional) defined contribution (NDC) schemes in four countries—Italy, Latvia, Poland, and Sweden—and takes stock of how these systems are faring 10 to 15 years after their introduction. It reviews and analyzes the various paths to reform, the detailed design of the reforms, the implementation process, and the outcomes.

The study addresses the main issues of adequacy and macroeconomic sustainability. The analysis shows that in all four countries, the full-career worker with average earnings can expect a gross earnings replacement rate of about 65 percent. Those with shorter careers can be at risk of lower living standards in old age. Early retirement, insufficient compensation for time out of the formal labor force for childbirth and for care of family members, and the absence of a joint annuity at retirement increase the likelihood of relative poverty among women who survive their partners in old age. Sweden sets a good example of support to women in conjunction with childbirth, avoiding a negative effect of this event on pensions and replacement rates. All four countries, however, lack rules for redistributing rights between partners in a couple.

The sine qua non of an NDC pension scheme is financial sustainability. Using a simple simulation model, this study examines the responses of Italy and Sweden to a permanent decline in labor productivity, an increase in longevity at retirement, and a permanent decline in the size of the youngest cohort. The analysis shows that Sweden's balancing mechanism ensures financial stability, although sometimes with a lag, whereas with the Italian design, where two or three negative shocks lead to deficits over long periods of time. Because pensions in payment are only price-indexed in Italy, Latvia, and Poland, these schemes will build up surpluses when wage-sum growth is positive (even without an explicit funding mechanism) but will run deficits when nominal wage-sum growth falls below the rate of inflation. For this reason, the issues of indexation and financial balance

Agnieszka Chłoń-Domińczak is an assistant professor at the Warsaw School of Economics and is at the Educational Research Institute, Warsaw. Daniele Franco is managing director for economics, research, and international relations at the Bank of Italy. Edward Palmer is professor emeritus of social insurance economics at Uppsala University, research fellow at the Uppsala Center for Labor Studies, and senior advisor at the Swedish Social Insurance Agency.

need to be revisited in those countries. Italy is the only country that automatically adjusts the retirement age to gains in life expectancy.

This study shows how the four countries have designed their NDC pension schemes and discusses the issues. The economic crisis that began in 2008 stimulated public debate about pension reform in Latvia, Poland, and Sweden. In Latvia and Poland, the economic crisis brought to the forefront the underfinancing of the overall reforms, which also included the introduction of financial defined contribution (FDC) schemes in parallel with the NDC schemes. This led to downscaling of the FDC components of the overall system. In addition, Italy's slow transition and initial political reluctance to adjust newly granted annuities to life expectancy—a central component of NDC—finally had to be addressed as the financial crisis deepened. In sum, the lessons emphasize the importance of getting the basic design right from the outset. Despite some political turbulence, the original four NDC schemes have survived, and in Italy, the design has been improved in response to the crisis.

NDC is now widely considered to be one of the alternatives that countries contemplating reform of their public pension systems should review (Holzmann and Hinz 2005).[1] Because it is a relatively new concept, there is an even greater need than usual to examine the pros and cons of various possible design approaches.

NDC as a Pension Reform Alternative

Prior to 1994, when the first NDC pension system was legislated in Sweden (see Palmer 2000, 2002; Könberg, Palmer, and Sundén 2006), it was generally thought that a sustainable defined contribution pay-as-you-go (PAYG) pension scheme was an impossibility. A decade later, NDC had been introduced in a number of countries. Inspired by Sweden's new model, Latvia (Fox and Palmer 1999; Vanovska 2004, 2006; Palmer et al. 2006) formulated and legislated an NDC reform that was implemented on January 1, 1996. Italy introduced NDC in 1995 (Franco 2002; Franco and Sartor 2006; Gronchi and Nisticò 2006). The Kyrgyz Republic, taking note of the spread of information about Sweden's 1994 legislation, introduced NDC in 1996, for new entrants only (Palmer 2006a, 2007). In 1999, Poland initiated its NDC reform (Chłoń, Góra, and Rutkowski 1999; Góra 2001; Chłoń-Domińczak 2002; Chłoń-Domińczak and Góra 2006), as did Sweden. In Sweden, however, implementation was delayed, coming seven years after the concept was presented to the public in 1992 and five years after the initial legislation in 1994. Elements of NDC can also be found in other more recently reformed pension systems—for example, in the pension system introduced in 2002 by the Russian Federation (Hauner 2008).[2]

NDC combines PAYG financing with an individual lifetime account structure; individual accounts are based on contributions paid throughout the person's working career. The government sets a contribution rate on earnings from employment and self-employment that, in principle, is fixed for all generations and is paid by individuals or by employers on their behalf. Pensions are granted as life annuities, calculated from the individual's account balance and his or her birth cohort's life expectancy at retirement.[3] An internal rate of return, based on the economic fundamentals of the system, steers the system toward long-term financial balance and ensures maintenance of a fixed contribution rate—in principle, forever. This, together with the use of life expectancy in computing the annuity, maintains long-term financial sustainability at a fixed contribution rate.

The direct link between contributions and benefits in NDC means that individuals are rewarded with a higher pension for every extra monetary unit of contributions paid. This yields horizontal equity—the basis of NDC's claim to fairness. Because every marginal unit of contributions gives rise to an equivalent pension right, NDC does away with the disincentive to contribute that characterizes nonfinancial defined benefit (NDB) schemes. NDC, like financial defined contribution individual account schemes, lacks distributional features.[4] Nevertheless, it does provide an appealing framework for introducing an explicit distribution, as the government can create noncontributory rights that are not based on the individual's earnings. An example that all NDC countries have adopted is child-care rights granted for a period following childbirth. These rights, however, must always be accompanied by a source of finance external to the otherwise financially self-contained NDC scheme. The fundamental logic of NDC is that every monetary unit of a liability has to have a financial counterpart (contributions from earnings or from the government). This is a principle that, when fulfilled, ensures long-term financial balance, other things being equal.

NDC should be supplemented with a minimum income (pension) guarantee as a buffer for persons who have a small earnings-related pension, or none. The guarantee can be formulated as a universal flat-rate pension that constitutes the basic pension for everyone (the case in Russia) or as a top-up that is means tested only vis-à-vis the NDC and other public pension benefits (e.g., in Latvia, Poland, and Sweden) or against all income (as in Italy).

Given the actuarial link between benefits and contributions in NDC, there is no need to set either a vesting period for eligibility or a fixed final retirement age (a feature built into NDB schemes). NDC gives individuals the freedom to choose when to retire, after a statutory minimum pension age that is designed to protect people from myopic decisions to leave the labor force at too young an age—a step that can lead to a low lifetime pension and a higher risk of poverty in old age as a single survivor.

At a time when reforms of PAYG pension systems were badly needed (World Bank 1994; Disney 1996), the emergence of NDC provided a structural-reform alternative to the otherwise piecemeal reforms whereby countries were attempting to come to grips with unfair distributional rules and unaffordable schemes that pushed costs onto future generations. Nevertheless, NDC can achieve the desired results only if the scheme is well designed and correctly implemented.

In brief, NDC schemes combine (a) desirable economic incentives for individuals, (b) flexibility in making retirement decisions, (c) transparency in redistribution, and (d) mechanisms that ensure financial equilibrium. This chapter discusses how these schemes have been implemented in the four selected countries. A general conclusion that emerges is that NDC, as it has been implemented in these countries, is financially sustainable and provides adequate benefits for the average career worker. There are, however, several design issues that are important to discuss.

The next section provides a history of the evolution of NDC in the four selected countries. Subsequent sections review implementation and country design choices, analyze the outcomes for career workers, look at long-term financial outcomes, and examine special issues that have arisen in the four countries. The final section presents general conclusions.

A Brief History of the Evolution of NDC in Four Countries

Perhaps the major lesson to be drawn from the experience of the four countries considered here is that implementation of NDC reforms requires extensive preparatory work, at both the technical and the political levels, as well as good communication with the public and the development of an efficient administrative framework. That said, there is no one best route. Or, more appropriately, there are several paths that can lead to the same destination.

FOUR PATHS TO REFORM

The reform paths chosen by the four countries reflect the context within which they were undertaken. Italy and Sweden are Western European countries that faced the need to keep social spending under control, given the prospects of progressive aging of the population and of economic growth that was expected to be lower than in previous decades. Latvia and Poland were former members of the Soviet bloc that in 1990 suddenly found themselves in the position of having to adapt the pension systems inherited from the Soviet-style command economy to an emerging market economy, and at a time of extreme disruption in the labor market. All four countries faced aging populations and the need to introduce pension rules that could remove disincentives and, at best, create incentives for participation in the formal labor market. Encouraging participation in the formal labor force was at the top of the policy agenda in both Latvia and Poland, but it was also important in Italy and Sweden, where high rates of immigration from countries with other cultural customs and practices created a clear risk of increasing informality in the expanding service sector.

Italy and Sweden. By the early 1990s, it was evident that Italy and Sweden badly needed to reform their defined benefit (DB) pension systems. In both countries, pension schemes were not in long-term financial balance. In Sweden, the existing DB formula, with only 30 years required for a full benefit that was based on an average of the best 15 years of earnings, was especially unfavorable for people with long working careers—typically, blue-collar workers (Ståhlberg 1990)—and needed to be changed for this reason alone. Nevertheless, the public debate in Sweden and in Italy was driven by the prospect of unaffordable increases in expenditures (Palmer 2000; Franco 2002; Franco and Sartor 2006; Könberg, Palmer, and Sundén 2006).

In 1992, Sweden's Working Group on Pensions published an outline of the NDC reform—essentially, the reform that was legislated two years later, in mid-1994. What was left undecided at the time was whether to base the internal rate of return on growth of covered earnings or on growth of covered per capita earnings. Eventually, the politicians in the working group chose the latter. This led to the development of the solvency ratio, or balancing mechanism, approach toward maintaining balance in the event of labor force decline—a situation not dealt with by indexation solely with covered per capita earnings—and to an accompanying definition of the contribution asset.

The delay in the implementation of the Swedish reform until 1999 reflected existing political circumstances. The representatives of the governing right-center coalition, as well as the Social Democrats in the Working Group on Pensions and their party members in the parliament, supported the reform, as did the major labor unions, the Employer

Confederation, and the pensioners' organizations. Nevertheless, important factions within Sweden's large Social Democratic Party were not convinced. This forced a political "time-out" when Social Democrats took over the government in autumn 1994. During the hiatus, the Social Democratic party leadership discussed the reform with the party's opposition factions. The delay brought implementation to a halt until well into 1996, when the Social Democratic Party voted in its annual national meeting to accept the reform.

Once the implementation process had begun in Sweden, notional accounts were calculated using computerized register data on individual earnings beginning in 1960 and a contribution rate of 18 percent, which was about the rate needed to pay for an NDC scheme, given the parameters at that time. Child-care credits for up to four years per child were created retroactively, and other noncontributory credits were estimated, also using individual register data. At the same time, subsidiary legislation concerning the taxation of pensions, the minimum pension guarantee, and a means-tested housing allowance for pensioners was developed, and the entire information technology (IT) system for the administration of pensions was replaced with new technology. What was important, and has remained important, for the Swedish reform was the political consensus among the five political parties that, from 1994 through 2010, accounted for more than 80 percent of the seats in the parliament. According to the agreement, any new legislation for the pension system must be agreed by the five parties that are part of the consensus.

Both Italy and Sweden were hit hard by a recession and exchange rate crisis in the early 1990s. The deep recession and the mounting government debt needed to salvage overextended welfare commitments helped impart a sense of the urgency of reforming the pension system to bring the economy into long-term structural balance. For both countries, the prospect of entrance into European Union (EU) and eventually the European Monetary Union (EMU) also required the reduction of deficit and debt levels.[5] The introduction of NDC schemes was a way of achieving this reduction while securing intergenerational balance and financial stability in pension commitments. It also offered a means of increasing creditworthiness and restraining the cost of sovereign debt.

It was against this backdrop that both Italy and Sweden began pension reform. Whereas Sweden reformed in one step, Italy took several. Italy's chain of reforms began with the Amato reform in 1992, in which the government introduced a number of parametric changes that had been discussed already in the 1980s (see Franco 2002; Franco and Sartor 2006). The adjustments in the pension system in 1992 were necessary to rapidly restore confidence in public finances. The Amato reform reduced pension liabilities at the time by around 25 percent (Beltrametti 1996; Rostagno 1996); increased the standard retirement age by five years; shifted benefit indexation from wages to prices; and linked benefits to life-time earnings rather than to the average of the last five years of employment for private sector employees and the final wage for central government employees. Although benefits were based on lifetime earnings, the defined benefit formula was retained. Moreover, eligibility for seniority pensions remained constant at 35 years of coverage for private sector employees; for civil servants, it was rapidly raised from 20 to 35 years.[6]

Italy's 1995 reform took the full step of introducing NDC accounts, with account values at retirement to be converted into an annuity using conversion coefficients based on an estimate of life expectancy. The coefficients used to compute the annuities were to be revised every 10 years, beginning in 2005, to reflect changes in life expectancy. As it turned out, this revision was not implemented until 2010. Finally, the new rules were to be implemented gradually, applying fully only to new entrants in the labor force. This concession was the weak point of the Italian NDC reform.

Additional changes were introduced over several years. A revision in 1997 affected those subject to the pre-NDC rules. In 2004, the eligibility requirement for seniority pensions was tightened, with implementation beginning in January 2008 (but there was some backtracking in 2007). [7] In 2007, the interval between the revisions of the annuity coefficients was reduced to three years, with the first update in January 2010. Then, in 2009, the parliament voted to link the minimum retirement age to life expectancy, effective from 2015. In 2011, the adjustment of the retirement age to life expectancy was scheduled for 2013. Consequently, both the conversion coefficients and the retirement age will be adjusted over time on the basis of the same estimate of life expectancy.

Further changes were introduced at the end of 2011, under the pressure of new tension in the sovereign debt market: starting from January 2012, NDC accounts were created even for older workers not previously covered by NDC due to the initial transition rules; the statutory retirement age was set at 66 years from 2012 for all workers except for women in the private sector, for whom the pension age gradually increases to 66 beginning in 2018; and the eligibility requirements for seniority pensions were significantly tightened, although not completely abolished.

The rapid introduction of NDC in 1995 represented a striking development in Italian pension policy. The new rules aimed at improving the incentive structure of the pension system and automatically adjusting benefits to reflect demographic and economic trends. Preparatory work was limited, however, and very little information was provided to the public (Gronchi and Aprile 1998). No report was issued examining the reform's implications for public finances, the labor market, or the future economic situation of pensioners. In fact, the formula underlying the conversion coefficients was not immediately published.

The lack of any broad debate was understandable in the difficult economic context of 1992, but this was not the case in 1995, when the policy focus shifted from expenditure control to a wider range of objectives. The failure to conduct an open and extensive debate had negative implications both on the technical side (e.g., the self-equilibrating mechanisms introduced in 1995 were partial and slow) and on the political side. In particular, the lack of a broad consensus based on a shared understanding of the reform principles may explain why subsequent governments introduced a number of changes that were not consistent with the initial approach, such as the removal of any flexibility in retirement for male workers, the postponement of the adjustment of newly granted pensions with new coefficients, and—most strikingly—the continuation of seniority pensions. For several years, there also remained a gap between the effective contribution rates, especially for the self-employed, and the (higher) imputed rates used in the computation of benefits. Together with the lack of an extensive effort to inform the public, all these factors diluted the message of the Italian reform. Moreover, short-term political considerations led to a very slow transition from the old to the new system, avoiding immediate cuts in replacement rates, but at the cost of postponing savings in expenditures. This era finally came to an end in 2012, in response to the financial market pressure on the Italian sovereign debt, about 20 years after the first phase in Italian pension reform.

Latvia. The point of departure for Latvia's NDC reform was Sweden's 1994 legislation, first presented to the Latvian government in late 1994. Latvia developed and legislated its version of NDC in 1995 and implemented it in January 1996. The Latvian reform was driven in part by the prospect of future financial imbalance accompanying the aging of the population and in part by the need to adopt a system that would function efficiently in the emerging market economy. An important component of the prereform discussion was the need to create incentives for workers to pay their contributions. At the time of the reform discussion in 1995, 30 to 40 percent of individual earnings was estimated to be unreported (Fox and Palmer 1999). The message of the new NDC reform was that, from the very beginning in 1996, benefits for new retirees would be linked directly to individual contribution records.

A unique feature of the Latvian reform was a model for the conversion of individual work records from the Soviet period through December 1995 into NDC accounts, which were constructed as individuals applied for pensions beginning in January 1996. Individual work histories were valued using measures of current earnings during 1996–99. However, given the disruption in the labor market in the aftermath of the collapse of the Soviet economy, this turned out to yield an unreasonably low valuation of previously acquired rights for persons who had erratic employment records in the 1990s. To help rectify this imbalance, a minimum guarantee for persons with 30 or more years of recorded work experience before 1996 was introduced, to remain in force through 2011.[8] Another key feature of the Latvian reform process was the increase in the minimum pension age, from 55 for women and 60 for men to 62 for both, beginning in 1994.

One of the main political selling points of NDC in the Latvian discussion, as has already been mentioned, was the hope that the incentives provided by the strong link between contributions and pensions would encourage a higher degree of formality. In the beginning, a pervasive feeling of hardship made it difficult for the general population to grasp the logic of the principles of the new NDC scheme (Vanovska 2006). By 2004, however, there was already evidence that the reform had the desired effect (Palmer et al. 2006). This is far from a universal claim for the success of NDC or defined contribution (DC) schemes, however. Coverage data for Latin America in Forteza, Lucchetti, and Pallares-Miralles (2009), for example, indicate that DC is not a general panacea for informality; Latin America is still struggling with serious coverage problems, despite widespread implementation of DC schemes.

In Latvia, in the initial years, there was a political struggle concerning the legislation to increase the pension age. The political reaction was to grant early retirement rights, which continued over several years. This allowed a gradual transition, using the new NDC scheme's age-related actuarial adjustments of newly granted pensions. It was difficult for workers to adjust to the need to postpone retirement in order to receive a higher benefit and for employers to adjust to the idea of employees' working longer. At first, most women claimed a benefit at the earliest possible age, which in the beginning was age 56, whereas it would have been advisable, considering the actuarial adjustment of their pensions, to work until age 60 or longer. In other words, despite information to the contrary, women continued to believe that an early pension was an "extra" benefit—instead of a clear road into poverty in old age. The low de facto retirement age in the early reform years in Latvia is a reason for the very low average benefit of pensioners a decade and a half later, as we shall see further on in this study.

Poland. At the other extreme, it took Poland until 2009 to achieve an increase in the de facto pension age. The experience in Latvia and Poland demonstrates clearly that once a policy supporting or encouraging early exit from the labor force is embarked on, it is diffi-cult to end it, and that although such a policy may satisfy short-term interests, it will have harmful long-term consequences.

From the early 1990s, Poland struggled with the disorganization of the labor market created by the transition from the planned to the market economy, which, in practice, meant that the infrastructure for collecting contributions and taxes, as well as the pub-lic's willingness to pay taxes ("tax morale"), disintegrated. The high rate of unemploy-ment and increased engagement in sporadic informal work resulted in political pressure to grant pension benefits to an onslaught of claimants who had been workers under the Soviet regime. Not surprisingly, this remedy led to an increasing deficit in the pension system. The government responded to the increase in expenditures with ad hoc measures, including reduction of the wage base used to calculate pensions. This measure was over-ruled by the Constitutional Tribunal, however, and by 1997, the social security contribu-tion rate had reached 45 percent of the gross wage (Chłoń-Domińczak 2002). Clearly, a thorough and systemic overhaul of the system was needed to achieve long-run financial stability. The need for reform was related to the projected financial deficits, the product of a combination of demographic aging and excessive early retirement stemming from an extensive system of generous early retirement privileges (Góra and Rutkowski 1998). Incentives were needed to encourage workers to prolong their working careers, and NDC appeared to reform-minded politicians to be the ideal solution. Moreover, the pension system required a complete overhaul to regain public trust.

The work on the Polish reform began in 1996. The reform proposal, including the transformation of the system to a mixed NDC–FDC one, was published at the begin-ning of 1997. The simple message of linking benefits to contributions and pensions to life expectancy turned out to have popular appeal for Poles. The split between the NDC and FDC components of the overall reform was proposed to use the current privatization revenues to finance structural reform, including the reform of the pension system.

There was a broad political consensus on the pension reform concept from the outset, and the work on legislation in 1997 (for the FDC scheme) and 1998 (for NDC) went on uninterrupted despite changes in the political constitution of the government and the par-liament. The new system, which was implemented in 1999, has since then been accepted and improved by all successive governments (Chłoń-Domińczak 2002; Chłoń-Domińczak and Góra 2006). The Polish reform discussion in the years preceding implementation of the system in 1999 is generally recognized to be one of the best efforts of its kind.

Poland had the superfluity of special rights typical of the region, and, as in Latvia, a major challenge was to phase these out. The special rights inherited from the old regime were generally granted to persons below the age of 55 and in particular occupations; they financed early retirement for these individuals. Of course, the idea of granting publicly subsidized rights to special groups, often owing to their bargaining power, runs counter to the idea of NDC. In Latvia, special rights acquired under the old regime were converted into NDC account values with practically no protest, possibly because of the generosity of the conver-sion rules (Fox and Palmer 1999; Vanovska 2004). This was not to be the case in Poland.

In Poland, reformers recognized the importance of converting special rights into NDC account values but ran into stark opposition from the trade unions. This impasse led to the development of the concept of bridging pensions, which took until late 2008 to establish in legislation. In the meantime, in 2005, the parliament decided to move one occupational group (the miners) out of the NDC scheme and back to the old PAYG defined benefit system, with generous early retirement options. This was a major setback for the principle of universality and for the idea that, to the extent that special rights can be motivated, their cost should be factored into the cost of the products or services in question and provided by external occupational supplementary schemes. The bridging pension system, in place from 2009 on, helped raise the de facto retirement age, which had remained at around 55 for women and below 60 for men for the two decades from the beginning of the transition in the early 1990s.

Transition under the four systems. Transition rules are important when phasing in NDC. In practice, they differed considerably among the four counties—a point taken up in a subsequent section. Here, it suffices to note that Latvia began to grant NDC benefits in the first year of implementation, 1996. Sweden began in the third year after implementation, 2001, granting prorated new and old system benefits. Poland paid its first benefits in 2009, when women born in 1949 reached the minimum retirement age of 60. The first NDC payments to men will begin in 2014, when men born in 1949 turn 65. Italy's NDC reform covered only younger birth cohorts. As a consequence, the number of NDC pensions is still very small in Italy; they are mostly benefits paid by the new scheme for employer-coordinated freelance work set up after the 1995 reform.[9] As has already been mentioned, it took until 2012 for all contributions to be included in the NDC framework.

What the NDC reforms in the four countries had in common was that they were undertaken against the backdrop of a sense of economic urgency. Latvia and Poland were pressed in the initial years by the economic and social chaos following the dismantling of the Soviet-style command economy, which created an excess supply of low-skilled older workers. Especially in Poland, the social security system—in particular, early retirement and disability pensions—provided a convenient way out, although this use of the system was clearly unsustainable. In fact, more than 80 percent of pensioners had retired well before the pension ages of 55 for women and 60 for men. The transition period would inevitably come to an end, however, as changes in the rules enabling early retirement became critical to halt the rise in the dependency ratio. The additional appeal of introducing NDC in Latvia and Poland was that it provided an incentive for younger workers to join the formal labor force. Reform was necessary to cope with the rapidly emerging opportunities for informal work.

THE RETIREMENT AGE

Italy, Latvia, and Poland all started their reform processes in the 1990s with relatively low statutory and de facto retirement ages. The statutory ages were 55 for women and 60 for men in all three countries. However, the widespread use of special rights in Latvia and Poland meant that the de facto pension age was much lower than the straightforward average of 57.5; for example, benefits could be claimed from age 40 by persons working in hazardous conditions. Seniority rules in Italy allowed for retirement, especially by men, before the standard retirement age. The average of age of exit was even lower, as a result of exit with disability. By contrast, in Sweden, where the minimum pension age was 60, the average age of exit from work, including other forms of exit such as disability, was 62 as early as the mid-1990s, before the NDC reform (Palme and Svensson 1999).[10]

In Sweden, the de facto pension age has continued to drift upward since the introduction of NDC, but there is no evidence either for or against a connection. In fact, there is a tendency to retire both earlier and later, creating a more pronounced dispersion around the mean. In 2009, 10 years after the introduction of NDC, the de facto pension age in Sweden was close to 63, whereas the minimum age at which an NDC pension can be claimed is 61 (SSIA 2009). Discussions of changes in the pension age have focused on increasing the age to which all Swedes have the right to retain their employment, from 67, at present, to 69 or 70, so that those who can and want to work at least this long can easily do so. Also, the Swedish NDC rules enable workers to combine 25, 50, 75 percent, or full benefits with any degree of employment after having passed the minimum age for claiming a public pension. This provision makes it easy to combine part-time work with part-time retirement.

In Italy, the 1992 reform increased the normal retirement age from 55 for women and 60 for men to 60 and 65, respectively, but seniority rules watered down the effect. In the NDC system introduced in 1995, individuals retiring with an NDC pension were initially allowed to retire between the ages of 57 and 65. In 2004, the minimum NDC retirement age was set at 65 for men, without any flexibility, and at 60 for women, with the possibility of postponing retirement to age 65. The new rules thus coincided with the requirements for those retiring under the pre-NDC regime. In 2004, seniority retirement, which was meant to disappear with the phasing out of the defined benefit regime, was instead extended to the NDC scheme. Both men and women with 40 years of contributions were allowed to retire at any age, and they were allowed to retire at age 61 (62 for the self-employed) if they had 36 years of acquired rights.

Taking on board the changes introduced in the last months of 2011, as of 2012 the statutory retirement age for those who started to work before 1996 (whose pension is partly computed with the pre-NDC rules) is 66 for all males and for females in the public sector. It is 62 for females in the private sector, rising gradually to the general level by 2018. However, female workers are allowed to retire earlier on a seniority pension with 41 years and 1 month of contributions while males need 42 years and 1 month of contributions (a reduction of benefits is envisaged for those retiring before 62). All these age criteria will be adjusted automatically to changes in life expectancy from 2013 onward. The first increase will be with three months, implying that the statutory retirement age in 2013 will be 66 years and three months. For those who are fully under the NDC rules (those paying contributions from 1996 onward), the retirement age will be 63, provided the pension is at least 2.8 times the amount of the welfare pensions for poor elderly individuals. This age limit will also be adjusted to changes in life expectancy. For both groups, at least 20 years of contributions are required.

Before legislating NDC in 1994, Latvia had already enacted a stepwise increase in the minimum pension age of women from 55 to 60, which at that time was the pension age for men. As the concept of NDC emerged in 1995, the motivation behind this measure became even more compelling. Under a defined contribution scheme, and with life annuities based on life expectancy at retirement, a low pension age increases the likelihood of falling into poverty in old age. This was especially a problem when the pension age was 55 for women, increasing the likelihood of a widowed woman's having to live a long life as a single survivor on an inadequate pension. Latvia revisited the issue after the reform. Since 2010, 62 years has been the minimum pension age for both men and women.

Polish reformers have struggled unsuccessfully to increase the minimum pension age of women to above 60. The initial 1997 proposal included the equalization of the minimum retirement age for men and women at 62. This proposal did not receive political support, and the final legislation retained age 60 for women and 65 for men. Another attempt was made in 2004 under the Hausner program, named for the deputy prime minister who proposed a series of structural changes to improve social expenditures, but this plan, too, was withdrawn because of political disagreement.[11] (For further details, see Chłoń-Domińczak and Góra 2006.)

In 2008, Poland's ombudsman claimed that different retirement ages for men and women was against the constitutional right of equal treatment and nondiscrimination. The Constitutional Tribunal did not share his opinion and, in July 2010, ruled that the difference in retirement ages is in accordance with the constitution. (Three judges, all women, disagreed with this decision.) Nevertheless, the tribunal recognized the need to equalize retirement ages of men and women and urged the parliament to start this process through appropriate legislation.

What Poland did succeed in doing within the framework of the reform was to withdraw widespread early retirement options, including those for women, who had been able to retire at age 55 with 30 years of seniority. Equalization of the retirement age for men and women is still needed. We return to this issue later.

Figure 2.1, produced by the national authorities for the European Union Ageing Working Group (AWG), shows the estimated effect of the NDC reforms on the average age of exit from the labor force. Note that the starting point is particularly low in Italy and Poland; the reforms are expected to set these countries on a path that will lead toward convergence with Sweden (except in the case of Polish women, unless the pension age is changed). Long-term projections are obviously difficult. In particular, it is difficult to model how people will react to changes in longevity and how they will use the flexibility allowed by NDC in deciding their retirement age. However, the broad trends are clear: the retirement age is increasing, and countries are likely to converge.

FIGURE 2.1 **Estimated impact of pension reforms on average age of exit from the labor force in 2060**

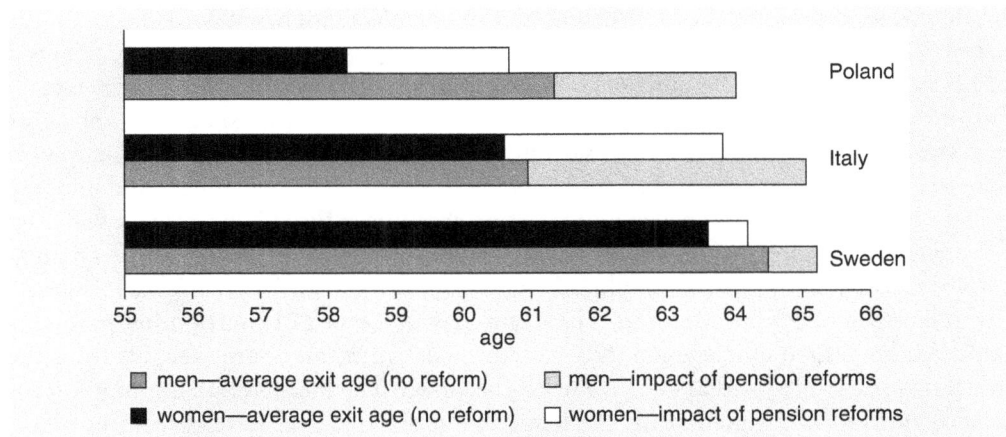

Legend:
- men—average exit age (no reform)
- women—average exit age (no reform)
- men—impact of pension reforms
- women—impact of pension reforms

SOURCE: European Commission and Economic Policy Committee 2009.

ADMINISTRATIVE AND COMMUNICATION ISSUES

In all four countries, the new legislation required the introduction of new information technology, staff training, and the development of communication strategies to inform the public about the principles of the new system.

Administration. NDC requires that information on contributions—the building blocks of personal accounts—be provided and recorded on an individual basis. The development of the administration of the system typically has to do with handling information flows concerning individual contributions and reconciling these with money flows.

The administrations in Italy and Sweden were already set up to collect and process the kind of information required. Latvia and Poland lacked systems that connected contribution payment flows with flows of individual information. In addition, these two countries came from a tradition in which client services were primitive, whereas NDC requires a strong focus on dissemination of information to the insured public.

In 1995, when the Latvian NDC reform was being designed, the social insurance administration was still an artifact from the previous Soviet years, without modern accounting, IT, or customer services, nor was there a head office to exercise leadership of the implementation of the reform. The first step was to create the State Social Insurance Agency, under which existing regional social insurance offices were connected to a new head office and formal guidelines were put in place for the relation between the government and the newly created independent state agency. Collection of contributions was moved from the "old" Social Insurance Agency to the tax authority, and the administration was reorganized to suit the new legislative environment. A new system for collecting personal information on contributions was implemented beginning in January 1996. The process of converting work records from previous years, as documented in personal workbooks, into "initial capital" for individual accounts began with persons claiming pensions from January 1996.

In Poland, the collection of contributions remained with the social insurance administration, but beginning in January 1999, collection routines moved from a structure in which gross contributions were paid by employers to one with payments consistent with information flows for individuals. Work history prior to 1999 is provided by the individual on applying for calculation of individual initial capital. During the preparation of the reform, communication between the government and the administration was inadequate. As the reform went into effect in January 1999, IT support for the administration was not designed sufficiently well to reconcile individual information with aggregate employer payments; in fact, it took about two years after the implementation of the reform to do this. The chaos thus created directed the public discussion away from the content of the reform and toward the perceived incompetence of the administration (Chłoń-Domińczak 2002). And once the mistake had been made, reconciliation of pension accounts in Poland was a lengthy process.

Finally, to improve the quality of information, employers (except for very small employers, as well as the self-employed) were required by law to transfer information electronically to the administration. The day-to-day processing of contribution payments achieved the desired efficiency in 2004, but even 10 years later, some records from the initial two years, 1999 and 2000, were not fully correct. The Polish lesson is important for other countries contemplating the implementation of NDC: the development of policy and of its administration must go hand in hand prior to implementation.

Communication to the public. The underlying principle of NDC, and the key message that has to be communicated to the pulic, is that an individual's benefits are determined by his or her contributions, a rate of return based on economic growth, and the individual's birth cohort's life expectancy at retirement. As has already been noted, one reason why countries opt to introduce NDC is to convey the message that individual benefits depend on individual contributions and the individual cohort's life expectancy. These features of NDC encourage participation in the formal labor force by those who have a choice of working informally. They also provide an incentive for postponement of exit from the labor force near the end of the working career because additional employment and delay of retirement reward workers with a higher yearly benefit in retirement.

The efficacy of a reform in achieving the goals of increased formality and delayed exit from the formal labor force at successively higher ages as longevity increases will depend on success in conveying the principles of NDC to the population. Information and communication are thus key to the success of an NDC reform. The Latvian, Polish, and Swedish reforms were accompanied by well-planned public information campaigns that helped introduce the logic of the reforms to the public. In Italy, by contrast, little effort was put into a communication strategy regarding the 1995 reform (see Franco and Sartor 2006).

The Latvian reform was introduced primarily with the help of television campaigns and radio programs, together with mass media coverage of the political debate in the parliament. In the years following the reform, the Latvian government and the newly formed State Social Insurance Agency devoted considerable resources to communicating the content of the reform and developing a modern, customer-oriented administration. From 1997 to 2006, the State Social Insurance Agency sent participants a yearly statement of contributions that had been paid for them. Beginning in 2007, the annual statement was replaced by provision of information on request. One shortcoming of implementation in Latvia was that the government never provided sufficient resources to register historical work books from before 1996 prior to a person's retirement. This means that people have only incomplete information for determining the pension they will get at retirement. They can, however, contact a local office for help with calculating, prospectively, the pension they will receive on the basis of previous work records, the conversion formula, and registered contributions since 1996.

In Sweden, there was a long process of communication with unions, pension organizations, other institutional interests, and the general public, beginning with the publication as early as 1992 of an overview of the basic elements of the reform proposal (Könberg, Palmer, and Sundén 2006). Sweden also became the leader in providing extensive information to individuals in tandem with the implementation of its NDC scheme. The Orange Envelope, a yearly account statement, was developed and has been sent to all participants from the outset, in 1999. In addition, the *Orange Report*, the annual report of the Swedish pension system, has been published since 2001. Swedes can also view information on their accounts through the Internet. This information can be combined with standard growth assumptions regarding future earnings or with more specific information provided by the individuals themselves to calculate possible pension levels at chosen retirement ages.

Supported by a media campaign, the Polish reform captured the attention of the mass media, giving rise to an extensive public discussion of the principles of defined contribution schemes—that is, of the principles of the reform. So, when reform came in

1999, the general public was well informed, and opinion polls showed popular support for the principles of NDC and FDC. Because of the IT problems at the outset of the reform, as already mentioned, information for participants could not be sent out until 2002, and at first it included only data on NDC contributions paid in the most recent calendar year. From 2006 on, it also included the value of the individual's NDC account at the beginning of the year and information on contributions paid in the previous calendar year. Beginning in 2008, the information sent to individuals has been very extensive, including information on NDC account values, the value of initial capital computed on the basis of rights acquired prior to 1999, contributions paid into the NDC and FDC schemes, and hypothetical pensions, given the individual's account value and assuming continued contribution payments in line with the past.

At the other extreme, in Italy, the information made available to the public was opaque, and there was no extensive debate preceding its implementation. It took until 2010 for the National Social Security Institute (INPS) to systematically inform individuals about the amount of contributions they paid in the past, and that was without any projection of the benefits they could expect. Long-term aggregate pension expenditure projections are regularly made available to the Italian public, but there is no special focus on the NDC scheme per se.

In the case of Italy, the fact that a large part of the workforce was not affected by the reform meant that it was difficult to introduce a single package of information for everyone. In addition, the reform was widely perceived as being incomplete, as indicated by the ongoing discussion on further reforms and by the changes actually introduced in the NDC framework after 1995. As a result, those immediately affected (i.e., younger workers) may have perceived the conditions of the contract as uncertain. Finally, as of the time of this writing, a systematic effort had not been made to explain to the general public the logic and construction of the new system.

In sum, each of the four countries encountered specific obstacles, whether political disagreement, administrative difficulties, or problems of transition from the old to the new system. And, as no one size fits all, the four countries adopted different ways of moving forward. Yet all fit into the conceptual framework of NDC.

NDC at Work in Four Countries

The design of the NDC schemes in Italy, Latvia, Poland, and Sweden exhibits both similarities and differences. These can affect future levels of benefits, as well as the overall performance of the schemes. In this section, we describe the coverage and design of the four systems.

COVERAGE

The NDC schemes in Latvia and Sweden are truly universal and cover the entire labor force. Universal coverage was a feature of both Latvian and Swedish social insurance long before their NDC pension reforms, so the implementation of their NDC schemes followed the established tradition. In Poland, by contrast, some parts of the workforce are not covered by the general NDC scheme, and in Italy, coverage conditions are not homogenous. The causes are the fragmentation of the pension systems prior to the implementation of

NDC and the inability—or unwillingness—of politicians to move away from established institutions, even though the reform process provided an opportunity to change path dependency.

Table 2.1 highlights the exceptions to universality in Italy and Poland. In Italy, the exceptions are for some groups of self-employed workers whose pensions are managed on a semiprivate basis. In Poland, exceptional status is given to farmers, miners, and some categories of public sector workers. The largest exception to the principle of universality in all four countries is Polish farmers, who constitute almost 20 percent of the country's working population. Most farm holdings are very small—too small, in fact, to earn a living from. The special status granted the farmers presents an opportunity for them to be excluded from paying contributions on farming activities and runs against the principle of a universal NDC scheme, setting a bad example for workers in other sectors. In addition, at present, contributions from farmers cover only about 5 percent of the costs of the separate farmers' pension system, whereas the benefit received is about 20 percent higher than the general revenue-financed minimum pension guarantee available to everyone else.

Initially, Poland's NDC scheme also covered people working in the armed forces (military, police, and so on), but in 2001, the government decided to take this group back into the noncontributory pension system, with pension rights granted after 15 years of service. In 2005, following demonstrations on the streets of Warsaw before the presidential and parliamentary elections, the miners also managed to gain a return to a more generous PAYG defined benefit scheme, with the possibility of retirement after 25 years of work underground. As these examples show, initial support for the pension reform weakened, especially for groups that traditionally enjoyed "special" status in the Polish labor market. This corroborates the well-known fact that once one group—in this case, farmers—obtains special rights, the door is opened for additional demands. To the extent that groups may have legitimate claims to special rights, these should, in principle, be financed through the market mechanism, that is, through private (occupational) pensions.

TABLE 2.1 **Coverage of the four NDC systems**

Year of implementation	Italy 1995	Latvia 1996	Poland 1999	Sweden 1999
Coverage	Employees and self-employed	Universal	Employees and self-employed	Universal
Exceptions	A few independent plans with a small number of workers, mainly professionals	No exceptions	Farmers (as of 1999) Judges and prosecutors (1999) Military (2001) Police (2001) Prison staff (2001) Border guards (2001) Miners (2005)	No exceptions

SOURCE: Authors' elaboration from country legislation and information from legislative experts.

In the case of miners, special rights awarded because of their harsh working conditions should not be subsidized by the government through special pension privileges; rather, they should be reflected in the prices of mining products, including the cost of paying for improvement of work environments.

INTEGRATION WITH OTHER PILLARS OF THE PENSION SYSTEM

In all four countries, the NDC pension is the main source of future pension income, but it is not the only one. In Latvia, Poland, and Sweden, the mandatory NDC component is supplemented by a mandatory financial defined contribution component (table 2.2). The division of contributions between NDC and FDC differs in these three countries. The largest share for NDC (86.5 percent of total contributions) is found in Sweden. Latvia at first aspired to split the overall contribution rate of 20 percent in 2010 evenly between NFC and FDC.

It had been clear from the beginning that Latvia could not afford to increase the FDC contribution rate beyond 6 percent without increasing the overall contribution rate to pay for both the old system and the NDC benefits (Palmer et al. 2006), together with a 10 percent contribution rate for the prefunded FDC scheme. The economic crisis that began in autumn 2008 showed the overall commitment to be too great, confirming the initial calculations. The government's response was to legislate, in 2009, a new split of 14 percent for NDC and 6 percent for FDC, starting in 2012, which means that 70 percent of overall contributions will go to NDC accounts. In Poland, about 63 percent of total contributions goes to NDC and 37 percent to FDC.

TABLE 2.2 **Contribution rates for pensions as a share of wages**
percent

	Italy	**Latvia**	**Poland[a]**	**Sweden**
Contribution rate for retirement savings	33 (employees) 20 (self-employed) 24 (atypical contracts)	20	19.5	18.5
NDC contribution	33 (employees) 20 (self-employed) 24 (atypical contracts)	14, from 2012	12.2	16.0
FDC contribution	Voluntary scheme	6, from 2012[b]	7.3	2.5
Existence of occupational and voluntary systems	Yes; initially low but gradually rising (20% of labor force in 2008)	Yes, but very low coverage	Yes, but very low coverage	Yes; high coverage

SOURCE: Authors' elaboration from country data.

NOTE: The contribution rates presented are as legislated in the countries. The wage base may differ because it includes part of the contribution paid by the employee.

a. Cohorts born between 1949 and 1968 may either leave their full old-age contribution (19.52 percent) in NDC accounts or split it between NDC and FDC. In the first case, the full contribution is also registered in the account. Beginning in April 2011, the contribution diverted to FDC accounts is 2.3 percent; it will gradually rise to 3.5 percent by 2018.

b. The contribution to the FDC scheme was reduced from 8 percent to 2 percent in January 2009; it was scheduled to increase to 4 percent in January 2011 and 6 percent in January 2012, but remained at 2 percent. It is expected to increase to 6 percent in 2013 and then to remain there.

Italy has a voluntary FDC scheme based on contributions for severance pay. Legislation was enacted in 1993 and in later years to develop supplementary pension funds. Governments have attempted to shift the contributions for severance pay benefits, which amount to 6.9 percent of each worker's gross earnings. Severance pay benefits are disbursed by employers to employees on the termination of an employment contract. Employees choose whether to retain the severance pay benefits or to join a pension fund, with an occupational defined contribution pension fund being the default option. Additional contributions can also be paid, usually on the basis of agreements between social partners. In 2010, about 20 percent of the labor force was enrolled in a voluntary supplementary pension fund.

TRANSITION MODELS

Given that most of the contributors covered by the new system had worked a significant part of their professional careers under the old pension systems, countries implementing NDC needed to find some way to honor past pension rights in creating NDC accounts and transition benefits. The rules embrace two main areas: the cohorts of workers to be covered by the new scheme, and either the transfer of accrued pension rights to the new regime or the conversion of acquired rights into NDC account values. Each country constructed the transition rules differently (table 2.3). In Latvia, Poland, and Sweden, the transition was relatively rapid, with Latvia being the fastest, followed by Sweden. In Italy, it was slow.

The second and third rows of table 2.3 make clear the principal differences in the implementation strategies of Latvia, Poland, and Sweden, compared with Italy. In Latvia and Sweden, the switch was mandatory for all. In Latvia, persons born in 1941 were fully covered by the NDC rules. In Sweden, persons born in 1938 were partially covered by the old system and partially by NDC, with full coverage coming first to persons born in 1954. In Poland, persons born in 1949 were the first to be covered by NDC, which meant that the first NDC pensions were paid out 10 years after the introduction of NDC in 1999—that is, in 2009.[12]

In Italy, the cohort of persons born in 1978 was the first entire cohort in which everyone is mandatorily covered by NDC. If the 1978 cohort members retire at age 65, this cohort will retire in 2043. Older cohorts were also covered by NDC if they had fewer than 18 years of recorded contributions prior to implementation in 1995. Consequently, a majority of the workforce was allowed to continue to use the pre-1995 pension rules. Moreover, the NDC regime in Italy applies only to contributions made from 1996 on, combined with a pro rata procedure for rights acquired prior to 1996; that is, acquired rights were not converted into initial individual account capital, as in Latvia, Poland, and Sweden. For a long time to come, then, many individuals will retire with a pension consisting of two components, one computed under the old rules and the other according to the NDC rules. This political choice, which was aimed at reducing opposition to the reform, shifted the cost-reducing impact of the reform considerably into the future. This was a factor contributing to Italy's fiscal stress in the economic crisis from 2008.

Until the law was changed beginning in 2012, the Italian approach also clearly diluted the behavioral message of NDC—that benefits are based on contributions. In 2010, 15 years after the introduction of NDC, pre-NDC pensions still represented the bulk not only of the stock of benefits but also of the flow of new benefits. It is not surprising that the slow transition was generally recognized by Italian experts to be the Achilles'

TABLE 2.3 **Cohorts covered by the NDC scheme**

	Italy	Latvia	Poland	Sweden
Coverage policy	From 2012, all contributions of all contributors are included in the new system. Those with 18 or more years of contributions can opt for the new system. For those working before 1995, pensions are calculated according to a mixed formula.	All contributors are in the new system from 1996 on.	Mandatory for people younger than 50 in 1999, with the exception of those who could retire before 2009 according to the old rules.	All persons born in 1938 and later are covered.
Oldest (first) birth cohort with NDC	Mandatory NDC: 1960	1941	1949	Persons born in 1938 are partially covered by NDC, and persons born in 1954 and later are fully covered, with prorating for cohorts in between.
First birth cohort for which all NDC years are based solely on actual contribution information	1978	1981	1981	1983

SOURCE: Authors' elaboration from country data.

NOTE: NDC = nonfinancial defined contribution.

heel of the Italian NDC reform (Franco and Sartor 2006). As has already been discussed, this deficiency was finally rectified with the 2011 legislation, applying from 2012.

In Sweden, notional capital for individual accounts was based on existing computerized individual earnings records from 1960 and based on a contribution rate of 18 percent.[13] In the Swedish transition formula, two pensions are calculated for persons born between 1938 and 1953, using both the old and the new rules. A person born in 1938 receives 4/20 of his or her pension from the NDC scheme and 16/20 from the old system. The relation changes by 1/20 for each new cohort, ending with persons born in 1954, who have 20/20 in the new system. The same "smoothing" effect could have been achieved with a much shorter transition period—say, 5 to 10 years.[14]

In Latvia, initial capital was computed for individual accounts on the basis of work histories (workbooks from Soviet times), valued with individual wages for 1996–99. This was a good idea in principle, but in practice the poor labor market in these transition years resulted in sporadic employment and, consequently, in low annual earnings for many. As a cushion, a special (higher) guarantee was granted to persons with at least 30 years of service. This special guarantee rule, which applied through 2010, set the level of the minimum benefit at the higher of either that deriving from the individual's capital at retirement, based on his or her own record valued with the individual's wages for 1996–99, or an amount equivalent to 40 percent of the average wage during the valuation period.

Poland, like Latvia, transformed past rights into initial capital. In Poland, the formula that was applied based initial capital on the value of a pension in the old system if it were to be computed and paid out at the end of 1998, given the individual's work record. This approach was chosen mainly because of the absence of sufficient individual records at the Social Security Institution (ZUS), which, prior to the reform, collected relevant data only in conjunction with a benefit claim. Because most of the individual records existing prior to 1980 had not been saved in any form, the creation of a value of NDC accounts based on earnings records, as in Sweden, was not possible.

The G-value (the divisor applied to calculate the annuity) that was used to convert acquired rights from the old system into NDC initial capital assumed a retirement age of 62. If G-values for 60 and 65 had been used to calculate initial capital, a woman with a work history identical to a man's would have been granted initial capital 30 percent higher than would a man the same age, since her benefit under the old system would have been paid out for a considerably longer time. As this was politically unacceptable, an equal G-value was used for men and women based on life expectancy at age 62. The lower retirement age for women, assuming that they claim their benefit at the minimum age, will lead to a low pension level for women in the new system, as they lose from the conversion. To prevent the sudden change in the benefit level, another transition rule is applied for women retiring between 2009 and 2013. During these years, pensions will be calculated using a mixed old-new formula, with a rising proportion of the NDC part of the benefit (from 20 percent in 2009 to 80 percent in 2013).

Assessment of the transition rules reveals issues and problems in Italy and Poland. In Italy, the youngest birth cohorts of workers can be covered either by the old system (with 18 or more years of contributions) or by the new system, which by definition is less generous for persons with fewer years of contributions. In Poland, a similar discontinuity appears between 49-year-olds covered by the new system and 50-year-olds, who remain in the old scheme, and it is only partially dealt with through the transition rules described above. These discontinuities obviously raise equity issues.

Conversion of pension entitlements acquired before the introduction of NDC into initial capital, as in Latvia and Poland, and into notional capital, as in Sweden, also means that life expectancy changes that occur after the introduction of the new scheme reduce the value of prereform rights. In practice, this diminishes the legacy costs of the old system in all three countries. This was not the case for Italy, where NDC rules apply only to contributions paid since 1996, so that until 2020, most new pensions will be paid on a pre-NDC basis and only after 2035 will most new benefits be paid fully on an NDC basis. In all four countries, individuals can mitigate the decline in the benefit ratio by postponing retirement.

INDIVIDUAL ACCOUNTS

Apart from the contribution rate, there are three elements that influence the value of an individual NDC account: (a) credits granted for noncontributory rights and payments made from general budget revenues to support rights associated with periods important from a social policy perspective, (b) the inheritance gain from account holders who die during the accumulation phase, and (c) indexation.

Credits granted for periods outside employment. All four countries recognize some periods outside employment that are important from a social or general policy perspective by crediting notional accounts with additional contributions, paid, in principle, from general public revenues (table 2.4).

All four countries cover periods of unemployment, as well as periods of maternity and parental leave, covered by public insurance programs. (In Italy, the latter is taken into account through a more generous coefficient used for pension calculation.) Except in Latvia, periods of mandatory military service are covered. Poland, Latvia, and Sweden credit years of care for disabled children; the credit in Poland is subject to an income test. Latvia and Sweden also cover periods of sickness, work injury, and disability that are covered by public insurance. Sweden credits periods of postgymnasium education and of care for sick children and extremely sick relatives at home under public insurance programs.

The Swedish model for old-age pension rights for persons receiving disability benefits is to impute contributions for insured periods of disability and pay them into the old-age pension system. These payments are made yearly from general tax revenues, are entered as a cost of the disability system in the country's accounts, and are part of the transfer from state revenues to the NDC pension fund. Disability benefits are converted into old-age benefits at age 65. In Latvia, transfers to finance social rights are carried out as transfers inside the social insurance budget, which in practice means they are covered by a surplus generated by contributions not earmarked for NDC. Disability benefits are converted into old-age benefits at the minimum pension age.

Italy and Poland do not pay contributions for periods of disability. In Italy, disability pensions are based on the notional capital at the time of disability, which is integrated taking into account the gap between the age of the individual when the pension is granted and the reference age of 60. From the point of view of system finances, granting people a higher than actuarially fair conversion is quite all right if the government covers the extra cost with general revenues. Gronchi and Nisticò (2006) point out that there is no correspondence between the disability benefit and the old-age pension rights of persons on disability benefits where this procedure has been applied. This means that the NDC scheme is underfinanced.

In Poland, the lack of a clear relationship between the two components of social insurance is even more acute than in Italy. When the disability benefit recipient reaches retirement age, the disability pension is converted into an old-age pension. If the disability pension is higher, the value of the old-age benefit is increased to the value of the disability pension, creating, as in Italy, an unfunded right. If, however, a person receives a disability pension for some time during the working career and then retires from work, years with a disability benefit are not taken into account, which creates a risk of lower benefits for people with prolonged spells of disability. In addition, the disability pension formula in Poland is similar to the old defined benefit pension formula. That means that for persons close to the retirement age, the potential disability pension is almost always higher than the old-age pension, creating a higher risk of disability pension take-up.

Sweden is the only country that actually transfers money to an NDC fund to fund all the social rights as they are granted, with a precise legal framework governing the procedure.[15] The Italian method of using more generous transformation coefficients for

TABLE 2.4 **Components of individual accounts during the accumulation phase**

	Italy	Latvia	Poland	Sweden
Notional rate of return	GDP growth	Covered wage bill growth	Covered wage bill growth	Per capita wage growth
Inheritance gains	Increase in general reserve	Increase in general reserve	Increase in general reserve	Distributed on a birth cohort basis to the accounts of survivors in the cohort based on their relative share in the sum of all accounts in the cohort
Additional credits to notional account				
Insured periods of unemployment	Yes; based on past wage, up to total of 5 years	Yes	Yes; based on unemployment benefit, only when eligible for benefit (around 12 months)	Yes
Maternity and parental leave	Contributions are accrued during periods of maternity leave. There is a more generous transformation coefficient for mothers.	Yes	Yes	Yes
Care of a disabled child		Yes	Yes; income tested	Yes
Conscripted military service	Yes		Yes	Yes
Insured periods of income loss due to sickness		Yes		Yes
Periods covered by public disability insurance		Yes		Yes
Insured periods of income loss compensated by public insurance for work-related injury or sickness		Yes		Yes
Care of seriously sick relatives				Yes
Postgymnasium education				Yes

SOURCE: Authors' elaboration from country data.

special groups (mothers and, as mentioned earlier, the self-employed) at retirement is a clear vestige of the old defined benefit scheme, as is the Polish model. In both cases, rights are not accompanied by a clearly defined means of external finance and in this sense break with the underlying principle of NDC. The situation is similar in Latvia. Hence, in Italy, Latvia, and Poland, the financing of these social rights relies on the state's upholding an implicit contract and providing any necessary injection of money when the time comes. The "missing" finances could be covered through redistribution within the insurance pool, but that would require the creation of rules to achieve this end, which would have distributional consequences. To sum up, in these countries, the source of finance for rights not based on individual earnings is not clearly specified, and there is a clear conflict with the NDC principle that every liability should have a counterpart in an asset.

Distribution of inheritance gains. A difference between a prefunded FDC and an NDC scheme lies in the way the capital accounts of persons who die during the accumulation period (the inheritance gains) are used. This difference is arguably consistent with what people believe is "right." That is, the design of a mandatory prefunded scheme may logically specify that the assets of deceased participants are to be inherited by that individual's survivors, but in the mandatory public NDC scheme, which is a PAYG scheme, it is logical to distribute the capital of the deceased to the surviving scheme participants. This can be done within the deceased's own birth cohort, in proportion to the surviving participants' shares in the total of the cohort's accounts, and this is, in fact, what is done in Sweden.

In the other three countries, no use of this money is identified, and it implicitly becomes a component of general public revenues. In Poland and Latvia, these revenues provide a source of finance for other insurance commitments with no specified source—for example, the legacy costs from the old system. An alternative that may be more in line with what people think is "right" is to use the money to finance a survivor benefit for surviving spouses or children (or both), but none of these countries has adopted this approach explicitly.

In Italy, the reform of 1995 basically extended the previous rules for survivors. A surviving spouse receives 60 percent of the deceased's pension. The pension amount is increased to 70 percent if the only recipient is a child. If there are more dependents, the pension is apportioned according to their number, with the ceiling being 100 percent of the deceased's entitlement. The method for computing transformation coefficients assumes that the insured has a spouse and implies a general transfer of rights from single persons to married couples. Although this is a common practice in defined benefit schemes, it is not an uncontroversial principle.

Indexation of accounts during the accumulation phase. The issue of indexation of notional accounts during the accumulation phase and benefits paid to pensioners is central to the success of an NDC scheme. To maintain financial equilibrium, the notional interest rate, or the internal rate of return, should be equal to the growth of the covered wage bill, which reflects average wage growth and changes in the labor force. This rate of return would be applied to all liabilities, that is, to workers' accounts and pensioners' benefits (accounts). As a result, the revenues (contribution assets) and liabilities of the pension system grow at the same pace. (See Palmer 1999, 2012; Valdés-Prieto 2000.) The four countries differ considerably with regard to the indexation of accounts during the accumulation phase. We next discuss how these countries handle indexation and the results of their choices, beginning with Latvia and Poland.

In Latvia and Poland, accounts are indexed using the rate of growth of the covered wage bill. In this way, economic growth is reflected in the growth of pension rights, as is (normally, infrequent) economic decline. For example, in Latvia, the annualized real rate of return on workers' accounts during the accumulation phase was 6.6 percent from 1997 through 2003 and 14.6 percent from 2004 through 2008. Then, as a result of the economic crisis that began in 2008, accounts were indexed downward in 2009 by 7.2 percent. According to the Latvian Ministry of Welfare, about 80 percent of the growth registered was attributable to per capita wage growth and the remainder to expansion of the covered labor force. The decline accompanying the recession was mainly driven by a dramatic fall in employment.

Initially, the indexation of notional accounts in Poland was based on the rate of inflation plus 75 percent of real wage growth in the economy. Because one of the most important political and social concerns of the new pension system is the adequacy of future benefits, the indexation rule was changed to 100 percent of wage-sum growth, but not less than the increase in prices. At the same time, indexation was changed from 1999, ex post, to comply with the new rules. The indexation of accounts was not very high initially, as a result of the low wage and employment growth observed during the first half of the first decade of the 21st century. In 2006–07, the labor market situation changed, with strong growth in both employment—the highest growth among European Union (EU) countries—and wages. Indexation of notional accounts peaked, resembling the situation observed in Latvia. Poland managed to maintain positive economic growth in 2008 and 2009, when most countries were experiencing negative numbers, and the NDC return remained positive.

The guiding principle behind Polish pension reform was security through diversity. Comparison of the NDC and FDC rates of return, presented in figure 2.2, shows that the Polish concept worked during the first decade of the plan; that is, when financial market

FIGURE 2.2 **GDP, wage growth, and NDC and FDC returns, Poland, 2000–09**
percent

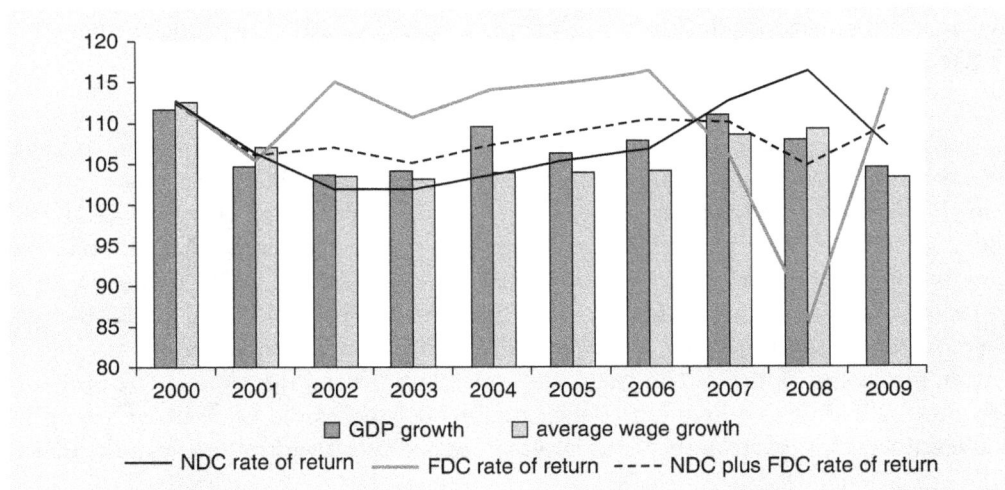

SOURCE: Authors' calculations from national statistical data.

NOTE: FDC = financial defined contribution; GDP = gross domestic product; NDC = nonfinancial defined contribution.

returns were higher, NDC indexation was lower—and vice versa. As a result, the overall rate of return based on the combined performance of the economy and the financial market remained relatively stable.

The Swedish balancing mechanism. Sweden weighed the advantages and disadvantages of indexing using a combination of the covered per capita wage rate and the rate of growth of the covered labor force, or of basing the internal rate of return solely on the per capita wage rate (Palmer 2000). The political preference was to index using growth in the average wage because this would maintain, at least in principle, a constant ratio of an average benefit to an average wage. This led to the development of a balancing mechanism (Settergren and Mikula 2006) based on a solvency ratio (the ratio of "contribution assets" to liabilities) to cover the downside risk of a declining labor force. Liabilities are exactly determined in an NDC scheme by the accounts of workers and pensioners. Assets, by contrast, consist of future contributions, which are unknown in any current period. Accordingly, a definition of contribution assets is needed. The Swedish model defines the projected contribution assets in terms of a measure of the time a unit of contribution money is in the pension system before it is paid out, based on outcome data from the period nearest the projection date (see SSIA 2009).

The estimate of the contribution asset is revised annually to derive a new solvency ratio. A solvency ratio below unity triggers a balancing index that reduces liabilities (workers' accounts and pensioners' benefits) to achieve a solvency ratio of unity. The mechanism is nonsymmetric and does not adjust upward, except that after a downward adjustment, the average wage indexation returns to the level that would have occurred if negative balancing had not been needed.[16] The Swedish balancing mechanism is thus a sort of gyroscope that steers the system toward financial equilibrium.

We note that in principle it is possible to employ a symmetric balancing mechanism, although no country has yet done this. This alternative has nevertheless been analyzed in the literature (Auerbach and Lee 2011). The advantage of symmetric balancing is that the system need not build up unnecessary funding, which leads to a welfare loss for current participants. This said, it is possible to create a band around a solvency ratio of unity, including the idea of incorporating a buffer fund for economic or demographic contingencies (as discussed in Holzmann, Palmer, and Robalino 2012), with balancing being triggered when the solvency ratio goes outside this band.

GDP as an indexation proxy for wage growth. In Italy, notional accounts are indexed in line with growth of gross domestic product (GDP), using a rolling three-year average. The question arises whether this form of indexation ensures stability of the pension system. The answer depends on the degree of correlation between the growth of GDP and the wage sum, or, more precisely, the covered wage sum, since that is what generates the internal rate of return in NDC. In the long run, the wage sum and GDP could grow more or less at the same rate, but history reveals considerable discrepancies between the two over long periods of time. The risk is that GDP will grow faster than the internal rate of return, producing rights not consistent with contributions and the internal rate of return and thereby leading to a long-term deficit that, by default, would be financed from general revenues. This is yet another issue that has not been dealt with explicitly in the Italian NDC discussion.

COMPUTING PENSIONS

In principle, the calculation of an NDC annuity can be a straightforward procedure: the individual's capital at retirement is divided by a factor that may be called a conversion factor (Italy), divisor (Sweden), or G-value (Poland). In Latvia and Poland, this factor is simply the life expectancy of the retirees in the individual's birth cohort at the time the individual retires (table 2.5). In Italy and Sweden, the factor includes an assumed rate of real wage growth: 1.5 percent in Italy and 1.6 percent in Sweden.[17] These numbers are based on the expectation that the countries will experience real long-run growth at something close to this rate. The Italian-Swedish model of front-loading benefits distributes money from years as an older-than-average pensioner to years as a younger-than-average pensioner.[18] This can be claimed to depict consumer time preference (people prefer to consume more now than in the future). At the same time, for a fixed amount of lifetime contributions, by shifting a fixed amount of life-cycle income to earlier years as a pensioner, this construction creates a risk of relative poverty for the older elderly. It also has distributional consequences within the cohort insurance pool.

In creation of the life annuity, the conversion factor is fixed using an age specified in the legislation for the NDC scheme. In Sweden, the minimum pension age is 61, but for a person retiring before age 65, the value of the annuity can be adjusted using new life expectancy information until age 65, at which time it becomes a fixed annuity for life. Of course, there is no reason why the life expectancy factor must be fixed at such an early age as 65. It is notoriously difficult to estimate life expectancy correctly, and postponement of the setting of the final fixed annuity factor until a later age has the advantage of incorporating an estimate that is likely to be closer to the final outcome. This is important because underestimation of life expectancy is a source of financial disequilibrium.

The effect of bearing the longevity risk for pensioners is highly dependent on the whole annuity package—on whether benefits are not indexed at all, indexed with prices, or indexed with some form of wage or wage-sum index, where the expected positive effect of indexation could counterbalance the likely negative effect of revised life expectancy projections (Alho, Bravo, and Palmer 2012). Note also that it is not reasonable for the very old in the population to bear the residual longevity risk. More generally, a way of spreading this risk to a wide base is to create an NDC bond, which transfers this risk to the general taxpayers (Palmer 2012). Finally, the question of who is to bear the residual longevity risk needs to be addressed explicitly in the creation of NDC schemes, which to date has largely not been the case.

Indexation of pensions. Pensions are price-indexed in Italy and Latvia. They are price-indexed in Sweden, too. But in Sweden, there is a yearly adjustment, in addition to price indexation, that adjusts benefits (both upward and downward) to the deviation of the actual rate of growth of the per capita wage from the norm of 1.6 percent per year that is factored into the divisor. In addition, if Sweden's balancing mechanism is triggered, as a result of the economic recession or a fall in financial asset values, there is a negative effect on overall indexation. Italy does not have any form of indexation of benefits besides prices, which means that it is at risk of developing a deficit in response to a chronic decline in the covered labor force—a risk examined and confirmed in the final section of this study.

TABLE 2.5 **Pension formulas**

	Italy	Latvia	Poland	Sweden
Denominator	Life expectancy adjusted with an imputed rate of return, set at 1.5%	Life expectancy (unisex) at retirement age	Life expectancy (unisex) at retirement age	Life expectancy adjusted with an imputed rate of return, set at 1.6%
Postretirement indexation	Price indexation	Price indexation from 2011 (previously, a combination of wages and prices)	Mixed price-wage indexation with at least 20% of wages	Price indexation plus discrepancy between real per capita wage growth and 1.6% rate of return (per capita wage growth) used to compute annuity; also, balancing when solvency ratio falls below unity
Retirement age (men/women)	65/60 (optional for women); individuals with 36 years of contributions can retire at 61	66/66 (men with 42 years and 1 month and women with 41 years and 1 month can retire earlier; a minimum age of 63 applies to all new contributors from 1996, provided their pension is at least 2.8 times a welfare pension, otherwise age 66; all ages are adjusted with increases in life expectancy)	65/60	65/65, but minimum age of 61 for retirement
Minimum qualifying period	20 years	10 years	None, but required for a minimum guarantee (25 years for men, 20 years for women)	One year of contributions based on earnings that surpass the floor for personal income taxation
Minimum pension guarantee				
Minimum benefit level	Social assistance pension (around 25% of average wage net of the income tax), paid from age 65	Depends on years of contributions above a minimum qualifying period; otherwise, a minimum state social benefit (45 Latvian lats per month)	In 2009, 675 Polish zlotys per month (about 20% of the average wage) The minimum benefit indexed like other pensions	2.13 base amount for single pensioners, 1.90 base amount per person for married couples; price-indexed (Base amount = 44,000 Swedish kronor in 2009, about 15% of the average wage)
Financing	General state budget revenues	General state budget revenues; constructed as a top-up to the NDC and FDC benefits together	General state budget revenues; constructed as a top-up to the NDC and FDC benefits together	General state budget revenues; constructed as a top-up to the NDC and FDC benefits together

SOURCE: Authors' elaboration from country data.

NOTE: FDC = financial defined contribution; NDC = nonfinancial defined contribution.

Poland has used various models to index pensions during the past 10 years. From the outset in 1999, when there were still no NDC pensioners, indexation reflected an estimate of ex ante inflation and part of real wage growth for some given number of years. This rule, however, proved to be quite generous because of regular overestimation of price and wage growth. Consequently, the ratio of an average pension to an average wage increased from 52.7 percent in 2000 to 57.6 in 2004. As of 2005, pension indexation is based on an ex post inflation value. Between 2005 and 2007, pensions were indexed only to prices, and indexation was triggered only when the price level had increased by more than 5 percent from the last year of indexation. As a result, in 2005 and 2007, there was no indexation of pension benefits whatsoever. Since 2008, mixed price-wage indexation has been employed, where the wage component is at least 20 percent of the preceding year's wage growth. The tendency toward frequent changes in indexation models is a problem, as it dilutes the message that NDC is an intergenerational contract with the same contract conditions for all generations.

Latvia has employed price indexation throughout most of the period. During 1996–99, when real economic growth had returned, the gain was shared with pensioners through extra indexation, as was noted above. The Latvian reform strategy originally called for the introduction of combined price-wage indexation of pensions, moving increasingly toward full wage indexation as the costs of the legacy from the old system declined (Palmer et al. 2006). In the early 2000s, the first steps were taken in this direction, but the economic crisis of 2008 led to the freezing of all indexation in 2009 and 2010. Latvia has since returned to pure price indexation.

The alternative of wage indexation. In principle, NDC schemes can index in accordance with the growth of the covered wage sum. In a demographic steady state, this is tantamount to indexing with the growth of the per capita covered wage. And, indexation of pensions with the per capita covered wage maintains the value of an average pension relative to an average wage, which is an attractive feature. Of course, straightforward indexation to the nominal per capita wage (i.e., the real wage per capita plus inflation) ignores the need to adjust benefits even to changes in the labor force component of the changing wage base. The asymmetric downside balancing mechanism covers this risk in Sweden, which has chosen per capita wage indexation. Other countries choosing the option of per capita wage indexation will also have to determine how to cover the risk of a declining labor force. In a more recent NDC reform, Norway (Christensen et al., chapter 4 in this volume) has opted to cover this risk with general revenues.

Price indexation, which is presently either the only component of benefit indexation (in Italy and Latvia) or the dominant one (in Poland and Sweden), creates a gradual decline over time in the ratio of an average benefit relative to an average wage. Price indexation maintains the purchasing power of pensions but leads to relative poverty for the poorest elderly pensioners. Single women are particularly at risk. So, given this risk, why haven't the NDC countries moved in the direction of wage indexation? The main reason is that the pre-NDC regimes employed price indexation of benefits, and countries could not afford the increase in pension costs that would have accompanied a direct switch to full-scale wage indexation.[19] With time, these countries can consider gradually introducing wage indexation, reducing considerably the risk of relative poverty among pensioners as they become increasingly older.

MINIMUM INCOME GUARANTEE

The primary goal of the public mandate of old-age pensions is to protect the elderly from poverty in old age. NDC contains no intragenerational income redistribution in its pension formula. As a result, it is likely that more people will earn pension rights below an acceptable minimum level under NDC than under traditionally designed defined benefit systems. NDC schemes, like FDC schemes, must therefore be supplemented with a minimum guaranteed income level. This can be formulated either as a minimum benefit, which, de facto, implies testing only against other public pension benefits (an administratively inexpensive option) or as a minimum income, which entails means testing against all sources of income.

In Latvia and Poland, the minimum pension age is also the age at which a guarantee can be claimed. In Sweden, this is not so: the minimum age for claiming an NDC pension is 61, whereas the minimum age for claiming the guarantee is 65. The minimum guaranteed benefit in Sweden and Poland tops up the NDC and FDC pensions and is financed from the general budget. This both makes redistribution more transparent and allows the government to use other sources of income (i.e., general tax revenues rather than social security contributions) to finance the minimum guarantee.

In Latvia, persons with a record of at least 10 years of paid contributions are entitled to a minimum guaranteed benefit (social pension) financed with social insurance contribution revenues. They receive 1.1, 1.3, 1.5, or 1.7 times the basic social pension amount for 11–20, 21–30, 31–40, or 41 or more years, respectively, of contributions. Persons with fewer than 10 years of contributions receive a social pension financed out of general tax revenues.

In Italy, the old defined benefit scheme included a guaranteed minimum level, which was particularly relevant for workers with poor work records and for recipients of disability and survivors' benefits. The new NDC regime does not envisage any guarantee. This means that the de facto guarantee is the social assistance pension paid to poor individuals 65 and over, which is less than the minimum level under the defined benefit plan. The relationship between the NDC pension and the social assistance pension has not yet been fully specified. We note that it is important that individuals be provided with an incentive to contribute to the system even if their NDC pension is relatively poor.

Individual Outcomes

The underlying feature of defined contribution schemes is the tight link between contributions and pensions. Here, we examine outcomes for individuals using the Pension Models of the Organisation for Economic Co-operation and Development (OECD) and the official country data in the model databank. These are the same data and methodology that underlie the OECD's publication *Pensions at a Glance* (OECD 2009) and the World Bank's *Pensions Panorama* (Whitehouse 2007).[20] The clear advantage of using this model is that results are based on the same calculation procedure, using the same set of assumptions (age of entrance, age of exit, wage growth, financial rate of return for financial schemes, and so on). By using the same assumptions for all four countries, we can examine and compare the underlying characteristics.

THE PENSION FOR A STANDARD WORKER

Figure 2.3 plots the relative pension level (the individual pension, given the calculation assumptions, divided by economywide average earnings) on the vertical axis and individual earnings in relation to average earnings on the horizontal axis. It thus shows the relationship between pensions and preretirement earnings. Pensions are pretax and, on a country basis, include the features shown in table 2.5.

The figure highlights the underlying characteristics of the countries' overall mandatory pension schemes. Generally speaking, a flat-rate benefit that is the same for all would appear as a horizontal line. A 45-degree line from an origin of zero would represent a one-to-one relationship between the individual's earnings (in NDC contributions on earnings) and pension, given a rate of return on accounts that equals the rate of growth of the average wage. A higher slope means that the rate of return is greater than the rate of growth of the average wage. The greater this difference is, the more vertical the slope will be.[21] Finally, since countries differ in their indexation of pensions, overall annualized lifetime returns also differ. In addition, in Sweden, quasi-mandatory occupational schemes take over above the contribution ceiling on the public NDC and FDC contributions. In the OECD calculations, Sweden is represented above the ceiling by the scheme for private sector white-collar workers, which is an FDC scheme (with an assumed rate of growth of 3.5 percent, compared with the NDC rate of 2.0 percent), explaining the increase in the slope for pensions based on higher earnings. The occupational scheme also

FIGURE 2.3 **Relation between lifetime earnings and pensions**

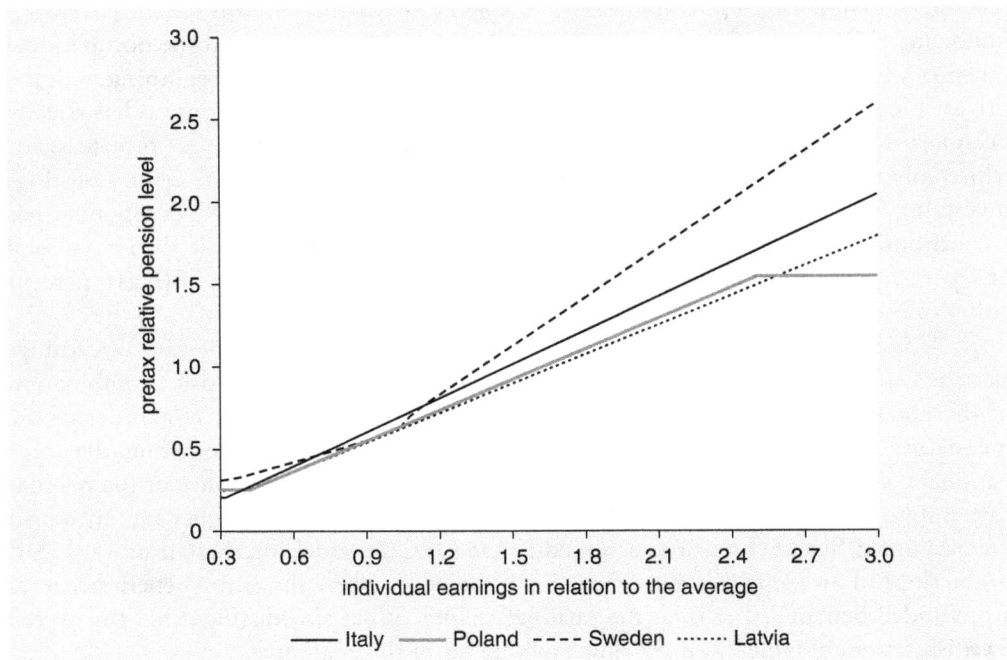

provides a small supplement to the public NDC and FDC schemes below the ceiling, which accounts for Sweden's top position in the figure.

The initial section of the curves for Latvia, Poland, and Sweden is flat or relatively flat, reflecting the guarantee benefit. In Sweden, as the relative contribution of a guarantee to the total pension tapers off, the curve tilts upward. As expected, all four countries' schemes exhibit a strong link between earnings and pensions. The figure also reveals several features of the particular national systems. First, we see that Polish benefits are capped at 2.5 times average earnings. Second, the Swedish curve has a kink at the average wage (unity on the horizontal scale), reflecting the fact that the guarantee top-up has tapered off wholly at this point. Third, the Italian curve is a straight-line relationship from the origin, since there is no guarantee in the Italian NDC system (although there is means-tested social assistance at the bottom, not depicted here).

As table 2.6 shows, the four countries have put together their pension packages very differently. Nevertheless, the expected outcome for the average pensioner is about the same from country to country.

Italy has an NDC pension with a contribution rate that, given the assumptions made, yields a 68 percent replacement rate at all income levels.[22] Latvia's combined NDC and FDC system (based on a 70–30 percent split of contributions) yields a pretax replacement rate of 60 percent, once the guarantee threshold has been passed. Similarly, the Polish system yields a replacement rate of 61 percent after the guarantee level is passed.

Sweden has four major quasi-mandatory occupational schemes that provide a small supplement to the public pensions beneath the ceiling on contributions to the public NDC and FDC schemes and the entire pension above the low ceiling of 1.1 times average earnings. (Coverage for workers in a sector or occupation covered by one of these schemes is mandatory, and employers are obliged to pay contributions for the coverage.) Following the introduction of the public NDC and FDC schemes, all the occupational schemes were converted to prefunded defined contribution schemes, beginning with the private blue-collar schemes in the mid-1990s. In the OECD calculations, as has already been noted, the occupational component is represented by the scheme for private sector white-collar workers, with a contribution rate of 4.5 percent below the ceiling earnings qualifying for the public benefit. The Swedish public mandatory FDC component has a contribution rate of 2.5 percent. The individual Swede in the example thus has a total of 7 percent contributions to two prefunded financial schemes, on top of the 16 percent going to NDC.

With these dimensions, the Swedish NDC scheme replaces 38 percent of earnings (for the OECD's typical worker retiring at age 65) up to the ceiling, and the combination of the mandatory and occupational prefunded schemes provides the remainder of the mandatory benefits, giving a total replacement rate of 62 percent. At the ceiling, the occupational component takes over completely, and so the relative importance of the mandatory public scheme for the overall benefit declines. Because of the higher rate of return for prefunded financial schemes assumed in the OECD model, there is an upward shift in the slope of Sweden's curve in figure 2.3 at the point where the entire benefit becomes a prefunded benefit—that is, at the earnings ceiling. What also distinguishes the overall Swedish system in table 2.6 is the slow tapering off of the guarantee.

Although Italy has no mandatory guarantee, it does have means-tested social assistance at the bottom. (Even Latvia, Poland, and Sweden have means-tested social assistance at the very bottom, as a safety net of last resort.) What the guarantee does, among other

TABLE 2.6 **Replacement rates for newly granted benefits**

Country and percentage of average earnings	Guarantee	NDC	FDC	FDC (OP)	Total Gross	Net
Italy						
0.30	0.00	0.68	0.00	0.00	0.68	0.99
0.50	0.00	0.68	0.00	0.00	0.68	0.75
0.75	0.00	0.68	0.00	0.00	0.68	0.75
1.00	0.00	0.68	0.00	0.00	0.68	0.75
1.50	0.00	0.68	0.00	0.00	0.68	0.77
2.50	0.00	0.68	0.00	0.00	0.68	0.78
Latvia						
0.30	0.24	0.22	0.38	0.00	0.84	1.08
0.50	0.00	0.22	0.38	0.00	0.60	0.80
0.75	0.00	0.22	0.38	0.00	0.60	0.80
1.00	0.00	0.22	0.38	0.00	0.60	0.77
1.50	0.00	0.22	0.38	0.00	0.60	0.73
2.50	0.00	0.22	0.38	0.00	0.60	0.70
Poland						
0.30	0.20	0.30	0.31	0.00	0.82	0.96
0.50	0.00	0.30	0.31	0.00	0.61	0.74
0.75	0.00	0.30	0.31	0.00	0.61	0.75
1.00	0.00	0.30	0.31	0.00	0.61	0.75
1.50	0.00	0.30	0.31	0.00	0.61	0.75
2.50	0.00	0.30	0.31	0.00	0.61	0.77
Sweden						
0.30	0.43	0.38	0.09	0.15	1.05	1.04
0.50	0.15	0.38	0.09	0.15	0.77	0.79
0.75	0.03	0.38	0.09	0.15	0.65	0.67
1.00[a]	0.00	0.38	0.09	0.15	0.62	0.64
1.50	0.00	0.28	0.07	0.41	0.76	0.81
2.50	0.00	0.17	0.04	0.64	0.85	0.88

SOURCE: OECD Pension Models.

NOTE: FDC = financial defined contribution; NDC = nonfinancial defined contribution; OP = occupational pension.

a. The ceiling on qualifying earnings is 1.1 times average earnings.

things, is to prevent the need for means-tested benefits for a segment of the low-income pensioner population. A means-tested benefit, however, is targeted; it takes into consideration all forms of income and at least some forms of wealth, which makes it more efficient. The most generous assistance is the least efficient, since it gives less incentive for a low-income earner to work longer to receive a higher benefit.

Under the 2009 tax schedules, average individuals in Italy, Latvia, and Poland have a higher replacement rate after tax than before tax—about 75 percent versus about 65 percent. In Sweden, the after-tax rate is about the same as the before-tax rate. The Latvian and Polish systems, with relatively large FDC components for all income levels, are assumed by OECD simulations to be more efficient in that they deliver higher benefits with a lower contribution rate than the Italian or Swedish systems. This does not take into account the higher volatility of financial markets returns. In the OECD calculations, Sweden achieves a higher level for the average earner with the help of an FDC occupational supplement, and Italy does the same through a contribution rate that is 33 percent instead of about 20 percent (the rate in Poland and Latvia). It should be noted that life expectancy in Latvia and Poland is considerably lower than in Italy and Sweden, and this, given similar pension ages, helps achieve similar replacement rates despite lower contributions.

NDC AND WOMEN

Early retirement. Women still enjoy special status in Poland, where they are allowed to retire at an earlier age (60) than men (65). Earlier retirement is seen as a right, but this is an artifact of the defined benefit view of pensions. If women exercise this right in a defined contribution scheme, it will have a significant impact on their pension levels because they will accumulate pension rights on their NDC accounts for a shorter period of time and because a lower retirement age means longer life expectancy and thus lower yearly annuity payments. As has already been emphasized, taking advantage of this right may be the entrance to relative poverty for widows in their older years.

Theoretical replacement rates calculated for new entrants in the labor market show that a lower retirement age significantly affects the pension level (table 2.7). [23] Retirement at age 60 decreases the replacement rate (with all assumptions other than the retirement age unchanged) by 17 percentage points in Italy and by 20 percentage points in Poland.

Generally speaking, although a woman and her retired husband may live adequately together on their combined pensions, a widow living alone on her own pension loses the economies of scale of a two-person household. This, along with price indexation at a time when workers' wages are increasing in real terms, contributes to creating relative poverty among elderly women. These consequences raise the issue of whether couples should be enabled (or mandated)

TABLE 2.7 **Theoretical replacement rates at retirement for new entrants into the labor force**

	Italy	Latvia	Poland	Sweden
Baseline: retirement at age 65	0.75	0.77	0.75	0.64
Women's retirement age (60)	0.58	n.a.	0.55	n.a.

SOURCE: OECD Pension Models.

NOTE: n.a. = not applicable.

to contract joint annuities at retirement within the NDC framework—something that none of the four countries considered here offers.[24]

Until the end of 2008, under the rules of the old pension system, Polish women could retire even earlier than age 55 if they had worked 30 years or longer. Most women made use of this opportunity, and the actual retirement age of women was close to 55, which is far from the present mandatory retirement age of 60. This early retirement opportunity was abolished beginning in January 2009. The fact that women could retire with a full benefit even before reaching age 55 under the old rules has been utilized by opponents to block efforts to equalize the pension ages of men and women at an age above 60. Yet an increase in the retirement age of women is needed to ensure that women retiring in the future receive adequate benefits. With the lower retirement age, given their shorter working careers and the wage gap, as many as 40 percent of women risk falling below the ceiling for the minimum pension guarantee if the level of guarantee were to remain at 20 percent of the average wage (Chłoń-Domińczak and Strzelecki 2010).

In Italy, women retiring with the old system rules were in the past afforded more flexibility than men in choosing the retirement age (they could retire with an old age pension between the ages of 60 and 65). This was frequently justified with reference to the fact that men were more likely to acquire the rights needed to qualify for a seniority pension prior to age 65. This is no longer the case, as we have already mentioned. From 2012, women in the public sector are subject to the same rules as men, and in the private sector from 2018.

Career breaks for child care. Another important gender issue is the impact on pensions of career breaks taken to provide child care. As described earlier, each of the four countries has rules intended to compensate for pension rights lost because of time taken off in conjunction with childbirth. The impact of career breaks on pension levels is illustrated in table 2.8. The Swedish scheme, with generous child-care pension rights, is the closest to being neutral; the potential loss is largest in the case of Latvia. For Poland, the combination of a lower retirement age for women and a career break for child care decreases the level of the replacement rate and increases the potential risk of low income at retirement.

The risk of loss of pension rights is to some extent mitigated by transfers from general contribution or tax revenues that take the form of additional contribution payments to individual accounts for periods of child care. Figure 2.4 illustrates the gross loss in the pension level resulting from a break in employment and the compensation in the form of public transfers paid for a period of maternity leave from work. Italy and Latvia provide relatively less compensation for absence from work for child care. Sweden is the most generous of the four countries, covering most of the gap.

TABLE 2.8 **Change in future net replacement rates depending on years spent out of the formal labor market to provide child care**
percent

	1 year	2 years	3 years
Italy	−1.4	−2.8	−4.2
Latvia	−1.8	−3.6	−4.2
Poland	−0.8	−1.7	−2.5
Sweden	−0.3	−0.5	−0.8

SOURCE: OECD Pension Models.

FIGURE 2.4 **Impact of public contributions on reduction of net loss of pension benefit because of child care**
percent

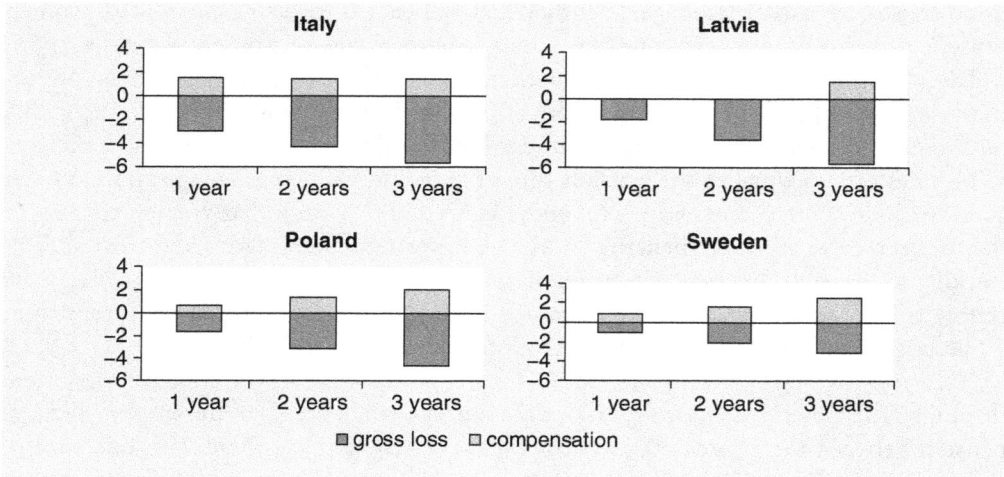

SOURCE: OECD Pension Models.

In Italy, compensation does not depend significantly on the number of years, which shows that there are few incentives in the pension system to spend more time out of the labor force in child care and to have more children.

The risk of having a lower pension because of fewer years at work or lower contributions to a pension scheme is greater for women because women tend to perform a larger percent of their work in the informal sector, caring for children and relatives. This is a structural characteristic of the labor market in most, if not all, countries, although the degree varies. It is a structure determined by cultural heritage. In addition to differences in formal labor force participation, women also tend to work part-time to a greater extent than men, and they often work in sectors dominated by their own gender, where wages are lower than in sectors where men dominate. For all of these reasons, it can be argued, as in Klerby, Larsson, and Palmer (2012), that countries should at least offer couples the voluntary opportunity to share NDC accounts or to create a joint annuity around the time of retirement. This would allow for a transfer of resources from men to women, strictly within the family—without externalities for others in the insurance pool—and would increase the income of survivors (normally, women) in old age. This alternative, which is relatively easy to implement within the individual account framework of NDC, needs to be considered in these (and other) NDC countries.

Long-term Financial Stability

The close link between contributions and benefits at the individual level in NDC mimics the logic of a fully funded scheme and ensures horizontal equity. At the macroeconomic level, intergenerational equity and long-term financial stability depend on how the system is designed in practice and the resulting response to demographic and economic developments. The question is, to what extent can the present makeup of the NDC schemes in the countries examined here fulfill the promise of long-term financial stability?

Generally speaking, in PAYG systems, current and prospective imbalances can be tackled either via ad hoc adjustments of benefits, entitlement conditions, or contributory rates, or through automatic adjustment mechanisms. The second solution can speed adjustment, avoiding the difficult and often lengthy process that all democracies face when cutting entitlements. That process may open the door for special interest groups to lobby for rules that benefit themselves—the sort of phenomenon that implementation of NDC is intended to eliminate.

Recourse to built-in stabilizers is not limited to NDC, but it is one of its key features. This is related to some of the main reasons underlying the introduction of NDC:

- NDC schemes were introduced after a decade or so of widespread parametric reforms of PAYG systems. The emergence and increasing popularity of NDC is a way of recognizing that in the face of large economic and demographic changes, benefits and entitlement conditions should follow "economic logic." Liabilities should not be allowed to grow faster in a long-run perspective by more than what prospective contributions can cover.

- Entitlements in NDC are transparent, and the adjustment mechanisms are spelled out in advance. With the rules of the game fixed, entitlements can be perceived as stronger than in standard PAYG schemes, where the counterfactual is a series of ad hoc adjustments that are unknown in advance. As in funded schemes, individuals are informed about the amount of their contributory "wealth"; they are also told that an individual's pension is strictly proportional to his or her account value (wealth) at retirement—a logic that can be perceived as fair. Whereas the ad hoc changes typical in DB regimes would thus be viewed as the state's defaulting on its contractual commitment, in NDC the contract consists of a defined (and legislated) process leading to a more certain outcome.

The effectiveness of the built-in stabilizers is one of the most important factors in the success of NDC reforms. The question is, how effective are the designs in the four countries? This section tackles the issue in four steps. First, it briefly examines the current financial prospects of pension systems in the four countries under consideration. Second, it considers whether the design of the NDC schemes can limit the occurrence of disequilibria in the four countries. Third, it examines what mechanisms are in play to correct disequilibria when they arise. Finally, it offers a schematic presentation of the time lags in the reaction to shocks in the four countries.

CURRENT FINANCIAL PROSPECTS

According to projections by the Ageing Working Group (AWG) set up by the European Union (European Commission and Economic Policy Committee 2009), during the period 2007–60 the ratio of pension expenditure to GDP is expected to decline in all four countries under consideration here (table 2.9).[25] By contrast, the EU average is expected to increase significantly. This is clear evidence that the four NDC countries have achieved long-term financial stability.

TABLE 2.9 **Changes in the ratio of public pension expenditure to GDP, 2007–60**
percentage points

Country or group	2007–20	2020–30	2030–40	2040–50	2050–60	2007–60
Italy	0.1	0.7	0.8	−0.8	−1.1	−0.4
Latvia	−0.3	0.7	0.3	−0.3	−0.7	−0.4
Poland	−1.8	−0.3	−0.2	−0.1	−0.3	−2.8
Sweden	−0.1	0.1	−0.1	−0.3	0.3	−0.1
EU-27	0.4	0.9	0.7	0.2	0.2	2.4

SOURCE: European Commission and Economic Policy Committee 2009.

NOTE: EU-27 refers to the 27 current members of the European Union.

The picture nevertheless varies considerably among countries. In Sweden, pension expenditure is projected to remain about constant in GDP terms. In Italy and Latvia, it is projected to increase until 2040, from a relatively high level in Italy and a relatively low level in Latvia, and to fall thereafter. In Poland, it is projected to fall continuously. In all four countries, there is a large expected increase in the dependency ratio. This will be offset by a sizable cut in the benefit ratio (benefits per person for a given retirement age) and by a substantial reduction in the coverage ratio, deriving from postponement of retirement to a higher age (table 2.10). On first view, these figures are an indication that NDC reforms have managed to get pension expenditure under control in a context in which populations are aging rapidly. However, the picture is less clear-cut than that.

A pattern in which, under current rules, pension spending is stable or declining suggests that these rules are financially sustainable. However, this does not necessarily imply that they are also socially and politically sustainable. According to the AWG projections, by 2060, the benefit ratio for the public pension schemes declines by 30 percentage points in Poland, 21 in Italy, 19 in Sweden, and 11 in Latvia. These results imply a sizable increase in the risk of relative poverty among pensioners.

The pensioners particularly at risk are the very elderly in countries in which pensions are indexed only, or mainly, to prices, with the result that the ratio of an individual's benefit to an average wage declines as the pensioner becomes older. This feature has been a recurring theme in this study. Advanced industrial societies do not appear to accept widespread old-age poverty, and this attitude may strengthen as the electoral influence of the elderly increases. Accordingly, increasing pressure for discretionary higher benefits can be expected.

In this respect, table 2.11 provides considerable food for thought regarding the future course of pension policy in these countries. The low macroeconomic replacement rates in the table reflect two assumptions used in the calculations. The first assumption behind the numbers is that workers will continue to retire at the present minimum ages of retirement, even though they will live much longer during the coming half century. This is not plausible and is not likely to occur. The second is that countries will continue to index pensions to prices. This is a difficult issue, and at the time of this writing there is no discussion of indexation in any of the countries discussed here.

TABLE 2.10 **Decomposition of the ratio of public pension spending to GDP, 2007–60**
percentage of GDP

Country or group	2007 level	Dependency ratio contribution	Coverage ratio contribution	Employment effect contribution	Benefit ratio contribution	Interaction effect	2060 level
Italy	14.0	10.4	−3.2	−1.1	−5.5	−1.0	13.6
Latvia	5.4	5.7	−1.6	−0.2	−3.9	−0.4	5.1
Poland	11.6	13.4	−6.3	−1.0	−7.1	−1.8	8.8
Sweden	9.5	5.6	−0.4	−0.4	−4.3	−0.6	9.4
EU-27	10.1	8.7	−2.6	−0.7	−2.5	−0.6	12.5

SOURCE: European Commission and Economic Policy Committee 2009.

NOTE: EU-27 refers to the 27 current members of the European Union.

TABLE 2.11 **Ratio of an average pension to an average wage, 2007 and 2060**
percent

Country	Public pensions		Public and occupational pensions	
	2007	2060	2007	2060
Italy	68	47	—a	—a
Latvia	24	13	24	25
Poland	56	26	58	31
Sweden	49	30	64	46

SOURCE: European Commission and Economic Policy Committee 2009.

NOTE: Sweden has a ceiling on contribution-based income. For employees in all sectors, a (nonpublic) occupational benefit takes over above this ceiling. To get a complete picture of the ratio of an average benefit to an average wage, one must thus include the occupational benefit, which has been omitted from this table. For all countries, the results are influenced by the assumed retirement age.

a. Italy has no occupational pension.

The guarantee of a minimum pension level is an instrument that the governments of Latvia, Poland, and Sweden can adjust to help low-income pensioners, but adjusting the guarantee does not deal with the general phenomenon that individual pensions decline relative to real wages as the pensioner ages. In principle, Latvia and Poland have room within their NDC systems to gradually move toward wage indexation of benefits, which would contribute significantly to alleviating this problem. Italy and Sweden have locked in this potential in their front-loaded benefits, which makes changing indexation more problematic.

The trend increase in longevity underlying the numbers also points to the need for continuous increases in the de facto retirement age. For example, Latvians are assumed in these calculations to continue to retire at age 62 for the coming 50 years, whereas it would be more reasonable to assume an increase in the normal pension age to well over 65 in the half century covered by the calculations. Likewise, Polish women are assumed to continue to leave the labor force at age 60. In fact, in Italy and Sweden—among the world leaders in life expectancy, health, and perceived well-being—it is not unreasonable to assume a normal retirement age of close to

69 or more within the next 40 years. This would pull the benefit ratios in table 2.11 up tremendously.

The low pension levels in 2007 in Latvia reflect at least two factors specific to that country, both of which were discussed earlier in the chapter. The first is that women were for many years still allowed to retire at ages just above 56, with early retirement privileges but with pensions that reflected the very high life expectancy at these ages. Most women did indeed retire at an early age, and the results reflect the consequences. Second, the economic upheaval created by the transition to the market economy, with the closing down of Soviet industry in the country, left many people, especially older working-age men, without or with only limited formal employment for the remainder of their working careers. This process, which went on for more than a decade, created many new pensioners who received only the minimum pension, which is about 25 percent of an average wage.

Italy is already moving in the direction of longer working lives via the automatic increase in the retirement age starting in 2013, in parallel to progress in life expectancy.[26] Clearly, the other three countries should follow this example. Sweden is presently discussing increasing the age to which employees have the right to remain at work to 69 or 70, which would make it much easier to remain in the workforce past the present right-to-work age of 67. This alone, however, may not achieve the goal of increasing the minimum pension age to match gains in longevity. Moreover, even if minimum pension ages were to remain unchanged, individuals may try to offset the decline in yearly payments by postponing retirement. An effect of this kind is already built into the calculations presented here, which means that the assumed voluntary increase in the retirement age is far from sufficient. In the end, the extent to which the de facto retirement age is adjusted upward depends on right-to-work legislation and on the attitudes of workers and employers. What should be noted is that the minimum age for claiming a public pension is an important signal to workers and employers alike.

PREVENTING FINANCIAL DISEQUILIBRIA

In an assessment of whether the design of NDC schemes prevents financial disequilibria from arising, three features are important: the rate of return on the notional capital accumulated by workers; the composition of the coefficient used to convert account values into pensions; and the indexation of pension benefits (table 2.12).

The rate of return on the notional account is determined, in Sweden, by the rate of growth of per capita wage; in Latvia and Poland, by the rate of growth of the contribution base; and in Italy, by the rate of growth of GDP. As already mentioned, the Swedish model is somewhat problematic because the growth of the average wage is likely to differ in the long run from the growth of contributions actually paid into the pension system, which is the rate that guarantees financial balance in steady state. The problem arises when labor force growth becomes negative. This potential source of disequilibrium (as well as others) is addressed in the Swedish system through an automatic balancing mechanism, discussed below.

As to the coefficient used in computing annuities, two issues are relevant: how life expectancy is taken into account, and what rate of return is applied to pension wealth after retirement. Coefficients are based on backward-looking assumptions in Italy, Poland, and Sweden and on forward-looking assumptions in Latvia. A backward-looking approach has the advantage of avoiding difficult assumptions about changes in life expectancy, since it

TABLE 2.12 **Factors influencing financial balance**

	Italy	Latvia	Poland	Sweden
Factors affecting the probability that disequilibrium will emerge				
Rate of return during the accumulation phase	GDP	Contribution base	Contribution base[a]	Per capita wages
Conversion coefficient used in creating the annuity				
Demographic assumptions	Backward looking	Forward looking	Backward looking	Backward looking
Rate-of-return assumptions in the computation of the annuity	1.5% real growth	None	None	1.6% real growth
Indexation of benefits, in addition to the consumer price index	No	No	Partial (20% of wages)	Per capita wage rate minus 1.6%
Mechanisms contributing to long-term financial balance				
Automatic adjustments in the notional rate of return on accounts	Yes	Yes	Yes	Yes
Automatic adjustment of retirement age	Yes	No	No	No
Automatic balancing when the solvency ratio falls below unity	No	No	No	Yes
Annuity coefficient update				
Cohort life expectancy	Yes	Yes	Yes	Yes
Frequency of adjustment	Every three years	Yearly	Yearly	Yearly
Automatic	Yes	Yes	Yes	Yes
Automatic adjustments in the annuity	No	No	No	Yes
Reserve fund[b]	No	No	No	Yes

SOURCE: Authors' elaboration based on country data.

NOTE: CPI = consumer price index; GDP = gross domestic product.

a. The real rate of return cannot be negative.

b. Only those reserve funds that are not invested exclusively in government bonds are considered.

simply reflects current data. However, because life expectancy keeps increasing, such an approach leads to long-term financial imbalance. It implies attribution to a person retiring now—say, at 65—the life expectancy of persons who are now 66 and older. But those who are now 66 and older belong to another generation and are likely to have a shorter life expectancy than persons currently retiring. A backward-looking approach can represent a viable solution only if there are counterbalancing mechanisms.

In the case of Italy, the conversion coefficients have been computed without taking into account part of the expenditure for disability and survivors' pensions. Specifically, it has not been considered that disabled workers will receive benefits in excess of those awarded on the basis of their contributions.[27] Pensions paid to survivors of deceased workers have also been disregarded. To achieve balance, the government must therefore transfer even more money to the system to cover these benefits. In other words, these pensions have implicitly—but unfortunately not explicitly—been considered as welfare benefits to be financed by the government budget.

The individual's account balance is paid out over the whole retirement period. As in prefunded schemes, a rate of return equal to the internal rate of return of the scheme should therefore be applied to remaining account values. This can be done in three ways:

1. The rate of return is estimated and is taken into account in the computation of the transformation coefficient, without changing the benefits ex post if the actual rate of return turns out to be different from the one implicit in the coefficient (Italy).
2. As in (1), but with the provision that, in case the actual rate of return turns out to be different from the one implicit in the coefficient, benefits will be adjusted accordingly (Sweden).
3. No rate of return is acknowledged in formulating the initial annuity, but pensions are indexed ex post at a rate equal to the internal rate of return of the system. Poland and Latvia have employed price indexation to date, and Latvia has discussed a transition to wage indexation.

Models (2) and (3) can be equivalent. If based on the actual internal rate of return, they would keep the net present value of benefits in line with the actual rate of return of the system. As has been noted, however, there is a distributional difference. Model (1) is problematic: it leads to permanent imbalances between revenues and outlays if the rate of return of the system turns out to be other than randomly different from the one implicit in the coefficient (which in the Italian case is fixed at 1.5 percent).

CORRECTING DISEQUILIBRIA

In principle, NDC remains in long-run financial equilibrium if the rate of return is adequately designed and if the errors in projecting the values of life expectancy used in computing annuities are random. This, in turn, means that there are two ways in which long-run disequilibria can arise: through an inadequate representation of the internal rate of return in indexing workers' accounts and pensioners' benefits, and through the occurrence of systematic errors in computing the value of life expectancy used to calculate life annuities (see Alho, Bravo, and Palmer 2012; Palmer 2012).

Since the contribution rate is defined, contributions are determined by the exogenous factors that shape the development of the wage rate and the labor force. Thus, changes that steer the system in the direction of financial equilibrium can be directed exclusively toward the accounts of workers, pensioners, or both. Disequilibrating forces that reflect systematic changes in the capacity to pay, such as a long-run decline to a lower permanent level of fertility, affect the capacity of the system to pay—in this case, once the smaller birth cohorts enter the labor force. This "disturbance" affects the capacity to pay pensions both now and in the future. Hence, it is important for the maintenance of financial equilibrium that both the benefits of pensioners and the account values of workers are scaled down through indexation. However, if the disequilibrating events that arise are a series of more or less random events that cancel each other out over time, such as impacts with zero expected value, long-run equilibrium will be maintained. In fact, this is an argument for creating a reserve fund to smooth out the effects of, especially, temporary downturns in the economy. Holzmann, Palmer, and Robalino (2012) discuss how this can be done. Finally, there is a potential source of disequilibrium connected to how the valuation indexes are constructed; for example, index values based on (averages of) lagged values lead to delayed adjustments.

The design of all four countries' NDC schemes is such that in the accumulation phase, accounts are adjusted automatically to changes in the internal rate of return. At the time of writing, only Sweden adjusts pensions to the internal rate of return. If the rate of return used is equal to the rate of growth of the contribution base, this ensures a steady-state balanced pension budget. If pensions are not adjusted, the equilibrating process can be very long, and balance may not occur at all. This is presently the case in Italy, Latvia, and Poland, where benefits are only price-indexed (with a small wage component in Poland). This outcome is obvious from the fact that the contributions needed to cover pension payments in any specific period (the period contribution rate) are equal to the ratio of pension payments to contributions.

All four countries have procedures for revising the coefficients: revisions are automatic and take place every year except in Italy, where they are to be made every three years. Increases in life expectancy would reduce new pension benefits via the new life expectancy conversion coefficients for each new retiring birth cohort. However, if these are systematically underestimated, continued reductions in mortality rates will not affect the levels of pensions once they are awarded. Only Sweden has an automatic mechanism that adjusts both accounts of workers and pensions already being paid to guarantee a near period-by-period balance between pension liabilities and pension assets.

ADJUSTMENT TO SHOCKS IN NDC SCHEMES: A SIMULATION

As was discussed above, properly designed NDC systems ensure that in the long run, pension outlays and receipts stay broadly in balance, irrespective of changes in macroeconomic and demographic trends. After a shock, however, the return to a balanced budget may require a certain amount of time.

To put these ideas into a more quantitative framework, we perform a very simple exercise, which we apply to the Italian and Swedish pension systems. [28] We consider an economy in which people enter the labor market at age 20 and work for 45 years. Afterward, they spend between 15 and 20 years in retirement; indeed, the exact moment of death is uncertain (and for simplicity is uniformly distributed) within this age bracket, so that the expected average life span is 82.5. In line with the most recent Europe-wide projections (European Commission and Economic Policy Committee 2009), we assume a constant macro labor input and an annual increase in labor productivity of 1.7 percent.

"Textbook" NDC. On this economy, we superimpose the simplest possible version of an NDC scheme: contributions to the notional account of workers are assigned a rate of return equal to the rate of growth of the contribution base, which is what is needed to keep the system in financial equilibrium. At retirement, the notional capital is transformed into an annuity in an actuarially fair way and using the best estimate of the remaining life span that is available at that moment. Pension benefits in the postretirement phase are also indexed to the contribution base.

We assume that the payroll contribution rate is equal to 25 percent of the wage. (The contribution level is, in any case, irrelevant for the dynamics.) In steady state, this implies that both pension outlays and social security contributions receipts are equal to about 16 percent of GDP.[29]

We consider three kinds of (permanent) shocks.

1. *A negative shock to the rate of growth of labor productivity,* which declines from 1.7 percent to 1.0 percent. This kind of shock is absorbed at once by the system: the growth rates of pensions and of notional capital are immediately reduced to a rate equal to those of labor productivity and of GDP. The pension budget remains balanced, and the ratio of pension expenditure to GDP stays constant.

2. *A positive shock to longevity,* with average life expectancy at retirement increasing by about one year. In this scenario, even our textbook NDC pension system suffers from imbalances in the short to medium run. Indeed, even if the coefficients of new pensioners are immediately updated so that they are actuarially fair given the new life expectancy, there is a stock of retirees who enjoy pensions that were calculated, at the moment of their retirement, using old transformation coefficients. This implies that, starting from the year of the shock, outlays will exceed revenues until none of these preexisting pensioners survive. The length of the transition period in our economy is about 15 years; just after the shock, expenditures increase to about 17 percent of GDP, and the deficit goes from zero to 1 percentage point of GDP. Afterward, expenditure falls to preshock levels, and the deficit returns to zero.

3. *A decrease in the rate of growth of the labor input.* Instead of setting the size of the new cohorts equal to that of the cohorts exiting the labor force, we assume that the size of the youngest cohort of workers decreases by 0.5 percent annually. In general, this has two opposite effects on the pension budget: it lowers revenues because it reduces the number of contributors, but it also diminishes expenditures because pension indexation (as well as the amount of the first pension benefits for those who retire in that year) depends on that parameter. The effect that prevails depends on the exact pension rules and on the parameters of the economy. In our simple economy, the effect is a very small and temporary surplus.[30] The surplus, which is in the order of magnitude of 0.1–0.2 percentage point of GDP annually, lasts until the last person who was already working at the moment of the shock retires (approximately 45 years).

These experiments highlight the different nature of the shocks: it is important whether the change affects equally all the cohorts working at the time of the shock and thereafter; whether it affects the youngest working cohort and all new-entrant cohorts thereafter but not other working cohorts at the time of the shock; or whether it affects cohorts randomly or cyclically or in some unsystematic manner. Furthermore, it is important whether the process continues "forever" or stops with a certain cohort. In experiment (1), the decline in the rate of growth of productivity affects the wages of all cohorts of workers from the moment it occurs. In experiment (3), the downsizing of the labor force occurs with the youngest cohort and all following cohorts, and full adjustment occurs only after the entitlements of all cohorts have been downsized.

Italian NDC. Real-world NDCs can be even more vulnerable to shocks than the textbook version studied in the previous section. An example is the Italian system, which differs from the textbook model in two main respects: (a) transformation coefficients are updated only with a lag (currently equal to three years), and (b) each pension is fixed in real terms for the whole postretirement period. This implies that, even in a steady state, pension expenditures will generally be equal to revenues only if the technical rate of return implicit in the transformation coefficients happens to be equal to the actual rate of growth of GDP. In Italy, such a rate of return, at 1.5 percent, has been incorporated in newly granted annuities from the start. It is not automatically changed when coefficients are updated, nor is there an annual adjustment process, as in Sweden, for annual deviations from this "norm."

- If, as in our baseline simulation, the rate of growth of GDP is reduced from 1.7 percent to 1.0 percent, it will generate permanent deficits of about 0.3 percentage point of GDP. Similarly, systematic growth above 1.5 percent induces permanent surpluses.

- The effect of our unexpected increase in longevity is broadly offset by the two corrective mechanisms: the revision of coefficients converting contributions into pensions and the revision of the retirement age. These tend to offset the effect of delayed retirement on the amount paid to new pensioners and neutralize the increase in the number of pensioners that would otherwise occur.

- Finally, a negative shock to fertility has a permanent negative impact on the balance of the pension system (–0.2 percentage point of GDP in the new steady state). The reason is that a permanent shock to fertility permanently decreases the rate of growth of the economy and of the wage bill, which is also the internal rate of return of the system. This is not taken into account by the Italian transformation coefficient, which still awards a 1.5 percent rate of return to new pensioners.

Swedish NDC. The Swedish NDC scheme differs from the textbook model in two main respects: (a) contributions are indexed to average wages, not to the wage bill; and (b) an automatic balance mechanism is in place. The mechanism works as follows: in each period, the liabilities and the assets of the system are computed. The former are calculated as the present discounted value of the rights matured by all current workers (the amount in their personal accounts) and by all current pensioners (the discounted values of their present and future benefits).[31] The assets are computed as the annual flow of contributions multiplied by a factor, the "turnover duration," that is designed to capture the money-weighted sum of the average number of years of contributions and the average number of years of retirement in the cross-section of workers.[32] If the solvency ratio—the ratio of assets to liabilities—is less than unity, the balancing index is triggered, and the indexation of accounts of workers and of pensions is reduced. The indexation is no longer equal to the growth of the average wage but, rather, to the growth of the average wage multiplied by assets divided by liabilities. The adjustment mechanism speeds up the return to a balanced budget after a shock to the system. In what follows, we describe the effects of the three above-mentioned shocks in a slightly simplified version of the Swedish NDC.[33]

1. The negative shock to the rate of growth of labor productivity is immediately absorbed by the system; the balancing mechanism is not triggered. [34]

2. The positive shock to longevity, without the operation of the automatic balancing mechanism, would have caused a deficit for about 15 years, starting from a value of 1.4 percentage points of GDP and then declining, as in the case. However, the increase in longevity triggers the balancing mechanism as liabilities become greater than assets (even if the turnover duration increases). As a consequence, the rate of return on the accounts of workers and the benefits of pensioners already in payment drops from 1.7 percent to slightly above zero. This trims the deficit from 1.4 percentage points of GDP to slightly over 1.0 percentage point and reduces its duration from 15 to 10 years. During this 10-year period, the asset liability ratio gradually increases, finally reaching unity again, and the same happens for the rate of return awarded to workers and pensioners, which gradually returns to 1.7 percent.

3. Finally, in the case of the negative shock to fertility, the presence of the automatic stabilizing mechanism plays an important role. The shock implies that the rate of return awarded by the system to participants (average wage growth) becomes permanently higher than the rate of return that is affordable by the system in the steady state (the growth of the wage bill). Without the stabilizing mechanism, there would be a growing deficit, which reaches about 0.5 percentage points of GDP on an annual basis in the new steady state. However, the shock implies an asset/liability ratio of less than unity in each future period, and in response, the balancing mechanism permanently reduces the rate of return awarded to participants, in line with the internal rate of return of the system.

Response to Economic Crises

Proponents of NDC claim that by locking the parameters of the system into a package that generates long-term financial stability, the system is insulated from the political risk inherent in defined benefit PAYG schemes. With the economic crisis of 2008, this assertion was put to its first real test.

Pensions are price-indexed only in Italy and Latvia; Poland has only a small real wage component. Negative growth reduces the future pension rights of current workers but does not reduce pensions already being paid. Pensions are nevertheless price-indexed, and, in principle, negative inflation should determine a downward adjustment in benefits.

Of the three countries, Latvia had negative inflation in 2009, but Latvian politicians were reluctant to deflate pensions and instead set a floor of zero on inflation adjustment of pensions.

In both Latvia and Poland, the economic crisis of 2008 led to political discussions concerning the reasonability of the extra tax burden created by the diversion of contributions to the buildup of the FDC schemes. In Latvia, this led to a legislated decrease in the portion of contributions transferred to the mandatory FDC scheme, from the planned 10 percent to 6 percent, which is the share that previous analyses showed Latvia could afford with an unchanged (or lower) contribution rate (see Palmer et al. 2006). This process could be viewed as correcting a decision that from the outset was highly questionable.

Poland was one of the few countries that went through the 2008–09 recession with positive real economic growth. Nevertheless, the economy slowed, and the public finance situation worsened. The decline in contribution revenues and an ensuing deficit meant that the Social Insurance Fund had to seek external funding of about 5 billion Polish zlotys from commercial banks.[35] This led to a proposal, finally set forth by the government at the end of 2010, to reduce the FDC contribution initially to 2.3 percent of wages and then gradually increase it to 3.5 percent. The remaining contribution rate of 5.0 percent (decreasing to 3.8 percent) would be passed to the PAYG system but would be recorded on hybrid individual accounts that would be adjusted in line with GDP growth and a cash payout of inheritance in case of death of the participant. The proposal triggered a hot debate on the performance of the pension system, with most experts, and public opinion as well, against manipulation of the system. Despite this debate, the change was legislated and entered into force as of May 2011. The change not only altered the proportion of contributions between the NDC and FDC parts of the scheme but also created two parallel NDC-type accounts, with different rules of indexation and inheritance. This diminishes both the ability to diversify risks in the scheme and the overall transparency of the system design.

In Latvia, early retirement pensions were reduced from 80 percent of the normal retirement pension to 50 percent, and, as of January 1, 2012, early retirement will no longer be an option. On December 21, 2009, the Constitutional Court ruled that the government's decision to reduce pensions was unconstitutional. Accordingly, the reduction was abolished, and reductions that had been made were repaid in April 2010. This sequence attests to the strength of the NDC commitment in Latvia. Even significant budget pressure was not sufficient reason to reduce benefits ad hoc.

This view of what "the fund" is applies to the Swedish NDC scheme, as well. However, unlike the other three countries, Sweden has an explicit NDC reserve fund. The valuation of assets is a function of the value of the reserve fund and a valuation of future contributions based on the money-weighted time a krona is in the system, on average—from the time it is paid in until it is paid out. In 2008, the value of the reserve fund fell with the general decline in the global equity market. At the same time, wage growth was close to zero. The overall effect of the recession was that the balance index fell below unity, to 0.9672 in 2008 and to 0.9570 in 2009 (SSIA 2009).

Reserve funds had been valued in the accounts at their market value on December 31 of each year. In response to the crisis, the parliament changed the valuation principle to a three-year moving average, which reduced the imbalance to 0.9826 in 2008 and to 0.9570 in 2009, thereby decreasing the necessary reduction in the initial years. Nevertheless, both workers' accounts and pensioners' benefits were reduced in accordance with this outcome. In reflecting on this rule-based decrease in pensions, it is important to consider, first, that with a return of the fund values to normal growth, and as the economy begins to grow strongly again, perhaps all of this loss will be made up with renewed indexation up to the original income index values. The question that arises is why Sweden has not built up a contingency reserve to cushion the effect on pension payments of temporary declines in assets. This was the first time the Swedish "brake" on indexation needed to be employed. Following some public discussion, the fact that the rule-based adjustment of NDC liabilities of workers and pensioners needed to be undertaken was accepted.

In sum, the rule-based systems weathered the stress test of strong recessionary pressure in Latvia, Poland, and Sweden. In Italy, there was no discussion specific to NDC, since the number of NDC pensions being paid is still very small. But the changes introduced to increase the retirement age (such as the automatic adjustment to longevity) can also be seen as a way of offsetting the impact of the crisis both on the budget and on individual pensions.

Conclusion

This study has discussed the circumstances under which NDC was introduced in four EU countries and has reviewed the pros and cons of the construction of these countries' systems. One finding is that the political processes leading to NDC went smoothly in all four cases, although with very different courses. If the introduction of NDC faltered somewhere, it was in Italy, where there was little communication of the content and goals of the reform to the public and where the transition process was so slow that people hardly realized a change had taken place. These circumstances may have undercut the goals of the reform.

Specific issues involved the cashing in or outright abolition of special rights. Sweden started in the position of having no groups with special privileges. Latvia had inherited a large list of special privileges from the Soviet system and dealt with these issues successfully from the outset by converting acquired rights into initial capital for personal accounts. It took Poland until 2008 to resolve these same issues, through legislation for bridging pensions for people with special rights from the old regime. Latvia and Sweden have the same retirement age for men and women, whereas Poland still has a retirement age of 60 for women and 65 for men, in spite of repeated political proposals for equal treatment. Italy grants to women in the private sector greater flexibility than to men and women in the public sector and also allows individuals with long contributory records to retire earlier. In Sweden, the only country where special privileges did not exist in the public defined benefit scheme that preceded NDC, the unisex age of exit from the labor force was more than 63 in 2010, with the normal age for claiming an NDC benefit being 65 (although it was possible to claim a benefit as early as age 61). The pension age has also been on a gradual upward path. The increase in the minimum pension age to 62 in Latvia has had the effect of raising the de facto age of exit from the labor force.

We have emphasized that with price indexation of benefits, the ratio of an aging cohort's benefit to the average wage for all workers declines as the pensioner becomes older. The question is whether this will be politically acceptable in the long run. A first conclusion on indexation is that straightforward wage-sum indexation of pensions will have to be considered. The second conclusion that emerges is that, because Italy and Sweden distribute the available real growth surplus in the creation of the initial annuity, future consumption may be discounted more than is optimal. Latvia and Poland do not distribute possible future real indexation to pensioners in the creation of the annuity; instead, they implicitly use this surplus for other purposes, such as increasing the long-term financial sustainability of the pension system—which was endangered by the deep economic crises of the past few years. A thorough analysis (e.g., Palmer et al. 2006 for Latvia) would reveal that the money is largely going toward the creation of the FDC schemes in these countries. This redistributes a portion of contributions that could have been used for higher NDC benefits to the FDC "savings" of workers—largely, but not exactly, the same persons, since the transfer has also occurred at the expense of current pensioners who do not benefit from it. The success of this strategy depends on the development of the NDC and FDC rates of return. In addition, this strategy has been pursued at the expense of older pension cohorts who cannot benefit fully or at all from the FDC scheme. A similar argument applies to Poland.

The sine qua non of NDC is financial stability. Using a simple simulation model, the study has examined the responses of Italy and Sweden to a permanent decline in labor productivity, an increase in longevity at retirement, and a permanent decline in the size of the youngest cohort. Sweden's balancing mechanism ensures financial stability, albeit sometimes with a lag, whereas under the Italian design, two of the negative shocks lead to deficits over long periods of time. Because pensions in payment are only price-indexed in Latvia and Poland, the NDC schemes create a surplus during periods with positive wage-sum growth (although without an explicit funding mechanism) and will run a deficit in periods when nominal wage-sum growth falls below the rate of inflation. In these countries, there is a clear case for considering an explicit reserve fund. Generally speaking, the issue of financial balance needs to be revisited in Italy, Latvia, and Poland.

The possibility of incurring large and long-lasting financial imbalances in NDC can be limited by careful design of the system. Once an imbalance has occurred, it can be remedied either via built-in stabilizers, such as those incorporated into the Swedish system, or by not distributing the entire internal rate of return, as in Latvia and Poland, or through periodic ad hoc adjustments, which is implicitly what Italy might be forced to do. In some circumstances, in the latter three countries, the government budget becomes the buffer fund. This may work in both sunny and stormy weather if the government maintains an accounting or fictive fund, which implies saving (reducing debt) in good times to increase debt in bad times. Of course, this reasoning works only if good and bad times tend to even out, which will not be the case in a world with a pronounced tendency toward persistent labor force decline. This risk requires explicit creation of the necessary automatic stabilizers.

In the case of NDC, the traditional political difficulties associated with tightening pension rules may be fostered by psychological difficulties arising from contributors' (mis)perception that the pension system as a whole is always in balance, insofar as individual benefits are linked to past individual contributions. If this misperception exists, it can be hard to convince the public that benefits have to be reduced because of an unexpectedly unfavorable macroeconomic or demographic scenario. Therefore, it is extremely important that stabilizers be built into the system.

What the four countries have not yet succeeded in bringing home to the population is that the NDC rate of return is just that—a rate of return, determined by economic and demographic developments. In practice, this means that even pensions are variable, although the variation will almost always be in positive numbers. Negative numbers may nevertheless arise temporarily, in conjunction with deep recessions that lead to a decline in the contribution base.

Changes in the conversion coefficients could be made ad hoc when the numbers turn negative, as they did in 2008–09 in most of the world. However, this breaks with the discipline—and trust in the discipline—of the NDC idea. A more promising avenue to explore would be to not fully distribute the internal rate of return during good times, in order to intentionally provide a buffer for bad times. The buffer could then be used to finance pensions in times of crisis, when the fundamentals of the system indicate that pensions should be reduced, as during the recession of 2008–09. This solution obviously requires a definition of good times and bad times. Many issues must be addressed in setting up a reserve fund. How large should the reserve be? How should it be built up from the start? How should the portfolio be managed? How should funds be distributed?

NDC is the basic earnings-related pension in all four countries. The analysis shows that, overall, the countries' mandatory systems provide gross income replacement rates at retirement for full-career workers, with average earnings of 60–65 percent and net replacement rates of about 75 percent in Italy, Latvia, and Poland, although the structures of their mandatory systems differ. The net replacement rate for the average earner in Sweden is about the same as the gross replacement rate. The Italian system is less efficient in that a higher contribution rate is required to achieve the same after-tax return as in Latvia, Poland, and Sweden. The reason is the substantial FDC components of the overall pension landscape in the latter three countries, with an assumed higher long-run rate of return.

Only Sweden has succeeded in fully compensating women for time out of the labor force in conjunction with childbirth and the initial years of child care. In addition, none of the three countries has legislated provisions to allow for sharing of accounts or creation of joint annuities. This is largely to the disadvantage of women. In Italy and Poland, the possibility for women to retire at an early age is yet another factor that puts women at risk of falling into poverty in old age. These are all relatively simple design features to change. In fact, one can make a case for generous parental as well as noncontributory pension supplements as a policy initiative to promote higher fertility and endogenously determined labor force growth.

NDC appears to have weathered the storm created by the deep recession of 2008–09. The three countries where the adjustment to the drop in the contribution base was absorbed by the overall budget (Italy, Latvia, and Poland) saw no strong political repercussions, although Latvian politicians put brakes on the overall effect of price deflation. Latvia also downsized the scale of the FDC scheme, but from an initial level that, arguably, was too high. The split was also changed in Poland. In Sweden, the adjustment was internal, within the NDC system, with downward revision of workers' accounts and pensioners' benefits.

In 2011, Italy responded to the financial market pressure to reduce its sovereign debt by accelerating the transition to full NDC. This entailed: tightening (although not fully abolishing) seniority rules for all workers and creating NDC accounts for contributions of persons not previously covered by the NDC scheme (pre-1996 contributors) for the remainder of their working careers. The statutory pension age was raised to 66 for all workers from 2012 (with a transitory period till 2018 for women in the private sector). From 2013 onward, the statutory pension age (as well as the minimum number of contribution years required for seniority pensions) will be automatically indexed to increases in life expectancy. Some of the features of an NDC scheme that guarantee long-term financial robustness (the construction of the internal rate of return, including explicit rules for handling deficits and surpluses) are still absent, but there are two corrective mechanisms (the revision of retirement age and the revision of the coefficients converting contributions into pensions) working in parallel to offset the impact of raising life expectancy. This is a unique feature of the Italian system. It would have been preferable to implement from the very outset a full NDC regime for all groups of workers and cohorts, but in the end—after a lengthy reform process—Italy now has a sustainable and homogeneous pension system providing the "right" economic incentives.

Notes

1. NDC is a main element in reforms in process at the time of writing in the Arab Republic of Egypt (see Maait and Demarco, chapter 5 in this volume) and in Norway (Christensen et al., chapter 4 in this volume).

2. The Kyrgyz and Russian NDC schemes are not discussed in this chapter. According to Hauner (2008), the Russian system suffers from inadequate design, including undervaluation of rights, which will yield too low benefits in the future, and a fixed life expectancy factor, which means that newly granted annuities do not follow the development of life expectancy.

3. For a more general presentation of the principles of NDC, see Palmer (2006b; 2012, chap.19).

4. It is not exactly true that NDC has *no* distributional features. For example, the widespread use of average life expectancy redistributes resources from men to women, given women's greater life expectancy. Redistribution can also take place across categories of individuals with different average life expectancies if the differences in categories reflect a systematic selection—for example, of persons with low human capital into sectors or occupations with low earnings.

5. Although Sweden did fulfill the deficit and debt reduction criteria, it chose to remain outside the European Monetary Union.

6. Seniority pensions allowed individuals to retire before the standard retirement age, once a certain contributory record had been achieved.

7. Altogether, the reforms introduced through 2004 reduced pension liabilities by about one-third (Franco and Sartor 2006).

8. If the average individual monthly covered wage is less than the average country covered wage between January 1996 and December 1999, the wage used for the NDC account will be increased to the average country level.

9. In 2009, NDC pensions represented about 5 percent of the number of new pensions and about 1 percent of the amount paid. Nearly four-fifths of the flow of new pensions was still paid out fully on the basis of the pre-NDC formula.

10. This was partly because the public defined benefit system replaced by NDC also had an actuarial reduction factor from a "full" pension age of 65.

11. Jerzy Hausner, who proposed this program, was also the Government Plenipotentiary for Pension Reform in 1997.

12. In Poland, workers covered by the new scheme could opt out to the old one if they had accrued their pension rights before the end of 2008; this deadline was postponed by two years from that initially proposed, as a result of preelection political decisions.

13. A rate of 18.0 percent, instead of 16.0 percent, was chosen because the additional 2.5 percent rate for the mandatory FDC scheme was first introduced in 1995 and calculations showed that acquired rights on an aggregate basis in the old scheme were comparable to those that would have accrued if people had had the same earnings history as in the old system, but with a contribution rate of about 18.0 percent. Initial capital also included imputed values of noncontributory child-care rights.

14. The old Swedish defined benefit scheme also had actuarially adjusted benefits, which made it very similar to the new NDC scheme in this respect.

15. Should the Swedish system break the solvency rule that assets are to be at least as great as liabilities, leading to a reduction of accounts, all account values are to be reduced proportionately.

16. Exactly how this is done in detail is explained in the appendix to the *Annual Report of the Swedish Pension System* (see, e.g., SSIA 2009).

17. The interested reader is referred to any of the annual reports of the Swedish Pension Agency, formerly the Swedish Social Insurance Agency (e.g., SSIA 2009).

18. In both Sweden and Italy, full or partial indexation to wage dynamics (coupled with lower initial benefits) would have been in conflict with the governments' objective of ensuring that individuals retiring at a specific age with a certain number of years of contributions would get the same replacement rate as before the reform. In Italy, the norm was 37 years of contributions at age 62. In Sweden, it was politically important that 40 years of contributions at age 65 would yield, initially, about a 60 percent replacement rate, with the realization that changing life expectancy for younger cohorts would alter this result,

19. In Latvia and Poland, there is a trade-off between wage indexation and the financing of the second-pillar FDC schemes during the transition, which, compared with a counterfactual of wage indexation, constitutes a tax on pensioners. See Palmer et al. (2006) for a discussion and analysis for Latvia.

20. We are indebted to the OECD, and specifically to Edward Whitehouse and Andrew Reilly, for providing these data.

    The assumptions of the model are as follows: real earnings growth is 2.0 percent; individual earnings are assumed to grow in line with economywide earnings; price inflation is 2.5 percent per year; the real rate of return on FDC schemes is 3.5 percent; the discount rate is 2.0 percent; and mortality rates are modeled using the World Bank and United Nations population database (Whitehouse 2007, 26–27).

21. In the OECD modeling exercise, the NDC components have a 2.0 percent real rate of return and the FDC components, a 3.5 percent rate of return. It should be noted that among the assumptions used is that of no employment growth, which means that average wage growth equals the covered wage-sum growth in the calculation. This has an impact on the results.

22. The Italian NDC sets a ceiling on yearly contributions. In 2009, contributions were not levied on incomes above 91,500 euros, which is slightly more than three times the average gross earnings of Italian employees.

23. The replacement rate reflects a country's contribution rate, which is higher in Italy and lower in Sweden. In Sweden, however, practically all workers also have an occupational supplement

that increases the average replacement rate below the ceiling on contribution income by about 10 percent.

24. See James (2012) and Klerby, Larsson, and Palmer (2012) for discussions of what countries could do to reduce the risk of poverty among older women within the NDC pension framework.

25. The estimates are provided by country experts using assumptions specified by the AWG.

26. Italy's innovation of automatic increases in the retirement age was introduced in 2009, so it is not taken into account in the AWG projections. However, because the change will both reduce the number of pensioners and increase benefits per pensioner, the overall effect on aggregate expenditure is likely to be small.

27. Gronchi (1998) estimates that this expenditure may represent 2 percentage points of earnings.

28. We thank Pietro Tommasino for his cooperation in developing this exercise.

29. This is a consequence of the assumption, in line with the AWG projections (European Commission and Economic Policy Committee 2009), that the share of labor in GDP is 65 percent, so that GDP itself is equal to the economy's wage bill divided by 0.65. Again, as in the case of the contribution rate, this assumption is irrelevant to the existence, timing, or magnitude of the dynamic responses of the system; it is only meant to add some degree of realism not just to the changes but also to the levels of our variables of interest.

30. In Valdés-Prieto's (2000) model, with no productivity growth and a rate of growth of labor input that is initially positive, the reverse is true, as shown by Breyer (2004) and acknowledged by Valdés-Prieto (2004). Our simulations start from a positive growth rate of productivity and a zero growth rate of the labor input.

31. The discount factor is given by the average wage. (Mortality rates are also taken into account.)

32. In our simulated economy, in the steady state before the shocks, the turnover duration is about 36 years.

33. For our purposes, the only relevant simplification is that in Sweden, the account increases with an average of lagged and current wages, but in our model, it increases in line with current wages. 1

34. In the real world, the shock would be absorbed slightly more gradually because indexation is based on a moving average of wages and not on current wages. However, the automatic balancing mechanism would also have been activated, and the impulse response path would have been very similar to the one described here.

35. A billion is a thousand million.

References

Alho, Juha, Jorge Miguel Bravo, and Edward Palmer. 2012. "Annuities and Life Expectancy in NDC." In *Gender, Politics, and Financial Stability*, chap. 22, vol. 2 of *Nonfinancial Defined Contribution Pension Schemes in a Changing Pension World*, ed. Robert Holzmann, Edward Palmer, and David A. Robalino. Washington, DC: World Bank and Swedish Social Insurance Agency.

Auerbach, Alan J., and Ronald Lee. 2011. "Welfare and Generational Equity in Sustainable Unfunded Pension Systems." *Journal of Public Economics* 95 (1–2): 16–27.

Beltrametti, Luca. 1996. *Il debito pensionistico in Italia*. Bologna: Il Mulino.

Breyer, Friedrich. 2004. "Comment on S. Valdés-Prieto, 'The Financial Stability of Notional Account Pensions.'" *Scandinavian Journal of Economics* 106 (2): 385–7.

Chłoń, Agnieszka, Marek Góra, and Michał Rutkowski. 1999. "Shaping Pension Reform in Poland: Security through Diversity." World Bank Pension Reform Primer Series 9923, World Bank, Social Protection Unit, Human Development Network, Washington, DC.

Chłoń-Domińczak, Agnieszka. 2002. "The Polish Pension Reform of 1999." In *Restructuring with Privatization: Case Studies of Hungary and Poland,* chap. 2, vol. 1 of *Pension Reform in Central and Eastern Europe,* ed. Elaine Fultz. Budapest: International Labour Office.

Chłoń-Domińczak, Agnieszka, and Marek Góra. 2006. "The NDC System in Poland: Assessment after Five Years." In *Pension Reform: Issues and Prospects for Non-Financial Defined Contribution (NDC) Schemes,* ed. Robert Holzmann and Edward Palmer, 425–48. Washington, DC: World Bank.

Chłoń-Domińczak, Agnieszka, and Pawel Strzelecki. 2010. "The Minimum Pension as an Instrument of Poverty Protection in the Defined Contribution Pension System: An Example of Poland." Munich Personal RePEc Archive (MPRA) Paper 25262, University Library of Munich, Munich.

Disney, Richard. 1996. *Can We Afford to Grow Older?* Cambridge, MA: MIT Press.

European Commission and Economic Policy Committee. 2009. "The 2009 Ageing Report: Economic and Budgetary Projections for the EU-27 Member States (2008–2060)." *European Economy* (European Commission) 2.

Forteza, Alvaro, Leonardo Lucchetti, and Monserrat Pallares-Miralles. 2009. "Measuring the Coverage Gap." In *Closing the Coverage Gap: The Role of Social Pensions and Other Retirement Income Transfers,* ed. Robert Holzmann, David A. Robalino, and Noriyuli Takayama, 23–40. Washington, DC: World Bank.

Fox, Louise, and Edward Palmer. 1999. "Latvian Pension Reform." Social Protection Discussion Paper 9922, World Bank, Washington, DC.

Franco, Daniele. 2002. "Italy: A Never Ending Pension Reform." In *Social Security Pension Reform in Europe,* ed. Martin Feldstein and Horst Siebert, 211–62. Chicago: University of Chicago Press.

Franco, Daniele, and Nicola Sartor. 2006. "NDCs in Italy: Unsatisfactory Present, Uncertain Future." In *Pension Reform: Issues and Prospects for Non-Financial Defined Contribution (NDC) Schemes,* ed. Robert Holzmann and Edward Palmer, 467–92. Washington, DC: World Bank.

Góra, Marek. 2001. "Polish Approach to Pension Reform." *Private Pension Systems* 3: 227–46.

Góra, Marek, and Michal Rutkowski. 1998. "The Quest for Pension Reform: Poland's Security through Diversity." Pension Reform Primer Series, Social Protection Discussion Paper 9815, World Bank, Washington, DC.

Gronchi, Sandro. 1998. "La sostenibilità delle nuove forme previdenziali ovvero il sistema pensionistico tra riforme fatte e da fare." *Economia Politica* 15 (2): 295–316.

Gronchi, Sandro, and Rocco Aprile. 1998. "The 1995 Pension Reform: Equity, Sustainability and Indexation." *Labour* 12 (1, March): 67–100.

Gronchi, Sandro, and Sergio Nisticò. 2006. "Implementing the NDC Theoretical Model: A Comparison of Italy and Sweden." In *Pension Reform: Issues and Prospects for Non-Financial Defined Contribution (NDC) Schemes,* ed. Robert Holzmann and Edward Palmer, 493–516. Washington, DC: World Bank.

Hauner, David. 2008. "Macroeconomic Effects of Pension Reform in Russia." International Monetary Fund Working Paper WP/08/201, International Monetary Fund, Washington, DC.

Holzmann, Robert, and Richard Hinz. 2005. *Old Age Income Support in the 21st Century: An International Perspective on Pension Systems and Reform.* Washington, DC: World Bank.

Holzmann, Robert, Edward Palmer, and David A. Robalino. 2012. "The Economics of Reserve Funds in NDC Schemes: Role, Means, and Size to Manage Shocks." In *Gender, Politics, and Financial Stability,* chap. 20, vol. 2 of *Nonfinancial Defined Contribution Pension Schemes in a Changing Pension World,* ed. Robert Holzmann, Edward Palmer, and David A. Robalino. Washington, DC: World Bank and Swedish Social Insurance Agency.

James, Estelle. 2012. "Gender in the (Nonfinancial) Defined Contribution World: Issues and Options" In *Gender, Politics, and Financial Stability,* chap. 10, vol. 2 of *Nonfinancial Defined Contribution Pension Schemes in a Changing Pension World,* ed. Robert Holzmann, Edward Palmer, and David A. Robalino. Washington, DC: World Bank and Swedish Social Insurance Agency.

Klerby, Anna, Bo Larsson, and Edward Palmer. 2012. "To Share or Not to Share—That's the Question." In *Gender, Politics, and Financial Stability,* chap. 11, vol. 2 of *Nonfinancial Defined Contribution Pension Schemes in a Changing Pension World,* ed. Robert Holzmann, Edward Palmer, and David A. Robalino. Washington, DC: World Bank and Swedish Social Insurance Agency.

Könberg, Bo, Edward Palmer, and Annika Sundén. 2006. "The NDC Reform in Sweden: The 1994 Legislation to the Present." In *Pension Reform: Issues and Prospects for Non-Financial Defined Contribution (NDC) Schemes,* ed. Robert Holzmann and Edward Palmer, 449–66. Washington, DC: World Bank.

OECD (Organisation for Economic Co-operation and Development). 2009. *Pensions at a Glance 2009: Retirement-Income Systems in OECD Countries.* Paris: OECD. http://www.oecd.org/els/social/pensions/PAG.

Palme, Mårten, and Ingemar Svensson. 1999. "Social Security, Occupational Pensions and Retirement in Sweden." In *Social Security and Retirement around the World,* ed. Jonathan Gruber and David Wise, 355–402. National Bureau of Economic Research Conference Report. Chicago: University of Chicago Press.

Palmer, Edward. 1999. "Individual Decisions and Aggregate Stability in a NDC PAYG Account Scheme." http://www.forsakringskassan.se.

———. 2000. "The Swedish Pension Reform Model: Framework and Issues." World Bank Pension Reform Primer, Social Protection Paper 0012, World Bank, Washington, DC.

———. 2002. "Swedish Pension Reform: Its Past and Its Future." In *Social Security Pension Reform in Europe,* ed. Martin Feldstein and Horst Siebert, 171–210. Chicago: University of Chicago Press.

———. 2006a. "Conversion to NDCs—Issues and Models." In *Pension Reform: Issues and Prospects for Non-Financial Defined Contribution (NDC) Schemes,* ed. Robert Holzmann and Edward Palmer, 169–202. Washington, DC: World Bank.

———. 2006b. "What Is NDC?" In *Pension Reform: Issues and Prospects for Non-Financial Defined Contribution (NDC) Schemes,* ed. Robert Holzmann and Edward Palmer. Washington, DC: World Bank.

———. 2007. "Pension Reform and the Development of Pension Systems: An Evaluation of World Bank Assistance." Kyrgyz Republic Country Study, International Evaluation Group (IEG), World Bank, Washington, DC.

———. 2012. "Generic NDC: Equilibrium, Valuation and Risk Sharing." In *Gender, Politics, and Financial Stability,* chap. 19, vol. 2 of *Nonfinancial Defined Contribution Pension Schemes in a Changing Pension World,* ed. Robert Holzmann, Edward Palmer, and David A. Robalino. Washington, DC: World Bank and Swedish Social Insurance Agency.

Palmer, Edward, Sandra Stabina, Ingemar Svensson, and Inta Vanovska. 2006. "NDC Strategy in Latvia: Implementation and Prospects for the Future." In *Pension Reform: Issues and Prospects for Non-Financial Defined Contribution (NDC) Schemes,* ed. Robert Holzmann and Edward Palmer, 397–424. Washington, DC: World Bank.

Rostagno, Massimo. 1996. "Il percorso della riforma: 1992–1995. Nuovi indicatori di consistenza e sostenibilità per il FPLD." In *Pensioni e risanamento della finanza pubblica,* ed. Fiorella Padoa Schioppa Kostoris. Bologna: Il Mulino.

Settergren, Ole, and Boguslaw D. Mikula. 2006. "The Rate of Return of Pay-As-You-Go Pension Systems: A More Exact Consumption-Loan Model of Interest." In *Pension Reform: Issues and Prospects for Non-Financial Defined Contribution (NDC) Schemes,* ed. Robert Holzmann and Edward Palmer, 117–48. Washington, DC: World Bank.

SSIA (Swedish Social Insurance Agency). 2009. *Orange Report. Annual Report of the Swedish Pension System 2008.* Stockholm: SSIA.

Ståhlberg, Ann-Charlotte. 1990. "ATP-Systemet från fördelningspolitiskt synpunkt. Expert rapport till Pensionsberedningen" [Distributional aspects of ATP. Expert report to the Swedish Pension Commission]. *Statens Offentliga Utredningar (SOU)* 1990: 78. Stockholm: Allmänna förlaget.

Valdés-Prieto, Salvador. 2000. "The Financial Stability of Notional Account Pensions." *Scandinavian Journal of Economics* 102 (3): 395–417.

———. 2004. "Response to Breyer." *Scandinavian Journal of Economics* 106 (2): 389–90.

Vanovska, Inta. 2004. "Pension Reform in Latvia: Achievements and Challenges." In *Reforming Public Pensions: Sharing the Experiences of Transition and OECD Countries,* 133–58. Paris: Organisation for Economic Co-operation and Development (OECD).

———. 2006. "Pension Reform in Latvia." In *Pension Reform in the Baltic States,* ed. Elaine Fultz, 143–266. Budapest: International Labour Office (ILO).

Whitehouse, Edward. 2007. *Pensions Panorama.* Washington, DC: World Bank.

World Bank. 1994. *Averting the Old Age Crisis: Policies to Protect the Old and Promote Growth.* World Bank Policy Research Report. New York: Oxford University Press.

Parallel Lines: NDC Pensions and the Direction of Pension Reform in Developed Countries

Edward Whitehouse

A number of countries have introduced nonfinancial (notional) defined contribution (NDC) pensions as a replacement for public pensions, usually of the defined benefit type. Among the member countries of the Organisation for Economic Co-operation and Development (OECD), Italy, Norway, Poland, and Sweden have done so, as has Latvia, which is not an OECD country but is a member of the European Union (EU). Other countries, too, have shown a great deal of interest in this approach to pension reform.

The motivations for these reforms differed. Undoubtedly, matters of political economy played a role: there was a desire to change the pension system and not merely to adjust parameters and rules. Also, it was thought that reductions in benefits on the ground that future pensions would be linked to changes in life expectancy would be more palatable to the electorate than cuts in another form.

This chapter highlights the economic issues associated with these changes. There are four main dimensions of pension schemes that we will focus on

1. Benefits should be based on lifetime earnings rather than on a subset of "best" or "final" years of pay.
2. Each extra year's contribution should give rise to an additional benefit, with no ceiling on the number of pensionable years.
3. Benefits should be reduced for people who retire early in their careers, to reflect the longer expected duration of payment, and should be increased for people who postpone retirement until later.
4. Benefits should be reduced as life expectancy increases, again to reflect the longer duration for which benefits would be paid.

These issues are considered in turn in the next four sections. They have important implications for the equity of the pension system and, in particular, for the treatment of people who retire at different ages or who have contributed for different lengths of time. They also impinge on questions of economic efficiency: How can the effects of the pension system in distorting individual work and savings decisions be minimized?

Edward Whitehouse leads the Pensions Team in the Social Policy Division of the Organisation for Economic Co-operation and Development. The views expressed are those of the author alone and do not necessarily reflect those of the OECD or of any of its member governments.

Different Types of Pension Scheme

Publicly provided earnings-related pension schemes fall into three broad categories: defined benefit (DB), points, and NDC. It is useful to compare the interrelationship between the three, using some basic algebra. Issues are simplified here by using simple, generic versions of the three models.

All three types of scheme are found in OECD countries. About 17 of the 30 member countries studied here have public DB schemes, and in another 3, private DB plans are either mandatory or quasi-mandatory—that is, they achieve near-universal coverage through industrial relations agreements.[1] Four OECD countries have points schemes, and three have NDC schemes. Seven countries have no public, or mandatory private, earnings-related schemes. Of these, three have mandatory or quasi-mandatory defined contribution (DC) provisions, while two lack any compulsory public or private arrangements for providing income replacement in retirement, relying instead on public, basic schemes. Indeed, most OECD pension systems have already achieved most of the four objectives listed above, but without adopting NDC.

A simple DB plan pays a constant accrual rate, a, for each year of service. The accrual rate is based on lifetime average revalued earnings. The pension benefit can therefore be written as

$$DB = \sum_{i=o}^{R} w_i (1+u)^{R-i} a,$$

where w represents individual earnings in a particular year (indexed i), R is the year of retirement, and u is the factor by which earlier years' earnings are revalued. In most OECD countries, u is the growth of economywide average earnings.

In a points system, pension points are calculated by dividing earnings by the cost of the pension point (k). The pension benefit then depends on the value of a point at the time of retirement, v. The pension benefit can be written as

$$PP = \sum_{i=o}^{R} \frac{w_i v_R}{k_i}.$$

A significant public policy variable is the method for uprating the value of the pension point, shown by the parameter x in the next equation. By writing the pension point value at the time of retirement as a function of its contemporaneous value, the equation becomes

$$PP = \sum_{i=o}^{R} \frac{w_i v_i}{k_i} (1+x)^{R-i}.$$

Under NDC, the inflow each year equals wages multiplied by the contribution rate. The notional capital is increased each year by the notional interest rate, n. At retirement, the accumulated notional capital is divided by a notional annuity factor, A, sometimes called the G-value. The pension benefit can be written as

$$NA = \sum_{i=o}^{R} \frac{w_i c}{A} (1+n)^{R-i}.$$

If the policy for valorizing earlier years' earnings is the same as the uprating procedure for the pension point and the notional interest rate ($u = x = n$), then the structure of the three equations is very similar. In this case, the accrual rate (a) under a generic DB scheme is equal to the ratio of the pension point value to its cost (v / k) and to the ratio of the NDC contribution rate to the annuity factor (n / A).

This relationship has two implications for the comparison of the three types of earnings-related pension schemes. First, the effective accrual rate can be calculated both for pension point schemes (as the ratio of point value to cost) and under NDC (as the ratio of the contribution rate to the annuity factor). Second, the valorization procedure in DB plans, the uprating policy for the pension point value, and the establishment of the notional interest rate are exactly parallel policies. Different choices of variables have the same effect in the various systems. Although the DB, points, and NDC systems can appear very different, they are in fact closely related variants of earnings-related pension schemes. The key difference is that NDC schemes have a built-in mechanism for adjusting benefits to changes in life expectancy—but, as discussed in detail below, the same thing can be achieved in DB and points schemes.

Like the three earnings-related schemes described above, defined contribution schemes—in which the pension benefit depends on individual contributions and the investment returns that these contributions earn—share the objective of providing income replacement during retirement. DC plans are mandatory or quasi-mandatory in eight OECD countries. Coverage by voluntary private pensions, which are increasingly of the DC type, is widespread (greater than 40 percent of the workforce) in another five countries.

An issue not addressed in this chapter is the financing of pension benefits. DC schemes are, by definition, fully funded at all points: the liabilities of the scheme are exactly equal to the assets in the fund. Some earnings-related schemes are also prefunded. In theory, all three types could be financed in one of three ways:

- By *full funding*, where the aim is for assets to be equal to the present value of liabilities
- By *partial funding*, where assets exist but are, by design, less than liabilities
- On a *pay-as-you-go* basis, whereby current revenues pay current benefits and there are no assets

For example, public DB schemes are partially funded in Canada and Finland and are pay-as-you-go (PAYG) in about half of the OECD countries, including Austria, Belgium, Greece, and Italy. (Mandatory and quasi-mandatory private DB plans are funded.) Points schemes are partially prefunded in France but are PAYG in Germany. NDC schemes are partially funded in Norway and Sweden but are PAYG in Italy. The question of the financing mechanism is separable from the microeconomic issues examined in this chapter and has been treated comprehensively elsewhere. (See the discussion and references in the concluding section.)

The next three sections focus on earnings-related schemes because the issues that are raised are relevant to DB, points, and NDC systems but not to DC plans. We then look at the evolution and spread of DC schemes in OECD countries and the implications for the sharing of life expectancy risk between generations.

Earnings Measures

Most OECD countries used to base individual pension entitlements under earnings-related schemes on individual earnings for a limited subset of best or final years of pay. In the past, of the 24 countries analyzed below, 15 used a subset of earnings. Pension reforms since 1990 have changed this position dramatically, as illustrated in figure 3.1. The figure shows the number of years of contributions (either best or final) that were taken into account in calculating pension benefits before and after pension reforms. It considers DB, points, and NDC schemes and the mandatory components of countries' pension systems, including mandatory private pensions. (DC schemes, in which benefits, by definition, depend on lifetime contributions, are omitted from the comparison.) Occupational plans that cover the bulk of the workforce, termed quasi-mandatory, are included. For example, private DB occupational plans are compulsory in Iceland and Switzerland and are quasi-mandatory in the Netherlands.[2]

Panel a shows countries in which there have been no changes to the earnings measure, except for changes arising from increases in the normal pension eligibility age. This group includes seven countries in which the entire career is taken into account, as well as Canada and the United States, where the pension is based on the best 35 years or so. It also includes Spain, which bases pensions on the final 15 years of earnings.

Panel b shows countries in which the earnings measure has changed. Eleven countries are moving or have moved from pensions based on between 5 and 20 years of earnings toward earnings over the whole career (or very close to that). They are Austria, Finland, Italy, the Netherlands (occupational plans), Norway, Poland, Portugal, the Slovak Republic, Sweden, Turkey, and the United Kingdom. France is moving from the best 10 years of earnings to the best 25 years of earnings in the public scheme, and the Czech Republic, to 30 years. The most recent country to change is Greece, from the best 5 of the final 10 years of earnings to the lifetime average.

Once these reforms are in place, almost no OECD countries will base pensions on earnings measured over a period significantly less than the whole career. This is a welcome improvement. Basing pensions on a limited number of best or final years tends to be regressive because the people whose best or final years of earnings are substantially above their career-average earnings tend to be those who earn the most. In countries with a large informal sector, such as Greece, use of a subset of career earnings furnishes a large incentive to underreport earnings in earlier years, and in others, such as Austria, it reinforces distortionary systems of seniority-based pay. Finally, basing pensions on a subset of years of earnings tends to encourage people to retire once earnings have peaked rather than move to lower-paid employment, which would reduce rather than increase their pension incomes.

It is interesting to note that the OECD countries that have adopted NDC—Italy, Norway, Poland, and Sweden—started from a position of basing pensions on 5, 20, 10, and 15 years of earnings, respectively. Another eight countries—Austria, Finland, Greece, the Netherlands, Portugal, the Slovak Republic, Turkey, and the United Kingdom—achieved the same result of moving from a subset to whole-career earnings while maintaining the existing structure of pension provision.

FIGURE 3.1 **Number of years of earnings used in the pension calculation**

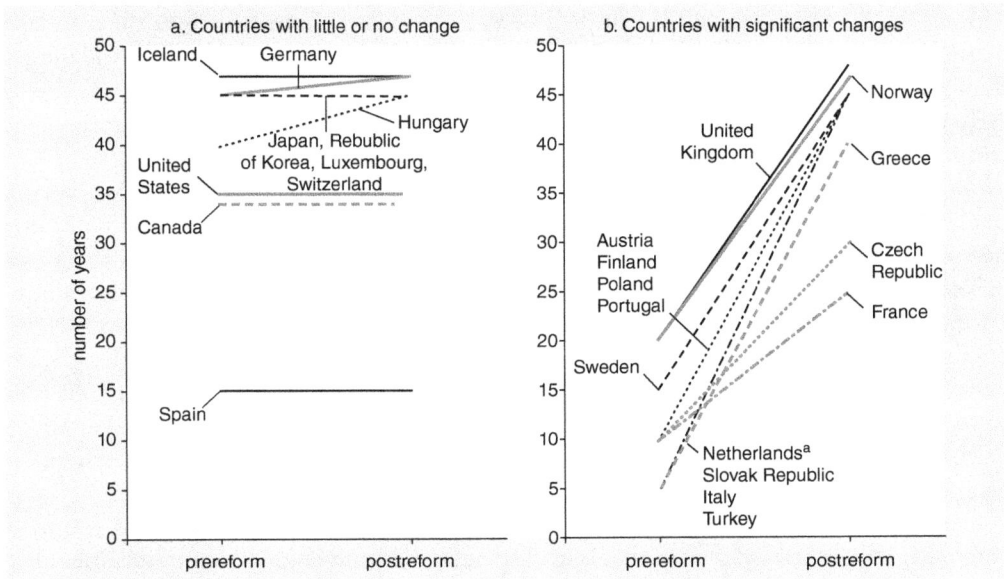

SOURCE: Author's elaboration based on OECD 2005, 2007, 2009, 2011; Whitehouse et al. 2009.

NOTE: Pensions are based on a full career, from age 20 to the normal national age of pension eligibility, and on pension ages for men where these differ from those for women. The change in the United Kingdom from best 20 years to lifetime revalued average was introduced in 1988 and so falls outside the earliest date (1990) considered here. However, since the scheme that was affected was not introduced until 1978, the impact of the reform was felt only from 1998 onward, and so the U.K. reform is included in the figure.
a. Occupational.

Pension Accruals

A small number of OECD countries have set limits on the number of years over which pension benefits can accrue in earnings-related schemes. In Greece, for example, the maximum pension replacement rate is achieved after 35 years of contributions, and only employment after age 65 confers any additional benefit. The pension entitlement in Greece may increase with additional work, but only if higher earnings replace lower earnings in the benefit formula. Similarly, the public pension scheme in the United States pays a full benefit with 35 years of contributions. There is a penalty if the pension is claimed early, but, as in Greece, extra years of contributions increase benefits solely because lower earnings drop out of the benefit formula. The maximum accrual is reached after 35 years in Spain as well.

The problem with these policies is that they discourage work once the maximum number of years has been achieved, and they are thus economically inefficient. Also, they are in a sense "unfair" in that contributions are levied but no additional benefit is earned. Two OECD countries have remedied this type of problem in their pension systems. Belgium has reformed the parameters and rules of the DB scheme. In Sweden, the full benefit had been reached after 30 years of contributions under the previous DB plan, but this is no longer the case after the introduction of NDC.

Pension Benefits and Choice of Retirement Age

Among the 30 OECD countries studied here, 22 permit retirement before the standard pension age. In most of these, benefits for early retirees are reduced to reflect the longer duration over which the benefit is paid. In three cases, there is no reduction in benefits for early retirees, if certain qualifying conditions are met. In a further three, early retirement without reduction is possible.

The size of the adjustments varies significantly, as is shown in figure 3.2, which tracks the adjustments in the relevant schemes of all 30 OECD countries.[3] Three countries—Finland, France, and Switzerland—appear twice in the figure because of having different schemes, with different rules, within the pension systems. The figure thus shows a total of 33 cases. In 12 of the 33 cases, there are adjustments that apply in specific circumstances, as indicated by the arrows on the bars. The figure shows the long-term parameters of the pension system, including changes that have already been legislated and are being phased in slowly. These can be thought of as the parameters that will apply to persons who entered the labor market in 2008 when they come to make their retirement decisions.

In most DB and points schemes, the adjustment shown in figure 3.2 is simply a parameter of the pension system that is readily extracted from descriptions of scheme rules: the benefit is permanently reduced by x percent for each year of early retirement. There are three exceptions in which this calculation is more complex—the Czech Republic, Norway, and Switzerland—but it is relatively straightforward to compute the benefit adjustment for early retirement on the same basis as for other countries. (The calculations are set out in the notes to table 3A.1 in the annex.) Similarly, the adjustment for early and late retirement in the NDC schemes of Italy and Sweden is not directly observed. (Poland does not allow early retirement.) The adjustment can, however, be calculated from the annuity rates or factors used to convert accumulated notional capital, which in turn are based on projections of mortality rates at different ages and the discount rates employed in the annuity calculation. (See the notes to table 3A.1.)

Returning to figure 3.2, the largest standard decrements are in Canada, which is increasing the rate from 6.0 to 7.2 percent, and in the public DB plans in Finland, where it is also 7.2 percent. However, larger adjustments are possible in the Czech Republic (for people who retire at the earliest possible ages) and in Spain, for people with a smaller number of contribution years. In Belgium, Luxembourg, and Mexico, there is no reduction in the minimum pension, provided that qualifying conditions regarding the number of years of contributions are met. Similarly, reductions of 5.0, 3.6, and 6.0 percent are applied in France, Germany, and Greece, respectively, but people with long careers, of 41, 45, and 37 years, respectively, can retire early without a benefit reduction.

The average decrement in the 25 schemes analyzed at the top of the figure is 4.4 percent for each year of early retirement.[4] This is just a little below the figure for the public scheme in Switzerland.

The age range that provides an early retirement window varies significantly among countries. Normal pension ages will vary between 60 and 68 in OECD countries once reforms are fully in place, with the average being age 65.2.[5] Early pension ages, just in the 22 countries that will allow early retirement, average 60.4 years, or 4.7 years earlier, on average, than the normal pension age in these countries. The earliest pension age, taking

FIGURE 3.2 **Reduction in accrued pension benefits per year of early retirement**
percent

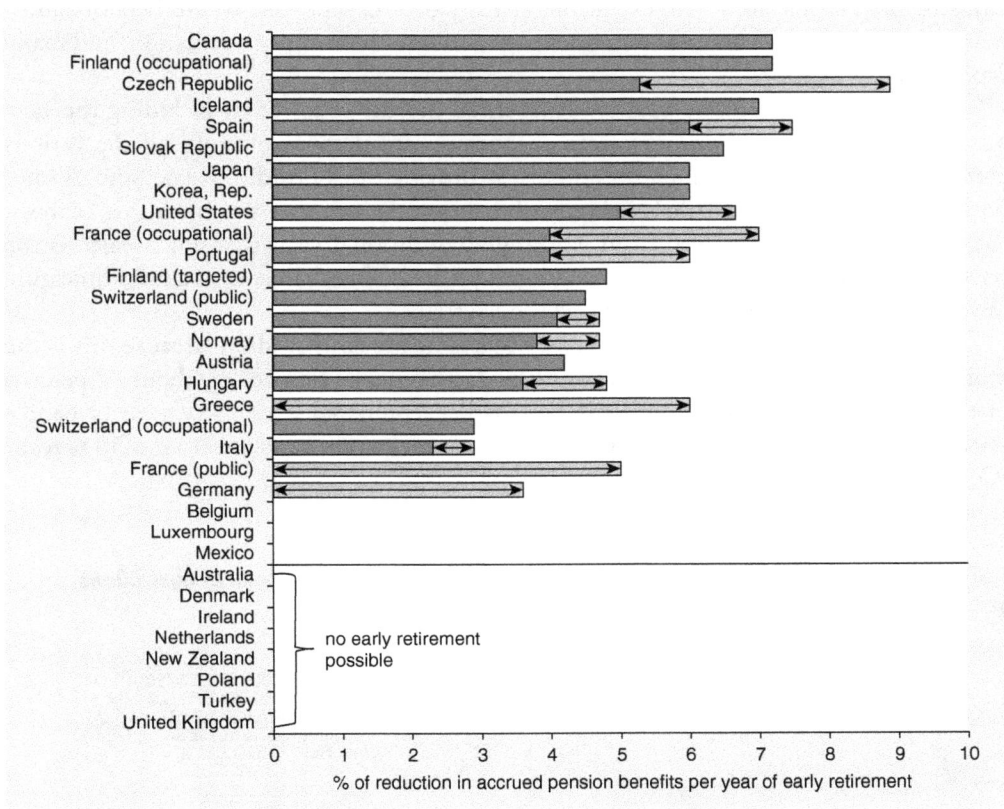

SOURCE: Table 3A.1 in the annex to this chapter.

NOTE: The arrows indicate cases in which various adjustments are possible, depending on the age of the individual or on the number of years during which contributions have been paid.

into account both the 22 countries that permit early retirement and the 8 that do not, is 61.8 years.

This parameter or indicator of particular pension schemes is just one aspect of the overall financial incentives to retire that are embedded in pension systems. Working an extra year rather than retiring early does result in a smaller reduction in benefits, reflecting the shorter duration over which the benefit is paid in most countries, but it also brings about other increases in pension entitlements. First, there is an effect that, like the benefit decrement, applies to pension entitlements already accrued. Deferring the pension claim for a year increases these entitlements through the parallel mechanisms of valorization (in DB schemes), the uprating of the pension point value (in points schemes), and notional interest rates (under NDC). Second, an extra year's contribution generally earns additional entitlement (with the exceptions outlined in "Pension Accruals," above). Third, where pensions are based on a subset of earnings over the career, higher earnings may replace lower earnings in the benefit formula. Such cases were outlined in "Earnings Measures," above.

It is important to bear in mind that this analysis covers only one scheme in 23 countries and two in 7 countries. The schemes analyzed are those for which these benefit adjustments are relevant. The exclusions consist of DC schemes, where benefits automatically change with choice of retirement age through the annuity calculation, and many types of social pensions.

A more comprehensive analysis of financial incentives to retire, including the various effects of a longer working career on pension entitlements and on all the various components of retirement income systems, is provided in D'Addio, Keese, and Whitehouse (2010) and OECD (2011). Figure 3.3 shows the key measure from this analysis: the change in pension wealth from working an additional year. (Pension wealth is the present value of the lifetime flow of pension benefits.) This change is a standard measure of retirement incentives embedded in pension systems.[6]

Figure 3.3 looks at the age range 60–65 (as in previous studies) because this is the main retirement window in OECD countries. Between ages 55 and 59, about 77 percent of the population participates in the labor market, compared with 23 percent of people ages 65–69. In the age range 60–64, labor-force participation rates are around 50 percent (OECD 2011, chap. I.2).

FIGURE 3.3 **Changes in gross pension wealth from working an additional year at ages 60–65**
percentage of annual gross earnings

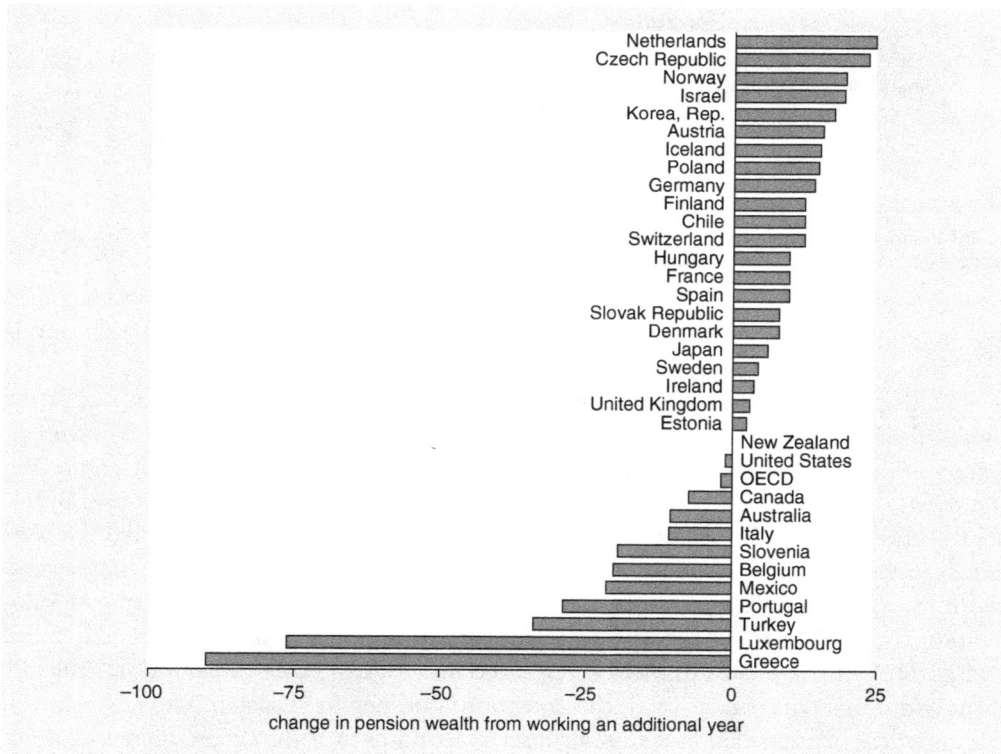

change in pension wealth from working an additional year

SOURCE: OECD 2011, chap. I.3; see also D'Addio, Keese, and Whitehouse 2010.

NOTE: OECD = Organisation for Economic Co-operation and Development.

The change in pension wealth is positive in 22 countries, negative in 11, and zero in New Zealand. The very large negative values in Greece and Luxembourg dominate the picture. These negative numbers arise because people in these countries are able to retire before age 65 without actuarial reduction in benefits. Similar effects are at work in Belgium, whereas in Portugal and Slovenia, the actuarial adjustments for retirement at different ages are relatively small.

Other cases of negative changes in pension wealth arise because of limits on the number of years needed to accrue a pension entitlement (35 years in the United States and 40 years in Canada). In the example of a full-career person working from age 20 on, the full benefit is already reached at or before age 60, which limits the return to continuing in work relative to other countries.

The rules for valorization of earnings in calculating benefits also have an effect. Most OECD countries valorize in line with the growth of average earnings, but a few do not. In the United States, for example, average earnings are used for valorization until age 60, with no adjustment from age 60 to age 62, and prices are used thereafter. Since the calculations are based on an assumption that earnings grow faster than prices, accrued pension rights grow more slowly than earnings after age 62 in the United States than in countries with earnings valorization. This effect is also at work in Belgium, where price valorization is used, and in Portugal, where valorization is 75 percent with price inflation and 25 percent with average earnings growth.

In Canada and Australia, the significant resource-tested benefits limit the returns to working longer because a larger pension under the earnings-related scheme (in Canada) or the DC scheme (in Australia) is partly offset by a smaller resource-tested benefit.

Where there is a small increment to pension wealth from working longer, the small size is often explained by the fact that mandatory pension benefits are relatively low. Ireland, Japan, and the United Kingdom, for example, are among the four countries with the lowest gross pension replacement rates for full-career workers. In Estonia and France, too, replacement rates are significantly below the OECD average.

The Netherlands is at the top of the scale, with an increase in pension wealth worth 24 percent of earnings for an additional year's work. This is because of the abolition of the early retirement programs that provided benefits from age 60 to age 65, coupled with the fact that the full-career replacement rate is one of the highest in the OECD. The Czech Republic has a high score here because of the relatively large actuarial adjustments for early retirement. Both factors are at work in Iceland. In other cases, such as Denmark and Poland, the relatively large increment in pension wealth is partly driven by the fact that it is not possible to claim benefits before age 65.

Turning to late retirement, figure 3.4 presents the results for increments to pensions for people who defer drawing their pensions until after the normal pension age, on the same basis as figure 3.2 for early retirement. Again, details on these rules are provided in table 3A.1 in the annex to this chapter. In only four countries is there no possibility of deferring the pension. Three of these, Luxembourg, the Netherlands, and New Zealand, allow people to combine work with receiving a pension. In the fourth, Ireland, income earned while claiming a pension can be subject to general means tests, and the basic pension is subject to an earnings test over the age range 65–66.

In six cases, deferral is possible but does not earn an increment to benefits already accrued. In Greece, additional pension is accrued at an accelerated rate. In Belgium and

FIGURE 3.4 **Increase in accrued benefits per year of deferral of pension claim after normal age** (percent)

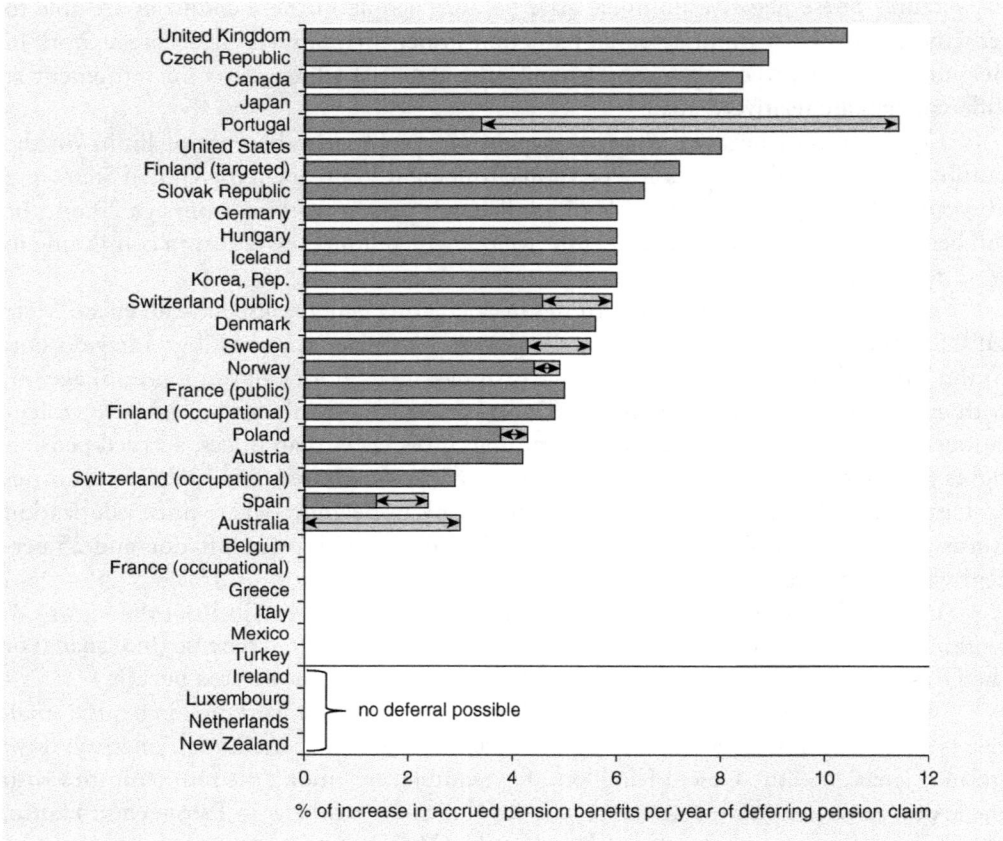

SOURCE: Table 3A.1 in the annex to this chapter.

NOTE: The arrows indicate cases in which various adjustments are possible, depending on the age of the individual or on the number of years during which contributions have been paid.

Italy, it is possible to combine work and receipt of a pension after the normal pension age without cost. Pensions are subject to an earnings test in Turkey, and in France, people who combine work and an occupational pension have to leave their usual job.

The average increment for deferring pensions (in the 29 cases where this is possible) is 4.8 percent. This is above the average decrement for early retirement. The largest increments are 8.4 percent in Canada and Japan, 8.9 percent in the Czech Republic, 10.4 percent in the United Kingdom, and a maximum of 12.0 percent in Portugal for people with very long careers.

Most OECD countries have taken steps in their recent pension reforms to encourage people to work longer. Austria, Belgium, Denmark, France, Greece, Hungary, and Italy have tightened the qualifying conditions for early retirement—the number of years of contributions required, or the eligibility age, or both. The Netherlands has removed tax incentives for private occupational early retirement schemes. Austria, Germany, Italy, and

Portugal have either introduced or raised the level of reductions in benefits for early retirees. Increments to benefits for late retirement were introduced or enhanced in Australia, Belgium, Spain, and the United Kingdom. Four countries—the Czech Republic, Finland, France, and the United States—adjusted incentives for both early and late retirement.[7]

Pension Benefits and Life Expectancy

The key difference between NDC and the other two types of earnings-related pensions is the automatic link between changes in life expectancy and the value of benefits. This feature was not shared by the simple generic versions of DB and points schemes that were presented above.

The link between life expectancy and benefits, however, does occur in funded DC schemes, where accumulated contributions and investment returns on account at the time of retirement are often used to buy an annuity at the time of retirement. The value of this annuity will depend on the estimate of life expectancy by the insurance company or other annuity provider.

Under the "traditional" form of public pension provision, pension entitlements were defined by some sort of formula. In theory, at least, this meant that the annual value of the pension was the same no matter what happened to life expectancy. DB schemes dominated both public and private pension provision in OECD countries in the second half of the 20th century. Over the past decade, however, this DB paradigm has been diluted, as pension systems around the world have become much more diverse.

The most significant change has been the expansion of private DC pension schemes. In some countries, these have replaced all or part of the public DB pension scheme. In others, a requirement to contribute to the DC plan was added on top of existing state pensions. Finally, in countries with widespread voluntary occupational pensions, employers have tended to shift these from DB to DC, or to a mix of the two.[8]

In DC schemes, the burden of changes in life expectancy is borne by individual retirees in the form of lower pensions. When people retire in a DC plan, the accumulated contributions and investment returns must be converted from a lump sum into a regular pension payment, known as an annuity. The calculation of the annuity will be based on the projected life expectancy of retirees at the time of retirement. Pensions will therefore be lower as people live longer. Of course, people always have the option of working longer to compensate. Doing so will augment benefits through additional contributions, returns on accumulated capital, and a shorter expected duration of retirement.

In DB schemes, by contrast, the cost of paying pensions for a longer time, as life expectancy increases, falls in the first instance on the pension provider—the government, for example. Ultimately, however, the cost must be financed by younger taxpayers and contributors. In practice, many recent pension reforms have cut future benefits, so that some of the cost of increased life expectancy is borne by future pensioners themselves in the form of lower pensions.

Nearly half of the OECD membership—13 countries out of 30—now incorporate an automatic link between pensions and life expectancy in their retirement income systems (table 3.1). A decade ago, only one country had such a link. The spread of this policy has a strong claim to be the main innovation in pension policy in recent years.

TABLE 3.1 **Four ways of establishing a link between life expectancy and pensions**

	DC	NDC	Benefit levels	Qualifying conditions
Australia	●			
Denmark	●			●
Finland			●	
France				●
Germany			●	
Hungary	●			
Italy		●		
Mexico	●			
Norway	●			
Poland	●	●		
Portugal			●	
Slovak Republic	●			
Sweden	●	●		

SOURCE: Whitehouse 2007.

NOTE: DC = defined contribution; NDC = nonfinancial defined contribution. The table covers the 13 member countries of the Organisation for Economic Co-operation and Development (OECD) that introduced a link to life expectancy in the pension system before 2010.

First, in the late 1990s, Hungary, Mexico, Poland, the Slovak Republic, and Sweden introduced private DC plans as a substitute for all or part of their public pensions. Australia and Norway added mandatory contributions to private DC pensions on top of existing public provision. Denmark has long had DC plans that cover nearly all workers (and so are considered quasi-mandatory in OECD analyses).

Second, Italy, Poland, and Sweden have substituted NDC for traditional DB public schemes.[9]

Third, some countries have retained DB or points-based public schemes while introducing a link between life expectancy and pensions. Finland, Germany, and Portugal will adjust benefit levels with life expectancy.

Finally, two countries, Denmark and France, intend to link qualifying conditions for pensions to life expectancy. In Denmark, the condition would be the pension age, and in France, the number of years of contributions needed for a full pension.[10]

To analyze the impact of these reforms on retirement incomes, one must first assess the degree of uncertainty about life expectancy in the future. The analysis is based on extrapolative methods, which have a better record of projections in the past than alternative (biological, for example) approaches. The dataset is based on mortality rates by sex and by a five-year age band for the Group of Seven (G-7) countries from 1945 to 2002. The distribution of the changes in these mortality rates in the past is used to simulate the potential changes in the future, using standard Monte Carlo techniques.

Table 3.2 presents the most important results. On average, in the OECD countries, life expectancy at age 65 was 15.1 years for men and 18.7 years for women. The median projection is that these life expectancy figures will increase by about 3.5 years over a 50-year period, to 18.5 years for men and 22.2 years for women. In the best 5 percent of cases, life expectancy at age 65 is projected to increase by five years or more and, in the worst 5 percent of cases, by around two years or fewer.

Before proceeding further, it is necessary to define two types of risk and uncertainty related to how long people live. The first, here termed *longevity risk*, applies to the period of retirement and to individuals. If there were no annuities (provided by DC plans or, implicitly, by earnings-related schemes), people might outlive their retirement capital because how long individuals will live is uncertain. The average length of life of a given

TABLE 3.2 **Life expectancy at age 65 in 2002; distribution of 50-year projections and change from baseline**

	Baseline (2002)	Distribution of projections (2052)				
		5%	25%	Median	75%	95%
Additional life expectancy (years)						
Men	15.1	20.1	19.1	18.5	18.0	17.1
Women	18.7	23.7	22.8	22.2	21.7	20.9
Change (years)						
Men	0.0	+5.0	+4.0	+3.4	+2.9	+2.0
Women	0.0	+5.0	+4.1	+3.5	+3.0	+2.2
Total life expectancy (years)						
Men	80.1	85.1	84.1	83.5	83.0	82.1
Women	83.7	88.7	87.8	87.2	86.7	85.9

SOURCE: Whitehouse 2007.

NOTE: Estimates for future changes are based on experience in Group of Seven countries since 1945, using the Human Mortality Database maintained by the University of California, Berkeley, and the Max Planck Institute for Demographic Research.

cohort of individuals is also uncertain, and this uncertainty is here termed *life expectancy risk*. During retirement, this risk is borne by the pension or annuity provider, but there may also be changes in life expectancy in the period between paying pension contributions and drawing benefits.

Two indicators of pension entitlements are important to the analysis of life expectancy risk. First, the pension *replacement rate* shows the value of the pension entitlement per period relative to the earnings of an individual. Second, *pension wealth* shows the lifetime value of pension benefits at the point of retirement.

In DB and points schemes, life expectancy risk is borne by pension providers. In theory, either governments or, in the case of occupational schemes, employers guarantee a level of benefits regardless of what happens to life expectancy. Ultimately, of course, the larger pension cost of longer life expectancy is passed on to taxpayers or shareholders. In these schemes, the replacement rate is constant whatever happens to life expectancy. But pension wealth increases as lives become longer because of the longer duration for which the benefit is paid. The DB scheme is here used as a theoretical benchmark. In practice, governments and pension providers have repeatedly changed pension systems, meaning that some of the cost of longer lives has been met by reducing benefits.

In DC and NDC schemes, by contrast, the life expectancy risk is borne by the individual. Up to the point of retirement, increases in projected life expectancy translate into lower benefits. In these schemes, pension wealth is constant whatever happens to the life expectancy of the cohort. But replacement rates are lower as life expectancy increases, conditional on the same age of withdrawal of the pension.

These two measures, replacement rates and pension wealth, provide benchmarks against which national pension systems can be evaluated. In practice, national pension systems are made up of a number of components. For some components, replacement rates are affected by changes in life expectancy; in this category are DC, NDC, and DB schemes with adjustments, as set out above. DB schemes without adjustments and basic pensions are, by contrast, generally not affected by changes in life expectancy. In some cases, resource-tested schemes and minimum pensions can offset the impact of changes in life expectancy. If, for example, DC pensions are lower, entitlements to minimum pensions may be higher. The analysis that follows covers all the components of retirement income provision.

The two benchmarks underpin a measure of the degree of life expectancy risk borne by individual retirees. This index is zero in the case where benefits per period are defined, and it is 100 percent in the alternative case, where contributions are defined and benefits per period therefore vary with life expectancy. (Formally, pension wealth is calculated under the different scenarios for life expectancy using the actual parameters of the pension system. The change in pension wealth between the low and high life expectancy scenarios is divided by the difference in pension wealth that would result in a hypothetical DC scheme that yields the same benefits as the country's actual scheme in the median life expectancy scenario.)

Figure 3.5 makes evident the huge diversity between countries in the way life expectancy risk is shared. The figure shows results for 12 (see note to figure) OECD countries where part of the pension system is linked to life expectancy. To repeat, this is a comprehensive analysis of pension systems covering all mandatory and quasi-mandatory schemes in each country. It is based on calculations of pension entitlements for people earning between 30 and 300 percent of the national average. These results are then weighted by the distribution of earnings and averaged.

FIGURE 3.5 **Effect of life expectancy risk in mandatory pension programs**
share of total life expectancy risk borne by individual retirees

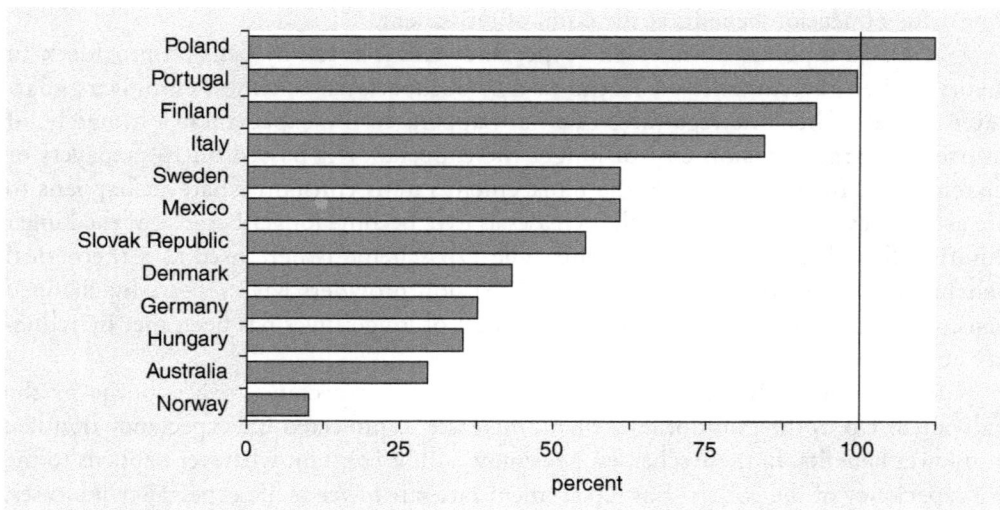

SOURCE: Whitehouse 2007.

NOTE: Based on weighted averages of pension entitlements and pension wealth calculated using the OECD pension models; see OECD (2009) for a discussion of these concepts. The complexity of the formula linking qualifying conditions to life expectancy in France is too great to allow a comparable calculation to be performed.

In Norway, because of the small mandatory contribution—just 2 percent of earnings—only 10 percent of the financial cost of longer lives is borne by retirees. In Australia, this proportion is about 30 percent; although 9 percent of wages is paid into the DC scheme, the means-tested public pension limits the impact of longer lives on pension entitlements. In Hungary, the public earnings-related pension, which is not linked to life expectancy, will continue to provide most retirement incomes.

At the other end of the spectrum, in Finland and Portugal, close to 100 percent of life expectancy risk is borne by individual retirees. In Poland, the share is more than 100 percent: individual retirees are projected to have higher lifetime benefits the shorter is life expectancy because of the way NDC pensions are calculated.

The differences between countries in the sharing of life expectancy risk are therefore mainly a result of the structure and design of the pension package, of which the option of NDC versus other forms of earnings-related pension provision (DB or points) is only a part.

Conclusion

This chapter has surveyed the three designs for earnings-related pension schemes found in OECD countries: DB, points, and NDC schemes. It has examined four significant advantages of NDC schemes that affect the economic efficiency and equity of the pension system. The first three are as follows:

- Benefits are based on lifetime earnings rather than on a subset of best or final years of pay.
- Each extra year's contribution gives rise to an additional benefit.
- Benefits are reduced, for a given age at claiming the pension, to reflect the longer expected duration of payment for people who retire early. Benefits are, similarly, increased for people who postpone retirement until later. Alternatively, people have to work longer to achieve the same benefit level as life expectancy increases.

The discussion has deliberately steered away from the heated debate about the financing of future pension benefits—that is, whether and to what extent these benefits should be prefunded or should be provided on a pay-as-you-go basis. All three types of scheme can be, in principle, and often are, in practice, financed through full or partial prefunding or pay-as-you-go mechanisms. This issue is separable from those addressed in this chapter.

The analysis looked at the various types of pension scheme from the perspective of an individual member.[11] It therefore focused on issues of economic efficiency—the extent to which the pension system distorts decisions to work and save—and on fairness, defined as the equal treatment of people who choose different retirement ages and contribute for varying numbers of years.

For example, pensions based on best or final earnings encourage people to leave the labor market once earnings have peaked (item 1 in the list above). Early retirement is also encouraged by schemes that do not provide additional pension benefits for an additional year of contributions once a certain number of years has been reached (item 2). Many schemes encourage early retirement through too low reductions in benefits for early pension claims or discourage later retirement by providing small increments for deferring the pension claim (item 3). These distortions to incentives to work and retire have been shown to have a significant effect on individual retirement decisions.[12]

All these factors give rise to substantial inequities among individuals. The people who benefit from pensions based on best or final earnings tend to be the better off. And if early retirement is encouraged through caps on the number of contribution years that earn benefits, or through small or zero reductions in benefits, those who do not retire at the earliest possibility opportunity are penalized.

NDC schemes are an example of good practice in all these areas, but well-designed DB or points schemes also share these characteristics. The effect of pension reforms in OECD countries has been that nearly all of them have now moved from best or final earnings to whole-career pay in calculating benefits. Many countries have fixed the problems caused by ceilings on the number of pensionable years, and they have introduced or enhanced reductions in benefits for early retirement and increments for late retirement. This has the important implication that the *microeconomic* benefits of moving to NDC, from the standpoint of economic efficiency and fairness, are minimal or even negative in almost all OECD countries. (This is a separate issue from the potential benefits at the macroeconomic level in terms of the stability of the finances of the pension system, as discussed above.) In only four OECD countries—Belgium, Greece, Luxembourg, and Spain—do pension schemes fall significantly short of best practice in at least two of the areas analyzed. Moreover, many OECD countries have retirement income systems to which NDC principles are simply not applicable: examples are Australia, Denmark, Ireland, the Netherlands, New Zealand, and the United Kingdom.

The final point considered in this chapter was this: benefits should be linked automatically to life expectancy as a way of spreading the costs of longer lives between generations and contributing to the long-term financial sustainability of the pension system.

This final issue needs to be treated separately from the other three because what constitutes best or good practice is less clear-cut. It is hard to see why people approaching retirement should not bear at least some of the cost of their generation's living longer than previous generations. After all, living longer is desirable. A longer life and a larger lifetime pension payout as a consequence of increased life expectancy confer a double advantage. The optimum amount of life expectancy risk that individual retirees should bear is therefore not zero. The obvious next question is, should 100 percent of the risk be shifted onto the pensions of new retirees? The issue is complex because each individual has a life cycle that includes periods as a contributor and as a beneficiary. There is a trade-off between greater certainty about retirement benefits and greater certainty about the amount of contributions or taxes paid when working.

Moreover, life expectancy risk is but one of many risks involved in pension systems. For DC pensions, the value of retirement income is also subject to investment risk. Furthermore, other objectives of the retirement income system, such as ensuring that low earners have an adequate standard of living in their retirement, may conflict with each other. Reducing already small pensions to reflect increases in life expectancy might risk a resurgence of old-age poverty.

Together, these factors suggest that individual retirees should bear some, but not all, life expectancy risk. Further work is needed to determine the optimum sharing of risk between generations.

The final message of this chapter is that analysis of pension policy cannot be piece-meal, looking at one component of the overall system of retirement income provision in isolation. For example, the earnings-related part of retirement income provision may embody the principles of equity and economic efficiency, but this work can be easily undone for a sizable part of the workforce that is entitled to means-tested, income-tested, or pension-tested benefits. For them, there is often no incentive to remain in work beyond the earliest possible age or to save voluntarily for their retirement, or these incentives may be severely curtailed. A comprehensive approach to pension policy analysis, covering all parts of the system, is essential.

Annex. Pension Benefits and Choice of Retirement Age

TABLE 3A.1 **Treatment of early and late retirees by pension schemes in OECD countries**

Country	Scheme	Early age	Reduction (%)	Normal age	Increase (%)
Australia	T	n.a.		67	0.6–3.6[a]
	DC	60	—	67	—
Austria	DB	62M/60F	4.2	65	4.2
Belgium	DB	60[b]	0	65	0
Canada	Basic/T	n.a.		65	
	DB	60	7.2	65	8.4
Chile	Basic/T	n.a.		65	
	DC	Any age[c]	—	65M/60F	—
Czech Republic	DB	60M/59–60F[d]	5.3/8.9[e]	65M/62–65F[d]	8.9[e]
Denmark	Basic/T	n.a.		67	5.6[f]
	DC	n.a.		67	—
Estonia	Points	60[g]	4.8	63	10.8
	DC	60	—	63	—
Finland	T	62	4.8	65	7.2
	DB	62	7.2/0[g]	65	0/4.8[h]
France	DB	56–60[i]	0/5.0	65	5.0
	DB (occupational)	55	4.0–7.0[j]	60	0
Germany	Points	63	3.6/0[k]	67	6.0
Greece	DB	Any age/55/60[l]	0/6.0[m]	65	0[m]
Hungary	DB	63	3.6/4.8[n]	65	6.0
	DC	63	—	65	—
Iceland	Basic/T	n.a.		67	
	DB (occupational)	62	7.0[o]	67	6.0[o]
Ireland	Basic/T	n.a.		66M/65F	n.a.
Israel	Basic/T	62[p]		67	
	DC			67	—
Italy	NDC	Any age/61[q]	2.3–2.9[r]	65M/60F	0/2.6–2.9[r]
Japan	Basic/DB	60	6	65	8.4
Korea, Rep.	DB	60	6	65	6
Luxembourg	DB	57/60[s]	0	65	n.a.
Mexico	Min	60[t]	0	65	0
	DC	Any age/60[t]	—	65	—
Netherlands	Basic	n.a.		65	n.a.
New Zealand	Basic	n.a.		65	n.a.

(continued next page)

TABLE 3A.1 **Treatment of early and late retirees by pension schemes in OECD countries (continued)**

Country	Scheme	Early age	Reduction (%)	Normal age	Increase (%)
Norway	DB	62	3.8–4.7[u]	67	4.9–5.4[u]
	DC	n.a.[v]		67	—
Poland	NDC	n.a.		65M/60F	4.3–4.8M/3.7–4.2F[w]
	DC	n.a.		65M/60F	—
Portugal	DB	55	4.0–6.0[x]	65	4.0–12.0[y]
Slovak Republic	Points	60[z]	6.5	62	6.5
	DC	60	—	62	—
Slovenia	DB	58[aa, bb]	1.2–3.6	63[cc]	0[bb]
Spain	DB	61	6-7–5[dd]	65	2.0/3.0[ee]
Sweden	T	n.a.		65	
	NDC	61	4.1–4.7[ff]	65	4.9–6.1[ff]
	DC	55/61[gg]	—	65	—
Switzerland	DB	63M/62F	4.5[hh]	65M/64F	5.2–6.5
	DB (occupational)	60M/59F[ii]	2.9[ii]	65M/64F	2.9[ii]
Turkey	DB	n.a.		65	0
United Kingdom	Basic/DB	n.a.		68	10.4[kk]
United States	DB	62	5.0/6.7[ll]	67	8.0

SOURCE: OECD 2011.

NOTE: DB = defined benefit; DC = defined contribution; T = targeted; n.a. = not applicable (early retirement or deferral of pension is not available); — = benefits are automatically adjusted for early and late retirement in DC schemes. The table is based on long-term parameters and rules and is confined to mandatory schemes, except for defined contribution plans. Where pension ages for men and women differ, they are shown as M/F. Data are rounded to one decimal place. Calculations for late retirement assume a maximum retirement age of 70.

a. The pension bonus is a single lump sum of 9.4 percent of the age-pension entitlement multiplied by the number of years of deferral squared. For comparison with other countries, it is expressed as a percentage of the age-pension benefit stream. The values shown are annualized for one and five years' deferral, respectively. Recent reforms replaced this bonus with a "work bonus," making it easier for people to combine work and receipt of a pension,

b. Early retirement with no actuarial reduction is possible once 35 years of contributions have been made.

c. Early retirement requires a DC benefit of at least 80 percent of the maximum targeted benefit and a replacement rate of at least 70 percent.

d. The pension age for women varies with number of children they have had.

e. There is a 3.6 percent reduction in the total accrual factor for the first two years of early retirement and 6.0 percent thereafter. There is an increment of 6 percent in the total accrual factor per year of late retirement. The figures shown are calculated for a full-career worker, who would have a total accrual factor of 67.5 percent at age 65.

f. The adjustment is based on the reciprocal of life expectancy at the age at which the pension is drawn. Projected life expectancy at age 68 for 2040 is 17.9 years.

g. The public pension can be claimed up to three years before the standard age (i.e., from age 60 in the long term), provided that people retire and meet the 15-year qualification requirement.

h. The adjustment applies from age 62 to age 63. Instead of adjustments, there is accelerated accrual in the earnings-related scheme of 4.5 percent of earnings per year of contributions between ages 63 and 68, compared with 1.5 percent at most ages. For late retirement, the adjustment shown applies from age 68 onward.

i. A full pension will require 41 years of contributions. Retirement from age 60 without benefit reduction is subject to this contribution condition. For those with long careers, retirement before age 60 ranges from retirement at 56 for people with 42 years of contributions and labor market entry before age 16 to retirement at 59 with 40 years of contributions and labor market entry before age 17.

j. A full benefit requires 40 years of contributions. The benefit is reduced by 4 percent for first three missing years and by 5 percent for the next two. Benefit reductions for retirement before age 60 depend on years of contributions.

k. Retirement at age 63 requires 35 years of contributions and is subject to 3.6 percent reduction. Early retirement is possible at age 65 (rather than 67) without actuarial reduction with 45 years of contributions.

l. Retirement at age 60 with 15 years of contributions and at age 55 with 35 years of contributions is subject to a 6 percent reduction per year earlier than age 65. Retirement with no reduction at any age requires 37 years of contributions. The recently announced reform will restrict early retirement to age 60.

m. Accelerated accrual (3.3 percent per year compared with 2.0 percent at younger ages) during deferral, but no increment to accrued benefits.

n. Early retirement requires 37 years of contributions.

o. Adjustment varies between schemes; typical rates are shown.

p. Early retirement pension is payable up to 5 years before the normal age if the number of years of contributions exceeds the
minimum qualifying period by at least 10 years. A partial early pension is payable from up to 5 years before the
normal retirement age if the number of years of contributions exceeds the requirement for a full pension by less than
10 years.

q. Retirement at any age is possible with 40 years of contributions and from age 61 with 36 years of contributions.

r. The adjustment for early retirement is calculated from government-provided transformation coefficients projected for
2048. After age 65, the transformation coefficient is constant, and so benefits do not increase for men retiring later.

s. With 40 years of actual (compulsory or voluntary) contributions, retirement is possible from age 57.

t. Early retirement at age 60 is conditional on 1,250 weekly contributions (approximately 25 years). A DC pension is available at any age if the pension is at least 30 percent above the minimum.

u. Calculated from government-provided figures for life expectancy divisors. For late retirement, higher increments are provided after age 70.

v. A debate is under way as to whether access should be allowed from age 62.

w. Calculated from projected (unisex) life expectancy at ages 66–70 for men and 60–65 for women.

x. Adjustment for early retirement is 6 percent per year, but with more than 30 years of contributions, the number of years
over which the pension is adjusted is cut by 1 year for each complete 3 years of contributions beyond 30 years. The 4 percent rate is an average over 3 years for a person with at least 30 years of contributions.

y. The increment depends on the number of contribution years, ranging from 4 percent for 15–24 years to 12 percent for
more than 40 years of contributions.

z. Early retirement is also conditional on the pension entitlement's exceeding 1.2 times the subsistence minimum.

aa. The age for early retirement is 58 years, conditional on having contributed for at least 40 years. For retirement before
the full pension age, reductions are 3.6 percent (a year) at age 58, 3.0 percent at age 59, 2.4 percent at age 60, 1.8 percent at age 61, and 1.2 percent at age 62.

bb. Additional years of contributions up to and after the full pension age attract a higher accrual rate. From the early to normal pension age, the annual accrual rate is 3.0 percent in the first year, 2.6 percent in the second, 2.2 percent in the third,
1.8 percent in the fourth, and 1.5 percent thereafter. For deferred retirement after the full pension age, the accrual rate is
3.6 percent for the first year, 2.4 percent for the second, and 1.2 percent for the third.

cc. Men with at least at least 20 years of contributions can retire at age 63. With 15 years of contributions, the pension age
is 65. For women, the full pension age will be 61 in 2023, conditional on 20 years of contributions.

dd. The size of the reduction depends on the number of years of contributions made: 7.5 percent (30–34 years), 7.0 percent
(35–37 years), 6.5 percent (38–39 years), and 6.0 percent (more than 40 years).

ee. The increment depends on the number of years of contributions: 2 percent for fewer than 40 years, and 3 percent for
40 years or more of contributions.

ff. The implicit adjustments are calculated from the annuity calculations using projected mortality rates for 2040, the 1.6
percent discount rate specified in legislation, and indexation of pensions in payment to wage growth minus 1.6 percent.
They also take into account the distribution of the account balances of people who die before claiming the pension, using
the same mortality rates.

gg. Early retirement at 61 under the mandatory DC scheme (premium pension) and from 55 under quasi-mandatory DC
occupational plans.

hh. A full pension requires 44 years of contributions for men and 43 years for women. For a full-career worker, approximately 2.3 percentage points of the 6.8 percent reduction for early retirement reflects a missing contribution year; the actuarial adjustment is the residual.

ii. Early retirement provisions vary between schemes: these are the legal minimums.

jj. Individuals' accumulated rights are converted into an annuity at the time of retirement. The annuity rate at age 65 will
fall to 6.8 percent. Each year of early retirement results in a reduction in the annuity rate of 0.2 percentage points. For late
retirement, schemes are free to set their own rules, but the government's guidance is to have the same 0.2 percentage
point change in benefits for each year of late retirement.

kk. A lump-sum payment of deferred pension plus interest can now also be claimed instead of a pension increment.

ll. The reduction is 6.67 percent for the first three years of early retirement and 5.00 percent thereafter.

Notes

Anna D'Addio, Andrew Reilly, and Monika Queisser of the OECD Social Policy Division provided useful input for this chapter. The author also gratefully acknowledges comments by the editors of this volume and by participants at the conference "Non-Financial Defined Contribution (NDC) Systems: Progress and New Frontiers in a Changing Pension World," jointly organized by the Swedish Social Insurance Agency and the World Bank.

1. When this chapter was first drafted, the OECD had 30 member countries. Chile, Estonia, Israel, and Slovenia joined later, in 2010.

2. The analysis does not cover voluntary private pensions, which have broad coverage (40 to 60 percent of the workforce) in Canada, Ireland, New Zealand, the United Kingdom, and the United States, nor does it include schemes for public sector workers, many of which are still based on best or final salaries; see Palacios and Whitehouse (2006).

3. Such a calculation is not relevant for DC schemes, where pensions are adjusted automatically for early and late retirement.

4. National figures are averaged, where appropriate, over varying circumstances.

5. See Chomik and Whitehouse (2010) for information on pension ages in OECD countries between 1950 and 2050, including legislated changes to be implemented in the future.

6. Gruber and Wise (1998, 1999), Blöndal and Scarpetta (1999), and Casey et al. (2003) all use this approach.

7. See Whitehouse et al. (2009) and Whiteford and Whitehouse (2006) for a detailed discussion of these reforms.

8. See OECD (2009), box 1.1, on the shift from DB to DC in private pension arrangements, and Queisser, Whiteford, and Whitehouse (2007) on the shift from public to private provision.

9. Norway's replacement of a points scheme with NDC, which began in 2011, occurred after this analysis was carried out, but it is included in a similar analysis in OECD (2011), chap. I.5.

10. In both Denmark and France, the status of these reforms is uncertain: they are the subject of political or industrial relations agreements. However, the policies analyzed here have been announced by the governments.

11. The individual's perspective is not the only one that matters. Many studies have looked at the position of pension schemes in aggregate; see, among others, Valdés-Prieto (2000); Breyer (2004); and Robalino and Bodor (2009). There is no space here to review this literature, which is also covered in other chapters in this volume.

12. See Gruber and Wise (1998, 1999); Blöndal and Scarpetta (1999); Casey et al. (2003); D'Addio, Keese, and Whitehouse (2010).

References

Blöndal, Sveinbjörn, and Stefano Scarpetta. 1999. "The Retirement Decision in OECD Countries." Working Paper 202, Economics Department, Organisation for Economic Co-operation and Development, Paris.

Breyer, Friedrich. 2004. "Comment on S. Valdés-Prieto, 'The Financial Stability of Notional Account Pensions.'" *Scandinavian Journal of Economics* 106 (2): 385–87.

Casey, Bernard, Howard Oxley, Edward R. Whitehouse, Pablo Antolin, Romain Duval, and Willi Leibfritz. 2003. "Policies for an Ageing Society: Recent Measures and Areas for Further

Reform." Working Paper 369, Economics Department, Organisation for Economic Co-operation and Development, Paris.

Chomik, Rafal, and Edward R. Whitehouse. 2010. "Trends in Pension Eligibility Ages and Life Expectancy, 1950–2050." Social, Employment and Migration Working Paper, Organisation for Economic Co-operation and Development, Paris.

D'Addio, Anna Cristina, Mark Keese, and Edward R. Whitehouse. 2010. "Population Ageing and Labour Markets." *Oxford Review of Economic Policy* 26 (4): 613–35.

Gruber, Jonathan, and David A. Wise. 1998. "Social Security and Retirement: An International Comparison." *American Economic Review* 88 (2): 158–63.

———. 1999. *Social Security and Retirement around the World.* Chicago: University of Chicago Press for the National Bureau of Economic Research.

OECD (Organisation for Economic Co-operation and Development). 2005. *Pensions at a Glance: Public Policies across OECD Countries.* Paris: OECD.

———. 2007. *Pensions at a Glance: Public Policies across OECD Countries.* Paris: OECD.

———. 2009. *Pensions at a Glance: Retirement-Income Systems in OECD Countries.* Paris: OECD.

———. 2011. *Pensions at a Glance: Retirement-Income Systems in OECD and G20 Countries.* Paris: OECD.

Palacios, Robert J., and Edward R. Whitehouse. 2006. "Civil-Service Pension Schemes around the World." Pension Reform Primer Series, Social Protection Discussion Paper 06/02, World Bank, Washington, DC.

Queisser, Monika, Peter Whiteford, and Edward R. Whitehouse. 2007. "The Public-Private Pension Mix in OECD Countries." *Industrial Relations Journal* 38 (6): 542–68.

Robalino, David A., and András Bodor. 2009. "On the Financial Sustainability of Earnings-Related Pension Schemes with Pay-as-You-Go Financing and the Role of Government-Indexed Bonds." *Journal of Pension Economics and Finance* 8 (2): 153–87.

Valdés-Prieto, Salvador. 2000. "The Financial Stability of Notional Account Pensions." *Scandinavian Journal of Economics* 102 (3): 395–417.

Whiteford, Peter, and Edward R. Whitehouse. 2006. "Pension Challenges and Pension Reforms in OECD Countries." *Oxford Review of Economic Policy* 22 (1): 78–94.

Whitehouse, Edward R. 2007. "Life-Expectancy Risk and Pensions: Who Bears the Burden?" OECD Social, Employment and Migration Working Paper 60, Organisation for Economic Co-operation and Development, Paris.

Whitehouse, Edward R., Anna Cristina D'Addio, Rafal Chomik, and Andrew Reilly. 2009. "Two Decades of Pension Reform: What Has Been Achieved and What Remains to Be Done?" *Geneva Papers on Risk and Insurance: Issues and Practice* 34: 515–35.

Seemingly Parallel Lines

Marek Góra

The problem facing us in the area of pensions is that what initially—say, a hundred years ago, when the key concepts of social security were developed—was meant to help very old workers has turned into a kind of ill-designed method of income allocation over the life cycle. Demography has played a cruel trick on social and economic thinking. We would have never designed any of the currently operating systems; they are a consequence of demographic developments taking place in rigid institutional settings that have not been able to adjust to changing circumstances. There is no way back—we cannot start from scratch. So, we try to solve the problem by restoring the sustainability of pension systems. Is that really possible, given social and economic constraints? Maybe the only thing to do is to neutralize the existing pension arrangements? If yes, then it makes sense to rethink the very basic concepts of pension economics and the contemporary meaning of the definitions of the social goals at which pension systems aim.

A huge amount of economic knowledge on pensions has already been accumulated. In chapter 3 in this volume, Edward Whitehouse provides a condensed but comprehensive review of approaches based on the best economic knowledge. That knowledge, however, was developed mostly for individual and group private programs, and the concepts were adopted and adjusted for public pensions. We lack clear concepts focused on social (public) arrangements, and that is one reason for the problems in discussing public pensions. Commonly, pay-as-you-go (PAYG) financing is public only, and "real" defined contribution (DC) schemes are private and have to be funded.[1] Applying that approach, we are, in many cases, intuitively at a dead end. We see pensions in the light of the opposition between PAYG and DC, whereas DC schemes, if they cover entire working populations, turn into public schemes and exhibit more similarities to other public arrangements than to private DC plans.

Whitehouse undertakes a comprehensive review of attempts to rationalize pension arrangements and their implementation in member countries of the Organisation for Economic Co-operation and Development (OECD). He analyses three possible arrangements in nonfunded public systems: defined benefit (DB) schemes, points systems, and nonfinancial (notional) defined contribution (NDC) schemes. He shows in an elegant way that the three are, in principle, similar, if not identical—if properly designed and managed, of course. In his view, NDC is a really good approach, but the other two can lead to the same outcomes. He cites examples of countries in which these non-NDC

Marek Góra is a professor at the Warsaw School of Economics, a visiting professor at the College of Europe, and a research fellow at the Institute for the Study of Labor (IZA) in Bonn.

schemes are helping to restore the long-term financial sustainability of the pension systems. But isn't it remarkable that it is mainly those European Union (EU) countries that have replaced their traditional DB systems with NDC or financial defined contribution (FDC) schemes, or a combination of the two, which have succeeded in substantially reducing expected pension expenditure? (See European Commission 2009.)

In his analysis of the various features of the three types of pension system, Whitehouse does not take into account such an important issue as labor mobility across countries. Traditional pension systems are complicated and are hardly translatable from one country to another, and workers who consider moving to another country do not know in advance what the effect of that move will be on their future pension incomes. Moreover, since national pension systems are undertaking permanent reforms, even if the worker were able to calculate the effect on the basis of current arrangements, future adjustments may totally change the picture. Workers, then, face an irremovable risk stemming from participation in national pension systems, and it applies not only to traditional systems but also to reformed DB or points systems. Actually, the more reforms are introduced within these systems, the more complex they become. DB and points systems do not give much hope for reducing that risk, and the creation of a pan-European pension system is probably too optimistic a goal. Only NDC and FDC can provide Europe with a chance of reducing the problem so as to contribute to stronger mobility within the fragmented European labor market.

Whitehouse discusses distortions caused by pension systems and compares their scale in the systems analyzed. I would go further and consider for additional discussion the following case. Assume that a worker pays 100 euros (€) into a public pension system. If that is a DB or points system, it does not generate any clear liability for the worker, who does not feel any effect of the liability, or only a weak effect. In the case of NDC and FDC, the worker pays the same amount, but in this case, a clear liability is created. We assume that in all four arrangements, the outcome, expressed as a financial benefit, is the same (€100 + x percent). Will the distortions be the same in all cases? I doubt it, because transparency matters.

Whitehouse concludes by saying that we should follow whatever way we choose, since all the possible choices go along parallel lines anyway. Are they really parallel? The mobility issue is one reason, although not the only one, for thinking the lines are not parallel. Here we come to the essence of the pension problem. Yes, I agree, all types of pension system arrangements are mathematically the same. I go even further and think that applies also to DC arrangements that cover entire working populations; if they do, they are public, even if they are funded.[2] Following Góra and Palmer (2004), I call them FDC schemes. Participation in a public system means buying today a part of future gross domestic product (GDP). If the share of today's contribution is the same as the share of the future benefit, then the system—if that applies to all participants—does not run a deficit and can be neutral (see Góra 2003, 2009).

The average replacement rate (z) is

$$Z = C \frac{1}{d},$$

where C is the real contribution rate and d is the demographic dependency ratio (the number of retirees per worker). Funding does not change that very basic formula, unless we take into account investment abroad. That holds true irrespective of any arrangement for a pension system. But does the formula, and do Whitehouse's arguments, really lead to a conclusion that all lines are parallel? Not necessarily. First, as we know, particular pension systems' arrangements can generate different externalities (positive as well as negative) and are exposed to different risks, at the individual as well as at the macroeconomic level. Possible positive externalities can be generated by funded arrangements (under a set of additional assumptions), which may contribute to stronger growth, especially in economies that are catching up. But political risks, especially in times of very high deficits and debts, are also unevenly distributed across various types of arrangements.

The lines are thus not parallel, mostly because NDC and FDC reduce pension expectations ex ante. The bad news for the young who are beginning or are in the course of their working careers is that the replacement rate—future pensions compared to wages—will be lower. Under DB and points systems, political decisions have to be made to adjust pension systems to the current and expected population structure. Unless the retirement age is increased, pensions are going to be lower as a consequence of demographic developments, irrespective of pension system design. Delivering the bad news is politically dangerous, so usually it comes too late. In consequence, working people get it ex post, which is much worse from all possible viewpoints, whether social, psychological, political, or economic.

One may say that politicians can always intervene and change the rules for public systems. That is true, but in DB and points systems, the rules are part of the system and are needed to make the system work. With NDC and FDC, the system can work without politicians' decisions. Moreover, in the case of NDC, politicians have no motivation to intervene because NDC automatically reduces the future replacement rate to the sustainable level—which is, after all, the goal of pension reform.[3]

We try to reform pension systems because they are too generous. That sounds terrible. It is being done to protect people in the working phase of their life cycles, but still, the message is sad. Even the best and most responsible politicians cannot simply tell that to the people because the real options are hardly acceptable to the public. This is one of the problems DB and points systems will not solve, while NDC and FDC may do the job, but at substantial political risk.

The lines are not parallel. If we keep in mind that trying to fix traditional pension systems is probably hopeless and that the only feasible goal is to neutralize them, then we see that the arrangements we analyze—DB, points systems, NDC, and FDC—can be divided into two groups:

- *Discretionary* schemes (political decisions needed), which adjust pension rights ex post (DB and points systems)
- *Self-operating* schemes (political decisions not needed), which adjust pension expectations ex ante (NDC and FDC)

The two situations differ greatly in reality, even if theoretically they can be proved to be very similar or identical. Self-operating systems restore intergenerational equilibrium. Discretionary ones can do the same, but that is much more difficult and requires people (politicians' constituencies) to stop believing in Santa Claus and allow politicians to reduce their pensions, or substantially increase the retirement age, or both. Self-operating systems do not block labor mobility; discretionary ones do. Self-operating systems are easy for participants to understand, whereas discretionary ones are typically very complicated and are not transparent. Self-operating systems treat all participants the same; discretionary ones leave the door open for various privileges.

The last difference mentioned above merits more discussion. Traditionally, as reflected in the design of discretionary systems, income allocation and income redistribution were to be reached in parallel. (By income distribution, I mean here horizontal distribution within a cohort.) Designing systems to support the very old (today, that would mean people in their 80s and 90s) was rational and doable. People nowadays start claiming benefits in their 60s, which means that the initial idea does not fit the reality. The pension systems are just income allocation methods, and their efficiency is reduced by their attempts to redistribute income. Neutralization of the problem means turning the existing public pension systems into a pure income allocation method. Income redistribution—which is very necessary in developed societies—could, and in my opinion should, be financed out of general reve-nues.[4] Self-operating systems fit that idea perfectly; discretionary ones do not.

A good way to design pension systems for the future entails finding appropriate methods that are effective in reaching each of the social goals separately: (a) NDC and FDC for income allocation, (b) general revenues for income redistribution, and (c) pro-bably, noncontributory solutions for people over age 80. If we try to manage the three goals together, the result is a conceptual disorder that prevents us from finding efficient solutions to the problems we face.

Whitehouse also discusses the issue of who bears the risk in various pension system arrangements. This is the last, but not the least, point discussed in my comment. The problem should be clearly attributed to the public system. If we stay in a fuzzy frame-work that does not distinguish clearly what is public (universal coverage) and what is private (individual decisions and responsibility), we cannot draw proper conclusions. The difference is fundamental. In private systems, the risk is taken by a participant or by a sponsor (employer), and in the public system, the risk is borne by the entire working population, which is in the role of sponsor. Everybody is on both sides of the relation-ship; each person is both a participant in the system (as a worker) and a sponsor (as a producer). Individualization of participation (not to be confused with privatization) does not change that.

Distribution of consumption over the life cycle matters. However, the proper question to be posed here is, in which part of life does an individual take the risk—as a worker, or as a retiree? An individual may run the risk of contributing too little, and society should prevent that by legislating the contribution rate at a level sufficient for a reasonable bene-fit, with the definition of "reasonable" a matter for public choice. An individual may run the risk of starting to withdraw benefits too early; society should legislate the minimum age for claiming the old-age benefit. The two decisions, however, have nothing to do with the type and design of the pension system itself.

Pension systems, in their commonly existing form, have lost their initial social goal, which in the past was to support the very old. Now, that concept is gone. The systems exist because of institutional inertia and a tendency we all have to believe in Santa Claus. National systems are in a trap, and DB and points system arrangements keep us in that trap even if we rationalize them toward more sustainable and less distortive solutions. Going that way can yield effects, as Whitehouse's chapter demonstrates. If, however, we really wish to solve the problem, we had better choose NDC or FDC (or both). The lines are not parallel. In the longer run, they are probably almost orthogonal.

Notes

1. Consequently, squeezing the PAYG part of a system and implementing pension funds is perceived as privatization of pensions.

2. The Latin meaning of *publicus* is social, covering the entire population, whereas the notion *private* assumes individual decisions and individual responsibility (risk).

3. In the case of FDC, politicians have strong motivation to intervene and act, but not because of the benefit (hence, total expenditure) level. FDC requires accrual accounting, which is not "politically friendly," whereas other arrangements allow pension system debt to be kept under the carpet by the use of cash accounting.

4. Not using the pension system as a channel to provide redistribution and using general revenues instead is rational for these reasons: the redistribution base is larger; labor does not bear all the cost; taxation is progressive, with the rich contributing more toward financing redistribution; and redistribution targets can be flexibly adjusted to changing social needs. Separating income redistribution contributes to turning a perception of contributions as taxes to a perception of contributions as savings, but time is needed to internalize the shift.

References

European Commission. 2009. *Sustainability Report 2009*. Brussels: European Commission.

Góra, Marek. 2003. "Reintroducing Intergenerational Equilibrium: Key Concepts behind the New Polish Pension System" (rev.). William Davidson Institute Working Paper 574, University of Michigan, Ann Arbor.

————. 2009. "Systemy emerytalne w krajach Unii Europejskiej: Problemy i kierunki zmian." In *Europejski Model Społeczny: Doświadczenia i Przyszłość,* ed. Dariusz K. Rosati. Warszawa: Polskie Wydawnictwo Ekonomiczne (PWE).

Góra, Marek, and Edward Palmer. 2004. "Shifting Perspectives in Pensions." IZA Discussion Paper 1369, Institute for the Study of Labor (IZA), Bonn.

Lessons from Pension Reforms

Krzysztof Hagemejer

The analysis in chapter 2 of nonfinancial (notional) defined contribution (NDC) reforms in Italy, Latvia, Poland, and Sweden, and the examination in chapter 3 of other reforms implemented in a number of member countries of the Organisation for Economic Co-operation and Development (OECD), are rich in information and allow insights into the nature of these reforms and some of their implications. All the reforms aim at establishing, in the public tiers of the pension systems, schemes that are still financed through a pay-as-you-go (PAYG) mechanism but are, at the same time, purely earnings related, with pension amounts calculated on the basis of adjusted earnings from the whole contribution career.

The analyses look at how pensions are calculated and examine the "outcomes" of the pension schemes—that is, benefit amounts and the degree to which income from work before retirement is replaced by a pension at retirement (replacement rate.) They examine various approaches to reform—for example, reliance on a purely earnings-related benefit formula that calculates the pension as a multiple of accrual rates, the number of years of contributions, and the average of adjusted earnings from the whole contribution career; use of a points system; or adoption of NDC schemes—and find that, despite their differences, the outcomes are equivalent.[1]

The use of adjusted lifetime earnings or contributions as a basis for computing pensions leads to lower pension levels and replacement rates than result under those defined benefit schemes that allow periods of lower income (e.g., the early stages of a person's work career) to be excluded from the calculation. Such reduction of pensions is not uniform, and it has redistributive effects. The losers are all those who, especially at early stages of their careers, had low earnings and haphazard earning patterns. It is easy to show that pension outcomes depend not only on the total amount of earnings, and thus on contributions paid during the whole work career, but also on when during the career those earnings and contributions were received and paid. A person who had a constant stream of earnings over his or her whole career will have a higher pension and a higher replacement rate than another person who had the same (unadjusted) sum of lifetime earnings and paid the same amount of contributions into the scheme overall but began working and paying contributions after a delay of several years, even though with higher earnings than the first person.

A person who defers the start of his or her work and contribution career to achieve a higher educational level may have the resulting loss in the future pension compensated by higher earnings—if the returns from this investment in human capital are high enough.

Krzysztof Hagemejer is chief of the Policy Development and Research Group in the Social Security Department of the International Labour Organization (ILO).

A contrasting case, in which there is little chance of compensation from higher earnings at later stages of the career, is that of persons who at young ages have to struggle to obtain formal employment fully covered by social security and, if they are employed at all, are usually in employment of a precarious character. Similarly, compensation in the form of higher future earnings is not usually awarded to those (mostly women) who have to care for children and therefore have spells when they are out of work, working part-time, or on parental leave.

To compensate for such losses in all these schemes, including NDC, different forms of honoring certain noncontributory periods are used. In three of the four NDC schemes examined in chapter 2, compensation is only a very small part of the loss of future pension entitlements. The exception is Sweden, where the proportion of loss compensated is higher than elsewhere.

NDC pension schemes, like financial defined contribution (FDC) schemes but also like any purely earnings-related scheme in which the pension calculation is based on adjusted whole-career earnings, do not just translate differentiation of earnings in the labor market into differentiation of pensions. Rather, these differences are actually amplified, and pension levels may be more differentiated than are earnings levels.[2]

Although one can say that FDC schemes with real individual accounts lack distributional features, the same cannot be so easily said about PAYG-financed NDC schemes. Returns on contributions paid differ depending on when higher contributions were paid over the working career. At the same time, actual contributions are paid into a "common pot," and thus it may happen that there is redistribution from people who had relatively low incomes and made relatively low contributions at early stages of their careers to those who already enjoyed higher earnings at the beginning of their careers. Much more research is needed into how the distribution of earnings over the working career relates to final pension amounts before one can claim that NDC and similar PAYG schemes offer horizontal equity, fairness, and transparency in redistribution.

The analysis and evaluation of various reforms presented in chapters 2 and 3 focus mainly on how the reformed schemes improve long-term financial sustainability and on the strength of the potential economic incentives for contributing and for delaying retirement. With respect to the latter, the incentives are seen as strong. Still stronger are the positive links between duration and amounts of contributions paid, and between age of retirement and pension levels. It is argued that the adequacy of the benefit level is determined by individual choice of retirement beyond a publicly fixed minimum retirement age and that in NDC there is no need to set a fixed "final" retirement age because individuals can be offered considerable flexibility concerning their age of retirement. The problem is that potentially strong incentives to work longer may not operate as expected in reality because there are other factors that determine whether and how long people can remain employed. These include the overall labor market situation and prevailing unemployment rates; the state of health of older workers, which is to a large extent determined by working conditions during their working careers; their family situations, such as the need to care for sick family members; their productivity, which is shaped by the degree to which they had a chance for lifelong learning to keep up with changing technologies; and the attitudes and choices of employers. Despite strong incentives to remain at work, older workers may be forced out of the labor market and left in poverty, with insufficient pensions. It is also becoming more and more obvious that even in NDC, there is a need to adjust the minimum legal retirement age upward, as employers may not retain older workers or invest in their training, knowing that at any moment the employees can decide to retire.

Chapters 2 and 3 deal much less with the core objectives of pension systems: the prevention of poverty and the securing of a minimum level of income security for individuals in old age, and income replacement that enables pensioners to maintain their standards of living after retirement. The notion of the adequacy of pension benefits relates to the degree of success in meeting these policy objectives in the pension system as a whole. In policy making, benefit levels cannot be just an "endogenous variable"; they provide an important measure of how policy objectives are met.

The reforms removed from the benefit formulas certain redistributive components aimed at protecting those with lower earnings and shorter careers against poverty. It is obvious that within any defined contribution (or similar) pension scheme, there is no built-in guarantee that the benefits will meet policy targets for adequacy. On the contrary, for a given contribution rate and a given rate of return, replacement rates will fall unless members of the scheme work long enough to match increasing life expectancy. Although these automatic downward adjustments in benefits can work as automatic financial stabilizers, this may be a trap, in that if the promised benefits become inadequate, the willingness of stakeholders to finance the system will deteriorate.

The chapter 2 authors claim that in all four countries that introduced NDC schemes, "the full-career worker with average earnings can expect a gross earnings replacement rate of about 65 percent." One of the main problems with this statement is that such a "full-career worker" with a 100 percent density of contributions over 45 working years may not exist at all, and certainly such a worker does not today and will not in the future represent an average or prevailing case in the contemporary labor market.

There are two parameters that allow improvement in the adequacy of replacement rates in the NDC scheme: the rate of return, and the contribution rate. Both can be increased; it is difficult to see why the fixed contribution rate should be "the cornerstone" of NDC, as chapter 1 puts it.[3]

To meet the objective of preventing poverty in old age, one should either preserve or restore the redistributive defined benefit formula (and use other mechanisms to ensure financial sustainability) or ensure that in the overall pension system there are strong noncontributory income guarantees such as a basic state pension, whether universal or means tested. Unfortunately, until now the existing mechanisms guaranteeing old-age income security in the countries that have embarked on NDC or similar reforms do not seem to be strong enough, and there is a risk of "a resurgence of old-age poverty," as chapter 3 warns. Chapter 2 calls for strengthening minimum benefit guarantees, but it accepts only the means-tested version, not even discussing universal basic pensions (which have proved very effective in many countries). Why? Because "it is important that individuals be provided with an incentive to contribute to the system even if their NDC pension is relatively poor." One can only wonder how strong an incentive a poor pension may be. An incentive becomes effective when it can offer something in exchange; an incentive to contribute in order to top up a basic universal pension may appear to be much stronger than when one is given a choice between a means-tested minimum pension and a not much higher "poor" NDC pension.

NDC schemes seemed to be an automatic (and not so obvious to the public, and thus politically easier) way of reducing pensions and inducing people to retire later. These schemes were supposed to diminish the need for involvement of policy making and social dialogue in the process—involvement that would slow the necessary decision making. The recent financial and economic crisis has clearly shown that belief in such automatic adjustment mechanisms is not very realistic. There is, and there always will be, a conflict between long-term concerns and shorter-term needs, and there has to be a compromise between the two. The same applies to long-term concerns about benefit adequacy: unless we are able to build into the system mechanisms that ensure not only financial stability but also adequacy of benefits, there will be a permanent need for discretionary interventions in the system.

What we thus need is not to keep politicians away from pensions—that is not only unrealistic but also undesirable; pension policy is part of overall social policy. We need to make sure that the decisions made by politicians are the right ones, harmonizing shorter- and longer-term needs, and balancing benefit adequacy with financial sustainability. A key prerequisite must be to ensure through democratic mechanisms the full participation of each group of stakeholders—workers, employers, and governments—in establishing the relevant standards and in creating and maintaining permanent structures through which pension systems may be monitored, verified, and adjusted in a responsible way (see Woodall and Hagemejer 2009).

Notes

1. Michael Cichon (1999) had shown this many years ago.

2. This was clearly shown in a recent study that analyzed expected replacement rates in the Polish pension system for different variants of allocation of contributions between PAYG and funded tiers (Lewandowski 2011).

3. In 2010, a World Bank report on public expenditure in Poland recommended that when the NDC tier starts to produce a surplus, part of the contributions should be channeled to the private pension funds "to improve the benefit level further" (World Bank 2010, 8). Why does a fixed contribution rate seem not to be a cornerstone of privately managed defined contribution plans?

References

Cichon, Michael. 1999. "Notional Defined-Contribution Schemes: Old Wine in New Bottles?" *International Social Security Review* 52 (4): 87–105.

Lewandowski, Piotr. 2011. "Komentarz do uzasadnienia zmian w systemie emerytalnym przedstawionego przez rząd 24 stycznia 2011 wraz z alternatywną propozycją zmian wysokości składki do OFE" [Comments on the grounds of changes to the pension scheme provided by the government on Jan. 24, 2011, together with an alternative proposal to change the amount of contributions to pension funds]. Institute for Structural Research, Warsaw. English summary available at http://ibs.org.pl/publikacja/komentarz_do_zmian_w_systemie_emerytalnym.

Woodall, John, and Krzysztof Hagemejer. 2009. "Maintaining Pension Levels in PAYG Schemes in Ageing Societies: Rules versus Discretion." Presented at a technical seminar on pensions, International Social Security Association, Paris, October 1–2.

World Bank. 2010. "Background Papers." Vol. 2 of Poland: Public Expenditure Review. World Bank, Poverty Reduction and Economic Management Unit, Europe and Central Asia Region, Washington, DC.

How Close to Best? Appraising the NDC Model as It Moves into Adulthood

Bernd Marin

Yes, indeed, the new nonfinancial (notional) defined contribution (NDC) family of sibling pension schemes is a group of most promising youngsters in their teens. They have high potential, holding promise of further development and of a bright future, unfolding multiple talents. Adolescent by now, NDC is uncontested as an innovative invention and as a good practice. For many experts, it surely holds out a more credible pledge than most of the alternative approaches to old-age security—defined benefit (DB) plans, fully funded financial defined contribution (FDC) schemes, and points systems—usually offer in terms of assurances.

What is controversial, though, is to what extent NDC systems are best practices under all circumstances. Can they serve as a yardstick of performance, or even outperform all others in the long run in most relevant aspects of output and sustainability? Is NDC an "ideal" pension framework in general, as Holzmann (2006) suggests? Or is it as incomplete and abortive as any other pension system, a position that, for instance, Barr (2006), Barr and Diamond (2006), and Börsch-Supan (2006) seem to lean toward? Can, and actually do, "well-designed" DB and points systems successfully mimic NDCs without adopting them, as Whitehouse argues in chapter 3 in this volume? Or is NDC, as I have argued and continue to think, as imperfect by definition and by virtue of lived experience as any other human institution, from democracy to families to social insurance, but without a viable better alternative so far? By implication, this would make NDC "close to ideal" or "close to best," depending on the specific molding and shape of its social security arrangement.

NDC will continue to be diffused but will not be copied wholesale everywhere in this copycat world of globalizing inventions. Yet it will remain a point of reference, if not a—more or less silently—admired role model of institutional design for mature and advanced welfare regimes and a developmental perspective for low- and middle-income countries. The particular beauty of its specific versions, in terms of both efficiency and fairness or equity, will continue to be debated according to highly diverse public policy preferences and idiosyncratic tastes, stemming from irreversible histories and related political cultures and path dependencies. But the very base common to all NDC systems remains a simple, solid, sound, and robust rock of core organizing principles, implementation constraints, and sustainability requirements.

Bernd Marin is executive director of the United Nations–affiliated European Centre for Social Welfare Policy and Research, Vienna.

Sustainability, the single most important distinctive feature of NDC, is often power-ful as rhetoric, but it may be poorly understood conceptually and is rarely operationalized empirically in a convincing way. Sustainable pensions imply management of resources so they can meet the demands of the present generation without decreasing opportunities for future generations. The purpose is to minimize the closure of future options or to maxi-mize the range of future choices. This does not mean leaving old-age security in the state in which it has been inherited—something that is neither possible nor desirable in view of demographic and socioeconomic challenges.

Sustainability is a constraint or limit on choices of developmental strategies ("not everything goes"), but it does not compel any single policy (there is no "one best way," "one size fits all," "no alternative"). There are multiple compatibilities of sustainable devel-opment, with different NDCs and with other pension arrangements. Highly divergent levels of, for example, sovereign debt, implicit liabilities, pension generosity, financing gaps, system dependency ratios, and contribution or accrual rates, corresponding to widely different political and social values—all are compatible with sustainability.

Thus, sustainability is defined as a precondition for pension maintenance in the sense of fiscal and social feasibility, not as a matter of cultural, ethical, or political desir-ability. It has to do with a viable old-age security system, not an ideologically desirable welfare system. Several levels of pension expenditures may be financially sustainable but not adequate and socially acceptable for retired or active people. And, vice versa, mas-sive and popular early retirement practices (for example, in some European countries, up to 90 percent of individuals retire before age 65) may be self-destructive habits that are unsustainable even in midterm time frames.

Intergenerational equity is central to sustainability, but this does not imply zero-sum conflicts between current and subsequent generations. In contrast to uses of capi-tal and credits for consumption *à fond perdu* (i.e., the resources are lost forever), new knowledge and institutional inventions such as NDC and other human capacities that are passed on to the next generation are enhanced rather than depleted by intensive current utilization. Investment in human development and social security, however, contributes to sustainability only if it is made at the expense of current consumption (including some legacy costs) and not by cutting spending that would add to future capacity.

NDC exhibits character (and style), in contrast to the many *bricolage*-type do-it-yourself DB pension edifices without building plans. These latter mostly result from painfully long series of patchy parametric repairs of often fundamentally flawed skeletal structures, very difficult to restore even through critical reconstruction. Given that suc-cessful reconstruction basically implies mimicking NDC within DB or points systems without adopting its overall architecture, as Whitehouse argues, why not take over the NDC institutional framework as a whole, as a total work of art of collective intelligence? This is what Holzmann and Palmer (chapter 1 in this volume) convincingly recommend: "go for an immediate transition to avoid future problems."

Chapter 2

The comprehensive analysis by Chłoń-Domińczak, Franco, and Palmer (chapter 2 in this volume) provides ample empirical evidence as to the wisdom of the advice offered in chapter 1. Latvia, Poland, and Sweden reformed rapidly and mandatorily, and thereby best, whereas Italy tried to buy time and build consensus through a slow, partly voluntary, and minority transformation that "turned out to be the Achilles' heel of the Italian NDC reform." As with justice, so reforms must not only be done but must be seen to be done. Italy's strategy of "disguised change," almost hiding the real agenda of far-reaching but long-postponed 1995 reforms, is somewhat self-defeating politically and technically, as the authors document in great detail.

Sweden, by contrast, has demonstrated how to use a "demographic window of opportunity" but also how to take time—including some years of political time-out—to reach the necessary broadest possible political consensus. Distinguished Swedish communication strategies such as the famed Orange Envelope, the *Orange Report,* and user-friendly Internet access that allows "individuals themselves to calculate possible pension levels at chosen retirement ages" certainly constitute a best practice that enables such political success. But even less effective communication of NDC has not prevented its achievement: according to the chapter 2 authors, "NDC appears to have weathered the storm created by the deep recession of 2008–09" and has done so everywhere.

The authors also show the impressive historical diversity and path dependency of NDC evolutionary patterns, far beyond a simple and uniform "one format fits all" model. Similar architectural design principles still allow for great pluralism in NDC systems. Much variety is seen in the indexation of notional accounts and benefits; in patterns of explicit redistribution within a piggy-bank framework; in the settlement of legacy costs and the (non-)acceptance or existence of inherited special privileges, coverage, and exemptions within a fundamentally universal system; in the quality of law enforcement and administrative infrastructure (most problematic in Poland); and in the structure of transition models, the speed of transformation, and the cohorts affected. The arrangements for individual accounts vary widely with respect to the calculation formula for the notional rate of return or other parameters, the handling of inheritance gains, or the numerous and diverging levels of generosity regarding pension credits for time off from work because of unemployment, sickness, disability, maternity and parental leave and caregiving, conscripted military service, and even tertiary education. All NDCs resemble each other but are as diverse as DB schemes, although in a much less arbitrary way and without violating basic sustainability requirements.

Despite significant variations in the share of contributions going to NDC as against FDC (50.0 percent, originally, in Latvia; 63.0 percent in Poland; and 86.5 percent in Sweden) and in the share of current contribution rates (from 12.22 percent in Poland to 33.00 percent in Italy), there is a remarkable convergence in expected gross replacement rates. These rates run between 60 and 68 percent for average workers, with net rates varying more, from 64 to 77 percent, as a result of different tax loads. The variation in rates implies highly differential effectiveness of pension system mixes in Italy and Sweden, for instance. These future individual outcomes should be adequate and broadly acceptable, in particular because they are comparable with those of other systems within the European Union (EU) but reinforce long-term financial and fiscal stability, in contrast to hardly affordable rises in pension expenditures elsewhere in Europe.

In spite of all the technical and administrative constraints, once an institutional NDC design has been set up and quasi-constitutionalized, many important and genuinely ethical and political choices have to be made in design choice and implementation procedures. An example is the distribution of the adjustment costs between active and retired people to address the fallout of the 2008 financial crisis (e.g., two-thirds to one-third in the Swedish balancing index). A second example concerns the conversion rules for transforming acquired pension entitlements into initial capital, where seemingly highly technical decisions—such as the choice of the G-value, the divisor used to calculate annuities—have severe distributional consequences along gender and generational lines, as well as by age group. A third example is the phasing out (or not) of special privileges for persons below the age of 55 and of the continuing exceptions from universal NDC coverage such as professionals in Italy or a long list of occupations—farmers, judges and prosecutors, military personnel, police, prison staff, border guards, and miners—in Poland.

These exceptions from coverage under the NDC approach in Poland are even more surprising, given the "extensive public discussion . . . of the principles of the reform" and the "popular" appeal to Poles of "the simple message of linking benefits to contributions and pensions to life expectancy"—in contrast, for instance, to the reception of this idea among Greeks or Austrians. Still, narrow sectional-interest protection prevailed, and Polish bridging pensions are a dunning remnant of the "cashing in" of nonabolished special rights—that is, of the structural corruption of an authoritarian past that extends far into the future. But the Polish system remains an exception among NDCs, whereas the clientelism and rent seeking of potentially "dangerous" or otherwise critical interest groups seem to be widespread among DB schemes and extend far beyond those countries with an authoritarian (Communist or Fascist) past.

One last remark on chapter 2: the authors justly state that "given the actuarial link between benefits and contributions in NDC, there is no need to set . . . a fixed retirement age." Unfortunately, instead of exploiting this innovative and libertarian competitive edge over all other mandatory public pension schemes, the authors adhere to a traditional benevolent paternalism. Setting a minimum age from which pensions can be paid to "protect people from myopic decisions . . . that can lead to a low lifetime pension and a higher risk of poverty in old age" is very conventional indeed and is not up to the most important potential of the new paradigm. The debate on the age of retirement, which is fully dispensable within NDC, is understandable in view of the heavy historical legacy in Italy, Latvia, and Poland, which began their reform processes with very low (and gender-unequal) legal and actual retirement ages. I am also well aware of the important signaling function of minimum and reference ages, but they could be made variable as required by account endowments. Fixed (higher) age thresholds should be restricted to poverty relief measures such as "guaranteed pensions" or conversion of disability benefits into old-age benefits (both of which are available in Sweden at age 65) or to benchmarks for people's "right to retain their employment" (currently 67, to be raised to 70 in Sweden, as in France).

But the truly innovative potential of NDCs still to be explored is that they could, and should, be used not just as old-age pensions but also as a kind of lifetime social security account. That is, people (after a significant contribution and vesting period, i.e., from midlife onward) could withdraw funds for sabbatical-like time-out periods up to a year every seven (or x) years during their working lives, at the cost of correspondingly lower accrued pension benefits in old age or of later retirement. For prevention of moral hazard, it is sufficient to make sure that money can be drawn from lifetime accounts only if coverage assets are sufficient to ensure a life annuity above the poverty level. Without an optional, elective retirement age and full liberalization of lifetime social security accounts by flexible choice, the liberating, choice-enhancing effects and "utopian potential" of NDCs will fall largely short of their reassuring "you get what you paid for" stabilizing force. The persuasive powers of system maintenance, financial stability, and sustainability by design, and of social insurance and personal freedom of choice, should not be abdicated to each other.

Chapter 3

In chapter 3 in this volume, Edward Whitehouse identifies four main areas of economic concern and observes "parallel lines" between NDC and the direction of pension reform in countries of the Organisation for Economic Co-operation and Development (OECD): "benefits based on lifetime earnings, rather than a subset of 'best' or 'final' years of pay"; "each extra year's contribution . . . giv[ing] rise to an additional benefit" and "no ceiling on the number of pensionable years"; an actuarial bonus-malus (reward and penalty) system for later and earlier retirement; and the reduction of benefits as life expectancy increases.

Whitehouse's bold summary statement—that "most OECD pension systems have already achieved most of the four objectives . . . but without adopting NDC"—may appear quite plausible at first glance. It also seems to be in line with an apparent disposition by the OECD's Social Policy Division to play down the innovative character of the Swedish and other NDC reform countries as against Anglo-Saxon ("Britain abroad") demogrant models or Franco-German points systems, or even traditional DB plans. But a second glance at his own evidence reveals that his interpretations may have been all too hasty and contradictory and that the conclusions may be overly favorable to ongoing DB reforms.

"Most . . . systems have . . . achieved most . . . objectives" is hardly half true, according to the evidence presented by Whitehouse himself: almost 40 percent of the DB systems still have no lifetime earnings calculations; many countries, including Canada, the Czech Republic, France, Spain, and the United States, remain far below the optimum standard; and others, such as Austria, that do reform adequately in principle will require many decades of transition before fully implementing this core requirement. Of the countries in the sample, 73 percent permit early retirement, 10 percent do so without any actuarial reductions (or increments) in accrued pension benefits with early (or later) exit, and 80 percent have penalties (or rewards) that are less, and in some case, much less, than actuarial levels. Early pension ages average age 60.4 years, or 4.7 years less than normal retirement age. The earliest, according to Whitehouse, is 61.8 years, but this number ignores the lower retirement ages for women even in OECD or EU countries such as Austria, Bulgaria, the Czech Republic, Estonia, Italy, Latvia, Lithuania, Poland, Romania, Slovenia, Turkey, and the United Kingdom—not to speak of the almost 20 European countries outside these bodies, such as Belarus, the Russian Federation, Ukraine, and many countries between the western Balkans and Central Asia.

I fully agree with Whitehouse that "the key difference between NDC and the two other types of earnings-related pensions is the automatic link between changes in life expectancy and the value of benefits . . . . Pensions will therefore be lower if people live longer," as long as they are not also "working longer to compensate." NDCs—and automatic NDCs only—provide what I call *lifetime indexing* against "age inflation"(Marin forthcoming); that is, an automatic coupling of the pension entitlements formula with gains in life expectancy to make the formula failproof when key parameters change significantly.

Whitehouse recognizes this unique selling proposition as a distinctive feature of NDCs but again plays down NDCs' decisive comparative advantage over all forms of DB and points systems. "Nearly half of the OECD countries—13 out of 30—now incorporate an automatic link between pensions and life expectancy . . . . A decade ago, only one country had such a link. The spread of this policy has a strong claim to be the major innovation in pension policy in recent years." Although I completely agree with the innovation claim in principle, the impression created of an innovation glass almost half full is fairly misleading. According to the data provided, in 69 percent of the cases the credit goes only to the new NDCs or to "DC plans as a substitute for all or part of their public pensions," not to traditional schemes being reformed accordingly.

Not quite 17 percent (5 out of 30) of the OECD countries studied have started to introduce an automatic link between life expectancy and pensions in their public DB or points systems, with the link running either to benefit levels (Finland, Germany, and Portugal) or to qualifying conditions. In contrast to fully operating DC and NDC schemes, lifetime indexing in the few DB countries adopting it will be partly implemented far into the future and partly linked to suboptimal parameters (contribution years in France, instead of pension age, as in Denmark). The "automatism" of lifetime indexing foreseen in a coalition government program has been defeated by agitated protest and stolid resistance against the supposed tyranny of soulless computers, bringing down the government and provoking snap elections in Austria in 2008.

Thus, in the overwhelming majority of cases of DB and points systems, the most necessary lifetime indexing adjustment so far does *not* work—not only not automatically; it does not work at all in 83 percent of the OECD domain, and where it starts to do so, it does not work immediately, consensually, properly, or as fully as needed. Consequently, in most OECD countries, pension systems continue, as Whitehouse observes, to distort decisions to work and save and to encourage people to leave the labor market early; they "give rise to substantial inequities among individuals," penalize those "who do not retire at the earliest possible opportunity," and so on. Although not all countries display all or most of these undoubtedly bad practices, Whitehouse's reasoning that in "only four OECD countries—Belgium, Greece, Luxembourg, and Spain—do pension schemes fall significantly short of best practice in at least two of the areas analyzed" and that "many OECD countries have retirement income systems to which NDC principles are simply not applicable: examples are Australia, Denmark, Ireland, the Netherlands, New Zealand, and the United Kingdom" sounds quite unconvincing in view of his own empirical evidence and his candid concession that "NDC schemes are an example of good practice in all these areas."

Though it is a—purely tautological—truth that "well-designed DB or points system schemes also share these characteristics," Whitehouse cannot even raise, let alone answer, the query as to why this happens so rarely, as he does not recognize its rarity in his own data but rather defines away failures. Thus, a critical review of his reasoning supporting the reform of DB and points systems and of the evidence provided for it turns out to be the single best argument, as regards outcome and process, in favor of the key recommendation by Holzmann and Palmer (chapter 1, in this volume) to "go for an immediate transition to avoid future problems," through a rapid adoption of paradigmatic NDC instead of parametric DB reforms.

Other observations in chapter 1 are equally pertinent. In view of the above observations concerning chapter 3, the first suggestion of the priority policy research agenda is most urgent: "assess the outcome of NDC schemes compared with the primary goals of pension systems, and compared with alternative scheme designs" to guarantee better informed and more objective appraisals. Regarding the historical legacies and transformation problems discussed in chapter 1, the proposal in that chapter to "identify and finance the transition costs, as they will hit you otherwise" is most topical. And, apart from two recent, more general, volumes on women and pensions (James, Edwards, and Wong 2008; Marin and Zólyomi 2010), this two-volume publication marks the first time that the gender dimension of pension reform with NDC has been systematically examined, in five studies by leading experts in the field, with good prospects for productive further research and productive political discourse.

References

Barr, Nicholas. 2006. "Notional Defined Contribution Pensions: Mapping the Terrain." In *Pension Reform: Issues and Prospects for Non-Financial Defined Contribution (NDC) Schemes,* ed. Robert Holzmann and Edward Palmer, 57–69. Washington, DC: World Bank.

Barr, Nicholas, and Peter Diamond. 2006. "The Economics of Pensions." *Oxford Review of Economic Policy* 22 (1): 15–39.

Börsch-Supan, Axel H. 2006. "What are NDC Pension Systems? What Do They Bring to Reform Strategies?" In *Pension Reform: Issues and Prospects for Non-Financial Defined Contribution (NDC) Schemes,* ed. Robert Holzmann and Edward Palmer, 35–56. Washington, DC: World Bank.

Holzmann, Robert. 2006. "Toward a Reformed and Coordinated Pension System in Europe: Rational and Potential Structure." In *Pension Reform: Issues and Prospects for Non-Financial Defined Contribution (NDC) Schemes,* ed. Robert Holzmann and Edward Palmer, 225–65. Washington, DC: World Bank.

Holzmann, Robert, and Edward Palmer, eds. 2006. *Pension Reform. Issues and Prospects for Non-Financial Defined Contribution (NDC) Schemes.* Washington, DC: World Bank.

James, Estelle, Alejandra Cox Edwards, and Rebeca Wong. 2008. *The Gender Impact of Social Security Reform.* Chicago: University of Chicago Press.

Marin, Bernd. Forthcoming. *Welfare in an Idle Society?* Vienna: European Centre for Social Welfare Policy and Research.

Marin, Bernd, and Eszter Zólyomi, eds. 2010. *Women's Work and Pensions: What Is Good, What Is Best? Designing Gender-Sensitive Arrangements.* Farnham, U.K.: Ashgate.

On the First Wave of NDC Schemes

Fritz von Nordheim

In chapter 2 in this volume, Chłoń-Domińczak, Franco, and Palmer document the experiences and dilemmas of four European Union (EU) countries—Italy, Latvia, Poland, and Sweden—that have converted their earnings-related pay-as-you-go (PAYG) public pension schemes to nonfinancial (notional) defined contribution (NDC) schemes. As is highlighted in the opening of their thorough discussion, NDC is one of the more revolutionary new designs to emerge from the past 15 years of pension reforms, and one that very few had thought possible.

In my view, the primary merit of NDC designs is that they have exploded the myths of public versus private and PAYG versus funded plans by demonstrating that key positive features of both systems could be constructively combined without importing their downsides. NDC has shown that the characteristics of economic efficiency, financial stability, and strong contributory and work incentives normally associated with private and fully funded (or financial) defined contribution (FDC) schemes can be emulated by public schemes, which are PAYG and universal. NDC therefore does not imply the double-payment problem, with a long buildup phase, and the fragmented coverage normally associated with fully funded private FDC schemes.

This means that governments do not need to move to fully funded private schemes and tackle all the problems and dilemmas inherent in them to achieve some of those schemes' key features of actuarial structure and financial stability. A notionally defined contribution scheme with individualized accounts in which a worker's entitlements are strictly linked to his or her contributions can deliver (most of) the same effects.

By smashing the myths that public PAYG or private funded schemes are inherently deficient, or inherently superior, in their ability to deal with the economic and demographic challenges involved in building good pension systems, NDC has returned us to the essential insight that the devil is in the details. Far more than the mere choice of whether to opt for one system or another, successful reforms are about details and the quality of preparation, design, implementation, and communication. NDC has helped us recover part of our common sense, which had been mired for two decades in bitter contention informed primarily by ideological political-economy preferences about market and state.

Fritz von Nordheim is a social protection expert specializing in pensions and policy responses to population aging. He currently manages the pensions and health teams in the Active Ageing and Pensions Unit of the European Commission's Directorate General for Employment, Social Affairs and Inclusion. The assessments and opinions expressed in this comment are attributable only to the author and cannot be presumed to reflect positions of the European Commission or its services.

Again, as amply demonstrated in chapter 2, which was written by sophisticated pension engineers, the mere generic features of NDC do not guarantee much success. The issue really concerns implementation and the choice of design details. Thus, as evidenced by the comparative discussion of the four country cases, the problem is how to handle the transition from the old to the new system, including the conversion of earned entitlements and the speed with which the new system is put in place. Unsurprisingly, administrative capacity and political preparation and follow-up have proved to be important. Similarly, the extent to which the goals are achieved will depend crucially on the context into which the NDC design has to fit: the other parts of the pension system and the capabilities and limits of the labor and financial markets on which it can draw.

In fact, details are so important that it is an open question whether Sweden's exquisitely fine-tuned and ambitiously communicated NDC scheme can really be discussed on a par with Italy's NDC system, especially because the generic design has been watered down and poorly implemented in Italy and key determinants of success in its external environment, such as the ability of Italian labor markets to deliver reasonably stable jobs with full pension coverage for the young, appear to have been neglected.[1] Furthermore, even a preprogrammed scheme, as NDC aims to be, cannot be insulated from politics. In the end, the outcome of any pension design will depend greatly on whether politics can deliver sensible solutions, and here the capabilities of the Swedish political system differ so much from the Italian that they seem to be creatures from different worlds. An important point is that Italy, so far, has largely failed to make its NDC system transparent and to communicate to people the inherent incentives for them to realize their pension preferences by adjusting their labor supply behavior. It therefore appears to be an open question to what extent key supposed benefits of NDC, such as people's working more and longer, can even be reaped.

Moreover, to enable NDC schemes to fulfill the poverty prevention function of a pension scheme, pure NDC principles have to be combined with a minimum-guarantee pension financed from general taxation. The Italian and Polish variants lack a poverty prevention floor and simply offload this key function onto the social protection net of last resort, social assistance. Similarly, financial stability cannot be guaranteed only by the microeconomic link between individual contributions and entitlements; it must be tackled at the macroeconomic level. This task does not just involve smart indexation and valorization and smart use of inheritances (how to distribute the entitlements of those who die early); it requires intricate mechanisms of shock mitigation and shock absorption such as are found in the Swedish scheme, with its rules about how to distribute the losses from economic downturns among all stakeholders.

Despite the very thorough treatment of the challenges and dilemmas of NDC in chapter 2, two important aspects are largely neglected: (a) the financial and labor market context in which these four NDC systems have to function, and (b) the way NDC constructs have weathered the shocks from the ongoing financial, economic, and public budget crisis, including the associated political reactions.

Judged on their present performance, the national labor markets of the four countries clearly have very different capacities to deliver the long and unbroken careers that NDC schemes presume will result from the rational worker's choice to supply his or her labor. If short-term, contract, "atypical" jobs proliferate for the young in a polarized labor market, and if a significant part of young workers spend 5 to 10 years in involuntary underemployment, they are off to an extremely poor start in a pension system built on DC principles, as is convincingly argued by Boeri and Galasso (2012). As for the relation to financial markets, it is important to point out that NDC designs usually also combine public PAYG and private funded systems in a more external sense by having a financial defined contribution scheme linked to them. It would therefore be important to discuss the rules on charges, investments, and risk mitigation and the difference in the performance of these funds over the business cycle.

Unfortunately, the implications of very different levels of savings ambition in the Swedish, Latvian, and Polish schemes and the possible design flaws in the latter two are not adequately treated. In hindsight, the decision to finance FDC pillars simply by shifting part of the social security taxes necessary for current pensions to the private schemes does not appear to be the smartest design for mandatory private pensions—in particular, because the scale in Poland and Latvia was so ambitious (6–8 percent of gross wages, versus 2 percent in Sweden), but certainly also because the tax revenues forgone were never explicitly replaced by equivalent new taxes or gradually replenished by voluntary contributions from the owners of the individualized accounts. Even in a situation of rapid economic growth, this would not seem to be a particularly wise or stable form of financing for a supplementary pension scheme that is supposed to be fully funded and thus to involve real savings in the sense of present consumption forgone.

Latvia and Poland, along with the other countries that introduced some form of mandatory private pensions, obtained a five-year, gradually decreasing, dispensation under the accounting rules of the EU's Stability and Growth Pact to camouflage the impact on their deficit and the debt position of this peculiar type of pension fund buildup. When the permission expired, around the same time as the crisis occurred, the true cost of having to pay for both future and present pensions no longer could be hidden in a general increase in state revenues associated with rapid economic growth, and the fallacy of the construction gave rise to frenzied political reactions. Having to issue extra state debt to finance pension savings may have been economic reality but did not appear too convincing, and ministries of finance acted accordingly. In several countries, they temporarily shifted contributions back to the financing of pensions in payment, and they are only now, if at all, resuming payments into the private schemes, on a significantly reduced scale. Thus, we can safely assume that the contribution to pension adequacy from the funded element will be markedly smaller and that a greater burden of provision will have to borne by the NDC scheme. Developments in Latvia and Poland represent variants of this briefly sketched drama, and it would have been good if Chłoń-Domińczak, Franco, and Palmer had accorded them greater attention.

Finally, I think it important to place NDC in the context of general trends in pension reforms, as Whitehouse does in chapter 3, and of the other innovations in pension design that the past decade of efforts has generated. In this perspective, NDC can be seen as having inaugurated a trend in reform of pension systems that not only implied an intentional move in official provision from largely single to multipillar arrangements with a greater role for prefunding but, importantly, introduced innovative attempts to overcome many of the economic-efficiency weaknesses of public PAYG and the social protection weaknesses of private funded schemes. Thus, the reforms moved public schemes from best years to career average earnings as the basis for benefit calculation and began introducing mechanisms to reduce benefits or raise pensionable ages in line with future growth in life expectancy at retirement. And, as private second- and third-pillar schemes were given larger official roles in national pension provision, reforms also sought to tackle some of the usual unfortunate aspects of private pensions. For example, fragmented and nonequitable coverage was mitigated through mandating, autoenrollment, and elimination of health criteria, and discretionary entitlement was remedied through obligations to cover all employees, full immediate vesting, and abolition of waiting time. Innovations such as mandatory private pensions in Central and Eastern Europe, occupational schemes with autoenrollment in the United Kingdom, and voluntary third-pillar schemes with subventions that enable low-income groups to join, such as Germany's Riester scheme, have challenged traditional perceptions of what private pensions entail. In the course of these fascinating developments, the initial uniqueness of NDC has become somewhat less special, as Whitehouse argues.

These caveats do not imply that NDC is not a revolutionary design with many solid merits and fully deserving of a celebration of its first 10 years. They merely underline that not even NDC can save us from all the dilemmas of real-life pension provision. Amid the important help from grand designs, to which NDC truly belongs, we will, unfortunately, still have to pay constant attention to details and changing circumstances and go on tinkering.

Note

1. For a discussion of this Achilles' heel of the Italian NDC, see Boeri and Galasso (2012).

Reference

Boeri, Tito, and Vincenzo Galasso. 2012. "Is Social Security Secure with NDC?" In *Gender, Politics, and Financial Stability,* chap. 15, vol. 2 of *Nonfinancial Defined Contribution Pension Schemes in a Changing Pension World,* ed. Robert Holzmann, Edward Palmer, and David A. Robalino. Washington, DC: World Bank and Swedish Social Insurance Agency.

PART II

Reforms under Implementation, Consideration, Contemplation

CHAPTER 4

Pension Reform in Norway: Combining an NDC Approach and Distributional Goals

Arne Magnus Christensen, Dennis Fredriksen, Ole Christian Lien, and Nils Martin Stølen

Reform of Norway's pension system began in 2001, when Prime Minister Jens Stoltenberg's first government appointed a Pension Commission that included representatives from the political parties. The commission reported its conclusions in 2004 (Norway, Ministry of Finance and Ministry of Social Affairs 2004). Further work resulted in two settlements in the parliament, in 2005 and 2007. These settlements indicated that a broad majority in the parliament supported a pension reform along the lines suggested by the Pension Commission, but with some adjustments (see Norway, Ministry of Labor and Social Inclusion 2006). They were followed in 2009 by a White Paper in which the new system and transitional rules were presented in more detail (Norway, Ministry of Labor and Social Inclusion 2009), and the new system was approved by the parliament in the spring of 2009.

Important features of the Norwegian pension reform are the adjustment of pensions for changes in life expectancy, flexible retirement starting at age 62 based on actuarial principles, and new rules for indexation of pensions, beginning in 2011.

Another part of the reform is a new model for accumulating pension entitlements that will be introduced gradually for cohorts born after 1954 and fully for cohorts born after 1963. The various elements are discussed in greater detail below.

Supplementary pensions and tax rules and their effect on pension levels and replacement rates are also examined here. The Norwegian tax structure is progressive, and certain forms of tax relief apply only to pensioners and, in particular, to those with low incomes. People who receive a minimum pension typically pay no tax at all, and tax effects therefore need to be taken into account in estimating replacement rates.

Finally, the chapter includes a discussion on how the new pension system affects sustainability, labor supply incentives, and income distribution.

Background of the Pension Reform

As in most member countries of the Organisation for Economic Co-operation and Development (OECD), the pension system in Norway will face substantial challenges in the

Arne Magnus Christensen is a senior adviser in the Norwegian Ministry of Labor. Dennis Fredriksen is a researcher at Statistics Norway. Ole Christian Lien is a senior adviser in the Norwegian Labor and Welfare Administration. Nils Martin Stølen is a researcher at Statistics Norway.

coming decades because of the expected aging of the population. When the public old-age pension scheme was established in 1967, there were about four people in the labor force for each old-age and disability pensioner. In 2008, this ratio had fallen to 2.7, and without reform, it was expected to decline to 1.8 in 2050, according to projections from Statistics Norway, the country's central statistical bureau.

The population above age 67 is expected to more than double by 2050, and the increasing share of elderly people will lead to a strong increase in pension expenditure. In addition, the average pension is expected to increase compared to the average wage in the coming years. One reason is increasing labor force participation among women, which leads to higher average pensions for new pensioners than for the group of old-age pensioners as a whole.

It is estimated that if the old system were retained, the National Insurance Scheme's expenditure on old-age and disability pensions, as a share of mainland Norway's gross domestic product (GDP)—excluding the petroleum industry and related services—would rise from about 9 percent in 2011 to 18 percent in 2050. The expenditure on old-age pensions alone was estimated to increase from 6 percent to approximately 14 percent of mainland GDP.

An aging population will pose substantial challenges for state finances in other fields such as health and care services for the aged. In particular, the increase in the number of people age 80 and older will contribute to a sizable increase in health and welfare expenditures, even though a gradual improvement of the health of this age group is likely to moderate the increase. A pension reform and other measures that provide incentives for older workers to stay in the labor force can contribute considerably to financing pensions and creating resources for good health care and community home services for the future elderly.

The old pension system had some unfair aspects in that people with the same lifetime income could receive very different pensions, while people with widely different lifetime incomes might receive the same pension. This happened because of the weak connection between income throughout a person's working career and the resulting pension. The rule setting a maximum 40 years of registered earnings for receipt of a full pension implied, for instance, that people working for more than 40 years would see no increase in their annual pensions. In addition, under the old system, people who had worked for several years could end up with minimum pensions, like persons who never had any labor income, because the minimum pension for low incomes was income tested by 100 percent against the income-related pension.

The opportunity to retire before the pensionable age of 67 was unevenly distributed. Large groups were covered by the collectively bargained early retirement scheme (Avtale Festet Pensjon, or AFP), which could be claimed from age 62 to age 66, but other groups had no opportunity for early retirement except on a disability pension. For people covered by the AFP scheme, the incentives to continue working after age 62 were rather weak because the size of the annual AFP pension was almost independent of the retirement age between ages 62 and 66 and was thus far from actuarially neutral. In addition, the old system did not include any actuarial adjustment for persons postponing retirement until after age 67.

Design of the New System

This section begins with an overview of the public old-age pension under the new system. It goes on to examine disability pensions, supplementary pensions, the collectively bargained AFP schemes, and the effect of taxation on retirees.

PUBLIC OLD-AGE PENSION

Design of the new income pension. Under the new system, pension entitlements accrue through income from work, or through other types of entitlements granted for special periods and circumstances (to be discussed below), between ages 13 and 75. Each year, individuals' pension entitlements deriving from income from work will increase by 18.1 percent, up to a ceiling of 7.1 times the basic amount.[1] The resulting amount is registered on individual notional accounts. Old-age pension expenditures will still be financed by the pay-as-you-go method. Because of the present low number of old-age pensioners, compared with the size of the labor force, the current estimated contribution rate sufficient to finance the system on a pay-as-you-go basis is much lower than 18.1 percent and will probably not correspond to this number before about 2040. Pension entitlements are adjusted each year in line with wage growth.

At the time of retirement, the annual pension is calculated by dividing the accumulated pension entitlements by an annuity divisor that mainly reflects remaining life expectancy. The annual pension increases as retirement is postponed, as a result of both higher pension entitlements and a lower annuity divisor. As life expectancy at retirement increases, new birth cohorts will have to remain in the labor force a little longer to achieve the same replacement rate as earlier cohorts.

During the reform process, it was discussed to what degree pensions should be proportional to lifetime earnings from work, or whether there should be strong redistributive elements. In the original proposal by the Pension Commission in 2004, the ceiling on the maximum level of individual earnings that could give rise to entitlements was somewhat higher, and the annual pension entitlements that would have been granted for earnings below the ceiling were somewhat lower, than in the model approved by the parliament in 2009. The initial proposal was criticized for having adverse distributional effects that would make low- and middle-income earners worse off than under the old system, and for this reason it was not adopted.

The new Norwegian income pension scheme and the NDC model. According to Börsch-Supan (2006), for a pension system to be classified as a nonfinancial (notional) defined contribution (NDC) system, fulfillment of four criteria is required:

1. An accounting mechanism that credits all lifetime earnings
2. A mechanism that links the final balance with the demographic and macroeconomic environment
3. An actuarial rule for converting the final balance into an annuity
4. Collaterization of claims on future benefits not with real capital but through promises by a government-related entity

In the new Norwegian pension scheme, criterion 1 is only partly met. Pension entitlements of 18.1 percent of earned income are given for all years between 13 and 75 years, but only up to a ceiling on annual income. This means that the link between pensions and lifetime earnings becomes increasingly weaker with higher earnings above the ceiling. This was seen by Norwegian politicians as a desirable distributional feature of the reform.

Criterion 2 is not met. Instead, the new income pension system will still be part of general public finances, and the individual pension accounts are therefore used *just* for calculating the pension. The nonfulfillment of criterion 2 implies that the government bears the risk of unfavorable demographic developments in the labor market—the risk of a declining working-age population, and the risk that life expectancy may be systematically underestimated. In addition, there is the macroeconomic risk of unfavorable labor force participation. If these or other adverse events occur, it is up to politicians to decide how taxes and government expenditures should be adjusted to balance public finances in the long run.

Criteria 3 and 4 are fulfilled fully. Criterion 3 implies that workers will have to face the risk of increasing life expectancy and that younger cohorts will have to consider postponing retirement to get a higher annual benefit in line with that of previous cohorts.

Pension entitlements for special periods and circumstances. Persons registered as unemployed, those conscripted for military service, and those with children under age six or who care for the elderly will be accredited pension entitlements according to specific rules.

In addition, compensation from national social insurance benefits for time spent away from work in conjunction with sickness or injury, or for periods with maternity or parental benefits, or for time in labor market work assessment programs, is considered pensionable income in the same way as is work income. Recipients therefore earn pension entitlements on the basis of their benefit income. In the new system, people receiving unemployment benefits will earn pension entitlements based on the labor income they had before becoming unemployed, which is an improvement over the previous rules.

Parents caring for children under age six can be credited with an "income" of 4.5 basic amounts, or about 75 percent of an average full-time wage. This constitutes a floor for pension earnings for people with low labor income and children younger than age six. Parents with children under age six who earn more than 75 percent of an average wage will not receive any extra pension entitlements for unpaid care. Either the mother or the father of the child, but not both, may receive child-care credits in any given year.

Military conscripts with more than six months of military service receive pension entitlements equivalent to 2.5 basic amounts per year, or about 40 percent of an average full-time wage. Military conscripts were not credited with pension entitlements in the old system.

The guaranteed pension. The guaranteed pension is a basic safety net in the new system that is meant to ensure an acceptable minimum pension level for people with little or no pension earnings. The new guaranteed pension is at the same level as the previous minimum pension and is differentiated according to marital status. In 2010, the minimum pension was 2.00 basic amounts for single pensioners and 1.85 basic amounts per person for married pensioners. The lower minimum pension for married pensioners reflects the lower cost of living as a couple. For single pensioners, the minimum pension in 2010 was about 33 percent of an average full-time wage. The minimum pension is exempt from tax, implying that it is even higher relative to the average full-time wage after taxes.

A 40-year residence period is required for receipt of a full guaranteed pension. The guaranteed pension will be income tested by 80 percent of the income pension. In other words, people with a low income pension who receive a guaranteed pension will keep 20 percent of their income pension and will thus receive a total pension above the minimum level.

The guaranteed pension alone can be drawn only from age 67. For people who receive both an earnings-related pension and some amount of guaranteed pension, it is possible to retire beginning at age 62, but both elements will be actuarially adjusted depending on the age of retirement. For people retiring fully or partially before age 67, the pension level must exceed the level of the guaranteed pension at age 67. The idea behind this requirement is that everybody should receive a pension at least equivalent to the minimum pension from age 67 on. A consequence is that a share of the population, especially among women, will have pension entitlements that are too low to enable them to retire at age 62. To increase the opportunities for early retirement, the new supplementary AFP pension scheme in the private sector is included in the pension entitlements when calculating the requirement. Whether to include other kinds of pensions that are paid out as annuities is under discussion. The guaranteed pension can be deferred until after age 67 and will then increase on the basis of actuarial adjustments.

Flexible retirement and the life expectancy adjustment. Until 2010, the retirement age was fixed at age 67 in the public old-age pension scheme. Most people did retire at that age, although it was possible to postpone retirement until age 70. Beginning in 2011, flexible retirement was introduced for the 62–75 age group in the public old-age pension scheme, on the basis of actuarial neutrality. An upper age limit of 75 was set to avoid very large differences in annual pensions paid out. The limit is harmonized with the new age limit for earning an income pension.

As of 2011, a life expectancy adjustment is applied to the pension for new pensioners. The annuity factors are determined for each cohort, mainly on the basis of remaining life expectancy. The factors are determined when the cohorts are age 61 and will not be adjusted later. Each cohort is assigned a separate annuity factor from age 62 until age 75. To mitigate the effects for the cohorts that will soon reach retirement age, a transitional rule has been introduced to ensure that the life expectancy adjustments at age 67 will not exceed 0.5 percent a year for the first cohorts retiring after 2011.

The old-age pension may be drawn wholly or partially beginning at age 62 and it is possible to withdraw 20, 40, 50, 60, or 80 percent of a full pension. Work and receipt of a pension can be freely combined without an earnings test; continued work after having started to draw a pension gives additional pension rights.

Indexation of pension entitlements and pensions in payment. Pension entitlements in the accumulation phase are indexed to wage growth. Previously earned pension entitlements consequently retain their value relative to the average wage in society. After retirement, the income pension being paid out will be indexed to wages, but a fixed factor of 0.75 percent a year will be subtracted. This factor is also taken into account when calculating the annuity factors for flexible retirement. This method of calculating the annuity factor is similar to that employed in the new Swedish NDC pension scheme.

The level of the minimum or guaranteed pension is adjusted by growth in wages but also by changes in the annual annuity factor at age 67. Projections from Statistics Norway indicate that life expectancy at age 67 is assumed to increase by about 0.5 percent a year. Hence, according to the projections, the guaranteed pension will be adjusted by wage growth but will then be reduced by a factor of about 0.5 percent a year because of the life expectancy adjustment.

The minimum pension was increased in relation to the average wage level in the years 2007–10 as a measure for achieving more equal income distribution and reducing relative poverty among old-age pensioners. This policy, however, had the effect of weakening the link between pensionable income and pension payments and increasing the number of old-age pensioners receiving a minimum pension. In the long-term projections of pension expenditures, an annual real wage growth of 1.5 percent has often been assumed, and in that case the guaranteed pension can be expected to grow by about 1.0 percent a year in real terms.

Transitional rules. Persons born in 1953 or earlier will earn their pension entitlements only according to the old rules. People born between 1954 and 1962 will earn their pension entitlements partly from the old scheme and partly from the new scheme, with a gradual increase in the share of pension entitlements from the new scheme for younger cohorts. People born in 1963 or later will earn their pension entitlements only according to the new rules.

Flexible retirement beginning at age 62 was introduced for new pensioners as of 2011, both for persons who earn their pension entitlements according to the old rules and for those who will be under the new rules. The new indexation of the old-age pension applies to all old-age pensioners from 2011 on.

DISABILITY PENSION AND OLD-AGE PENSION FOR FORMER DISABILITY PENSIONERS

Under the old system, the disability pension and the old-age pension were interconnected, and disability pensioners usually kept their pensions unchanged when they were transferred to the old-age pension at age 67. The disability pension was indexed in line with wage growth.

Disability pension rates are high in Norway; about 11 percent of the population age 18–67 is on disability pension. At age 67, about 40 percent of new old-age pensioners are former disability pensioners, and the decisions made on how to treat earlier disability pensioners during old age will have large economic consequences.

As a part of the pension reform, the government proposed in 2011 a new disability scheme and a new model for calculating the old-age pension for those disabled earlier (Norway, Ministry of Labor 2011). The proposal was accepted by the parliament, and the new rules will be introduced from 2015. The disability pension will then be determined more as a short-term benefit whereby people receive a percentage of their final predisability salary. New disability pensioners will receive a 66 percent replacement rate, and disability pensions will be taxed like earnings, implying higher taxation than for current disability pensioners. The net effect of the reform is a slight increase in average disability pensions after taxes, in comparison with the old system.

As in the old system, disability pensioners will be transferred to the old-age pension at age 67, and their old-age pensions will be indexed the same as for other old-age pensioners. Persons receiving disability benefits cannot work longer after age 67 to enhance their pensions to make up for the dynamics of life expectancy adjustment. This group is therefore given an addition to their pension that compensates for half the growth in the life expectancy factor after 2010. The goal of this rule was to ensure disability pensioners about the same development in their old age pension as non-disabled persons. By 2018, the life expectancy adjustment of the old-age pension for earlier disability pensioners is to be evaluated in light of whether the nondisabled do compensate for the life expectancy adjustment by working longer.

The economic calculations of the reform in this chapter were undertaken before the new rules for disability pension and old-age pension for former disability pensioners were determined. In the calculations, it was assumed that when disability pensioners become old-age pensioners at age 67, their pensions will be subject to a life expectancy adjustment similar to that for nondisabled persons who retire at that age. The partial compensation for the life expectancy adjustment for earlier disability pensioners may somewhat increase the costs of the new system in comparison with the calculations shown in "Labor Supply, Sustainability, and Distributional Effects," below.

SUPPLEMENTARY PENSIONS

In addition to the public old-age pension, employees in Norway receive supplementary pensions through their employers. Before 2006, each company could choose whether to offer a supplementary pension to its employees. In 2006, supplementary pensions were made mandatory by law, to ensure that all workers would have some pension income in addition to the public pension system and to facilitate a more equal distribution of supplementary pensions. Employees in the public sector have had occupational pensions for a very long time.

Supplementary pension schemes exhibit huge variation with respect to benefit levels, duration of benefits, indexation, and whether the schemes are defined benefit or defined contribution, but there are some requirements that must be met to receive preferential tax treatment. From 2006 on, minimum requirements for the supplementary pension schemes have been introduced—mainly, that the contributions in a defined contribution scheme must amount to at least 2 percent of wages between 1 and 12 basic amounts and that the duration of the pension payments must be at least 10 years. For defined benefit schemes, the benefits must be of at least equivalent level. Before the reform, the supplementary pension could not, with some exceptions, be drawn before age 67. As part of the reform, the minimum retirement age for private supplementary pensions is 62, as of 2011.

COLLECTIVELY AGREED EARLY RETIREMENT SCHEMES (AFP)

Between 1973 and 2010, the retirement age in the public old-age pension scheme in Norway was 67 years, but the collectively agreed early retirement schemes (AFP) made it possible for about 70 to 80 percent of wage earners to retire between ages 62 and 66. AFP is a result of tripartite cooperation between the employers' and employees' organizations and the government and is partly financed by the government. It was first established in 1989 and has been gradually developed since then. All employees in the public sector and about 60 percent of employees in the private sector are covered by an AFP agreement. The annual benefit level was independent of the retirement age and of about the same size as the public old-age pension.

The AFP schemes in the private sector were reformed for those beginning to draw pensions from 2011 on. The new AFP is paid out as an addition (typically, slightly more than 20 percent) to the public old-age pension for the retiree's entire remaining lifetime. It is adjusted for remaining life expectancy at the age of retirement in the same way as is the public old-age pension. Furthermore, it can be combined with work income without an earnings test.

In the public sector, no agreement on a similar reform was reached, and AFP still remains a pension that is paid out from age 62 to age 66. It cannot be combined with the public old-age pension. If a person continues working while receiving a public sector AFP pension, that pension will be reduced proportionally. The incentives to work after age 62 for public sector employees are therefore weaker than for other employees. Public sector workers may, at least in some cases, receive a higher pension at age 62 than private sector workers. Public sector pensions will be adjusted for life expectancy from age 67, and as of 2011, they are indexed in the same way as public old-age pensions.

TAXATION

The Norwegian tax structure is progressive, and the marginal tax rate increases with income up to a level of about 160 percent of average wage. Since replacement rates of pensions normally are well below 100 percent, the progressive tax structure implies that replacement rates will be higher after taxes than before taxes.

In addition, certain forms of tax relief apply only to pensioners. New tax rules for pensioners, effective starting in 2011, reduce the marginal tax rates for workers who combine work and receipt of a pension after age 62. The favorable taxation of pensions compared with labor income is maintained, and the strong redistributive elements in the taxation of pensions are maintained and even strengthened.

The social security contribution rate paid by the individual is currently 7.8 percent for wage income and 4.7 percent for pension income (disability pension, old-age pension, and supplementary pensions). The contribution rates paid by employers are between 0 and 14.1 percent. These contribution rates were originally meant to finance all social security benefits, including the old-age pension. Currently, however, they are much too low to finance social security. All social security benefits in Norway, including the old-age pension, are actually financed by the pay-as-you-go method as an integrated part of public finances. Although these taxes are termed contribution rates, there is, in reality, no explicit contribution rate for social security in the Norwegian tax system.

Future Pension Levels and Replacement Rates

In what follows, we present pension calculations for typical cases, to reflect the main effects of the pension reform on individuals. Most of the calculations have been made for an unmarried person from the 1949 cohort—the first cohort to be fully affected by the new flexible retirement age from age 62—and an unmarried person from the 1980 cohort, to illustrate the effect of the new model for accumulating pension entitlements and the possible effect of the life expectancy adjustment in the long run. When calculating the life expectancy adjustment, we have assumed that life expectancy will evolve in line with the "medium" alternative in the population projections by Statistics Norway. This alternative is only one of several projections of future mortality, but it is considered the most likely estimate. For simplicity, all the cases are based on a person who began work at age 24 and who has had a fixed wage level relative to the average wage level in society during his or her working career. The average wage level in Norway in full-time equivalents is designated AW; AW100 means a fixed annual income of 100 percent of AW, and so on.

In the cases for which after-tax replacement rates have been calculated, we have assumed that the tax structure will be the same as in 2011 but that all threshold values will be adjusted in line with average wage growth. Total pension expenditures are expected to rise rapidly in proportion to total wages in the next decades, as is shown in the discussion of sustainability, below. One can therefore question whether it will be possible to maintain tax rates at the current level in the long term. Pension expenditures would have risen even more without the pension reform, and the need for tax increases would have been even more pressing. When comparing after-tax replacement rates before and after the pension reform, we have assumed the same tax structure in both cases.

Figure 4.1 illustrates the relationship between average annual income and the average pension after the pension reform for those who are covered by the new scheme for pension entitlements. Both are measured in terms of AW. The income pension is linear with annual income up to the ceiling. Those with no or low pension entitlements will, in addition, receive a guaranteed pension. The minimum pension applies only to those with no pension entitlements at all, and the pension will exceed the minimum level even for those with very modest pension entitlements. In this example the guaranteed pension applies up to quite high wage levels, about 70 percent of the average wage, AW.

EFFECT OF POSTPONING RETIREMENT

As is illustrated in figure 4.2, the replacement rates in Norway's new pension scheme rise rapidly when retirement is postponed. For the case AW100 for the 1949 cohort, the replacement rate is about 36 percent for retirement at age 62 and 61 percent for retirement at age 70. If we take both the guaranteed and the income pension together, replacement

FIGURE 4.1 **Before-tax overall public pension (income and guaranteed pensions) as a percentage of the average wage**

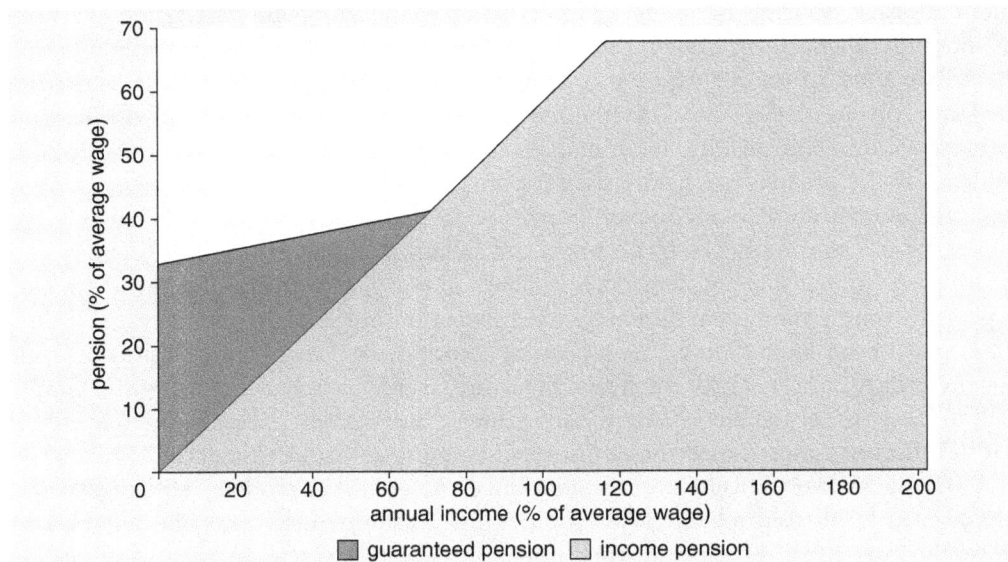

SOURCE: Authors' calculations from national data.

NOTE: The calculations assume a working career of 43 years and life expectancy of 83 years from the retirement age of 67.

FIGURE 4.2 **Before-tax overall public pension (income and guaranteed pensions) as a percentage of the average wage**

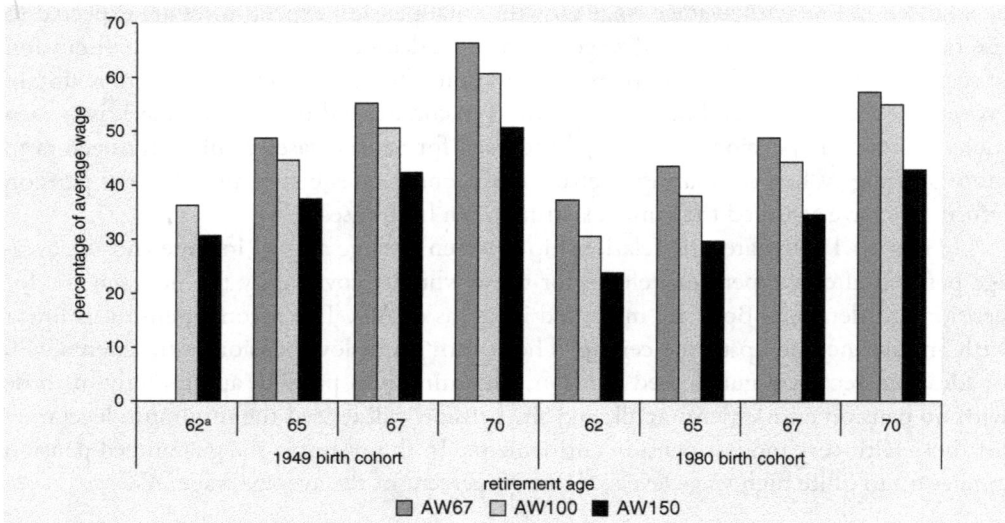

SOURCE: Authors' calculations from national data.

NOTE: The calculations assume a working career of 43 years, with retirement at age 67 and life expectancy of 84 years for persons born in 1949 and 87 years for persons born in 1980. AW100 indicates 100 percent of average wage, and so on.

[a] Conditions for retirement are not filled in this case.

rates decline as the average wage increases. The effect is similar regardless of cohort or retirement age and regardless of whether people are affected by the old or the new model for accumulating pension entitlements. This is the result of the distributive effects of the guaranteed pension and of the ceiling on annual pension-qualifying income. The replacement rates also decrease for younger cohorts owing to increasing life expectancy, given the assumption of a fixed age of 67 for claiming a benefit.

The effect of the life expectancy adjustment can also be illustrated by comparing replacement rates before and after the reform, as is done in table 4.1. The comparison is made for different earnings levels and for replacement rates at a retirement age of 67, which was the pension age before the reform. The life expectancy adjustment alone is expected to contribute to a reduction in pension levels, when the pension is drawn at age 67, of about 3 percent for the 1949 cohort and about 24 percent for the 1980 cohort. The new scheme for pension entitlements is somewhat more generous than the old scheme for a person working more than 40 years—the calculation in the table is based on 43 years. The cohort born in 1949 will have a pension according to the old entitlement rules, but for the cohort born in 1980, the new scheme for pension entitlements will offset almost half of the effect of the life expectancy adjustment. Furthermore, people can compensate for the effect of the life expectancy adjustment by postponing retirement.

People with no pension entitlements and those with very modest entitlements who are covered by the old scheme for accumulating pension entitlements are only able to draw the guaranteed pension starting at age 67. The guaranteed pension level will be adjusted according to expected remaining life expectancy at the age of retirement. The recipients of this pension can therefore, like other pensioners, obtain a higher annual pension by postponing retirement.

TABLE 4.1 **Replacement rates of the total old-age pension (including guaranteed pension) before taxes, for selected birth cohorts and earnings levels, before and after the reform**
percentage of average wage

	1949 cohort			1980 cohort		
	AW67	**AW100**	**AW150**	**AW67**	**AW100**	**AW150**
Before reform	56.8	52.0	43.5	56.2	51.2	38.8
After reform	55.1	50.5	42.3	48.7	44.2	34.4
Relative change	–2.9	–2.9	–2.9	–13.5	–13.7	–11.3

SOURCE: Authors' calculations from national data.

NOTE: AW = average wage. A retirement age of 67 is assumed. AW100 indicates earnings of 100 percent of average wage, and so on.

The guaranteed pension, when drawn at age 67, will constitute 32 percent of AW for the 1949 cohort. For the 1980 cohort, this figure is estimated to drop to 27 percent, as the guaranteed pension is indexed somewhat lower than average wage growth. Those who receive a guaranteed pension will in most cases pay no income tax. After taxes, the guaranteed pension is therefore estimated to constitute as much as 45 percent of AW for the 1949 cohort and 37 percent for the 1980 cohort.

Life expectancy adjustment will lead to higher annual pensions when retirement is postponed, but there will also be an effect from increased pension earnings. Table 4.2 illustrates the relative magnitude of these two effects for people covered by the new scheme for pension entitlements. Between ages 62 and 67, the real value of the annual pension will increase by about 7.5 percent for each year retirement is postponed. About two-thirds of this increase is attributable to the actuarial effect and about one-third to the pension earnings effect.

At higher ages, the actuarial effect will contribute even more for each year retirement is postponed. This is because postponing retirement one year reduces remaining life expectancy at the age of retirement relatively more when the person is already at a high age. When retirement is postponed from age 62 to age 75, the actuarial effect will contribute as much as four-fifths of the increase in annual pension.

If life expectancy evolves as in the "medium" alternative from Statistics Norway, it can be shown that people in general will have to work longer and postpone retirement by about one year for every 10 birth cohorts to compensate for this effect. The 1980 cohort is expected to have to postpone retirement by about four years to receive the same replacement rate as if life expectancy had remained unchanged after the reform.

OVERALL EFFECT, INCLUDING SUPPLEMENTARY PENSIONS

As has already been noted, since 2006, all Norwegian employees have accumulated entitlements to supplementary pensions. In addition, 70 to 80 percent of employees are covered by the AFP scheme when they approach retirement age. It is therefore useful to include these two types of pensions when calculating replacement rates to arrive at more realistic and complete replacement rates for large groups of the population. The cases in this section are based on a person who works in the private sector and is covered by the new AFP pension scheme. We assume that the person has contributed since 2006 to a private defined

TABLE 4.2 **Decomposition of the effect of postponing retirement on the replacement rate of the old-age pension for the 1963 birth cohort in the case AW100, by retirement age**
percentage of average wage

	62	67	70	75
Replacement rate when retiring at 62 years	33.7	33.7	33.7	33.7
Increase attributable to pension earnings after age 62	—	4.5	7.3	11.8
Increase attributable to actuarial effect	—	9.8	19.8	49.5
Total replacement rate	33.7	48.0	60.8	95.0

SOURCE: Authors' calculations from national data.

NOTE: — = not applicable, AW = average wage. A life expectancy of 85 years is assumed. AW100 indicates 100 percent of average wage.

contribution supplementary pension scheme at the same level as the minimum requirements.

In the long run, when people have been contributing to the supplementary pension for their total working career, the public old-age pension will constitute about two-thirds of the initial total pension in these examples. AFP and supplementary pension will each constitute about one-sixth. The assumption here is that payments of the supplementary pension are made for 10 years, whereas the AFP pension is paid out for the entire lifetime. The present value of the lifetime AFP pension will therefore be higher than for the mandatory supplementary pension at the minimum level in these examples.

Replacement rates without the pension reform are fairly similar for all cohorts and retirement ages, as shown in table 4.3. The rates are slightly higher for younger cohorts and for the highest retirement ages, but this is an effect of the supplementary pension. Since we have assumed that contributions to the supplementary pension started in 2006, the contribution period will be longer for younger people and for people who choose to postpone retirement. In reality, many people contributed to a supplementary pension scheme before it became mandatory in 2006, and in those cases, the difference between cohorts will be smaller or will disappear.

After the pension reform, the replacement rates will be highly dependent on retirement age, as a consequence of the adjustment of pensions in accordance with remaining life expectancy. Whereas the increase in replacement rates when retirement is postponed from age 62 to age 70 was only about 2 to 3 percentage points without the reform, the rates will increase by as much as 26 to 28 percentage points after the reform. In other words, the economic incentives to continue working and delay retirement will improve dramatically as a result of the reform both for those entitled to private sector AFP and for those not entitled to AFP. Increasing life expectancy will lead to lower old-age pensions at a given retirement age, but in the examples, this effect will be counteracted by increased supplementary pensions resulting from longer contribution periods.

As shown in table 4.4, when supplementary pensions and AFP are included, the pattern is still similar to that in figure 4.2, with replacement rates decreasing as the former wage level increases. This outcome is mainly a result of the distributive elements of the public old-age pension scheme. However, the ceiling on annual income for accrual of pension entitlements for the new income pension also applies to pension entitlements for the new AFP scheme in the private sector.

TABLE 4.3 **Replacement rates after taxes for case AW100 when AFP and supplementary pensions are included, by birth cohort and retirement age**
percentage of average wage

	1949 cohort				1980 cohort			
	62	65	67	70	62	65	67	70
Before reform	63.3	63.9	64.4	65.3	68.4	69.5	70.4	71.6
After reform	56.8	65.7	72.2	83.5	57.3	65.8	72.8	84.6

SOURCE: Authors' calculations from national data.

NOTE: AW = average wage. The calculations assume a life expectancy of 84 years for persons born in 1949 and 87 years for persons born in 1980. AW100 indicates 100 percent of average wage.

TABLE 4.4 **Replacement rates after taxes for selected wage levels, with AFP and supplementary pensions included, by birth cohort and retirement age**
percentage of average wage

	1949 cohort				1980 cohort			
Former wage level	62	65	67	70	62	65	67	70
AW67	—[a]	74.5	81.0	92.3	68.3	75.2	80.7	90.0
AW100	56.8	65.7	72.2	83.5	57.3	65.8	72.8	84.6
AW150	48.5	56.7	62.6	72.8	48.1	55.6	61.8	72.1

SOURCE: Authors' calculations from national data.

NOTE: AFP = Avtale Festet Pensjon, AW = average wage. The calculations assume a life expectancy of 84 years for persons born in 1949 and 87 years for persons born in 1980. AW100 indicates 100 percent of average wage, and so on.

a. Conditions for retirement are not fulfilled in this case.

At a retirement age of 70, the difference between the AW67 and the AW100 cases is quite small for the 1980 cohort. The reason is that the additional pension entitlements in the AW67 case are counteracted by an 80 percent reduction in the guaranteed pension. This implies that the incentives to work are somewhat weaker for low-income earners than for average and high-income earners, but they are still stronger than before the reform.

Because of the progressive tax structure and the special tax relief measures for pensioners, the replacement rates will be considerably higher after taxes than before taxes in all cases—typically, 10 to 15 percentage points higher. The tax relief measures for pensioners are targeted at low-income pensioners, and the differences in replacement rates between low-income and high-income pensioners are therefore higher after than before taxes.

Replacement rates clearly improve from postponing retirement under the new scheme, and this provides an incentive to work longer. Even though incentives to postpone retirement are substantially improved under the new system, a large percentage of the population is not affected by the new flexible pension rules based on actuarial adjustment of benefits. Of the population that reached age 67 in 2009, 41 percent had already retired on disability pension, and this group will in the future still be transferred to the old-age pension at age 67. This figure also includes people with a part-time disability pension, but most disability pensioners have drawn a full pension at age 67. In addition, 19 percent of the population is entitled to the public sector AFP scheme, which has not been reformed, and does not have actuarial adjustment of benefits. Public sector workers are also mostly not affected by the incentives to work longer.

The rest of the population (40 percent of the total) falls into two groups: 16 percent is entitled to the private sector AFP scheme, and the remaining 24 percent is not entitled to AFP. The incentives to work longer are mainly the same for these two groups because the private sector AFP scheme has been reformed in the same way as the public old-age pension scheme. Those without AFP are mostly people who work for private sector companies not covered by the AFP scheme, self-employed persons, or people who do not work at all.

Labor Supply and Sustainability

In the process of preparing a new pension system for Norway, various alternatives were assessed by analyzing their potential effects on average benefits, retirement age, pension expenditures, labor supply, and contribution rates. Statistics Norway's dynamic micro-simulation model MOSART (see Fredriksen 1998) has been used in these analyses to incorporate all the details in the pension system when evaluating the effects.

ADVANTAGES OF ANALYSIS BY MICROSIMULATION

As advocated by Orcutt, Merz, and Quinke (1986), a microsimulation approach is especially useful for policy analysis where different parts of the population may face different rules and where there may be substantial problems of aggregation in calculating the total effect on government budgets of changes in tax or pension systems. The main strength of microsimulation is that it can represent a socioeconomic system by a sample of decision units and then model the behavior of these units. Contrary to what is possible in a macroeconomic approach, detailed and complicated tax and benefit rules may be exactly reproduced. Aggregated numbers are obtained by multiplying the variable of interest for each unit by its sample weight and then summing up across the sample.

A dynamic microsimulation model is especially suitable for analyzing the mechanical effects of changes in the pension system on individual pension entitlements, benefits, and government pension expenditures. An obvious limitation is that behavioral effects may only be included in a simple way, and to incorporate general equilibrium effects, a macroeconomic approach is necessary, as has been worked out by Holmøy and Stensnes (2008). These authors also include the partial effects of a reduction in payroll taxes, compared with the reference scenario, that will be possible as a consequence of lower pension expenditures. However, the direct effects will always be of interest because they often constitute the most important elements, and they are used as a point of departure for the more comprehensive analyses.

From a representative sample of the population in a base year, the MOSART model simulates the future life course for each person in this initial population. The life course is simulated by possible transitions from one state to another, as determined by transition probabilities that depend on each person's characteristics. These transition probabilities are estimated from observed transitions in a recent period. Events included are migration, deaths, births, marriages, divorces, educational activities, retirement, and labor force participation. Public pension benefits are calculated from labor market earnings and other characteristics included in the simulation. Old-age pensions, disability pensions, survival pensions, and early retirement pensions are included in the model.

The analysis in this paper is mainly calibrated to the empirical picture of Norway in 2009, and the demographic assumptions are in accordance with Statistics Norway's demographic projections made in June 2010. In the "medium" demographic alternative, a fertility rate of 1.95 and net immigration decreasing from about 40,000 persons per year in 2009 to about 22,000 persons per year after 2016 imply modest growth in the size of the younger and middle-aged cohorts toward the end computation year 2050. As a result of the rather high immigration in the near future, in combination with further increases in life expectancy at birth of about six to seven years by 2050, the aggregate population is expected to increase.

LABOR SUPPLY EFFECTS

The Norwegian pension reform is expected to stimulate labor supply in two ways:

- A clearer connection between earlier labor incomes and accumulation of entitlements means an implicit reduction of marginal tax rates. As pointed out by Lindbeck and Persson (2003) and Lindbeck (2006), this change may stimulate persons of working age to work more.

- The actuarial design of the new system means a closer link between private incentives and the social costs of early retirement, which may stimulate people to postpone retirement.

Much uncertainty attends the quantification of the effects on labor supply of the Norwegian pension reform. A central finding in the empirical labor market literature, as pointed out by Blundell and MaCurdy (1999), is that the effects tend to be the strongest for retirement decisions. The illustrations in the preceding section of how replacement rates for typical cases increase when retirement is postponed show that the incentives may be strong. As a consequence, the labor supply effects of the reform are expected to be large on the extensive margin.

Smaller effects are expected among those of working age. Stensnes (2007) uses the MOSART model to compute the change in the present value of future pension benefits by exposing a cross-section of the model population to a small and transitory income shock in one specific period. The simulations indicate that the reform will reduce implicit marginal tax rates on labor incomes by about 5 percentage points, on average, as a result of a closer link between pension entitlements and former earnings. Use of a marginal compensated elasticity of about 0.5 from earlier empirical analyses yields a rough estimate of the increase in the supply of person-hours as a result of the reform of 2.5 percent. We assume that the effect on person-hours may be equally divided between an increase in the number of employed persons and average working hours of 1.25 percent each. Although this division of the effect for people of working age is a subject for discussion, it is of minor importance for the main effects of the reform.

In Norway, old-age retirement occurred within the age interval between ages 67 and 70 for the period 1973–2010, for all those who did not exit earlier with disability and early retirement rights. With no actuarial advantage to staying longer, most people participating in the labor market at age 67 have chosen historically to retire within a few months after reaching the age of 67. Therefore, it has only been possible to make a simple estimate of how retirement age might be affected by a shift toward a more actuarial pension system. Because early retirement carried no negative consequences for future pension benefits under the old early retirement scheme (AFP), that system favored early retirement. This is confirmed by empirical analyses by Hernæs, Sollie, and Strøm (2000); Røed and Haugen (2003); Hernæs and Iskhakov (2009); and Hernæs and Zhiyang (2009). Inclusion of actuarial adjustments in the new pension system is expected to have a considerable positive effect on the participation rates of elderly workers.

The estimation of the effect of retirement decisions on labor supply is documented in Fredriksen et al. (2005) and conforms very well to the empirical analyses above. For the approximately 30 percent of the labor force that is working in the private sector and is covered by early retirement schemes (AFP), average retirement age is estimated to increase by 1.2 years after an intermediate period. As a result of the wage negotiations in 2009, the old early retirement scheme for the 30 percent of the labor force working in the public sector continues to be in place. Employees in the public sector are thus only modestly affected by the reform. For the 40 percent of the labor force not covered by AFP, average retirement age is estimated to decrease by 0.3 years. Average retirement age for the three groups (private sector covered by AFP, public sector, and those in neither category) is estimated to increase by 0.24 years in 2015 before the effect of increased life expectancy is included. As a result of the life expectancy adjustment mechanism, retirement is expected to be postponed more when life expectancy increases.

Disability pensioners account for about 40 percent of the age 67 population. They will be transferred to the old-age pension scheme at an age set by the government—currently, 67 years. Retirement for employees in the public sector is also expected to be modestly affected by the increase in life expectancy. It is estimated that about 50 percent of the employed (the majority of whom work in the private sector) may, on average, postpone retirement by two-thirds of a year as life expectancy increases by one year. Because of increased entitlements from postponed retirement, this is almost sufficient to maintain the level of yearly pensions. The remaining 20 percent of the population is assumed to postpone retirement in line with the increase in life expectancy. For persons not disabled at age 62, average retirement age may increase by a half year as life expectancy increases by one year.

In sum, because of the actuarial nature of the benefits in the new system, the reform is expected to increase employment and reduce the number of old-age pensioners. Increasing life expectancy means that the effects become larger as time goes by, as illustrated in figure 4.3. Based on the estimated employment effects, by 2050 the total labor force is estimated to be 5.5 percent, or 180,000 persons, higher than it would have been in the old system, and the number of old-age pensioners (including early retirees) will decline by about the same number. More than 4 percent of the increase in the labor force compared with the old system is attributable to postponed retirement; the effect on people of working age is estimated at 1.25 percent. If the corresponding effect on working hours is included, total labor supply is estimated to increase by 6.8 percent.

FIGURE 4.3 **Projections of the labor force under the old and the new systems**
thousands of persons

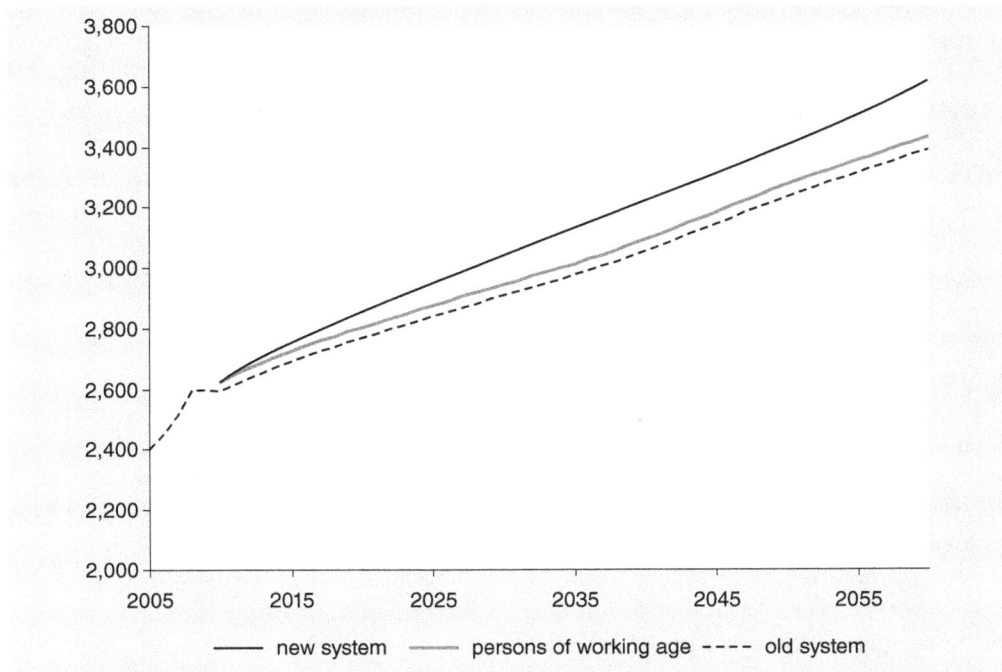

SOURCE: Statistics Norway.

SUSTAINABILITY

The expenditures of the public pension scheme are financed on a pay-as-you-go basis, and, as has been established above, pension contributions and expenditures are integrated components of the Norwegian state budget. Although payroll taxes and a pension premium on labor incomes are features of the Norwegian tax system that originally were intended to cover the total pension expenditures in the National Insurance System when it was introduced in 1967, the revenues from these taxes have been far from sufficient. This was also the case before the revenues from the petroleum sector made a positive net contribution to government budgets. However, because of the current low number of old-age pensioners compared with the size of the labor force, the present estimated contribution rate for old-age pensions is much lower than the accrual rate of 18.1 percent, and the actual costs will probably not correspond to this number before around 2040.

Norway's Government Pension Fund–Global (the successor to the Government Petroleum Fund) is a general public fund that is determined by petroleum revenues, returns from the global financial markets, and a fiscal rule stating that the deficit in the ordinary government budget should, on average, correspond to a real return stipulated as 4 percent of the fund. Although the fund is not directly related to the pension system, the large petroleum revenues and the fiscal rule render public finances in Norway very favorable compared with those in other OECD countries. The net worth for the government sector, which mainly consists of the capital in the Government Pension Fund–Global, is estimated to reach 156 percent of GDP by the end of 2012.

As is shown in figure 4.4, the number of persons in the labor force relative to the number of old-age and disability pensioners is expected to decrease from 2.6 in 2010 to about 1.7 in 2060 under the assumptions from the old pension system and using the "medium" demographic assumptions from 2010. The increasing dependency ratio is partly caused by higher life expectancy, but an even more important factor is that the large cohorts of persons born just after World War II will retire in the current decade, replacing rather small cohorts of pensioners born between the two world wars. As a result of postponed retirement and slightly higher participation rates under the new pension system, the decline in the ratio between persons in the labor force and number of pensioners may be reduced, leading to an estimate of about 2.0 in 2060.

Under the "aging" alternative scenario based on higher growth in life expectancy, falling fertility, and low net immigration, the ratio between the labor force and the number of pensioners may fall to 1.7 in 2060 even with the new system. Under the assumptions behind the "young" scenario, the ratio may only be reduced to 2.3. The main discrepancy between the different demographic alternatives stems from the great uncertainty about the size of immigration. Immigrants to Norway are rather young, and their numbers have increased significantly during recent years owing to a tight labor market in Norway and the enlargement of the European Union to include Eastern European countries. In the projections, labor market participation rates for immigrants are assumed to be lower than for Norwegians of the same age and gender.

FIGURE 4.4 **Ratio of the number of persons in the labor force to the number of old-age and disability pensioners, projected under different demographic scenarios and for the new and old pension systems**

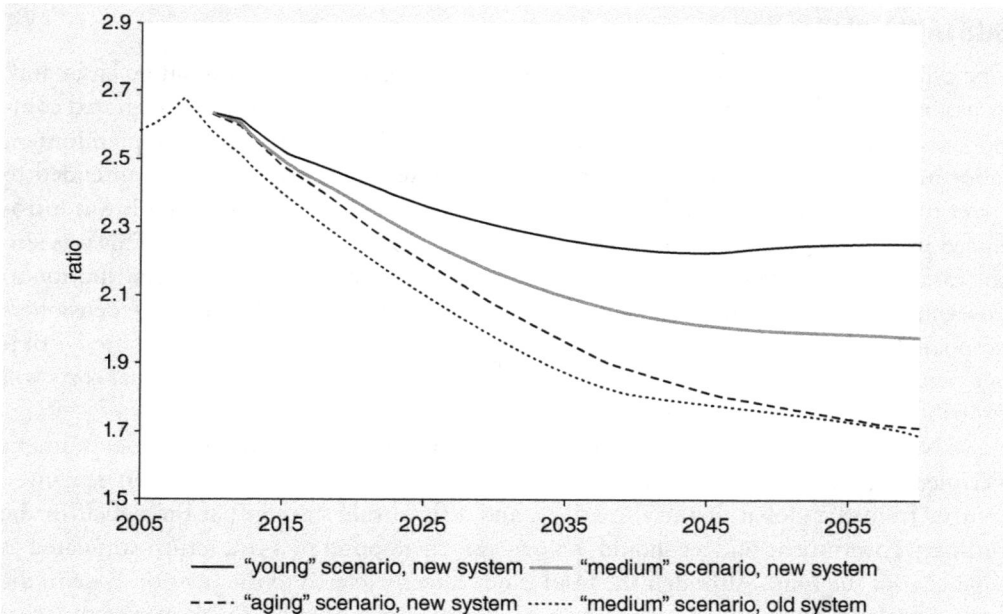

SOURCE: Statistics Norway.

In a pay-as-you-go system, in which public pension expenditures are financed by current tax revenues, the ratio of the number of workers to the number of pensioners has a significant impact on the fiscal balance sheet. One measure of the fiscal burden of the public pension scheme is the contribution rate, defined by Disney (2004) as "the average rate [on earnings] that would be required to finance current spending on public pensions without budgetary transfers or the accumulation or decumulation of public pension funds." Under the standard pay-as-you-go formula, the contribution rate (*CR*) may be calculated as the ratio of public pension payments (*PP*) to labor income (*LI*). Gross pensions are taxed in Norway, but more leniently than labor incomes, and therefore an appropriate contribution rate most in accordance with the Disney definition may formally be calculated as

$$CR = \frac{PP}{(LI + \gamma * PP)}.$$

The right-hand numerator represents nominal public pension expenditures, and the denominator is the relevant tax base. The parameter γ represents the more lenient taxation of pension incomes compared with labor incomes and is estimated at about 50 percent under the current tax regime. The contribution rate can be interpreted as the tax rate sufficient to finance pension expenditures, assuming that the entire tax burden falls on labor and pension incomes. Calculation of alternative contribution rates without correction for taxation of pension benefits would be of minor importance for discussing the effects of the reform

The estimated contribution rates for old-age pension expenditures in the National Insurance System, under the old and new systems and using different assumptions regarding growth in life expectancy, are shown in figure 4.5. If the old system had been maintained, the estimated contribution rate for old-age pension expenditures would have more than doubled, from 10.7 percent in 2010 to 20.8 percent in 2050. Because of the advantageous ratio between the number of employed and the number of old-age pensioners, the present contribution rate is much smaller than the accumulation of pension entitlements of 18.1 percent in the more NDC-like new system. Even in the long run, under the new system the contribution rate necessary to finance the payment of old-age pensions is lower because gross pensions are taxed in Norway and are thus included in the denominator in the definition above. Furthermore, income above the ceiling is included in the contribution rate but does not confer pension entitlements. Financing of the guaranteed pension for people with low income and entitlements for child care, however, works in the opposite direction, by raising the tax rate needed.

As shown by Stensnes and Stølen (2007), the life expectancy adjustment is the main tightening element of the new system. This is also evident from figure 4.5; assumptions about higher life expectancy yield only a modest increase in the contribution rate under the new system, compared with the old. Lower indexing of pension benefits than wage growth after the age of retirement also reduces future old-age pension expenditures, whereas a more generous model for earning pension entitlements works in the opposite direction.

Pension expenditures will continue to increase in relative terms in the coming decades, partly because the baby-boom generation born after World War II will be reaching retirement. Even under the new system, the contribution rate for old-age pension

FIGURE 4.5 **Estimated contribution rates for old-age pension expenditures under the old and new systems and with different assumptions regarding growth in life expectancy**
percent

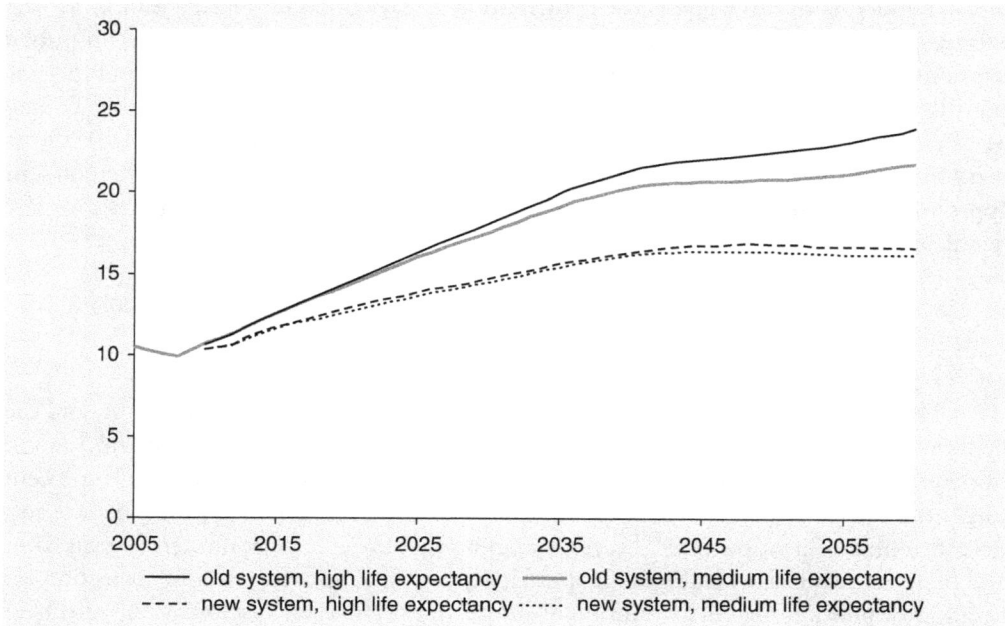

SOURCE: Statistics Norway.

expenditures is estimated to increase to 16.4 percent by 2050. After 2050, a fertility rate of 1.95 in the "medium" alternative for demographic projections, in combination with net immigration and adjustments of pension benefits for further growth in life expectancy under the new system, implies an almost constant contribution rate for old-age pension expenditures.

When claims on future benefits are not collaterized with real capital (Börsch-Supan's criteria 4 for NDC systems), and old-age pension expenditures are under pay-as-you-go financing, as part of general public finances, an isolated discussion about sustainability of the pension system is not of major importance. In Norway, actual contribution rates for old-age pension expenditures will have to rise in coming years, when the relative size of the old-age cohorts compared with working-age cohorts increases from a relative low number. To ensure sustainability in public finances, Norwegian politicians will then have to decide whether the corresponding growth in expenditures should be met by higher taxes or by a tightening of other public expenses.

Distributional Effects

Although the new model for accrual of pension entitlements means a closer connection between former labor incomes and pension benefits, important distributional elements remain. The guaranteed pension; the ceiling of 7.1 basic units for accrual of pension entitlements, while collecting contributions on earnings above the ceiling; and the accrual of pension entitlements for unpaid child care and for military conscripts are the most important elements. As a result, even under the new system, old-age pension benefits are more equally distributed than are former labor incomes. Because the closer link between former earnings and accrual of pension entitlements leads to smaller redistribution effects than under the old system, these effects have been important parts of the discussion about the design of the new system. By using the MOSART model to consider the distribution of benefits between individuals, we move beyond the stylized calculations presented above. The microsimulation approach permits a more accurate description of the distributional consequences of the pension reform, and the model may be used to show behavioral and other effects before and after reform.

It is, however, convenient to restrict the distributional analysis to the consideration of pension benefits, leaving aside how the pension premiums paid by the employed are distributed among individuals. In Norway, old-age pensions are fully integrated into general tax revenues and expenditures within the government budget. The pension reform will permit lower taxes or higher public expenditures, or both, in the future than if the old system had been maintained, and that is likely to have distributional consequences, depending on how politicians choose to meet imbalances. These consequences are excluded from our analysis because their inclusion would necessitate speculative assumptions about future policy decisions.

To focus on the distributional effects from the model for accrual of entitlements as presented in figure 4.6, one can conveniently look away from indexation and the actuarial adjustment through the flexible pension scheme. The reformed system replaces an almost fixed retirement age of 67 with an individual retirement choice from age 62 on. If we include labor supply effects, changes in annual pensions will be a poor approximation for changes in welfare because they will also reflect voluntary shifts in retirement ages.

In the figure, the annual pension benefit under the old and new systems is broken down by pension income percentiles in 2050. A more favorable model for accrual of entitlements (before taking into account the lower indexing of benefits than of wage growth and the adjustments for increasing life expectancy) means that nobody seems to lose, given these assumptions. Because adjustments for life expectancy and indexation are the cost cutters of the reform, whereas the system for accumulation of entitlements partially increases expenditures, figure 4.6 gives a good indication of distributional consequences, but it is misleading regarding the level of entitlements and also from a fiscal perspective.

For the bottom two deciles, pension levels will improve somewhat. This is mainly because the old system applies 100 percent means testing of the special supplement against the income-based pension, whereas the guaranteed pension in the new system is means tested against the income pension at only 80 percent. As a consequence, almost no minimum-benefit pensioners are left when pensioners with entitlements from the old system are all dead. However, after about 2020, the fall in the share of minimum-benefit pensioners may be more than counteracted by an increasing share of pensioners who receive a partial guaranteed supplement under the new system.

The pension level for old-age pensioners between the second and fifth deciles is almost unaffected by the reform before taking into account the lower indexing of benefits in relation to wage growth and the life expectancy adjustments. Elements of the modification of the accrual model seem to counteract each other. The top five pension income deciles will experience an increase in the pension level, reflecting both the increased accrual

FIGURE 4.6 **Estimated pension benefits in 2050, by pension income percentile**

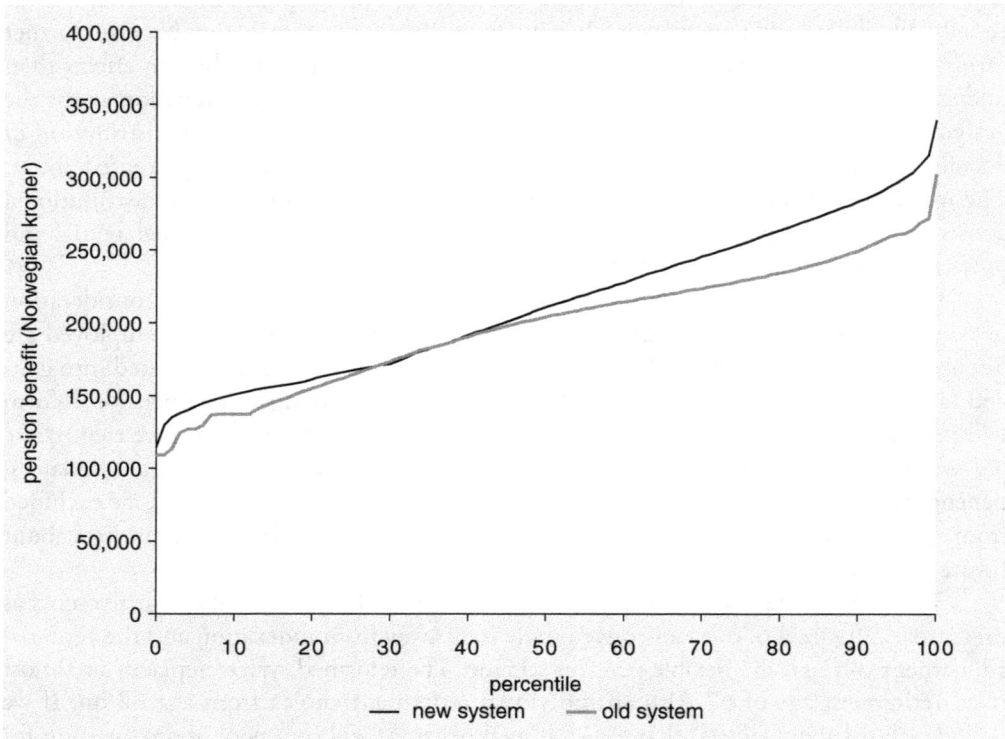

SOURCE: Statistics Norway.

NOTE: Benefits are shown for a constant 2008 wage level before indexation and before exposure to the life expectancy adjustment divisor.

coefficient for pension entitlements and the sharpened actuarial properties of the system in general. The gains are largest for the highest income groups.

Overall distributional effects from the public old-age pension system, including behavioral effects, are shown in figure 4.7, which presents total old-age pension benefits according to the corresponding total lifetime earnings, by income group and by gender. The comparison is based on the simulated earnings over the life cycle of persons born during the 1990s and is illustrated for the old and new pension systems. For the earlier disabled, we have calculated lifetime earnings as the incomes they could have earned, assuming that they had continued to work until age 67 with the same relative income as when they became disabled.

Along the *x*-axis, we measure lifetime labor market earnings in average yearly wages. In each panel, the depicted points show the average lifetime earnings for different deciles and the corresponding old-age benefits received relative to these earnings. Because women earn less than men, the points for females are to the left of the points for males for the corresponding deciles, except for the lowest. The points for the new system are to the right of the corresponding points for the old system as a consequence of assumptions about increased labor supply as a result of the reform, particularly because of postponed retirement.

FIGURE 4.7 **Ratio of total old-age pension benefits to total lifetime earnings, by gender and under the new and old systems**

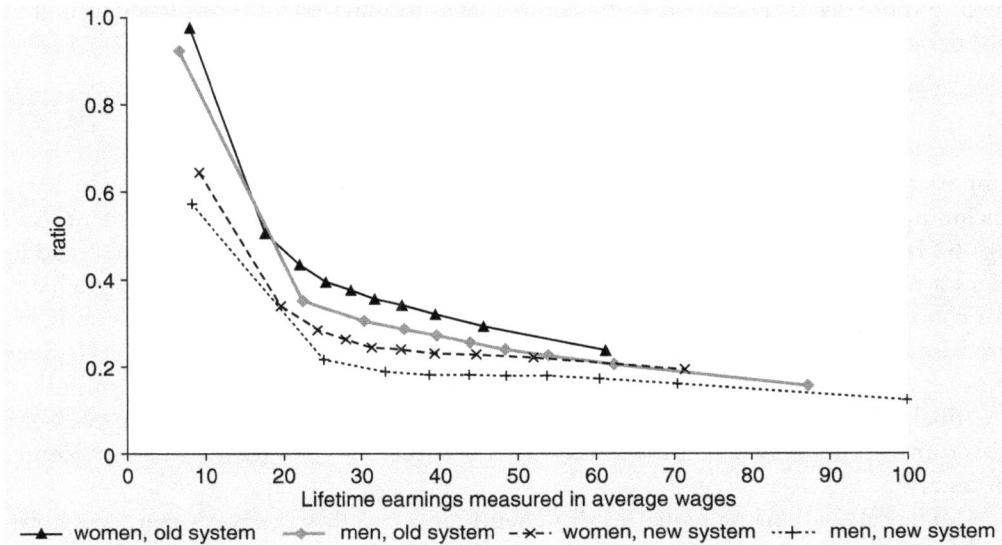

SOURCE: Statistics Norway.

NOTE: Benefits are shown for a constant 2008 wage level.

People with the highest incomes (and educational levels) are assumed to postpone retirement longest, and men are assumed to delay retirement more than women. Under the new system, the highest male decile during the working period earns, on average, 100 average yearly wages. The first decile, on average, earns only about 7 average yearly wages, probably because those persons have had only a few years of work in their working lives, and the immigrants among them may have worked only a few years in Norway. Because of the minimum pension, under the old system the total old-age pension for the lowest decile is of the same magnitude as total lifetime earnings. For the highest decile of men, total benefits constitute only 16 percent of their lifetime earnings under the old system. It is evident that the public old-age pension system to a large degree redistributes incomes from persons with high earnings to persons with low earnings, and from men to women. Aside from the minimum or guaranteed pension, the ceiling for yearly earnings is the main distributional element.

The large fall in average old-age pensions compared with lifetime earnings in the lower deciles under the new system is caused by a drop in average pensions for the earlier disabled in relation to wages resulting from the life expectancy adjustment after the disabled are transferred to old-age pensions at a fixed age of 67. Because the decision made in 2011 on a more generous life expectancy adjustment for persons making a transition from a disability benefit to an old-age benefit at age 67 has not been taken into consideration in the calculations underlying the figure, the drop in average pensions for the lower deciles is somewhat exaggerated.

Compared with the effects outlined above, the pension reform is of minor importance for redistribution from men to women, and women benefit from the redistribution caused by the guaranteed pension and the ceiling in the module for accrual of entitlements. Women in the lower deciles lose, on average, less from the pension reform than men in those deciles because they are compensated to some extent by a higher accrual of entitlements for time spent in unpaid child care.

Conclusion

Important elements in the Norwegian pension reform were introduced beginning in 2011, including adjustment of pensions for changes in life expectancy, flexible retirement from age 62 based on actuarial neutrality, and new rules for indexation of pensions. In addition, a new model for accumulating pension entitlements will be introduced gradually for cohorts born after 1954 and fully for cohorts born after 1963. Future pension rights are based on an amount corresponding to 18.1 percent of earnings from work. The new Norwegian scheme is only quasi-NDC in the sense that there is no mechanism linking the final balance with the demographic and macroeconomic environment. Instead, the government budget will be used as the shock absorber, to the extent that this becomes necessary.

The calculations presented in this chapter indicate that Norway's pension reform will lead to a strong improvement in economic incentives to continue working and to delay retirement, in comparison with the old system. Postponing retirement by one year will typically increase the annual old-age pension by about 7.5 percent. About two-thirds of this effect is attributable to the actuarial adjustment and about one-third, to the accumulation of additional pension entitlements in the new system. These incentives, however, only apply to a part of the population; about 40 percent of Norwegians retire on disability pension before age 67, and this group is mainly unaffected by the economic incentives of the reform. Public sector employees are also not fully affected by the incentives because of the AFP early retirement plan for the 62–66 age group. The public sector AFP scheme, which has poor work incentives, will remain largely unchanged in the near future.

Life expectancy adjustment will lower pensions at a given retirement age if life expectancy continues to increase. Given mortality projections from Statistics Norway, we find that future generations must postpone retirement by about one year for every 10 birth cohorts to fully compensate for this effect.

Without the pension reform, the ratio of the number of workers to the number of old-age and disability pensioners could be expected to decrease from 2.7 in 2008 to about 1.8 in 2050. Together with increasing replacement rates as a consequence of the maturing of the old system, this development would have caused the financial burden of the old system to double between 2008 and 2050.

Under the new system, the contribution rate, interpreted as the tax rate sufficient to finance future old-age pension expenditures, may be limited to 16.4 percent by 2050, compared to 10.7 percent in 2010. The life expectancy adjustment is the main tightening element of the new system. Lower indexing of pension benefits compared to wage growth after the age of retirement also reduces future old-age pension expenditures. In contrast, a more generous model for earning pension entitlements works in the opposite direction. Pension expenditures will continue to increase in relative terms in the coming decades, partly because of the effect of the baby-boom generation that was born after World War II and is now reaching retirement.

The new model for accrual of pension entitlements implies a closer link between earnings from work and pension benefits. If distributional effects are compared without taking into account adjustments for increasing life expectancy and lower indexing of benefits, persons with high incomes and long working careers seem to gain from the reform. However, a means-tested guaranteed pension and a ceiling on annual income for accrual of pension entitlements provide two important distributional elements. Strong redistribution of income from persons with high earnings to persons with low earnings, and from men to women, is therefore maintained after the reform.

Note

1. The old National Insurance Scheme used as its measurement unit what was called the basic amount. In 2010, when the average wage for a full-time employee in Norway was about 455,000 Norwegian kroner, one basic amount was equivalent to 74,721 kroner, on average. The average wage level was thus about 6.1 basic amounts, and the ceiling on pension earnings was approximately 115 percent of an average wage. The basic amount is adjusted annually in line with wage growth.

References

Blundell, Richard W., and Thomas MaCurdy. 1999. "Labor Supply: A Review of Alternative Approaches." In *Handbook of Labor Economics,* vol. 3A, ed. Orley C. Ashenfelter and David Card, 1559–1695. Amsterdam: Elsevier Science.

Börsch-Supan, Axel H. 2006. "What Are NDC Pension Systems? What Do They Bring to Reform Strategies?" In *Pension Reform: Issues and Prospects for Non-Financial Defined Contribution (NDC) Schemes*, ed. Robert Holzmann and Edward Palmer, 35–56. Washington, DC: World Bank.

Disney, Richard. 2004. "Are Contributions to Public Pension Programmes a Tax on Employment?" *Economic Policy* 19 (39, July): 267–311.

Fredriksen, Dennis. 1998. *Projections of Population, Education, Labour Supply and Public Pension Benefits: Analyses with the Dynamic Micro-Simulation Model MOSART.* Social and Economic Studies 101. Oslo: Statistics Norway.

Fredriksen, Dennis, Kim Massey Heide, Erling Holmøy, and Ingeborg Foldøy. 2005. *Makroøkonomiske virkninger av pensjonsreformer* [Macroeconomic effects from pension reforms]. Report 2005/2. Oslo: Statistics Norway.

Hernæs, Erik, and Fedor Iskhakov. 2009. *Effekter på arbeidstilbudet av pensjonsreformen* [Effects of the Norwegian pension reform on labor supply]. Report 3/2009. Oslo: Frisch Centre.

Hernæs, Erik, Marte Sollie, and Steinar Strøm. 2000. "Early Retirements and Economic Incentives." *Scandinavian Journal of Economics* 102 (3): 481–502.

Hernæs, Erik, and Jia Zhiyang. 2009. "Labour Supply Response of a Retirement Earnings Test Reform." Memorandum 25/2009, Frisch Centre, Oslo.

Holmøy, Erling, and Kyrre Stensnes. 2008. "Will the Norwegian Pension Reform Reach Its Goals? An Integrated Micro-Macro Assessment." Discussion Paper 557, Research Department, Statistics Norway, Oslo.

Lindbeck, Assar. 2006. "Sustainable Social Spending." *International Tax and Public Finance* 13 (4): 303–24.

Lindbeck, Assar, and Mats Persson. 2003. "The Gains from Pension Reform." *Journal of Economic Literature* 41 (March): 74–112.

Norway, Ministry of Labor. 2011. "Prop. 130 L (2010–2011) Proposisjon til Stortinget (forslag til lovvedtak) Endringer i folketrygdloven (ny uføretrygd og alderspensjon til uføre)" [White Paper forwarded to the Parliament 27 May 2011, Amendments to the National Insurance Act (New disability benefits and old-age pension for disabled)]. Ministry of Labor, Oslo.

Norway, Ministry of Labor and Social Inclusion. 2006. "St. Meld. Nr. 5 (2006–2007) Opptjening og uttak av alderspensjon i folketrygden" [Report No. 5 to the Parliament (2006–2007) Earning and drawing old-age pension from the National Insurance Scheme]. Ministry of Labor and Social Inclusion, Oslo.

———. 2009. "Ot. Prp. Nr. 37 (2008–2009) Om lov om endringer i folketrygdloven (ny alderspensjon)" [White Paper forwarded to the Parliament 13 February 2009: Amendments to the National Insurance Act (New Old-Age Pension)]. Ministry of Labor and Social Inclusion, Oslo.

Norway, Ministry of Finance and Ministry of Social Affairs. 2004. "Modernisert folketrygd: Bærekraftig pensjon for framtida" [A modernized national insurance scheme: Sustainable pensions for the future]. Ministry of Finance and Ministry of Social Affairs, Oslo.

Orcutt, Guy H., Joachim Merz, and Hermann Quinke, eds. 1986. *Microanalytic Simulation Models to Support Social and Financial Policy.* New York: North-Holland.

Røed, Knut, and Fredrik Haugen. 2003. "Early Retirement and Economic Incentives: Evidence from a Quasi-Natural Experiment." *Labour* 17 (2): 203–28.

Stensnes, Kyrre. 2007. "Equity versus Efficiency in Public Pension Schemes: Microsimulating the Trade-off." Discussion Paper 515, Research Department, Statistics Norway, Oslo.

Stensnes, Kyrre, and Nils Martin Stølen. 2007. "Pension Reform in Norway: Microsimulating Effects on Government Expenditures, Labour Supply Incentives and Benefit Distribution." Discussion Paper 524, Research Department, Statistics Norway, Oslo.

Tarmo Valkonen

The recent pension reforms in Nordic countries are similar in many ways. The forerunner was Sweden, which introduced a nonfinancial (notional) defined contribution (NDC) scheme. Finland and Norway copied from Sweden's system such features as the accumulation of pension entitlements on the basis of lifetime earnings, flexible retirement based on actuarial neutrality at the margin, and adjustment of monthly pensions for life expectancy. All the old systems rewarded early retirement, and their links between earnings and pensions were weak. Redistributive elements were often arbitrary. Moreover, the pension systems were deemed to be financially unsustainable because of the aging of the population. The outcome of the reforms is expected to be higher labor supply during the working years, later retirement, and lower expenditure. But only the Swedish NDC is designed to be financially and politically sustainable in the long term.

Chapter 4, by Christensen, Fredriksen, Lien, and Stølen, provides a detailed description of the recent Norwegian pension reform and assesses its influence on redistribution, working incentives, and sustainability. The main redistributive elements are the flat guaranteed pension, which is reduced by 80 percent when income pension increases, and the low income ceiling applied on accrual of the income pension. Progressive income taxation fortifies the redistribution from high-income to low-income people.

It is instructive to discuss separately the incentives on marginal labor supply and retirement. The incentives to work more hours or to earn higher wages are weakened mainly by the redistributive elements described above. Their influence is well presented in figure 4.1 in chapter 4. The link between wage income and pension benefits is strong only for those workers whose wage is close to the average. The incentives created by the new life expectancy adjustment vary among birth cohorts, but the adjustment is expected to cut the pensions of current middle-aged workers more than their contributions.

The reform abolished some incentives to retire early, but by their very nature, the new actuarial rules certainly do not encourage later retirement. Furthermore, these new rules apply only to part of the population. Public sector workers still retain their old early retirement scheme, which pays an extra pension when a person retires between the ages of 62 and 66. The eligibility rules for disability pensions are such that 40 percent of pensioners have left the labor force prior to age 67 using this route. Pensions are taxed at lower rates than wages, which further spurs early retirement. The authors describe the improvement in incentives as dramatic but project that the average retirement age will increase by only 0.24 years by 2015.

Social security contribution revenues are not high enough to finance pensions even now, when the old-age dependency ratio is low. The life expectancy adjustment markedly limits the future increase in pension expenditures if projections of longer lifetimes are realized. Generational account analysis shows, however, that the government's fiscal gaps are

---

Tarmo Valkonen is research director at the Research Institute of the Finnish Economy (ETLA).

large even after the implementation of pension reform (Hagist et al. 2011). That study estimates that total tax revenues must be increased permanently by 5 to 12 percent. There is no agreement on how the future increase in the pension expenditure will be financed, and political risks for a new pension reform remain. An important aspect of any incentive scheme is whether it can be trusted.

The government combined the existing social security fund and the Government Petroleum Fund into a new Government Pension Fund. This operation did not improve the sustainability of the general government, and no link between pension expenditure and the use of the new fund was established.

The reform influences the contributions paid and the pension benefits received in a complicated way, depending on, among other things, whether the individual works in the private or public sector, the individual's birth cohort and life expectancy, the wage earned, and whether the person's lifetime earnings profile is flat or rising. For example, current middle-aged, well-educated individuals are likely to lose from the lifetime calculation of entitlements and the life expectancy adjustment and to gain less from the improved incentives resulting from the ceiling on accruals.

The authors address the redistributive outcomes by presenting replacement rate calculations and results from the microsimulation model MOSART. Their table 4.1 shows that the reductions in the replacement rates of old-age pensions are small and are of the same magnitude for low- and high-income groups. The MOSART results presented in their figure 4.6 indicate that almost all income percentiles have larger pension benefits in 2050 but that the highest-income groups gain most. These simulations do not consider changes in behavior, the impact on premiums, new indexation, or the life expectancy adjustment. Another calculation, presented in figure 4.7, shows the total effects of the reform on the pension benefits of the cohort born in 1990. Lifetime pensions are proportional to lifetime earnings. Now, all income groups lose and the losses are largest for the low-income groups. The calculation includes life expectancy adjustments and the assumed increase in the labor supply.

These apparently conflicting results raise many questions, even though they are explained in detail. Moreover, intra- and intergenerational assessments of redistribution are only partial if they are measured without considering the changes in the contribution rate and the complicated interaction between progressive taxation and the pension system. For example, the deductibility of pension contributions in the progressive income tax structure influences both redistribution and incentives.

The reform is estimated to increase the retirement age by about four months, if the influence of the life expectancy adjustment is excluded. The authors assume that for persons not disabled at age 62, the average retirement age increases by a half year as life expectancy increases by one year. Total labor supply is expected to be 6.8 percent higher in 2050, mainly because of the assumed strong link between smaller monthly pensions and the retirement decision. Another noteworthy point is that the assumed increase in the retirement age does not improve the long-term financial sustainability of the pension system, even though it increases government revenue.

Simulation analysis of the corresponding Finnish reform suggests that the increase in the labor supply resulting from a life expectancy adjustment may be surprisingly small (Lassila and Valkonen 2008). The adjustment creates conflicting incentives: implementation of the reform reduces the additional pension benefit gained by a marginal increase in the labor supply but also yields a higher net wage because of lower contributions. Moreover, forward-looking individuals have no reason to react to the negative income effect created by the life expectancy adjustment simply by postponing retirement.

One of the main aims of the reform was to change the behavior of individuals, but the methods applied by the authors of chapter 4 are insufficient to analyze whether this really takes place. It is difficult to analyze changes in lifetime labor supply and retirement age without a numerical life-cycle model. If one wants to study welfare effects, including the value of leisure, use of the model is unavoidable. If this feature is not taken into account, an increase in the retirement age would always be the most preferable policy. A stochastic version of the model can provide distributional outcomes. An even more ambitious approach is to use a numerical overlapping-generations model that traces the life cycles of people born at different times and aggregates the outcomes using demographic data.

The authors of chapter 4 compare the elements of the reform to the criteria for an NDC system listed by Börsch-Supan (2006). The comparison shows that the new system is still based on a defined benefit principle, which allocates the macroeconomic and demographic risks (except the longevity risk) to current young and future taxpayers.

To sum up, the trade-off between working incentives and redistribution is improved after the reform because the redistribution is now less arbitrary. But the basic conflict still exists, and the political choice in Norway has been to emphasize redistribution at the cost of efficiency. The authors suggest that there will be a strong increase in the retirement age as a result of the introduction of the life expectancy adjustment. This is an assumption rather than the result of a profound analysis. There is also still uncertainty concerning how financial sustainability of the system will be restored, and this uncertainty will affect political discussions and individual provision for old age until it is resolved.

References

Börsch-Supan, Axel H. 2006. "What Are NDC Pension Systems? What Do They Bring to Reform Strategies?" In *Pension Reform: Issues and Prospects for Non-Financial Defined Contribution (NDC) Schemes*, ed. Robert Holzmann and Edward Palmer, 35–56. Washington, DC: World Bank.

Hagist, Christian, Bernd Raffelhüschen, Alf Erling Risa, and Erling Vårdal. 2011."Long-Term Fiscal Effects of Public Pension Reform in Norway: A Generational Accounting Analysis." Discussion Paper 49, Research Center for Generational Contracts, University of Freiburg, Germany.

Lassila, Jukka, and Tarmo Valkonen. 2008. "Longevity Adjustment of Pension Benefits." In *Uncertain Demographics and Fiscal Sustainability*, ed. Juha M. Alho, Svend E. Hougaard Jensen, and Jukka Lassila, 137–60. Cambridge, U.K.: Cambridge University Press.

Egypt's New Social Insurance System: An NDC Reform in an Emerging Economy

Mohamed Maait and Gustavo Demarco

The Arab Republic of Egypt operates one of the most expensive social insurance and pension systems in the Middle East and North Africa region. Contribution rates for old age, disability, survivors', health, work injury, and unemployment insurance absorb 41 percent of the payroll. Nevertheless, poor and often negative real returns on investments and inappropriate use of the available reserves have imposed on the country's Treasury a burden of ad hoc support to the system, to finance deficits, annual pension increases, and special benefits. In addition, the weak link between contributions and benefits provides little incentive to pay into the system's defined benefit (DB) scheme, in which pensions are based only on final salary. As a result, the system is not financially sustainable, and financial projections indicate increasing deterioration in the medium-to-long term.

The system has not only failed to provide an adequate living standard for pensioners and their survivors but has also fallen short of many of its other objectives. The government recognizes the need for a reform that can align the social insurance and pension system with current and future economic, demographic, and social realities and so enable it to support future growth instead of becoming an unbearable burden on the Egyptian economy and the Treasury. It was against this backdrop that a reform law was enacted by the parliament in June 2010.

The reformed system will be mandatory for new entrants to the labor market and voluntary for current workers, starting from July 2013.[1] The current pension system will continue operating on a defined benefit basis for those current members who choose not to transfer to the new system. This means that it will take about 75 years for all living birth cohorts to be covered by the new pension system rules. The new pension system combines a defined contribution (DC) component and a redistributive, noncontributory component. The transition is partial in the sense that it is only applicable to old-age and end-of-service indemnity benefits. Coverage for unemployment, work injuries, survivorship, and disability prior to reaching the retirement age is still based on defined benefit rules and includes minimum guaranteed benefits determined by law.

Mohamed Maait is deputy minister of finance in the Egyptian government, head of the Egyptian Government Actuarial Department (EGAD), and vice chairman of the National Organization for Social Insurance (NOSI)–Egypt. Gustavo Demarco is lead economist in the Middle East and North Africa Region of the World Bank.

The new pension model adopted is based on the principle that multipillar schemes serve multiple objectives—sustainability, transparency, efficiency, and solidarity. To achieve these goals, it combines nonfinancial (notional) defined contribution (NDC) and financial defined contribution (FDC) schemes—the latter with central administration of funds but with decentralized fund management.[2]

Although the criteria adopted to define the parameters of the NDC component in Egypt are relatively consistent with current international experience, the small number of cases and brief histories available do not provide conclusive evidence of best practices, and benchmarks are still only indicative. Implementation, regulation, and institutional capacity building in Egypt will demand increasing effort in the near future. With regard to the FDC component, the main challenges are associated with the very limited experience with managing and investing the assets to fulfill the dual goal of maximizing returns and minimizing risk.

Background of the Reform

Egypt's current social insurance and pension system was created more than 50 years ago to administer old-age, disability, and survivors' pensions; work injury, unemployment, sickness, and maternity benefits; and various forms of cash transfers. It is regarded as one of the most comprehensive social insurance and pension systems, not only in Africa, but also among all Arab and developing countries. In fact, almost 9 of every 10 economically active Egyptians, including casual and seasonal workers, are legally covered by one of the pension schemes within the system.[3] The legal framework has generally satisfied several of the criteria for a good social insurance system, such as redistribution, fairness, certainty, adequacy, and coverage.

The current system is administered by the National Organization for Social Insurance (NOSI) through two separate funds: the Government Social Insurance Fund (GSIF), which covers government workers (civil servants, the armed forces, and security personnel), and the Public and Private Social Insurance Fund (PSIF), for workers in public and private enterprises, self-employed persons, casual workers, and (on a voluntary basis) Egyptians working abroad.[4]

A number of programs, mostly administered by or under the supervision of the Ministry of Finance or the Ministry of Social Solidarity, provide social assistance to the poor who do not fall within the scope of the social insurance schemes. These and other developments of the Egyptian social insurance system reflect the importance that the government of Egypt has accorded social protection.

The system, however, is regarded as one of the most expensive in the region. Its contribution rates are equivalent to 41 percent of the payroll, with 26 percent paid by employers, 14 percent by employees, and 1 percent by the Treasury. Even though coverage extends to about 26 million members, representing 33 percent of the Egyptian population, there are significant differences between legal coverage and effective coverage, particularly for casual, seasonal, and rural workers and in the case of unemployment insurance. Demographic, economic, and social trends since the 1970s have affected the financial situation of the social insurance and pension system. In addition, the system's structure faces internal problems, such as high levels of evasion—a consequence of the high contribution rate—and a very low actual replacement rate in relation to the total salary received before retirement. The high contribution rates lead both employers and employees to escape from enrolling in the system and to become part of the informal sector, which currently exceeds 14 million workers. The absence of a direct link between the value of the contributions collected and the value of the benefits paid[5] has contributed significantly to the high level of contribution evasion.

The current defined benefit programs have a replacement target of 80 percent of the average salary over the last two years of work for government and public sector employees and over the last five years of work for private sector employees with 36 years of contributions. Benefits are primarily funded by contributions collected from employers and employees and by returns on the invested funds, but there has been substantial financial support from the Treasury, amounting to about 35 percent of total pensions paid in 2009. The Treasury's total legal responsibilities toward the system in 2009 reached 70 percent of the total benefits paid in that year. Moreover, there is no automatic indexation of pensions, and annual adjustments are mostly financed by the Treasury.

The existing pension system was initially built on a fully funded basis, but it is currently viewed as a partially funded system, with accumulated reserves of about US$75 billion.[6] These reserves are invested in government debt instruments (bonds, Treasury bills, and implicit government debt) and in National Investment Bank (NIB) debt instruments. To date, this has not been a successful investment strategy.[7] Like other prefunded pension schemes, the Egyptian pension funds generated surpluses during their early years of operation, and these reserves, in accordance with the legislation, were deposited with the NIB. Low and negative real returns over the period 1975–2005, as a result of inefficient investment policies, eroded the reserves, compromising their capacity to finance future liabilities (table 5.1).

TABLE 5.1 **Average annual rates of return on Egyptian pension fund assets compared with annual inflation rates, fiscal years 2001/02–2010/11**

Fiscal year	Total value of pension funds' investments (LE billions)[a]	Average rate of return on investments (%)	Nominal inflation rate (CPI) (%)	Real rate of return on investments (%)
2001/02	167.3	9.7	2.7	+7.0
2002/03	189.6	9.2	4.2	+5.0
2003/04	213.0	8.9	16.5	−7.6
2004/05	239.2	9.0	4.8	+4.2
2005/06	264.1	9.0	7.7	+1.3
2006/07	270.0	8.3	9.5	−1.2
2007/08	284.7	8.3	18.3	−10.0
2008/09	296.3	8.3	11.8	−3.5
2009/10	308.0	8.1	11.8	−3.7
2010/11	311.0	8.4	11.1	−2.7

SOURCE: Egyptian Ministry of Finance.

NOTE: CPI = consumer price index; LE = Egyptian pound.

a. Government debts, which do not earn any rate of return, are omitted.

The poor or negative real rate of returns on investments, added to the inadequacy of the parameters of the defined benefit pension scheme for ensuring long-term sustainability, have obliged the Treasury to provide ad hoc support to the system, particularly to finance deficits, annual pension increases, benefits granted by law or by presidential or governmental decisions, and special benefits accorded to some groups of the insured population. Consequently, the system is not financially sustainable; the existing assets and future contributions will not be sufficient to finance the existing system's current and future liabilities. In reality, the current system is gradually becoming a pay-as-you-go (PAYG) scheme rather than the fully funded system it was designed to be. As shown in figure 5.1, which is based on scenarios using the World Bank's pension projection tool, PROST, the consolidated balance of both pension funds was in deficit in the baseline year 2007—a situation that will increasingly deteriorate in the long term if there is no reform.[8]

Consistent with these results, recent valuations indicate that the pension funds are running an increasing actuarial deficit, reaching LE 182 billion (equivalent to about US$35 billion) by 2075. This represents 17.5 percent of fiscal year 2008/09 gross domestic product (GDP). The actuarial report also indicates that to keep the promises of the PAYG system, contribution rates for old-age, death, and disability pensions should be increased from the current level of 26 percent (15 percent from the employer, 10 percent from the employee, and 1 percent from the Treasury) to an impossible level of 67 percent of the payroll by 2075. In any case, NOSI would not be able to finance most or any of the Treasury's liabilities without additional sources of income.[9] Given such clear warnings, in 2005 the government

FIGURE 5.1 Expected consolidated balance of the Arab Republic of Egypt's current pension funds, to 2075

percentage of GDP

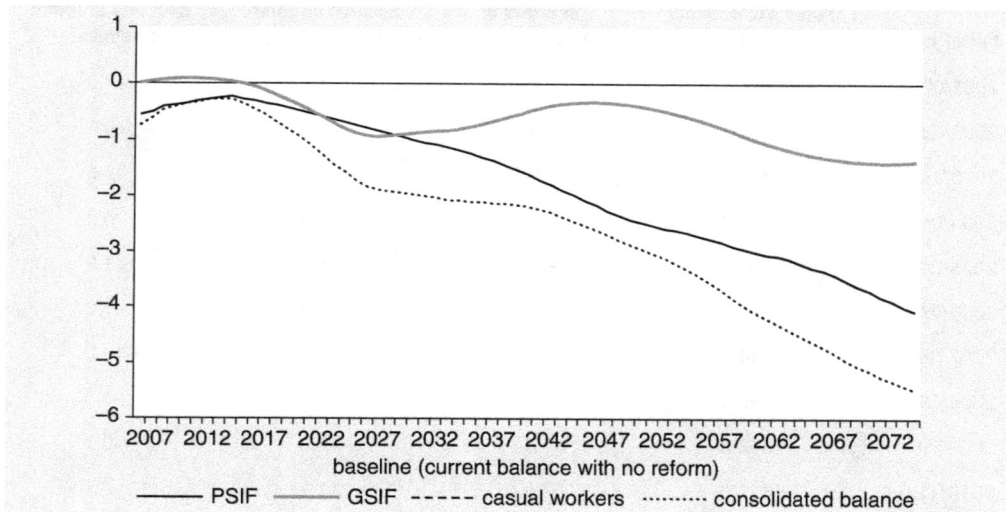

baseline (current balance with no reform)

——— PSIF   ——— GSIF   – – – – casual workers   ·········· consolidated balance

SOURCE: Egyptian Ministry of Finance.

NOTE: GDP = gross domestic product; GSIF = Government Social Insurance Fund; PSIF = Public and Private Social Insurance Fund.

began considering a structural reform of the social insurance and pension system as a way of moving toward dealing with the system's expected financial crisis in the near future.

The current pension system in Egypt also faces problems associated with changes in the demographic and economic structure of the country—for example, the increasing longevity of pensioners and the increasing share of the private sector in the economy. The latter is a significant factor in the contribution evasion problem.

Although the Egyptian case furnishes a good example of a comprehensive social insurance reform, this chapter mainly focuses on the pension component of the system. Other elements of the reform, such as unemployment insurance, are also discussed briefly below, as they too are to be financed through a combination of NDC and FDC components.

Motives for Reforming the Egyptian Social Insurance System

Numerous and diverse weaknesses in the current social insurance and pension system moved Egypt's Ministry of Finance (MOF) to explore options for reform. A major driver for reform was the actual and projected imbalance of the pension system. Other important adjustments will be needed, as well, and addressing them will require a complex reform.

The objectives of the reform include, in addition to long-term sustainability and fiscal neutrality, (a) providing effective income protection for lower-income earners through coverage extension; (b) improving incentives for middle- and higher-income earners by tightening the link between contributions and benefits; (c) introducing automatic mechanisms for adjusting for longevity increases and inflation; (d) inducing the self-employed to join and contribute to the system; (e) modernizing management, governance, institutional infrastructure, and procedures to improve administrative and investment capacity; (f) introducing effective mechanisms to protect the unemployed; and (g) providing a basic pension income and increased pension amounts for those with no or very low pension incomes at retirement.

The new scheme was designed to achieve the following goals:

- Financial viability over the long term
- A more equitable distribution of retirement income among workers
- Direct links between benefits and the level of earnings over the worker's lifetime, enabling individuals to understand more easily the pension rights they have earned
- Greater ability to support an evolving labor market and a growing modern economy
- Maintenance of the living standards that pensioners were enjoying before retirement by encouraging saving toward retirement
- Better protection against poverty in old age for all individuals and their dependents, regardless of their working history

An initial approach to the reform process was to assess alternative scenarios for parametric reform of the current system. The following scenarios were considered:

(a) reduction of the current accrual rate of 0.45 to 0.55; (b) gradual increase of the current retirement age of 60 to 65; and (c) replacement of the current benefit formula for old-age pensions by extending the period for averaging pensionable income to the last 20 years of service. Figure 5.2 presents the results of PROST projections for each scenario and for a combination of scenarios.

In all scenarios, the deficit increases during the first two decades, reflecting the fact that the new rules apply initially to a small part of the labor force. Although the parametric reform would improve long-term financial sustainability, the Egyptian government considered it unacceptable from a political-economy perspective, and passing such a reform might prove difficult. The evaluation of political feasibility is an interesting example of why more complex systemic reforms sometimes prove more acceptable than parametric reforms. This counterintuitive result deserves a separate, more technical, analysis, but it is useful to note that with the introduction of automatic mechanisms for adjusting longevity risk and the tight link between contributions and pensions, the hot political debates on retirement age and accrual rates are no longer in the headlines of the reform discussion, and public debate is significantly decompressed.

In addition to these important political-economy considerations, parametric reform scenarios, although they are feasible means of improving the system's financial sustainability, do not fully address the other challenges facing the system. These include (a) high evasion associated with the very high costs of social insurance; (b) a low pensionable salary ceiling (LE 1,750 in fiscal year 2010/11), resulting in a replacement rate

FIGURE 5.2 **Financial projections for various reform scenarios, the Arab Republic of Egypt, to 2075**
deficit as percentage of GDP

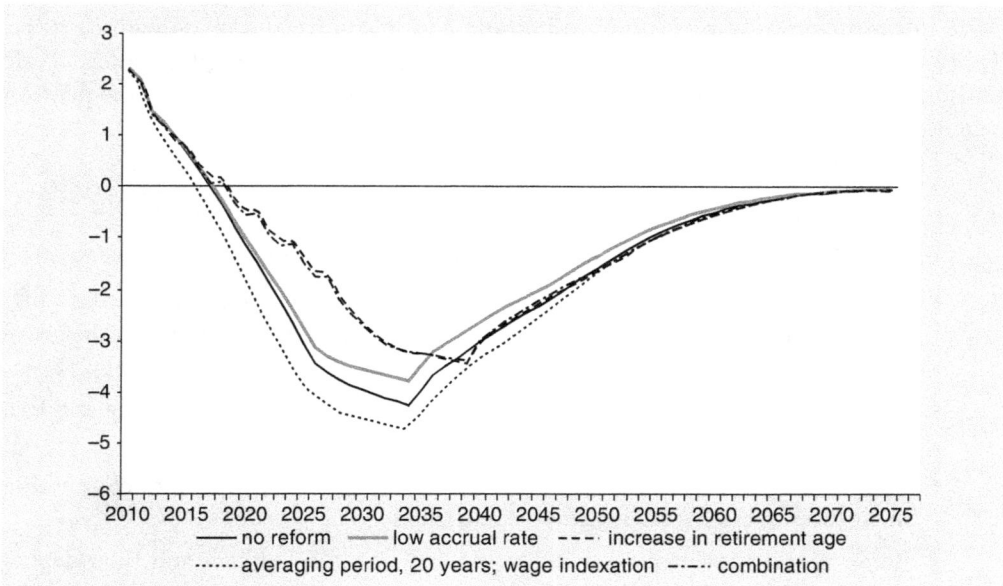

SOURCE: Egyptian Ministry of Finance.
NOTE: GDP = gross domestic product.

of less than 35 percent for a significant proportion of members, most of whom rely on the state pension system as their only source of income after retirement; (c) very high administrative costs (about 5 percent of total annual benefits); (d) increasing life expectancy and changes in the demographic profile; (e) generous survivorship schemes that are extended to a large number of beneficiaries and reach in some cases 150 percent of the pension value; (f) the inefficiency of current social insurance for unemployment; (g) discretionary pension adjustment in the absence of automatic indexation, which erodes real pensions in times of high inflation; (h) a low rate of return on the invested assets, as about 90 percent of the system's reserves are in different types of government debt instruments; (i) practical difficulties in the way of significant expansion of pensions for casual, seasonal, and informal workers, and very low levels of benefits, even though most of the benefits are highly subsidized; and (j) a very complicated defined benefit system, with different structures for every sector of the labor force or segment of the population and different definitions of insured salaries (for example, basic and variable salaries).[10]

In light of these considerations, the Egyptian government undertook some parametric reforms in 2009 but then submitted a systemic reform proposal. The parliament enacted the reform in June 2010.

The Transition Model

The systemic reform will affect new entrants into the labor market and those switching from the current (old) system. There will be also a gradual parametric reform of the old system, which is expected to operate for another 75 years.

The reform will close the current system to new members. Beginning on July 1, 2013, participation in the new NDC–FDC social insurance and pension system will be mandatory for all new entrants into the labor market and for other persons with no previous record of contributions. Those already covered before the introduction of the new system will have the option of remaining in the old system or switching fully or partially to the new system.[11] Those who change completely to the new system will receive pensions from both systems—a pension based on rights acquired according to the old system rules up to the time of the transfer, but calculated at the time of retirement, and a pension from the new system based on rights acquired after switching. Those who change partially to the new system will also receive pensions from both systems—from the old system based on rights acquired under the system rules before and after moving to the new system, and from the new system based on rights acquired after switching. The option of transferring to the new system will be given to current members of the old system for a period of one year from the date the new system starts operating. A further parametric reform of the old system will complement the systemic reform, with the objective of gradually correcting some of the problems and weaknesses of the old system.

In considering the transition from the existing nonfinancial defined benefit PAYG scheme to NDC and FDC, countries have employed two approaches. One is to convert the acquired rights of all workers—perhaps with the exception of the very oldest—into initial capital in the new NDC scheme. This was the path taken, using different models, in the original NDC countries, Latvia, Poland, and Sweden. The other approach is to introduce NDC only for new entrants and other persons who were not covered by the old scheme. This is similar to the path followed by Italy, and it is this route that Egypt has chosen.

The Italian model has been criticized by a large number of experts, including Italians, because it leaves most workers under the old regime in the initial decades. This dilutes the central message of NDC, that "what you get is what you pay for," since the scheme applies to so few workers in the beginning. Nevertheless, Egypt decided to make the change to the new NDC and FDC schemes optional for participants already covered under the old scheme, for two reasons. One is that some people may mistrust the government's intentions in creating the new scheme. If participation is optional, skeptics can choose to remain in the old system. The other is that it is currently unconstitutional to compel a member of the old system to switch to the new system. Egypt's chosen transition model was the best fit for Egypt's current circumstances and is what will be most understandable and acceptable to the Egyptian population.

The transition model of converting workers' acquired rights into initial capital in the new NDC scheme would not be acceptable to most of the Egyptian population and would open the door for huge public arguments regarding the way initial capital is calculated for each person. It would be difficult to convince the low-capital person of the reasons for his or her low value and the calculations behind it. The new system would be placed in the very bad position of trying to persuade 18 million people (the currently insured members) to accept their initial capital values. Doing so is regarded as impossible for many reasons, one of which is that the reform represents a significant philosophical and strategic shift in the country's understanding of pensions. For a long time, pension rights were seen to be acquired according to defined benefit final salary rules and dependent only on the number of contributory years and the final salary. In addition, the percentage of uneducated people in Egypt is still very high, and it is difficult for the less-educated population to understand the transitional model.

It should be noted that for the time being, the goal is not to encourage all the people, particularly those over age 45, who are now in the old system to switch to the new system. As mentioned above, it is unconstitutional in Egypt to make switching obligatory or to discriminate between people according to age or sex or to exercise any other sort of discrimination in setting the transfer arrangements. Furthermore; the transfer would be administratively very complicated and would simply move many problems from the old system to the new system. Finally, the members of the old system would create a huge burden for the new system and would not be satisfied with what they would receive in the near term—a situation that might kill off the reform at the beginning. It is believed, however, that there will be possibilities of additional reform after the new system starts operating, which might include arrangements for shortening the transition period.

Structure of the New Social Insurance and Pension System

The design of the Egyptian social insurance and pension reform is based on the following principles:

- All current workers are to be allowed to remain in the current system, and their accrued rights are considered acquired rights.

- Pension benefits should be adequate and affordable.

- A minimum level of retirement income should be guaranteed to all citizens above a reasonable age (65).

- The administration of the system should be effective and efficient, with reasonable costs.

- Employees' and employers' social insurance contributions should be reduced to encourage job creation.

- The reform should strengthen the link between contributions and benefits and encourage people to save more toward retirement.

The structure of the new system has the following characteristics:

- *Universal coverage* of the working population, regardless of workplace or profession. Segments of the population that are not covered today will become covered under the new system. These include members of unions in certain professions, casual and seasonal workers, farmers, skilled and unskilled workers in the construction industry, and many others. All these groups will be subject to just one unified system, with the same rules. The new system also eliminates the special privileges given to groups of participants in the current system.[12]

- A *mandatory shift from a nonfinancial defined benefit scheme to a defined contribution component* that is structured as a combination of FDC and NDC plans for new entrants and persons with no previous coverage record. This feature is coupled with the possibility of a voluntary transfer for persons with a previous contribution history at the time of the introduction of the new system. The total contribution rate to the new system (for the NDC, FDC, and solidarity accounts) will be reduced to 30.5 percent; 19.5 percent is paid by the employer and 11.0 percent, by the employee.[13] In the old system, the contribution rate was 41 percent; employers paid 26 percent, employees paid 14 percent, and the Treasury paid 1 percent (table 5.2). The contribution rate is distributed as follows: work injuries and health insurance, 4.0 percent; NDC accounts, 16.0 percent; FDC accounts, 7.0 percent; and solidarity accounts, 3.5 percent. It should be noted that under the current system, contributions are calculated only on the pensionable salary, with a ceiling roughly equal to the annual national average salary, rather than on the total salary.

- A *universal basic pension* equal to 18 percent of the after-tax national average salary. The basic pension is noncontributory and is financed by the Treasury.

- The *integration of all social insurance risks, such as old age, disability, survivorship benefits, work injuries, death, unemployment, and health, into a full, comprehensive system*. It was important for gaining the public's approval of the new system to ensure that the system will cover all the social risks that the current system does.

- A *clawback mechanism,* which provides an additional proportional benefit to members who made partial contributions toward their old-age, death, and disability pensions during their active lives.

TABLE 5.2 **Contribution rates under the Arab Republic of Egypt's old and new social insurance and pension systems**
percent

Risks covered	Current system		New system (based on total salary)	
	Employer	Employee	Employer	Employee
Old age, death, and disability[a]	15.0	10.0	13.0[b]	9.0
End-of-service indemnity	2.0[c]	3.0[c]	0.5	0.5
Work injury	3.0	0	1.0[d]	0
Unemployment	2.0	0	2.0	0.5
Health insurance	4.0	1.0	3.0	1.0
Flat-rate pension[e]	0	0	0	0
Total	26.0	14.0	19.5	11.0

SOURCE: Egyptian Ministry of Finance.

a. The Treasury provides a 1 percent subsidy for these three risks for the entire covered working population under the current system only.

b. Of the total of 13 percentage points, two percentage points go to a solidarity account.

c. From the basic salary only.

d. Increased cost for occupations with higher associated risks.

e. The total cost is paid by the Treasury

- A *gradual increase in the normal pension age,* from 60 to 65 over the following 17 years, and introduction of a uniform pension age in all the schemes (old and new) beginning in 2027.[14]

- *Universal benefits for everyone,* based on contributions to the DC system and on a redistributive noncontributory basic pension, when the NDC and FDC schemes are eventually mature (in the sense that all workers are under only the new system).

- An *innovative scheme of unemployment insurance savings accounts combined with a solidarity account.*

- *Institutional and administrative reforms.*

The model adopted is based on the principle that multipillar schemes serve multiple objectives—sustainability, transparency, efficiency, and solidarity—through a combination of defined benefit and defined contribution methods (Holzmann and Hinz 2005). The new NDC and FDC schemes are the core of the overall reform program. Although eligibility conditions were adjusted to reflect demographic trends, the new pension system will largely rely on NDC and FDC accounts to finance old-age pensions and unemployment insurance benefits.[15]

A significant change in the functioning of a pension scheme is associated with the shift from a defined benefit to a defined contribution scheme, and this is the main reason why the literature differentiates systemic from simple parametric reforms. Once the decision is made to move to a defined contribution scheme, the next design issue is NDC versus FDC. Although the comparison between the two systems is not trivial, it is generally accepted that FDC can offer higher returns, but at the risk of higher volatility in returns. In addition, the savings from the new system are usually required to finance the transition, and this is more clearly accomplished with NDC. Egypt decided to adopt a mix of NDC and FDC to combine the advantages of both schemes, although this choice may add complexity to the administration of the system. The concept is accepted by the people, who understand the NDC part as the risk-free investment and the FDC part as the risky investment. From the system's point of view, the NDC component is the PAYG part, and the FDC component is the funded part of the system.

The new three-pillar mandatory system is expected to be able to address demographic, financial, and institutional challenges by putting in place diversified mechanisms to achieve an optimal risk-return combination adapted to the specific circumstances of Egypt's labor market and economy. By establishing a close relationship between contributions and pensions, DC pensions are also expected to discourage evasion and induce individual savings.

In addition to the flat-rate (basic pension) minimum income guarantee at retirement age (65) and the clawback mechanism, the reformed Egyptian social insurance scheme retains the defined benefit structure for the survivors', disability, unemployment, and work injury benefits and for replacement of salary in case of temporary sickness or work injury. The defined benefit component serves the main objective of avoiding the risk of poverty (particularly if risks occur in the early work years) and is highly redistributive.

One of the most important features of the design of the new system is the establishment of solidarity accounts for all members, to cover the risks of death, disability, unemployment, and work injury. The solidarity accounts will fund the minimum guaranteed benefits determined by the law regulating these benefits, should an individual's account be insufficient.

The objective of transparency will be served by closer correlation between contributions and benefits, by the creation of individual records with a complete history of contributions for each worker, and by the adoption of an automatic pension adjustment mechanism. The new system will gain efficiency from a more effective institutional framework, with consolidation of processes to take advantage of economies of scale, clear definition of critical processes such as investment of reserves, and transparent pricing for each of the risks covered by the social insurance system.

An essential element in gaining public approval for the reform was the coverage by the new system of all the risks and benefits included under the old system. These risks, however, will be managed in a significantly different way, as the following sections briefly explain.

OLD-AGE, DEATH, AND DISABILITY BENEFITS

Old-age benefits. The new system aims at a replacement rate of 65 percent, or 75 percent of the last total salary before retirement.[16] The actual replacement rate at retirement will depend on many factors, including collected contribution amounts and the duration of contribution, the interest rate earned on the NDC accounts, the rate of return on the invested assets, the rate of increase in wages, the life expectancy of the insured member and the member's survivors, the expected future rate of return on the invested assets, and future inflation rates.

Old-age, death, and disability pensions will be funded through the establishment of DC individual accounts for each member. Into these accounts, 20 percent of a worker's total salary will be deposited: 9 percent from the employee, and 11 percent from the employer. This percentage will be distributed between the NDC account (65–80 percent) and the FDC account (35–20 percent). For the self-employed and for Egyptians working abroad, the contribution rate will be 20 percent of the amount of insured salary that individuals choose under the new system.[17] Enrollment in the new system for Egyptians working abroad will be optional, as it is in the old system.

The balance of the NDC account will earn an annual interest rate equal to the annual average interest rate on government bonds and Treasury bills issued during the year. The balance of the FDC account will be invested in a diversified portfolio and will be assigned the average rate of return realized on total invested FDC and solidarity account balances. System members will not be able to choose portfolio investments or fund managers.

Among the most important goals of the new social insurance and pension system are to enhance the relationship between the contributions collected and the benefits paid and to increase the net replacement rate at retirement to prevent poverty and maintain the member's living standard after retirement. Accordingly, studies have been performed to estimate the expected replacement rate under the new system.[18] Table 5.3 provides an example of the expected old-age benefits under the new system. The system guarantees that the overall rate of return earned on the individual DC account (NDC and FDC) over the whole contributory period will not be less than the average inflation rate over the same contributory period.

The studies have been also performed for different contribution rates and different retirement ages and with the total balance of both (NDC and FDC) accounts, which represents the present value of the insured's accrued pension at retirement.[19] Figure 5.3 presents the results of an analysis performed for the expected replacement rate on retirement at various ages and contribution rates and with some different actuarial assumptions.

The figure emphasizes the basis for the reform—that is, a stronger relationship between contributions and benefits—and shows the effect of different retirement ages on the expected replacement rate.

TABLE 5.3 **Example of the expected pension replacement rate under the Arab Republic of Egypt's new system, by retirement age**

	55	60	63	65
Last salary (LE)	1,423	1,996	2,445	2,799
Value of first pension (LE)	649	1,297	1,994	2,651
Replacement rate from gross salary before retirement (%)	46	65	82	95
Replacement rate from net salary before retirement (%)	57	81	102	118

SOURCE: Egyptian Government Actuarial Department (EGAD).

NOTE: LE = Egyptian pound. Estimates are for a new entrant at age 25 with a starting salary of LE 200 per month, assuming an average salary increase during the working life of the employee of about 8 percent per year and an average rate of return on the invested DC accounts up to the date of retirement of about 8 percent per year. The calculations of the value of the pension take into account future life expectancy and expected future life expectancy improvements, the expected future inflation rate, and the expected future rate of return on investments.

FIGURE 5.3 **Expected replacement rates at selected retirement ages and contribution rates, the Arab Republic of Egypt**

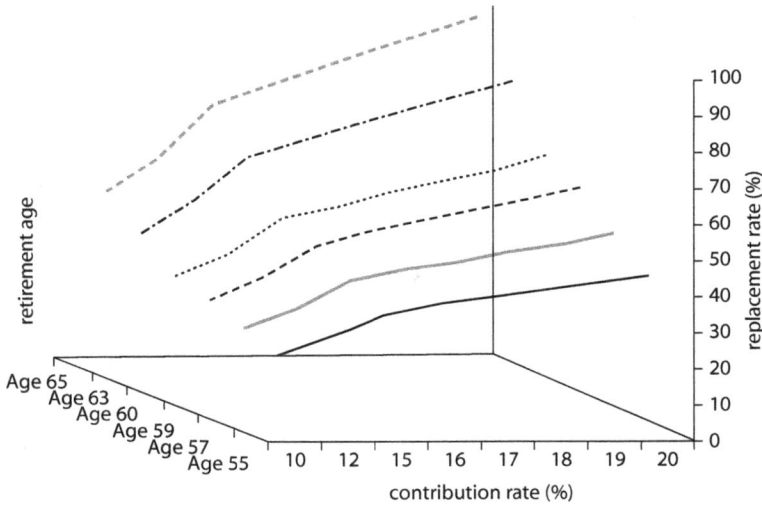

SOURCE: Egyptian Government Actuarial Department (EGAD).

Benefits for worker death and disability. The new system guarantees a survivors' benefit for a worker's death, or a disability benefit of not less than 65 percent of the average total gross salary over the last two years before death or disability, or 25 percent of the average national salary, whichever is greater. This benefit is more generous than the current system offers.

A solidarity account will be established as a pool fund for all insured members and will be financed by a 2 percent contribution rate paid by employers from the total salary of the employees.[20] The solidarity account balance will be invested in the same way as the FDC accounts.

Pensions for workers' death or disability will be financed from the total balance of the NDC and FDC. If that balance is insufficient to pay the minimum guaranteed pension, the solidarity account will be used to make up the shortfall. The new system will maintain the current additional benefits offered in the event of death or disability, such as funeral expenses and death grants, and will be financed from the solidarity account.

Survivors' benefits. The main principles of survivors' benefits in the current system are preserved in the new system: to ensure the protection of the dependents of the deceased member and to protect the rights of the insured. The new system retains the same eligibility conditions for widows, sons, daughters, parents, and siblings as in the current system. The new system also defines the cases of combined pensions, interrupted pension payments, and resumed pensions.

In the case of the insured person's death while employed or after retirement, the survivors are eligible to receive pensions and other survivors' benefits according to the rates specified in the current system, from the beginning of the month of death. The pension paid to survivors is normally equivalent to 100 percent of the deceased's pension and sometimes exceeds 100 percent.

End-of-service indemnity. The end-of-service indemnity is a one-time payment made at the time of the member's retirement or death. In the current system, it is a defined benefit payment of one month for each contributory year of the amount of the first pension (basic salary pension only), with a minimum of 10 months in the case of death or disability incurred while employed. This benefit is currently financed by a contribution rate of 5 percent of the basic salary only; 3 percent is paid by the employee, and 2 percent is paid by the employer.

This benefit is retained in the new system because of trade union pressure to preserve all the benefits of the old system, but it is managed in a different way than in the current system. That is, it is financed through the establishment of end-of-service-indemnity DC individual accounts for each member, into which 1 percent of the total salary is deposited in equal shares from the employee and the employer. This percentage will be distributed between the NDC and the FDC accounts in the same way as the individual accounts for old-age, death, and disability benefits. For the self-employed and for Egyptians working abroad, the end-of-service-indemnity benefits will be optional.

The total balances of the end-of-service-indemnity NDC and FDC accounts will be given to the insured member at retirement or to the survivors in case of death. It will be mandatory to use this balance first to increase the old-age or early retirement pension to at least a minimum of 50 percent if the pension is less than that value.

Unemployment insurance. Unemployment insurance benefits begin the eighth day after a person becomes unemployed and continues to be paid until the day before the person enters on a new job or according to the length of the contributory period before the spell of unemployment, whichever is shorter, as shown in table 5.4.[21]

TABLE 5.4 **Unemployment insurance, Arab Republic of Egypt**

Length of the contributory period before becoming unemployed (years)	Maximum length of unemployment compensation (months)
1 to < 2	6
2 to < 3	7
3 to < 4	8
4 to < 5	9
5 to < 6	10
6 to < 7	11
7+	12

SOURCE: Egyptian Ministry of Finance.

The compensation amount is a monthly sum of 65 percent of the average net salary during the last 12 months prior to unemployment, and it diminishes by 3 percent monthly. This unemployment insurance is financed by allocating 70 to 75 percent of the unemployment contribution rate of 2.5 percent (2.0 percent paid by the employer and 0.5 percent paid by the employee) to the individual DC unemployment account (NDC and FDC); the rest is allocated to the unemployment solidarity account for all members.

The balances of these accounts will be invested in the same way as are the old-age, death, and disability DC and solidarity accounts.

Unemployment compensation will be paid from the DC unemployment individual accounts balance (NDC and FDC) first. If the balance proves insufficient, the solidarity account will be used to make up any shortfall.

Any outstanding balance remaining in individual unemployment accounts will be given to the insured member at retirement or to the survivors in case of death, or it can be used to increase the amount of the old-age or early retirement pension. It will be mandatory to use this balance first to increase the old-age or early retirement pension to a minimum of 50 percent if the pension is less than that value.

WORK INJURY BENEFITS AND HEALTH INSURANCE FINANCIAL COMPENSATION

The new system offers the member a replacement for his or her salary during a period of absence from work owing to work injury or temporary disability caused by sickness. If a work injury leads to total and permanent disability, a pension is paid equal to 100 percent of the average net monthly salary in the last two years before the injury, in addition to the old-age pension, as determined according to the balance of the NDC and FDC accounts and age at retirement. The cost of such benefits is financed by a 1 percent contribution rate paid by the employer into the work injury and health insurance solidarity account. This solidarity account will be invested in the same way as the old-age, death, and disability solidarity account. In the case of partial and permanent disability that does not prevent the employee from continuing work, disability compensation and a pension determined according to the level or the percentage of disability will be paid. Should temporary disability resulting from illness become total and permanent disability, the worker death and disability benefits will be paid.

BASIC PENSION AND THE CLAWBACK MECHANISM

In addition to the financing mechanism, the new pension system includes universal benefits complementing the contributory DC component with a redistributive noncontributory component. This latter component is designed to provide protection against poverty in old age for all citizens who have reached age 65 and who do not receive any pension or income from other sources. The benefits offered in this component are in the form of noncontributory basic pension income.

The universal basic pension is a flat rate equal to 18 percent of the after-tax national average salary. Many studies were performed to determine the value of a flat rate that would represent an acceptable cost (as a percentage of GDP). It was found that 15 percent of the gross national average salary is the best fit. When the reform was brought before the parliament, much debate ensued on the use of gross rather than net (after-tax) national average salary. Accordingly, the studies were premised on maintaining the same cost. It was found that the equivalent percentage of after-tax national average salary is 18 percent, which is the appropriate percentage for keeping the cost within an acceptable level for the Treasury.[22]

The clawback mechanism provides an additional proportional benefit to members who made partial contributions toward their old-age, death, and disability pension accounts during their active lives. The benefits offered by this mechanism provide for an increase in the pension for those with a very low pension at retirement age or for their survivors. The increase in the member's pension as a result of applying the clawback mechanism equals the amount of the basic pension (18 percent of the after-tax national average salary) minus 33 percent of the pension amount calculated according to normal pension rules.

The total cost of the basic pension and the clawback mechanism is financed by the Treasury. Actuarial estimates show that this will impose a sizable financial burden on the Treasury in the short and medium terms but that in the long term, it will be balanced by the elimination of the subsidy of 1 percent of total insured salary for old-age, death, and disability benefits currently paid by the Treasury. Actuarial studies by Ministry of Finance staff show that the total cost of the basic pension and the clawback mechanism in 2010 will be about 0.12 percent of GDP.[23]

The preceding detailed description of the structure of Egypt's new social insurance and pension system is summarized in table 5.5, which demonstrates that this structure fulfills the principle of a multipillar system that serves multiple objectives through the combination of these pillars.

Financial Sustainability of the New Egyptian Pension System

The new pension system will be sustainable because its parameters are designed in a consistent manner, with the objective of long-term equilibrium. Figure 5.4 illustrates the projected financial situation of the new pension scheme in comparison with the current scheme, using PROST tools to estimate project revenues and expenditures, under the following assumptions:

1. *Old scheme:* no reform of the current system.

2. *New scheme:* a number of suggested scenarios based on changing the assumptions related to contribution rates to the financial and notional accounts and the investment return from the invested assets (see figure 5.5):

TABLE 5.5 **Structure of the Arab Republic of Egypt's new pension system**

	Basic pension, noncontributory component	Individual pension accounts, mandatory contributory component	Supplementary pension schemes, voluntary contributory component
Contributors	None	Employees and employers	No restrictions
Beneficiaries	Elderly age 65+ with no source of pension or income	Retired employees and their survivors	Plan members
Mechanisms	Budget transfers	Defined contributions (NDC and FDC)	Pension plans provided by employers and financial institutions
Financing	General revenues	Mandatory contributions	Voluntary contributions or tax

SOURCE: Authors' elaboration from national data.

NOTE: FDC = financial defined contribution; NDC = nonfinancial defined contribution.

FIGURE 5.4 **Financial projections (current PAYG balance, including investment income), current and new insurance schemes, the Arab Republic of Egypt, 2010–75**

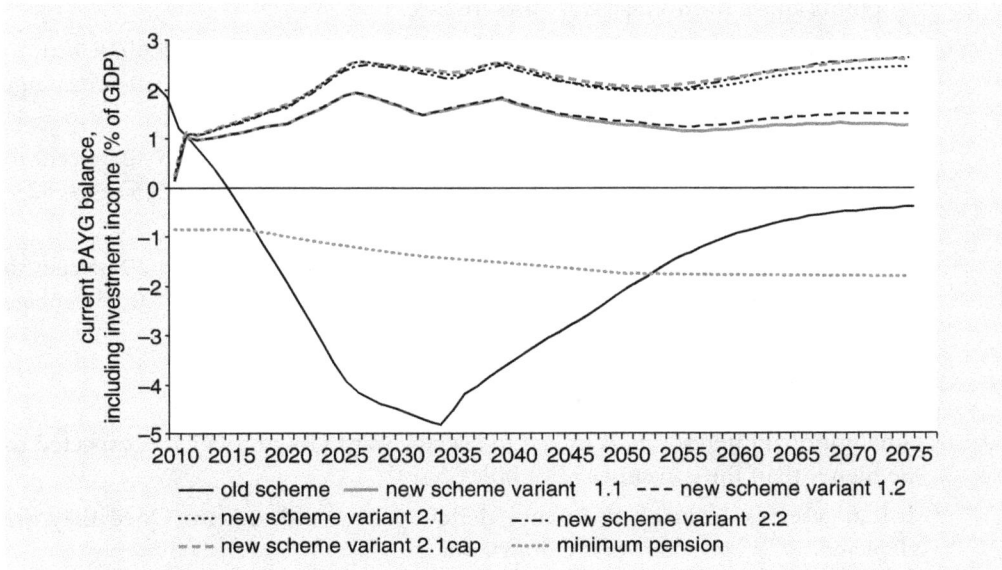

SOURCE: Egyptian Ministry of Finance.

NOTE: GDP = gross domestic product; PAYG = pay as you go.

FIGURE 5.5 **Financial projections (consolidated current PAYG balance, new and old schemes) for insurance system reform schemes, four variants, the Arab Republic of Egypt, 2010–75**

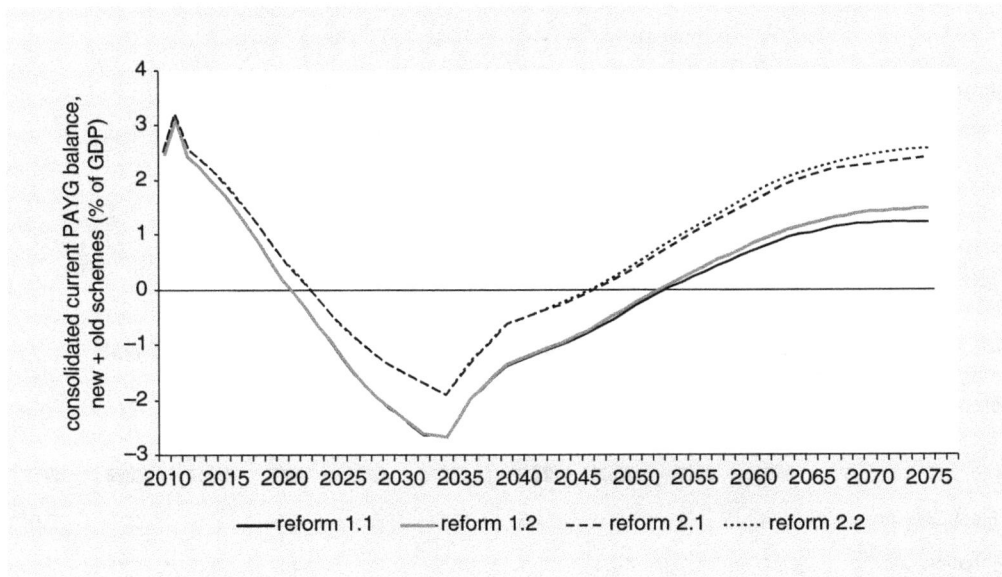

SOURCE: Egyptian Ministry of Finance.

NOTE: GDP = gross domestic product; PAYG = pay as you go.

- Variant 1.1: 60 percent of the contribution rate goes to NDC and 40 percent to FDC; the interest rate earned on FDC individual accounts is 2.5 percentage points above the average wage growth rate.
- Variant 1.2: 60 percent of the contribution rate goes to NDC and 40 percent to FDC; the interest rate earned on an FDC individual account is 1.0 percentage point above the average wage growth rate.
- Variant 2.1: 80 percent of the contribution rate goes to NDC and 20 percent to FDC; the interest rate earned on an FDC individual account is 2.5 percentage points above the average wage growth rate.
- Variant 2.2: 80 percent of the contribution rate goes to NDC and 20 percent to FDC; the interest rate earned on an FDC individual account is 1.0 percentage point above the average wage growth rate.

Additional assumptions are as follows:

- The notional interest rate is linked to average wage growth, which is expected to be higher than the consumer price index (CPI).
- Initial reserves are used to finance deficits in the old system. Once they are depleted, NDC reserves will be drawn on.
- Retirement age increases gradually, according to table 5.6, to reach age 65 by 2027.

TABLE 5.6 **Retirement age, the Arab Republic of Egypt**

Year	Age
2015	61
2018	62
2021	63
2024	64
2027	65

SOURCE: Egyptian Ministry of Finance.

TABLE 5.7 **Expected real GDP growth rates and inflation rates, the Arab Republic of Egypt, selected years, 2007–75**
percent

	2007	2008	2009	2010	2011	2012	2013	2014	2020	2075
Real GDP growth	7.1	7.2	5.0	4.5	7.0	6.5	6.5	6.5	3.7	2.5
Inflation rate	11.0	11.7	14.1	9.1	6.1	4.5	4.0	3.5	3.0	3.0

SOURCE: Egyptian Ministry of Finance.
NOTE: GDP = gross domestic product.

The macroeconomic assumptions are summarized in table 5.7.

As figure 5.5 illustrates, for a period of around 25 years or more after the introduction of the new system, there will still be a need for transfers from the state to finance fully the consolidated system. This reflects the effects of the transition model of the new social insurance and pension system and the fact that the new rules apply initially to only a small part of the labor force.

Implementing the NDC–FDC Combination: International Experience and Options for Egypt

From the financing perspective, the most important elements of the reform are (a) a clear separation between the insurance (contributory) and the redistribution (noncontributory) objectives and (b) the shift to the defined contribution method in the contributory component. Adoption of the DC models makes it possible to address the problems related to financial insolvency, nontransparent redistribution, and weak incentives that pervade traditional defined benefit PAYG pension systems. It was important, however, to decide whether the shift would be to NDC or to FDC. After comparing the advantages and disadvantages of both schemes, the government chose to adopt a combination of the two. This would mean that the members of the new social insurance system could benefit from the investment of part of the funds without saturating the small Egyptian financial markets and could, at the same time, continue to be an important source of funding for paying for the liabilities of the current system.[24] The decision to use both NDC and FDC responds to the objective of minimizing financial risks while allowing for a level of market investments for the pension funds.

International experience with the use of NDC has a fairly short history and is not very extensive geographically. Among the few countries that have adopted this model, Latvia, Poland, and Sweden are frequently used as benchmarks. Their schemes have been in operation for 10 to 15 years, which provides some experience. Chłoń-Domińczak, Franco, and Palmer (chapter 2 in this volume) include Italy among the countries in the "first wave of NDC reforms," and they analyze the differences among the four countries in critical design issues. In the case of the Egyptian reform, key areas to which international experience proved relevant were (a) the mix of NDC and FDC; (b) the population to be covered by the new rules; (c) the institutional organization of the NDC and FDC schemes; and (d) the technical definitions of the benefit formula.

With the exception of Italy, the reference countries adopted a combination of mandatory NDC and FDC components, with 63 to 86 percent of total contributions designated for the NDC scheme. The new Egyptian system will eventually transfer one-third of the contributions paid for each individual to the FDC scheme and the other two-thirds to the NDC scheme. The amount allocated to each account will not be fixed at the beginning but will be within a range of 65 to 80 percent for the NDC scheme, with the rest going to the FDC scheme. This will afford flexibility in dealing with changes within the system and the market.

The division of contributions between the NDC and FDC schemes takes into consideration the capacity of the Egyptian financial sector to absorb large flows of savings and the need to ensure smooth financing of the old scheme's liabilities. For a period of about 25 years after the introduction of the new system, transfers from the state budget will still be needed, in addition to contributions from the old and new systems. The decision ultimately to allocate two-thirds of the total contributions of the old-age, death, and disability plans to the NDC accounts is not very different from the practice in the benchmarks. The fact that the system is only applicable to new entrants means that there will be a gradual start during the first couple of decades while, at the same time, the capacity of the Egyptian financial market is growing. In addition, it will be possible to consider international investments, with time.

The second important design issue is that of the population to be covered under the rules of the new NDC and FDC schemes. Countries have used alternative strategies to move part or all of the labor force to the new scheme. At one extreme, Latvia transferred all contributors to the new system, whereas in Italy, only new entrants and younger workers have to join the new scheme. The model adopted in Egypt, which applies the new rules to new entrants, is closer to the Italian model.

There are advantages and disadvantages in each approach, the obvious basis of comparison being the speed with which the impact of the reform is felt and the financial implications of the transition from the old to the new system. It is worth mentioning here that people may not notice that, in practice, almost 40 birth cohorts will not be covered by Egypt's reform or will be only partly covered. This means that there will be little or no incentive effect on payment of contributions in Egypt, yet this incentive effect was a major reason why countries such as Latvia and Poland, with large informal sectors in the 1990s, found NDC so attractive, and why Latvia chose a full, immediate transition covering all contributors. Even Sweden's transition was relatively rapid; everyone had a component of the new NDC–FDC schemes from the outset. The Egyptian choice, like the Italian one, favors a slow transition path to the new rules, but the consequence is that the expected impact will only become effective in the long term. This political strategy was important in Egypt to put the initial reform through. As we have already noted, it is well understood in Egypt that the new system will definitely be revisited after the system starts operating.

The third critical design element relates to the organization and administration of the NDC and FDC schemes. The main decision concerned the choice between centralization and decentralization of the FDC component. International experience with FDC reforms shows that marketing costs associated with individual pension plans may undermine the positive effects of the reforms (Impavido and others 2010). In addition, there are economies of scale associated with larger funds, especially if investment rules or fund investment strategies lead to similar portfolios. To eliminate this negative effect, the Egyptian reformers opted for a central administration with a decentralized investment process. This setup will avoid having multiple operators and schemes and will enable administrative efficiencies through economies of scale by combining similar elements within a centralized administrative structure. A central pension administration will be responsible for the overall administration of the system, including the decision to outsource fund management for the FDC and social solidarity components. This choice is expected to result in substantially lower administrative costs than those observed in individual pension plans in Latin America and in Central and Eastern Europe. The main challenge is to avoid diseconomies of scale and to achieve significant modernization and improvement of the managerial capacity of a highly centralized agency built on the legacy of the two old pension funds.

TABLE 5.8 **Valorization of NDC accounts during the accumulation phase and indexation of pension benefits in the four original NDC countries**

Country	Notional rate of return on accounts during the accumulation period	Pension indexation
Italy	Growth rate of GDP	CPI indexation
Latvia	Growth rate of the covered wage bill	CPI indexation (with an eventual transition to mixed CPI-wage indexation)
Poland	Growth rate of the covered wage bill	CPI indexation (with an eventual transition to mixed CPI-wage indexation)
Sweden	Growth rate of covered per capita wage (There is additional adjustment when the NDC scheme's liabilities exceed assets and the balancing ratio falls below unity. This can be followed by an increase once assets exceed liabilities again, until the per capita wage index reaches the level where it would have been without adjustment.)	Price indexation. In addition, the index is adjusted for the discrepancy between real per capita wage growth and 1.6 percent real rate of return in per capita wage growth. Additional adjustments are provided for, as described in the first column.

SOURCE: Chłoń-Domińczak, Franco, and Palmer, chapter 2 in this volume.

NOTE: CPI = consumer price index; GDP = gross domestic product.

The fourth issue, that of the technical definition regarding the benefit formula, open doors to several options regarding revalorization and indexation. There is no uniform approach among the countries adopting NDC.

The generalized idea that the growth rate of the covered wage bill is the best proxy for the sustainable internal rate of return of a PAYG pension system follows from Samuelson's classic paper (1958).[25] In principle, both the accounts of workers during the accumulation period and the benefits of pensioners during the payout phase can be valorized with the rate of growth of the wage sum. Table 5.8 summarizes how the original four NDC countries valorize accounts during the accumulation period and index pensions during the payout period. For valorization of accounts during the accumulation period, Latvia and Poland selected the growth rate of the covered wage bill; Italy chose a long-term proxy for wage-sum growth, the GDP growth rate; and Sweden chose the per capita covered wage and developed an automatic balancing mechanism to maintain financial balance in the eventuality of labor force decline. In other words, the four original NDC schemes adhere closely, albeit not perfectly, to the principle of valorizing accounts of workers according to the growth of the covered wage sum, however they diverge from this norm in their selection of pension indexation.

Why did these countries stray from their principles in their choice of pension indexation? In Latvia, Poland, and Sweden, pensions granted prior to the reform were price-indexed, whereas the reform made it possible to index NDC pensions to the covered contribution base. However, even with Latvia's rapid transition, it would take about 20 years to reach a state in which the bulk of new pensions came under NDC rules. Indexation with wage-sum growth would thus have dramatically increased the costs of paying the old-system pension legacy—something these countries could not afford. The alternative for Latvia and Poland was to continue with price indexation, with a gradual transition to wage-sum indexation. This explains why Latvia and Poland are gradually introducing the wage-sum index for pensions and why Sweden has chosen instead to index using the covered per capita wage, with balancing.

Sweden has good reason to expect labor force growth in the future, with its relatively high fertility rate and positive net migration. To allow, nevertheless, for the possible downside of a declining labor force, Sweden uses a balancing index that is triggered when the solvency ratio—the ratio of assets to liabilities—falls below unity. The solvency-ratio approach also covers other possible technical deficiencies, including underestimation of longevity in the creation of annuities. Chłoń-Domińczak, Franco, and Palmer, in chapter 2 in this volume, demonstrate that the Swedish balancing mechanism reliably returns the system to equilibrium financing after a demographic or economic shock.

The initial Egyptian choice for valorization of NDC accounts, and for the discount rate, is the rate of interest paid on GDP-indexed government bonds, defined as

$$r_t = \bar{r} + \Omega + \alpha(g_t - \bar{g}),$$

where r_t is the rate of return on the GDP-indexed bonds at time t; $\bar{r}$ is the interest rate paid on a corresponding plain-vanilla bond; Ω is an indexation premium; g_t is the realization of the GDP growth rate for period t; $\bar{g}$ is the expected GDP growth rate; and α is an indexation coefficient that determines the extent of GDP indexation. The notional interest rate earned on individual accounts is identical to the rate of return offered on the GDP-indexed bonds used for asset accumulation in the NDC scheme. The rationale for this decision is that making the notional interest rate and the rate of return on the government bonds identical removes all financial uncertainties from the NDC scheme in cases of macroeconomic, demographic, or labor market–related shocks.

In the approved final version of the new Egyptian pension system, NDC individual accounts will grow at the rate of r, where r is the average annual interest rate on government bonds and Treasury bills, with a guaranteed minimum rate equal to GDP growth. The pension will be indexed with the CPI. This method of indexing individual NDC accounts and pensions differs from the methods used in, for example, Sweden, Poland, and Latvia, as follows:

- Sweden valorizes the NDC individual accounts with the rate $(g + p)$, where g is the growth rate of the real average covered per capita wage, deflated by p, and p is the rate of price inflation (the CPI).

- Latvia and Poland valorize the NDC individual accounts with the rate $(g + \lambda + p)$, where λ is the rate of growth of the covered labor force.

- The Egyptian method of indexing the NDC individual accounts may be more costly than the corresponding Swedish and Polish methods. This is because it is expected that $r > (g + \lambda)$, where this excess indexation = $r - (g + \lambda)$. In the long run, this method of indexation might lead to a deficit in the system because it can result in retirement annuities that are higher than the system can afford. However, with only price indexation of annuities, given real wage growth, wages will increase faster than pensions, and this might reduce the living standard of pensioners relative to workers in the long term, even though price indexation of benefits yields benefits that have constant purchasing power. The financial stability of the NDC scheme will thus depend on the net result of the overvaluation of accounts and the undervaluation of pensions.

In general, indexation with $(g + \lambda + p)$ is what an NDC scheme can afford. With a declining labor force, which is almost certain to be the case in the future in most parts of the world, NDC nevertheless yields a positive rate of return as long as $g + p > -\lambda$. What is more, it can be argued that the GDP growth rate is only a proxy for the covered wage-sum growth, whereas the covered wage-sum growth is the actual financial base of the NDC scheme and of financial stability. The growth of the covered wage base, however, can be expected to differ considerably from GDP growth because the national account GDP statistics are normally based on other measures of economic activity (output, sales, and so on) that have nothing to do with the covered wages. Also, typically there is a considerable difference between output, sales, and the like and wages actually reported, which is what contributions to the pension system are based on. Hence, indexation based on GDP can diverge greatly from indexation based on the covered wage sum.

The following points sum up important factors considered in the choice of indexation in Egypt:

- Historical experience shows that the annual inflation rate is not always lower than the average annual interest rate and sometimes exceeds it.

- According to the structure of the pension system in Egypt, there is a very long chain of beneficiaries of a deceased spouse. The annuity can thus be regarded as a perpetual annuity, indexed with the consumer price index. This construction means that survivors of the deceased will have considerable protection in the Egyptian framework, which is important in the Egyptian context, where women's labor force participation is relatively low.

- Although indexation of accounts during the accumulation phase with r may give a higher annuity than wage indexation would, indexation of annuities with the consumer price index will generate lower costs compared with the counterfactual of wage indexation. The possible lower cost of not wage-indexing annuities can eventually provide a source of finance for partially covering the excess cost of annuities associated with the survivor component.

- One of the main reasons that Egypt chose to index NDC with a financial return and annuities with the CPI is that this method commands public recognition and approval. The main goal of the government at the time of introducing the new system to the public was to ensure that it would be appreciated, understood, and accepted by the citizens. Nevertheless, the indexation method applied in the new Egyptian system is soon to be revisited and assessed.

An idea worth considering for the future is the issuance of "NDC bonds" (see Palmer 2011), which could be set up as follows:

- NDC bond shares would be issued to cover individual account values.
- The NDC bond shares would be indexed with $(g + \lambda + p)$.
- The government would promise, at retirement, to transform these bonds into an annuity, which also has a nominal rate of return of $(g + \lambda + p)$.

- By promising to honor the NDC bonds, the government would also cover the systematic longevity risk (or, systematic underestimation of life expectancy).

This alternative can be further studied and considered by the Egyptian government even before the implementation of the new system.

The final, approved version of the new Egyptian social insurance and pension system contains many changes that have not yet been fully examined and financially assessed because of time constraints and the pressures during the period when the reform was introduced. Some of the critical changes incorporated in the final version are the indexation of NDC individual accounts with the average annual interest rate on government bonds and Treasury bills, with a guaranteed minimum rate equal to GDP growth; pension indexation using the CPI; and the introduction of an overall minimum guaranteed rate of return on individual DC accounts (both NDC and FDC) equal to the average inflation rate over the whole contributory period. A further study and assessment of these and other changes to the reform and the associated parameters should be undertaken soon, and a new document containing the findings should be presented as a research paper following the study.[26]

Conclusion

This chapter has highlighted the circumstances that led the government of Egypt to prepare a comprehensive social insurance reform program. The proposed system, enacted by the parliament in June 2010, includes a combination of defined benefit, NDC, and FDC schemes, with a view to taking advantage of the principle of diversification, maximizing the system's fulfillment of its objectives, and limiting the system's exposure to financial risks while allowing for a level of market investment for the pension funds.

The combination of NDC and FDC schemes is not new; in fact, most recent NDC reforms include an FDC component. What is different about the Egyptian experience is the envisioned use of the combined DC accounts to finance pensions, unemployment insurance, and end-of-service indemnities.

The decision to adopt a central administration of the defined contribution accounts is a common feature of all NDC reforms and is expected to minimize the impact on costs that is observed in some decentralized individual pension plans. The adoption of a centralized administrative framework for the FDC scheme that purchases fund management but does not perform the other functions of pension administration on the private market is a unique feature of the Egyptian reform, and one that should dramatically restrain administrative costs.

With regard to the NDC component, the main challenges are associated with the wealth of design options and the limited international experience with these choices. The Egyptian authorities have adopted reasonable criteria for defining the parameters of the NDC component, but implementation, regulation, and institutional capacity building will demand increasing effort in the near future.

Egypt opted to make a gradual transition to the new rules. Whereas most other NDC reforms chose less gradual approaches, Egypt is less in need of producing rapid results because the current social insurance and pension system is still rather immature. A substantial improvement in the transparency and efficiency of reserve management is needed to make effective use of this transition-supporting mechanism. The Egyptian design of the reform, which includes additional features such as solidarity accounts, indexation of the NDC accounts and of pensions, and guarantees may need to be revisited and further examined in the near future.

Notes

The authors thank Nareman Farag Mofeed, actuarial analyst and coordinator at the office of the Egyptian minister of finance and assistant to Mohamed Maait, for her technical assistance in the preparation of the preliminary version of this chapter. The authors also thank the editors of this volume for their support and views, which are highly appreciated. The chapter includes elements from several documents produced as part of technical assistance by the World Bank to the government of the Arab Republic of Egypt. Those notes were written by a team of World Bank staff and consultants, including Christopher Bender, András Bodor, Tatyana Bogomolova, Mario di Filippo, Marc Goldwein, Carlos Grushka, Richard Hinz, Anca Mataoanu, David A. Robalino, Helga Salinas, Oleksiy Sluchynsky, and Edward Whitehouse.

1. It had been planned to begin implementing the new Egyptian social insurance and pension system in January 2012, but because of political and economic circumstances and the critical situation that followed the January 25, 2011, revolution, it has proved impossible to introduce the new system before July 2013. The change in the date of introduction required that the law be amended before January 2012, and so a new implementation date, July 2013, was legislated at the end of 2011.

2. The present administration will manage both the old and the new social insurance and pension systems.

3. The legal underpinning of the Egyptian system consists of (a) Provision 79 (1975), for civil servants and public and private sector employees; (b) Provision 108 (1976), for employers, self-employed persons, and the like; (c) Provision 50 (1978), for Egyptians working abroad; (d) Provision 112 (1980), for casual and seasonal workers and the informal sector; and (e) Provision 64 (1980), for alternative private social insurance and pension systems.

4. The GSIF covers about 6 million insured members, and the PSIF covers about 12 million insured members. The total number of current beneficiaries (pensioners and survivors) in both funds is about 8 million.

5. Pension benefits are calculated by multiplying the accrual rate (0.45) by the number of contributory years and multiplying the product by the average salary over the last two to five years of service.

6. One US dollar = six Egyptian pounds (LE). One billion is 1,000 million.

7. As of June 30, 2011, the system's accumulated reserves amounted to about LE 450 billion. Government debt instruments represent about 77 percent of the reserves (with 50 percent in government bonds and Treasury bills and 27 percent in other implicit government debt financing). NIB debt instruments make up 13 percent of the total, and the rest is in a diversified portfolio of different classes of assets.

8. The assessments, calculations, and studies undertaken by the staff of the Egyptian Ministry of Finance, with the cooperation of the World Bank team and using the World Bank PROST model for determining the interest rate for both the NDC and the FDC, were based on the initial version of the new Egyptian pension legislation. Because of many critical political considerations, the final legislation approved by parliament differed slightly from the proposed legislation on which the calculations were based.

9. In fiscal year 2011/12, the Treasury allocated about LE 28 billion to support the system, out of the total national budget of about LE 570 billion.

10. For casual, seasonal, and informal workers, a flat-rate pension of LE 145 per month is paid against a flat-rate contribution of LE 1 per month for 120 months, under relatively lax qualifying conditions. Given the scale of the subsidy and the number of participants, the scheme has structural similarities to a universal flat-rate scheme.

11. Switching fully means changing to the new system with one's full salary—that is, covered and uncovered salary under the current system. Switching partially means switching to the new system with only the part of the salary that is not covered under the current system.

12. If the government continues to accord special privileges to some groups, it will have to pay the cost of these additional benefits to the system.

13. This contribution rate includes 5 percent for social health insurance, which is part of the social insurance risks covered under the system. To enjoy the health insurance benefits, or to receive a benefit for temporary disability as a result of sickness or a work injury, a person has to be insured by the social insurance system.

14. The normal retirement or pension age is the age at which the majority of the insured population retires; it is determined by law. People are allowed to retire at any age prior to the normal retirement age as long as they satisfy other conditions, such as a minimum contributory period of 30 years in the new system or 20 years in the old system.

15. The adjusted eligibility conditions include a gradual increase of the normal retirement age to 65; an increase of the minimum contributory period for early retirement to 30 years; a minimum early retirement age of 55; and the use of an annuity factor determined at the time of retirement that includes an allowance for future life expectancy improvements. These eligibility conditions were adjusted to ensure the financial sustainability of the new system and its ability to deal with future demographic and economic changes.

16. The 65 percent replacement rate is calculated on the gross salary before taxes and the social insurance contribution of about 20 percent. The replacement rate therefore represents about 81.25 to 87.50 percent of take-home pay.

17. Those members pay a flat rate of 20 percent because there are no employer contributions.

18. The replacement rate was calculated using the total balance at retirement in both NDC and FDC accounts. The balance represents the expected present value of annual pension installments, assuming an average annual rate of return on invested assets of 8 percent and an average annual increase in pension payments of 6 percent. The mortality rates used in this study are taken from the actuarial English life table "(55) Mortality Tables for Annuitants" (Institute of Actuaries 1980, 71) but are adjusted to reflect expected future improvements in life expectancy.

19. The collected contributions, returns on the invested assets, and pension payments are all tax exempt. This has been the case in the current system, and it was difficult to change it at the time of introducing the reform to the public. Revisions may be necessary in the future.

20. All the system's solidarity accounts will be subject to actuarial valuation every five years at maximum, according to the law. If any of these accounts is not financially sustainable, a modification in the financing structure must be made and presented to the parliament for approval.

The 2 percent contribution rate will be paid for members who are under age 34. For those age 35 and older who decide to transfer from the current system, this percentage will be increased according to the member's age and will be used to make up the shortfall, as described in the text.

21. The data in the table are from the social insurance legislation.

22. The reason for choosing to make the value of the flat-rate basic pension a percentage of after-tax national average salary rather than use the average recorded covered salary is simply to be more transparent and to gain the public's trust.

23. The clawback mechanism is already being implemented, starting on July 1, 2010. Implementation of the basic pension mechanism will begin with the introduction of the new social insurance and pension system on July 1, 2013. The total cost of the clawback mechanism plus the basic pension as a percentage of GDP is estimated to reach about 0.29 percent in 2015.

24. The amount of reserves available for investment will be the sum of the balances of the FDC accounts and solidarity accounts, which together will represent roughly 35–45 percent of the total balance of the NDC, FDC, and solidarity accounts.

25. Note that Samuelson's model is a simple one, with fixed life expectancy and a pension that is a fixed percent of the wage. The growth of "the" pension follows the growth of "the" wage, in a neoclassical growth context and in an equilibrium context.

26. Taking into consideration the difference between the initial version of the reform that was simulated by the World Bank PROST model and the final approved version of the reform, we think that PROST might not be capable of modeling all the features of the approved version of the reform. For example, PROST does not allow for the existence of solidarity accounts. Accordingly, either a new model will be needed to incorporate all the features of the new social insurance and pension system, or the PROST model will need to be amended to take account of these features; this, however, may not be possible. The changes will have to be incorporated into the initial version of the system that was modeled by PROST. The approved version of the reform will have to be reassessed and necessary modifications made to ensure the achievement of the reform's objectives.

References

Holzmann, Robert, and Richard Hinz. 2005. *Old Age Income Support in the 21st Century: An International Perspective on Pension Systems and Reform.* Washington, DC: World Bank.

Institute of Actuaries. 1980. *Formulae and Tables for Actuarial Examinations.* Oxford: Institute of Actuaries and College of Actuaries. http://www.actuaries.org.uk/research-and-resources /documents/formulae-and-tables-actuarial-exams-1st-edition.

Impavido, Gregorio, Esperanza Lasagabaster, and Manuel García-Huitrón. 2010. *New Policies for Mandatory Defined Contribution Pensions: Industrial Organization Models and Investment Products.* Washington, DC: World Bank.

Palmer, Edward. 2011. "Generic NDC: Equilibrium, Valuation and Risk Sharing with and without NDC Bonds." Department of Economics Working Paper 2011:3, Uppsala University, Sweden.

Samuelson, Paul A. 1958. "An Exact Consumption-Loan Model of Interest with or without Social Contrivance of Money." *Journal of Political Economy* 66 (6): 467–82.

CHAPTER 5
COMMENT

Jorge Miguel Bravo

Chapter 5, by Mohamed Maait and Gustavo Demarco, summarizes the financial, economic, social, and demographic conditions that motivated proposals to reform the Arab Republic of Egypt's social insurance system. It elaborates on the appropriateness of a nonfinancial (notional) defined contribution (NDC) scheme—a key element in the structure of the new pension system—in a middle-to-low-income country and discusses the main options and constraints that have been taken into account in implementing the new system, including political-economy issues.

As a result of adverse demographic, economic, and social trends, a small contribution base, high levels of contribution evasion, uneven income distribution, and poor investment performance, the Egyptian pension system was considered financially unsustainable for taxpayers and contributors in the medium and long terms. It was regarded as incapable of fulfilling the main goals of any pension system: appropriate coverage, adequacy of retirement benefits, financial sustainability and affordability, economic efficiency, administrative efficiency, and predictability of benefits in the light of various risks and uncertainties. The actual large unfunded liabilities that are being accumulated imply a massive transfer of resources from future generations to current generations that cannot continue forever.

In the exploration of options for the reform, an interesting point concerns the economic and political desirability of systematic versus parametric pension reforms in middle- and low-income countries. It is well understood that parametric reforms (changes in the contribution rate, accrual rate, retirement age, and so on) can achieve (limited) success in improving the long-term financial sustainability of pension systems in this group of countries. The Egyptian government nevertheless decided to adopt a defined contribution (DC) system that combined NDC and financial defined contribution (FDC) schemes. It did so in the recognition that the successive parametric reforms needed to adapt to changing macroeconomic and demographic conditions would undermine the credibility of policy makers, would increase distrust in the system, and, most important, would not provide the "right" incentives, particularly with respect to labor supply and retirement and saving decisions. Some of the critical issues concerning the current defined benefit, pay-as-you-go (PAYG) scheme were that it did not provide enough incentives to continue working instead of choosing (premature) retirement; failed to reduce either the degree of informalization of the economy or the high level of contribution evasion and strategic wage manipulation; did not reinforce the link between contributions and benefits to promote transparency and stimulate participation in the labor supply (a crucial element in labor markets characterized by rigid structure and high level of taxes); and did not increase the sense of ownership of the assets accumulated in the system, and so augment the certainty that each person's contributions would likely yield a benefit.

Jorge Miguel Bravo is a professor in the Department of Economics, University of Évora, Portugal, and an invited professor at Université Paris IX, Dauphine. He also serves as coordinator of the Observatory of Biometric Risks of the Portuguese Insured Population, Portuguese Insurers Association.

The introduction of a combined DC system is regarded as an opportunity to control the pension expenditure level and ensure long-term financial sustainability and predictability of benefits. In contrast to the existing system—in which the absence of an automatic indexation mechanism for pension benefits makes adjustments arbitrary, uncertain, and likely to induce losses in the purchasing power of pensions, especially in volatile inflation scenarios—the adoption by the Egyptian NDC system of an automatic pension adjustment mechanism that internalizes (at least partially) changes in economic and demographic variables is likely to reduce benefit uncertainty. However, given the high volatility in wages and in labor force coverage rates observed in most developing countries, and in light of the unknown long-term demographic trends, it is advisable to have a buffer fund to mitigate the effects of these uncertainties on pension benefits. Unlike NDC systems implemented in other countries such as Sweden, the Egyptian system does not seem to preclude a buffer fund for systematic system risks, and it does include a sort of partial mutualization mechanism for unsystematic risks in the form of solidarity accounts.

In structuring the new social security and pension system, the Egyptian government opted for a multipillar scheme with universal coverage and integration of all risks; a mandatory shift from a nonfinancial defined benefit system to a defined contribution system comprising both FDC and NDC components for new entrants; a universal basic pension; higher normal retirement ages; institutional reforms; a redistributive mechanism for members with depreciated contribution careers; and a new scheme for unemployment insurance. The adoption of a unified DC scheme and, most important, the corresponding paradigm shift, should facilitate the integration of the heterogeneous schemes now in place—the Government Social Insurance Fund and its counterparts—and must be taken as an opportunity to involve previously excluded working populations in the system. In addition, the new paradigm will facilitate the tracking of the system's implicit liabilities and the portability of pension rights, thus contributing to improved financial stability and providing additional incentives for sound and transparent management of fiscal policy and for increased mobility in the labor market.

Another important aspect of the reform has to do with the implementation of redistributive poverty prevention mechanisms that are more transparent and more efficient than now exist and that eliminate discretionary and political manipulation, balance transfer costs, and avoid giving people the wrong incentives. These mechanisms are present in the basic pension and clawback mechanism, in the benefits for worker's death or disability, and in the unemployment and work injury benefits. The reform improves on the clear segregation between the funding sources of the contributory and noncontributory components of the system. My only question is whether the relatively generous nature of some of the benefits is actually sufficiently funded in the system by either the mutualization scheme (defined by the solidarity accounts) or the general budget, in the case of the universal basic pension. The flat-benefit approach adopted for the universal basic pension is simple to understand and easy to implement, in as much as it reduces to a minimum the eligibility conditions (i.e., individuals age 65 without any other income sources) and simplifies the means-testing evaluation procedures. Anyway, the integration of retirement and nonretirement benefits in the same system has never been an easy task. That being so, the efficiency and effectiveness of the proposed solution have to be confirmed once the system starts operating in full.

The implementation of an NDC and FDC system places great demands on institutional capacity. Administrative processes and information technology have to be put in place; individual records have to be collected and kept in a safe and well-structured data warehouse system; interaction with other government agencies, such as tax authorities, and with other administrative processes (payroll systems) has to be guaranteed; and transformation of DC accounts into annuity amounts requires the existence of appropriate prospective life tables. Regarding this last topic, actuarially correct cohort life tables that accommodate expected increases in life expectancy, employ sound methodologies, and use reliable demographic data are needed, and this is something that is not guaranteed to exist right now and should not be taken for granted. These life tables should be consistent with those used in the private sector. The implementation of the new pension system thus has to be accompanied by sound institutional reforms that create the conditions for success.

My last comment refers to the political-economy questions involved in the final definition and implementation of the new Egyptian social insurance system. Probably the greatest advantage offered by an NDC-type reform in any country, but particularly in developing countries, is the perception of permanency, and hence credibility and reliability, that it imparts to the social security system. The receipt by workers of regular statements tracking their rising notional account balances reinforces this sense of permanency and ownership. The sense of property rights creates a lock-in effect that prevents politicians from intervening to arbitrarily reduce or confiscate the notional capital accumulated in the NDC accounts. In other words, by reducing the need for governments to intervene regularly to adjust pension system parameters, the political risk of policy change in response to political pressures associated with public pension systems is significantly reduced.

Given this, the authors recognize that several aspects of the Egyptian reform—in particular, of the transition model chosen and the implementation choices selected—were made to gain public approval and support and are not sustained by technical studies, economic theory, or international experience. One example is the indexation mechanism of the NDC and annuities that, in the authors' words, "is soon to be revisited and assessed." Another is the guaranteed rate of return on the individual DC accounts. The notion that the way the system was finally calibrated is not sustainable in the short run and will inevitably have to be revisited just a couple of years after it starts operating is definitely not a good way to commence. Lessons learned from the Latvian pension reform show that when the benefits under the new scheme prove very different from public expectations, a chorus of disapproval will place intense pressure on politicians to revisit the pension reform to reinstate the generosity of benefits that was removed by the required adjustments. This could ultimately lead to the erosion of the DC-based pension reform.

China: An Innovative Hybrid Pension Design Proposal

Zheng Bingwen

This chapter presents a proposal for a new reform of the Chinese pension system that is based on individual accounts (introduced in 1997) and incorporates a hybrid design combining a nonfinancial (notional) defined contribution (NDC) component and a financial defined contribution (FDC) component. The proposal takes account of the specific Chinese institutional and cultural context. The system would also incorporate a noncontributory pension to complement the benefits of individuals with limited savings capacity. It represents an innovation in pension design that differs both from the Swedish NDC model and from China's present pension system, in which a direct link between contributions and benefits is lacking.

The main objectives of the proposed reform are to reduce the fragmentation of the current scheme while expanding its coverage, to address problems of financial sustainability, and to improve incentives and equity by creating a stronger link between contributions and benefits without incurring large transition costs. As in the original design of China's urban pension system, the reformed system would back its liabilities by both pay-as-you-go (PAYG) and financial assets.

The next two sections describe the development of China's current public pension scheme and the principal challenges that it faces. Subsequent sections outline the proposed hybrid scheme, examine the issues associated with the introduction of a social pension, and offer conclusions. The annex describes the models, data, and assumptions employed in the projections presented in the chapter.

China's Existing Pension System

At present, China's basic public pension system consists of the urban public pension system, which combines defined benefits with individual accounts; the farmers' pension system; and a scheme for workers in the public service sector (civil service) and public undertakings (PSS&UTs), which is financed from general revenues. (See Zheng 2009a.)

The urban public pension system, which was set up in 1997, is a hybrid system that combines defined benefit pensions, financed on a PAYG basis, with fully funded defined

Zheng Bingwen is the director-general of the Center for International Social Security Studies (CISS) at the Chinese Academy of Social Sciences (CASS), Beijing, and the director-general of the Institute of Latin American Studies (ILAS) at CASS. He is currently a member of China's National Social Insurance Standardization Technology Commission. The views expressed are the author's alone, and the accuracy of the data is the author's responsibility.

contribution (DC) pensions. The system was originally financed by an 11 percent contribution rate paid by the employee and a 17 percent contribution rate paid by the employer. The funded (FDC) component, however, was not implemented initially. Liaoning Province, in 2001, and Jilin and Heilongjiang Provinces, in 2004, were the first to introduce the FDC component, with budgetary support from the central and local governments. By 2006, 10 pilot provinces were funding individual accounts. Since then, implementation has stagnated, in part because of the costs of transition. In fact, the contribution rate for the FDC pillar has been reduced from 11 to 8 percent, paid entirely by the employee. The contribution rate going to the defined benefit PAYG system has been increased from 17 to 20 percent and is paid entirely by the employer. During the period 1997–2010, fund reserves increased from 24.5 billion yuan (Y) to Y 1.53 trillion.[1]

The country's rural areas contain 720 million people, or 54.3 percent of the country's total population of 1.33 billion.[2] In 1992, the government introduced in rural areas a fully funded DC public pension scheme, which has been referred to as the "old farmer pension." Originally, the system was supposed to be financed solely through individual contributions, but by the end of 2008, the number of participants in the plan was only about 56 million (down from just over 80 million in 1998), of whom about 5 million were pensioners. By then, the fund's reserves had reached Y 49.9 billion, up from Y 16.6 billion in 1998.

In August 2009, the central government announced a "new farmer pension" system funded by individual contributions, collective assistance, and government subsidies. There are five levels of individual contributions: Y 100, Y 200, Y 300, Y 400, and Y 500 per year. Individual participants opt for the level at which they want to contribute. Benefits consist of two parts: a basic pension equal to Y 55 per month and a monthly contributory pension equal to the balance in the individual account divided by 139—the same formula as that used for pensions in the urban system. By the end of 2010, coverage of the new farmer pension extended to 103 million participants, of whom 28.6 million were pensioners.[3] Total income was Y 45.3 billion, of which contributions amounted to Y 22.5 billion. Expenditure was Y 20.0 billion, and the cumulative fund reserve was Y 42.3 billion.

PSS&UT participants accounted for 8 percent of national coverage. This system cost Y 235.4 billion in 2010, or about 0.7 percent of gross domestic product (GDP).[4]

Although there are three core parts to the national pension system, hundreds of thousands of smaller schemes have been set up by local municipalities to meet the demands of migrant peasant workers or of special industrial zones. These local plans contribute to the fragmentation of the pension system, affect labor mobility, increase administrative costs, and create inequities among population groups. In addition, the lack of a direct link between contributions and benefits and the presence of implicit redistributive arrangements make all the schemes financially unsustainable and can reduce incentives to contribute, hindering expansion of coverage (see Zheng 2009b).

Main Challenges Facing China's Public Pension System

A reform of the Chinese pension system would have to overcome a number of difficulties:

- Low coverage levels
- Fragmentation that compromises efficient redistribution and the financial sustainability of pension schemes across provinces

- Low levels of portability that impede the mobility of the labor force
- A nontransparent link between contributions and benefits that reduces incentives to participate and contribute
- Low rates of return on investments.

Each of these problems is discussed in turn in this chapter.

LOW COVERAGE LEVELS

The three mandated pension systems of China cover, altogether, only 35.7 percent of the national labor force, or 264 million workers out of the workforce of 740 million.[5] In urban areas, coverage is 35.8 percent (190 million workers out of a workforce of 530 million, including rural workers); if participants in PSS&UTs are taken into account, urban coverage is 43.4 percent. Coverage in rural areas is 35.3 percent (about 74 million workers out of a workforce of 210 million). Under the current design of the system, it would be difficult to expand coverage further.

Among the 225 million migrant peasant workers, 140 million move from province to province, and most are employed in urban areas. At the end of 2010, only 33 million workers were participating in the basic public pension system.[6] This implies that about 197 million workers (90 + 140 − 33) in urban areas, or about 50 percent of the effective labor force, are not covered by the pension system. As was noted above, coverage in rural areas has been almost stagnant.

There are many reasons behind low coverage rates. One of the most important is that many workers are likely to have limited or no saving capacity and cannot afford the contribution rates required by the public pension system. Furthermore, individuals might have low incentives to enroll and contribute because of insufficient information about the benefits of long-term saving and the operations of the pension fund; because of the complicated procedures for enrollment and for drawing pensions; or because of lack of trust in the system, with its nontransparent benefit formulas and eligibility conditions.

HIGH LEVELS OF FRAGMENTATION

The Chinese pension system is inherently redistributive. Under current arrangements, however, redistribution is implicit, can be regressive, and is conditioned on the level of development of the region. There is no single fund in which pension reserves are accumulated. Rich provinces in eastern China with a greater share of high-income workers are better able to generate surpluses that can finance implicit subsidies for basic pensions than are poorer provinces in central and western China. Even within provinces, there is a high level of fragmentation in the allocation and management of funds. Only Beijing, Shanghai, Shanxi, and Tianjin Provinces have been able to pool funds within the province.

Changing the system under the current implicit and nontransparent redistributive arrangements would be very difficult and would lead to moral hazard. Counties in which individuals have shorter career histories because they enroll later or retire early would likely receive a larger share of subsidies that would be financed by counties where employees work and contribute longer. An important precondition for improving pooling across counties is therefore to make redistribution explicit. This will require a transparent and direct link between, on the one hand, contributions and, on the other, benefits and subsidies, which should be allocated on the basis of individual income levels rather than of career paths. (For a discussion about implicit and explicit redistribution in social insurance systems, see Ribe, Robalino, and Walker [2012], chapter 7.)

LIMITED PORTABILITY

In part because of limited risk pooling and low coverage rates, and in order to meet the needs of migrant workers, local governments, particularly in the developed cities in coastal areas where such workers concentrate, have set up schemes of their own for migrants and urban freelance employees. The result is further fragmentation of the pension system and a proliferation of programs that have different contribution rates and offer different benefits. There are seldom portability arrangements between these local schemes, and it is difficult for migrant peasant workers to transfer acquired rights from one to the other. As a result, many decide not to participate in the system. This constitutes a barrier to the mobility of labor that has greatly restrained the formation of a nationwide labor market.

LACK OF TRANSPARENCY AND WEAK INCENTIVES TO ENROLL AND CONTRIBUTE

The pension system lacks transparency, and difficulties in understanding the complicated formula used to calculate pensions discourage participation. The general problem is the total disconnect between the present value of contributions and the present value of future benefits. The replacement rate has been falling steadily, leading to further loss of confidence. Furthermore, the contribution rate for the urban pension system is too high—even higher than in northern European welfare economies. Many small and medium-size enterprises find it difficult to bear this cost, especially when other social insurance costs are taken into account.

LOW RATES OF RETURN ON INVESTMENTS

The fragmentation of investible funds makes it difficult to formulate an efficient investment portfolio and increases administrative costs. Partly as a consequence, effective rates of return are low. Public pension funds are scattered among more than 2,000 funds, with more than 2,000 local social security agencies responsible for their management. The general practice has been to deposit most of the funds in local banks and a smaller amount in government bonds. The annual average return rate has long remained less than 2 percent per year in nominal terms.[7] By comparison, between 2001 and 2008 the consumer price index (CPI) grew at an annual average rate of 2.2 percent, and, since 2008, the annual rate has been well above 5.0 percent.

Proposal for a Hybrid System

All the difficulties of China's public pension system described originate from the ad hoc designs of the various schemes, in which pensions are disconnected from contributions and redistribution is implicit and nontransparent. One way out of the present impasse of a "simple" combination of defined benefit (DB) and DC funding is to move toward a hybrid DC system that relies on both nonfinancial and financial assets.

The hybrid scheme operates as follows: (a) both the employee and employer contributions go into an individual account; (b) on the employee's retirement, the individual account assets are transformed into a lifelong pension using a DC formula; (c) the individual account assets are divided into two parts, one invested in financial assets and the other in PAYG assets; (d) by mixing the real return (the return on the financial assets) with the notional return (the internal return on the PAYG asset), a nominal fixed return of at least 8 percent is achieved, which is the declared interest rate, similar to the lending rate of banks; (e) the new system will apply equally to all participants, thus closing the gap between urban and rural residents and improving equality; and (f) the new system will unify the county schemes, eliminating the fragmentation of the public pension system.

This policy design is in full accord with the strategic objective put forward by the 17th National Congress of the Communist Party: to cover China's entire urban and rural population with a social security system by 2020. The design assumes a transition to the hybrid combination of social pooling and individual accounts, beginning in 2009. The transition period is 2009–20.

FUNDING THE INDIVIDUAL ACCOUNTS

The individual account consists of two parts: the FDC component, which depends on financial assets, and the NDC component. An important decision regarding the FDC component is how to invest accumulated savings. Under current conditions in China, it would not be cost-effective to allow account holders to make their own investment decisions, as they do in Chile and in Hong Kong SAR, China. The model proposed, instead, is of the centralized investment or provident fund type. Once the level of pension liabilities that needs to be backed by financial assets has been defined, a single institutional investor will take over the design and implementation of the investment policy. (There would be no need to separate FDC funds from the surpluses of the NDC.)[8] The proposal envisions that the central government would be responsible for the investment management of all the assets in the accounts, which would be pulled across funds.

An important gain from the move to a DC pension system is that the pooling of funds becomes easy to implement, as there is no longer implicit redistribution within the system. All workers, regardless of where they are, will know what their pension savings are and what rate of return they will receive on their investments—whether the assets are invested centrally or at the county level becomes irrelevant to them. From the point of view of the pension system, it is no longer important whether some of the surplus in a given county is used to pay pensions in another. At the end, all the liabilities of the county's plan members are backed by a combination of financial and PAYG assets. This system also eliminates the obstacles to making acquired pension rights fully portable nationwide. It is completely transparent and easy to understand and calculate, no matter where participants work and where they retire, because the benefit level has nothing to do with residence or household status. Similarly, there is no discrimination on the basis of residency documents; rather, there is equal national treatment. The public pension card could, under this plan, be used nationwide not only for the purpose of collecting pensions but also for banking.

Turning to the level of funding, we propose scenarios that depend on the level of the contribution rate. The current rate of 28 percent is too high for the existing pension system; it is detrimental to the expansion of coverage; and it can negatively affect firms' competitiveness. The proposal is therefore to maintain the employee contribution at the current 8 percent but to reduce the employer's contribution. Three cases can be considered for funding formulas at the end of a transition period:

- An 8 percent employer contribution (for a total, counting the employee's 8 percent share, of 16 percent), with 5 percentage points allocated to the FDC.
- A 12 percent employer contribution (total of 20 percent), with 5 percentage points allocated to the FDC.
- A 16 percent employer contribution (total of 24 percent), with 5 percentage points allocated to the FDC.

The decline in the employer contribution would be gradual and could be spread over a period of 11 years after the start of the reform. For instance, for the 8 percent + 8 percent plan, the employer contribution could be reduced by 1 percentage point per year, diminishing from 20 percent to, eventually, the final level of 8 percent. During the transition period, the difference between the observed contribution rate and the targeted contribution rate would continue to be used to pay current pensions; that is, the excess contribution would be allocated to the NDC rather than to the FDC component. (See table 6.1, which describes a reform with 2009 taken as the starting date.) At the end of the transition period, the entire employer contribution would be allocated to the FDC system.

Projections have been made to show how the reserves of the three plans would evolve over time. For plan 1, by the end of the transition period, the pension fund would record incomes of Y 2.7 trillion, expenditures of Y 2.0 trillion, and total reserves of Y 8.8 trillion, accounting for 13.1 percent of GDP (see table 6.2). After subtracting the reserves that would need to be invested in financial assets, there should be a balance of about Y 1.1 trillion, which would also need to be managed. Under plan 2, reserves would reach 16.7 percent of GDP, but there would be a funding gap of about Y 1.1 trillion. This gap, however, could be closed in subsequent years. In plan 3, reserves would reach 20.6 percent of GDP in 2020, and excluding the financial assets, there would be a cash surplus of Y 1.5 trillion. The long-term projections show that in all three of the FDC cases, the targeted level of funding can be achieved, leaving reserves that could be used to manage eventual liquidity shocks.

ENROLLMENT, CONTRIBUTIONS, AND SUBSIDIES FOR THE SELF-EMPLOYED AND FARMERS

An important design feature of this hybrid combination of NDC and FDC is that it facilitates the enrollment of self-employed persons, including farmers without employers. Table 6.3 lists four categories of workers: wage employees in the private sector and public enterprises; wage employees in the civil service; self-employed persons in urban areas and in nonfarm activities; and farmers. For the first two categories, contributions would continue to be paid by the employee and the employer on the basis of earnings. The proposal allows employers to pay additional contributions, with a ceiling on covered earnings of up to three times the average earnings in the locality.

TABLE 6.1 **Three plans for employer contributions and social pooling, with 8 percent employee contribution, for the transition period, 2009–20** percent

Plan	2009	2010	2011	2012	2013	2014	2015	2016	2017	2018	2019	2020
Plan 1 (8% + 8%, 5% funded)												
Social pooling	11.0	10.0	9.0	8.0	7.0	6.0	5.0	4.0	3.0	2.0	1.0	0.0
Employer	19.0	18.0	17.0	16.0	15.0	14.0	13.0	12.0	11.0	10.0	9.0	8.0
Plan 2 (8% + 12%, 8% funded)												
Social pooling	7.3	6.6	6.0	5.3	4.6	4.0	3.3	2.7	2.0	1.3	0.6	0.0
Employer	19.3	18.6	18.0	17.3	16.6	16.0	15.3	14.7	14.0	13.3	12.6	12.0
Plan 3 (8% + 16%, 8% funded)												
Social pooling	3.7	3.4	3.0	2.7	2.4	2.0	1.7	1.4	1.0	0.7	0.4	0.0
Employer	19.7	19.4	19.0	18.7	18.4	18.0	17.7	17.4	17.0	16.7	16.4	16.0

SOURCE: Author's calculations.

NOTE: Shares of employee and employer contributions for a plan are expressed as, for example, 8% + 8%, where the first number refers to the employee contribution.

TABLE 6.2 **Financial sustainability of the three proposed plans during the transition period, 2009–20**
trillions of yuan, except where specified

	Annual income	Annual payment	Balance for year	Cumulative balance	Cumulative balance as % of GDP	Balance after funding
	(1)	(2)	(3)	(4)	(5)	(6)
Plan 1 (8% + 8%, 5% funded)						
2009	0.91	0.64	0.26	1.00	3.47	0.86
2014	1.57	1.11	0.46	2.97	7.58	1.42
2017	2.21	1.74	0.47	5.78	10.84	1.48
2020	2.67	2.01	0.66	8.79	13.09	1.11
Plan 2 (8% + 12%, 5% funded)						
2009	0.91	0.64	0.27	1.01	3.49	0.76
2014	1.65	1.11	0.51	3.15	8.04	0.64
2017	2.47	1.76	0.68	6.73	12.61	−0.19
2020	3.22	2.03	1.15	11.25	16.75	−1.07
Plan 3 (8% + 16%, 5% funded)						
2009	0.92	0.64	0.28	1.016	3.53	0.77
2014	1.73	1.12	0.61	3.37	8.59	0.85
2017	2.74	1.78	0.96	7.74	14.52	0.83
2020	3.78	2.05	1.73	13.80	20.62	1.52

SOURCE: Author's calculations.

NOTE: GDP = gross domestic product. For each plan, the employee contribution (the first share) is a uniform 8 percent; the employer contribution varies. In column 1, annual income consists of the 8 percent individual contribution, an 8 percent employer contribution, 8 percent social pooling, and an 8 percent contribution by freelance employees and farmers. It includes a 5.8 percent real investment return on the account assets. Column 2 shows actual expenditures, and column 3 shows the difference between income and expenditure in the given year. Columns 4 and 5 show the cumulative balance, in amounts and share of GDP, including the 5.8 percent real investment return of the account assets. Balance after funding (column 6) refers to the balance over the previous years after funding the individual accounts in accordance with the targeted percentage.

For the self-employed, two issues have to be considered. First, on average, these workers are likely to have lower saving capacity than wage employees. Second, it is not possible to make a reliable estimate of their earnings. The proposal therefore provides flexibility in the level of the individual contribution. The base for contributions by the self-employed could be set at 50 percent of average earnings in the locality, and the contribution rate could range between 50 and 100 percent of the statutory individual contribution. This contribution rate, however, is unlikely to generate an adequate pension in old age. The proposal, therefore, is to allow the pension institution to credit the employers' share directly into the individual account. This policy, of course, generates liabilities that would not be covered by financial or PAYG assets and that would need to be made explicit and properly financed, as described below. One mechanism for reducing these liabilities would be to target the subsidies on the basis of means that could be estimated using proxy tests. A similar approach would be taken in the case of farmers except that, because their total earnings are likely to be even lower than those of the self-employed in some cases, their individual contribution could be zero.

Simulations suggest that even in the absence of additional revenues, the subsidies could be financed within the system. This would be an implicit tax on the contributions

TABLE 6.3 **Features of 12 participating groups in 4 categories covered by the hybrid pension plan**

Class and group	Description	Group features, individual contribution rate, and source of employer contribution
I. Employees		
1	Employees of state-owned enterprises	Private sector employees pay contributions according to the statutory percentage. Their employers, regardless of their nature, are to make their own contributions in the prescribed percentage according to law. Migrant peasant workers in various categories of enterprises shall be treated as the enterprises' employees.
2	Employees of private enterprises	
3	Employees of collective enterprises	
4	Employees of enterprises funded by foreign entities or by entities in Taiwan, China; Hong Kong SAR, China; and Macao SAR, China	
5	Migrant peasants working in enterprises in groups 1–4	
II. Public servants		
6	Public servants	Public servants, teachers, and employees working in public undertakings are employed by the state, and the principle of contributions made by both the state and the employee applies. The individual is to make the statutory contribution, and the state is to make the full contribution as an employer.
7	Teachers	
8	Employees in undertakings (a) with financial subsidies and with shortage subsidies and (b) without financial subsidies	
III. Urban freelance employees		
9	Self-employed industrial and commercial households and their employees	Participants in these three groups do not have employers. The contribution otherwise made by employers is to be credited into their accounts according to law. In view of these workers' limited capacity for contributing, their contribution base should be set at 50 percent of the average annual wages of the previous year.
10	Urban freelance employees	
11	Urban residents without jobs	
IV. 12. Farmers		Farmers are typical participants without employers. The employer contribution is to be paid as a credit into the account, and the individual contribution base is to be calculated from the average annual net income in the previous year in the locality.

SOURCE: Author's elaboration.

of current plan members, who, in the absence of the subsidies, could receive higher benefits for the same contribution (i.e., a higher rate of return on contributions). The second, more transparent and explicit, financing alternative would be to rely on government transfers, with the central and local governments sharing the costs. The central government could, for instance, contribute a fixed amount equivalent to 50 percent of the employer's contribution rate, multiplied by economywide average earnings, multiplied by the number of beneficiaries. The local government would make up any shortfall in the account. Financial projections of the cost of the transfers suggest that the fiscal burden would be manageable. Costs would increase rapidly over the first few years but would stabilize at about 0.5, 0.8, or 1.0 percent of GDP by 2050, depending on the plan (see table 6.4).

TABLE 6.4 Financial subsidy for pensions for farmers and urban freelance employees, amount and share of GDP, 2009–70

| Year | Plan 1 (8% + 8%) | | | | Plan 2 (8% + 12%) | | | | Plan 3 (8% + 16%) | | | |
| | Subsidy amount (100 million yuan) | | | | Subsidy amount (100 million yuan) | | | | Subsidy amount (100 million yuan) | | | |
	Farmers	Others	Total	% of GDP	Farmers	Others	Total	% of GDP	Farmers	Others	Total	% of GDP
2009	287	66	354	0.12	431	99	530	0.18	574	133	707	0.25
2014	1,588	784	2,372	0.56	2,382	1,176	3,558	0.84	3,176	1,568	4,744	1.12
2020	2,006	2,426	4,432	0.66	3,008	3,639	6,648	0.99	4,011	4,852	8,864	1.32
2030	2,714	4,502	7,216	0.58	4,072	6,753	10,825	0.87	5,429	9,004	14,433	1.16
2040	4,322	6,946	11,268	0.56	6,483	10,419	16,902	0.83	8,644	13,893	22,536	1.11
2050	6,513	10,619	17,132	0.52	9,769	15,928	25,697	0.78	13,025	21,238	34,263	1.04
2060	11,336	14,915	26,251	0.49	17,004	22,373	39,376	0.73	22,671	29,830	52,502	0.98
2070	20,758	21,353	42,111	0.48	31,137	32,030	63,167	0.72	41,516	42,706	84,223	0.96

SOURCE: Author's calculations.

NOTE: GDP = gross domestic product. Shares of employer and employee contributions for a plan are expressed as, for example, 8% + 8%, where the first number refers to the employee contribution. "Others" refers to urban freelance employees.

TRANSFORMING ACQUIRED RIGHTS INTO INITIAL CAPITAL AND CALCULATING ANNUITIES

For individuals who are in the current system and have accumulated pension rights, the proposal is that, on retirement, part of their individual account be reconstructed in order to "make up" their contributions between the time of enrollment and the time of the reform. The methodology suggested is to simulate past contributions (since, in many cases, full records might not be available) and to credit a given interest rate. Starting with the reform, new contributions would simply be credited to the NDC and FDC accounts.

The benefit might be paid either as a lump sum (for a minority number of people) or as a life annuity—essentially, monthly payments during the person's lifetime. For the latter, the authorities responsible for calculating and paying pensions could establish a National Administration of Basic Pension Fund Investment and Management (NABPFI) to assume the risk of issuing the annuity. The annuity could be indexed with wages (e.g., 60 percent of the growth rate of annual covered wages).

For survivors' pensions, there are two possible cases. If the plan member dies before retirement age, the savings in the account would be treated the same as any other asset and would be inherited according to normal inheritance rules or according to the terms of the member's will (or both). Simulations show that even if notional capital is converted into cash to make payments to survivors, there would be no major impacts on the financial situation of the fund (see table 6.5). In essence, the percentage of the amount inherited by the dependents in the balance is very small, standing at around 0.2 percent in the three plans. If the plan member dies after retirement, what happens to survivors will depend on the type of annuity that was issued. If the plan member wants the pension to revert to a given dependent on the member's death, a joint annuity would have to be issued.

As a reference, estimates of replacement rates for single annuities at age 60 for the three plans are 41 percent (plan 1), 52 percent (plan 2), and 62 percent (plan 3). Joint annuities, by definition, would involve lower pensions.

PRINCIPLES FOR DETERMINING THE INTEREST RATE

The proposal considers two different periods for the determination of the interest rate credited to the individual accounts. During the first period—the first 10 years of transition—the nominal interest rate would be fixed at about 8 percent, which is the rate at which the wage bill is expected to grow during that period. Simulations show that an 8 percent interest rate is indeed sustainable in the three plans. The interest rate is to be announced by the central government and is a national standard rate that is credited to all the accounts every month. It is open and transparent and may be checked or consulted at any time by telephone or Internet.

After the transition period, the pension fund will start paying the sustainable rate of return of the system, which is a weighted average of the growth rate of the PAYG asset and the return on the investment on financial assets. In the simulations, the latter has been estimated at about 5.8 percent real per year.[9] The notional rate in the NDC scheme could be approximated by the growth rate of the average covered wage.

TABLE 6.5 **Effect of inheritance of individual assets on the fund balance in the hybrid scheme, 2009–70**

Year	Number of deceased members	Amount inherited by dependents (Y hundred millions)	Fund balance without inheritance (Y trillions)	Fund balance with inheritance (Y trillions)	Share of the amount inherited by dependents (%)
Plan 1 (8% + 8%)					
2009	509,927	0	1.0349	1.0349	0.2
2014	1,113,763	87.4314	3.6764	3.6532	23.8
2020	1,191,634	240.4365	12.7597	12.5835	18.8
2030	1,631,190	1,361.4538	50.2754	48.9146	27.1
2050	1,662,235	7,035.9238	280.9642	264.2942	25.0
2070	1,476,722	17,222.3465	945.1541	854.4841	18.2
Plan 2 (8% + 12%)					
2009	509,927	0	1.0591	1.0591	0.2
2014	1,113,763	87.4314	4.2018	4.1787	20.8
2020	1,191,634	240.4365	17.1196	16.9435	14.0
2030	1,631,190	1,361.4538	71.5040	70.1432	19.0
2050	1,662,235	7,035.9238	389.9343	373.2643	18.0
2070	1,476,722	17,222.3465	1,301.9817	1,211.3116	13.2
Plan 3 (8% + 16%)					
2009	509,927	0	1.0865	1.0865	0.2
2014	1,113,763	87.4314	4.7592	4.7361	18.4
2020	1,191,634	240.4365	21.6109	21.4347	11.1
2030	1,631,190	1,361.4538	92.9634	91.6025	14.7
2050	1,662,235	7,035.9238	499.6171	482.9471	14.1
2070	1,476,722	17,222.3465	1,661.0102	1,570.3401	10.4

SOURCE: Author's calculations.

NOTE: Shares of employee and employer contributions for a plan are expressed as, for example, 8% + 8%, where the first number refers to the employee contribution. The last column shows the result derived from dividing the amount inherited by the dependents by the fund balance without inheritance.

GRADUAL INCREASE IN RETIREMENT AGE

In the reformed system, the calculation of the pension, through the annuity formula, would automatically take into account the remaining life expectancy at retirement. As a result, for the same number of years of contributions, individuals retiring early would receive lower pensions than individuals retiring later. To encourage individuals to work longer and thus receive higher pensions, the proposal also considers a gradual increase in the minimum statutory retirement age. The increase could be accomplished stepwise, so that by 2020, the retirement age for female employees would be set uniformly at 60 and for male employees at 65.

Introducing a Social Pension

Although the proposed reform is expected to gradually expand the coverage of contributory pensions, many elderly persons will still lack a pension during the transition period. In addition, even among those enrolled in the pension system, short contribution periods can lead to pensions that are insufficient to maintain an adequate standard of living.

To address these problems, the proposal calls for the introduction of a social pension financed from general revenues that would be paid to all individuals older than age 65. The pension could be universal (a flat transfer to all elderly persons) or, to reduce costs, it could be tested against pension income. Thus, for individuals receiving a contributory pension, the social pension could be reduced proportionally. The social pension would reduce the need to subsidize the contributions of the self-employed and farmers. The initial level of the social pension for urban residents could be set at Y 200 per month and that for rural residents, at Y 50 (in 2009 prices). The social pension could be adjusted once a year by being indexed with 100 percent of the growth rate of economywide average earnings.

Simulations show that the cost of the social pension could be sustainable even if the pension is universal. In the first five years after the reform, total expenditures would remain below or close to 0.5 percent of GDP (see table 6.6). As the number of beneficiaries increases (see figure 6.1), expenditures could exceed 0.8 percent of GDP by 2020. Since the number of people benefiting from the social pension after 2040 is expected to decline gradually, expenditures would also diminish, stabilizing at 0.6 percent of GDP in 2070.

It is important to note that because the introduction of a social pension will increase household incomes, there may be a reduction in social assistance (*dibao*) expenditures.

Conclusion

This chapter has described a proposal to reform the Chinese pension system on the basis of a hybrid NDC–FDC design. The discussion showed that the proposed reform can address the main challenges of the current system by (a) enabling the unification of fragmented programs at the county level and thus improving redistribution, portability of benefits, and labor mobility; (b) increasing the level of funding of the current system; (c) addressing the problem of financial sustainability; (d) improving transparency and the incentives that individuals have to enroll and contribute; and (e) creating the conditions for expanding the coverage of pensions to the entire labor force.

In the proposed reform, employee and employer contributions would be deposited in individual accounts. The liabilities of the system would be backed by two types of assets: PAYG assets (the NDC component), and financial assets (the FDC component). Over the long run, the hybrid system would pay a rate of return on contributions that is a weighted average of the notional interest rate paid by the NDC and the rate of return on the investment of financial assets. Under some designs, the NDC rate could be fixed in real terms to reduce exposure to macroeconomic and demographic risks.

An important feature of the reform is that it enables the expansion of the pension system to cover wage earners in the informal sector, the self-employed, and farmers. In part, this can be achieved by creating a direct link between contributions and benefits, which is expected to improve incentives to enroll and contribute. To facilitate the enrollment of the self-employed, one proposal is to subsidize part of their contributions (e.g., the employers' part). The reform also considers the introduction of a social pension for all elderly persons older than age 65, which would diminish the need for contribution subsidies. Finally, the reform aims at reducing the employer's contribution rate, which is expected to stimulate the creation of jobs in the formal sector.

The chapter has paid considerable attention to implementation. In particular, it has emphasized the need to give sufficient thought to transition arrangements. One issue is

TABLE 6.6 **Projections of social pension expenditure, 2009–21**

Year	Urban					Rural					Total	
	Beneficiaries (10,000 persons)	Amount (yuan per month per person)	Expenditure (0.1 billion yuan)	% of GDP	Replacement rate (%)	Beneficiaries (10,000 persons)	Amount (yuan per month per person)	Expenditure (0.1 billion yuan)	% of GDP	Replacement rate (%)	Total expenditure (0.1 billion yuan)	% of GDP
2009	3,078	200	739	0.26	9.1	7,448	50	447	0.16	14.3	1,186	0.41
2010	3,279	224	881	0.28	9.1	7,587	56	510	0.16	14.9	1,391	0.45
2011	3,462	251	1,042	0.31	9.1	7,732	63	582	0.17	15.4	1,624	0.48
2012	3,706	280	1,244	0.34	9.1	7,913	70	664	0.18	15.9	1,908	0.53
2013	3,927	311	1,463	0.37	9.1	8,082	78	753	0.19	16.4	2,216	0.57
2014	4,163	343	1,714	0.40	9.1	8,336	86	858	0.20	16.7	2,572	0.61
2015	4,380	377	1,983	0.43	9.1	8,596	94	973	0.21	17.1	2,957	0.65
2016	4,581	413	2,272	0.46	9.1	8,825	103	1,094	0.22	17.3	3,366	0.68
2017	4,811	450	2,601	0.49	9.1	9,180	113	1,241	0.23	17.5	3,841	0.72
2018	5,029	489	2,949	0.51	9.1	9,495	122	1,392	0.24	17.5	4,341	0.75
2019	5,265	528	3,335	0.54	9.1	9,831	132	1,557	0.25	17.5	4,891	0.79
2020	5,493	567	3,740	0.56	9.1	10,175	142	1,732	0.26	17.5	5,472	0.81
2021	6,349	607	4,626	0.64	9.1	10,421	152	1,898	0.26	17.3	6,524	0.90

SOURCE: Author's calculations.

NOTE: GDP = gross domestic product.

FIGURE 6.1 **Beneficiary populations covered by the social pension, 2009–2110**

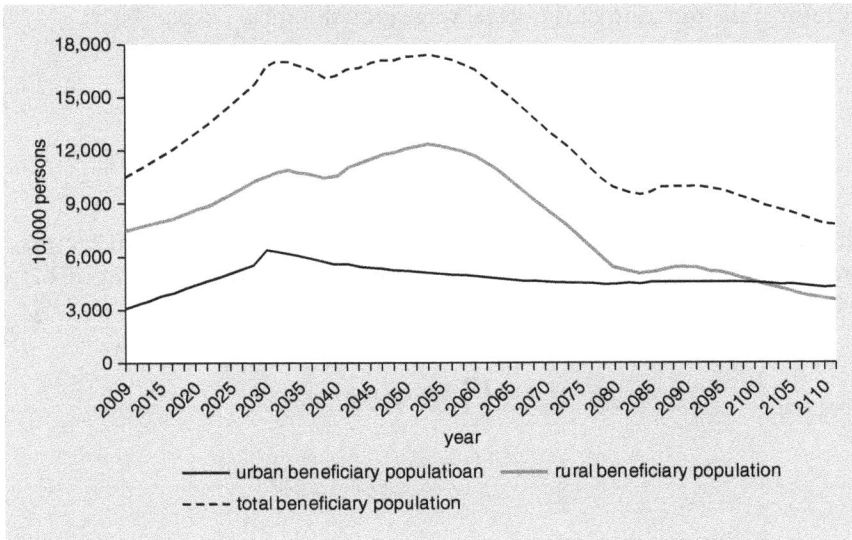

SOURCE: Author's calculations.

the calculation of acquired rights for current plan members. The proposal here is to reconstruct contribution histories in order to compute the initial level of capital to be transferred to the new hybrid pension system. The reform proposal also recommends gradual changes in the contribution rate and the targeted level of funding and in the statutory minimum retirement age. Simulations based on an actuarial model suggest that the fiscal costs of the reform would be affordable and that over the long term, the financial sustainability of the pension fund would be guaranteed.

Annex. Projection Models and Assumptions

This annex describes the models, data, and assumptions employed in the simulations reported in this chapter. Three models are discussed, covering replacement rates, the fund balance, and the funded ratio.

REPLACEMENT RATE MODELS

Final value of contributions. For a typical worker who retired in year t, the notional capital value of the first year of retirement (i.e., the final value, FVI, of all contributions), is

$$FVI_t = \overline{W_{a,t-b+a}} * \sum_{i=a}^{b-1} c * \theta_{t-b+a+1}^{t-b+i} * \vartheta_{a+1}^{i} * \gamma_{t-b+i+1}^{t-1}, \tag{6.1}$$

where a is the starting age of the insured as a plan member; b is the statutory retirement age; $\overline{W_{a,t-b+a}}$ is the wage at the starting age of the insured; c is the contribution rate to individual accounts; and $\theta^{t-b+i}_{t-b+a+1}$ is the wage growth index attributable to social factors. This last term is the function of the social wage growth rate w_j, expressed as

$$\theta^{t-b+i}_{t-b+a+1} = \prod_{t-b+a+1}^{t-b+i} (1+w_j)\,(i \ne a)$$

$$\theta^{t-b+a}_{t-b+a+1} = 1\,(i = a). \tag{6.2}$$

The term ϑ^i_{a+1} is the wage growth index attributable to personal factors, which is a function of the seniority wage growth rate ψ_i according to length of service, expressed as

$$\vartheta^i_{a+1} = \prod_{a+1}^{i} (1+\psi_i)\,(i \ne a)$$

$$\vartheta^a_{a+1} = 1\,(i = a), \tag{6.3}$$

and $\gamma^{t-1}_{t-b+i+1}$ is the interest rate index attributable to the declared interest rate α_j, which is credited to individual accounts in each fiscal year, as follows:

$$\gamma^{t-1}_{t-b+i+1} = \prod_{t-b+i+1}^{t-1} (1+\alpha_j)\,(i \ne b-1)$$

$$\gamma^{t-1}_{t} = 1\,(i = b-1). \tag{6.4}$$

Present value of pensions. For a person who retired in year t, the present value (PVE) of the total pension can be expressed as

$$PVE_t = B_t + \frac{B_t(1+k_{t+1})}{1+\beta_{t+1}} + \cdots + B_t \prod_{t+1}^{t+e_b-1}\left(\frac{1+k_h}{1+\beta_h}\right) = B_t * \left[1 + \sum_{j=t+1}^{t+e_b-1} \prod_{t+1}^{j}\left(\frac{1+k_h}{1+\beta_h}\right)\right], \tag{6.5}$$

where B_t is the pension in the first year after retirement (i.e., the pension in year t); e_b is the average life expectancy after retirement; k_h is the adjustment factor set at 60 percent of the social average wage growth rate in the previous year (i.e., $k_h = 0.6w'_{h-1}$); and B_h is the discount rate, equal to the system's internal rate of return, assumed to be $B_h = a_h$.

Replacement rate. Based on the principle of actuarial neutrality, the following equality holds:

$$FVI_t = PVE_t.$$

Substitution of formulas (6.1) and (6.5) into this equation yields

$$\overline{W_{a,t-b+a}} * \sum_{i=a}^{b-1} c * \theta^{t-b+i}_{t-b+a+1} * \vartheta^i_{a+1} * \gamma^{t-1}_{t-b+i+1} = B_t * \left[1 + \sum_{j=t+1}^{t+e_b-1} \prod_{t+1}^{j}\left(\frac{1+k_h}{1+\beta_h}\right)\right]. \tag{6.6}$$

Then B_t, separated into its components, is

$$B_t = \frac{\overline{W_{a,t-b+a}} * \sum_{i=a}^{b-1} c * \theta_{t-b+a+1}^{t-b+i} * \vartheta_{a+1}^i * \gamma_{t-b+i+1}^{t-1}}{1 + \sum_{j=t+1}^{t+e_b-1} \prod_{t+1}^{j} \left(\frac{1+k_b}{1+\beta_b}\right)}. \tag{6.7}$$

Finally, we obtain the replacement rate R_t,

$$R_t = \frac{B_t}{W'_{t-1}} = \frac{\overline{W_{a,t-b+a}} * \sum_{i=a}^{b-1} c * \theta_{t-b+a+1}^{t-b+i} * \vartheta_{a+1}^i * \gamma_{t-b+i+1}^{t-1}}{\overline{W'_{t-b+a}} * \theta_{t-b+a+1}^{t-1} * \left[1 + \sum_{j=t+1}^{t+e_b-1} \prod_{t+1}^{j} \left(\frac{1+k_b}{1+\beta_b}\right)\right]}, \tag{6.8}$$

where $\overline{W'_{t-1}}$ is the social average wage in the year before retirement and $\overline{W'_{t-b+a}}$ is the social average wage in the first year after enrollment.

FUND BALANCE MODELS

Pension fund income. Because contributions to social pooling will be continued until 2020, we build fund income models for social pooling and individual accounts, respectively.

The fund income from individual accounts is

$$I_t = \mu * \sum_{i=a}^{b-1} c * \overline{W_{a,t-i+a}} * \theta_{t-i+a+1}^{t} * \vartheta_{a+1}^i * \left(\frac{\overline{N_{i-1,t-1}} + \overline{N_{i,t}}}{2}\right), \tag{6.9}$$

where μ is contribution density (the ratio of the number of participating workers to the number of contributing workers); $\overline{N_{i-1,t-1}}$ is the number of contributing workers age $i-1$ at the end of year $t-1$; and $\overline{N_{i,t}}$ is the number of contributing workers age $i-1$ at the end of year t.

The fund income from social pooling is

$$I'_t = \mu * \sum_{i=a}^{b-1} c'_t * \overline{W_{a,t-i+a}} * \theta_{t-i+a+1}^{t} * \vartheta_{a+1}^i * \left(\frac{\overline{N_{i-1,t-1}} + \overline{N_{i,t}}}{2}\right). \tag{6.10}$$

The term c'_t is the contribution rate to social pooling in year t, where $t \geq 2020$ and $c'_t = 0$.

Pension fund expenditure. In the transition period 2009–20, the average replacement rate for retired workers is assumed to be 55 percent, according to current standards. After 2020, the new replacement rate under a hybrid combination of social pooling and individual accounts will be calculated for new pensioners. Therefore, in the pension expenditure model, we no longer distinguish between social pooling and individual accounts but use a unified formula:

$$E_t = \sum_{i=b}^{\omega-1} \mu * R_{t-i+b} * \overline{W'_{t-i+a}} * \theta_{t-i+a+1}^{t-i+b-1} * \left(\frac{\overline{N'_{i-1,t-1}} + \overline{N'_{i,t}}}{2}\right) * \phi_{t-i+b+1}^{t}, \tag{6.11}$$

where E_t is expenditure, ω is the age limit of survival, and $\phi_{t-i+b-1}^t$ is the adjustment index, expressed as

$$\phi_{t-i+b+1}^t = \prod_{t-i+b+1}^{t} \left(1+k_h\right)\left(i \neq b\right)$$

$$\phi_{t+1}^t = 1\left(i = b\right). \tag{6.12}$$

Annual balance of the pension fund. The annual balance (M_t) of the pension fund is

$$M_t = I_t + I_t' - E_t + F_t, \tag{6.13}$$

where F_t is the financial transfer from the central and local governments.

Cumulative deficit or surplus of the pension fund. The cumulative deficit or surplus (G_t) of the pension fund is

$$G_t = M_t + G_{t-1} * \left(1+r_t\right), \tag{6.14}$$

where r_t is the actual investment return rate of the pension fund.

FUNDED RATIO MODELS

The implicit pension debt (IPD) is equal to all the unpaid entitlements at some point, expressed as

$$IPD_t = \sum_{x=a}^{b-1}\left(\overline{N_{x,t}} * \sum_{i=a}^{x} c * \overline{W_{a,t-x+a}} * \theta_{t-x+a+1}^{t-x+i} * \vartheta_{a+1}^i * \gamma_{t-x+i+1}^t\right). \tag{6.15}$$

The funded ratio is expressed as

$$\delta_t = \frac{G_t}{IPD_t}. \tag{6.16}$$

BASIC DATA AND ASSUMPTIONS USED IN THE MODELS

Number of insured employees and pensioners. The projection proceeds in four steps:

1. Establishment of a dynamic equilibrium equation of the population and the projection of the national population by age and gender from 2005 to 2070. All hypotheses about fertility rates, life expectancy, mortality rates, and so on are from direct references or are the results of calculations by the author based on data from the *2005 China 1% Population Sample Survey* (NBS 2007) and *World Population Prospects: The 2006 Revision,* issued by the Population Division of the United Nations (United Nations 2007).
2. Construction of the age-structure curve for the urban-rural migration, according to recent census data and projections of the urban population by age and gender from 2005 to 2070, and given the hypotheses about urbanization rates that emerge from selected research results.

TABLE 6A.1 **Basic parameters of population and economic data**

Indicator	2009	2010	2011	2012	2013	2014	2015	2016	2017	2018	2019	2020	2030	2040	2050+
Urbanization rate (%)	48.6	50.0	51.0	52.0	53.0	54.0	55.0	56.0	57.0	58.0	59.0	60.0	65.0	68.0	70.0
Labor force participation rate (%)	67.5	67.5	67.8	68.0	68.3	68.5	68.8	69.0	69.3	69.5	69.8	70.0	70.0	70.0	70.0
Unemployment rate (%)	4	4	4	4	4	4	4	4	4	4	4	4	4	4	4
Average retirement age	55.0	55.0	55.5	56.0	56.5	57.0	57.5	58.0	58.5	59.0	59.5	60.0	65.0	65.0	65.0
Actual investment return rate (%)	5.8	5.8	5.8	5.8	5.8	5.8	5.8	5.8	5.8	5.8	5.8	5.8	5.8	5.8	5.8
Declared interest rate (%)	8	8	8	8	8	8	8	8	8	8	8	8	*	*	*
Nominal GDP growth rate (%)	8	8	8	8	8	8	8	8	8	8	8	8	5	5	5
Nominal wage growth rate (%)	12.0	12.0	11.5	11.0	10.5	10.0	9.5	9.0	8.5	8.0	7.5	7.0	5.0	5.0	5.0

SOURCE: Author's calculations and projections from Chinese data.

NOTE: GDP = gross domestic product. The discrete data in the table are determined by linear interpolation. Unemployment rates are derived from the current registered unemployment rate. After 2020, the declared interest rate (α_t) is equal to the weighted sum of return rates of the funded and unfunded components of the account (indicated in the table by an asterisk, *). The former is equal to the actual investment return rate (r_t); the latter is approximately equal to the wage growth rate (W_t). The formula can be expressed as $\alpha_t = r_t^* \delta_t + W_t^* (1 - \delta_t)$, where δ_t is the funded ratio.

3. Projection of the urban employed population by age and gender from 2005 to 2070, on the basis of labor force participation rates and unemployment rates from China's Fifth Census.
4. Estimation of the number of new insured employees needed to achieve the government's goal of full coverage in 2020. The numbers are projected by age and gender from 2005 to 2020 on the basis of the current age and gender structure of new insured workers. The total number of insured employees and pensioners by age and gender from 2005 to 2070 is derived by the use of the dynamic equilibrium equation for the insured population.

Average starting age of the insured. According to sample survey data in five cities—Beijing, Chengdu, Dalian and Shanghai, and Xi'an—the average starting age of the insured in 1999 was 16. The data are from the project on China's Old-Age Social Insurance Fund Measurement and Management, sponsored by the Social Security Institute at China's Ministry of Human Resources and Social Security. Projections from the project put the average starting ages of the insured at 16 in 2001, 17 in 2005, and 18 after 2010.

Taking into consideration China's goal of full coverage in 2020, the new insured employees from now until 2020 include not only new workers entering the workforce but also workers who have been employed for many years. In this chapter, the average starting age of the insured employee is assumed to be 17 in 2004 and prior years. One year of age is then added per year until 2014, when the starting age is age 27. If one assumes that the coverage works well, one year of age is subtracted every year until 2020, when age 21 is reached, after which this value remains unchanged.

Growth rate of seniority wage. On the basis of the survey data and research literature by Chinese scholars, the following assumptions are made: the annual growth rate of the seniority wage is 1.5 percent from age 22 to age 40 and 1 percent from age 41 to age 60. For individuals younger than age 22 and older than age 60, the rate is zero.

Other indicators. Table 6A.1 presents other relevant indicators.

Notes

The author thanks Qi Chuanjun, researcher for CISS and ILAS at CASS, for his calculations and actuarial computations for this chapter, and Grayson Clarke, international expert for fund management in the European Union–China Social Security Reform Cooperation project, for his comments on an earlier draft. Robert Holzmann and David A. Robalino of the World Bank have been very helpful in slimming the text to the elements critical for presentation to an interested international pension community.

1. A billion is 1,000 million; a trillion is 1,000 billion.
2. NBS, *National Economic and Social Development Statistics Bulletin,* 2008.
3. The data cited are from China, MHRSS, *Statistical Bulletin of Human Resources and Social Security Undertakings Development,* 2010.
4. See China, Ministry of Finance, *Final Financial Statement of National Expenditure,* 2008, available at Ministry of Finance website, http://yss.mof.gov.cn/yusuansi/zhengwuxinxi/caizhengshuju/200907/t20090707_176723.html.

5. Calculations are by the author and are based on data in *China Statistical Yearbook 2010*.

6. China, MHRSS, *Statistical Bulletin of Human Resources and Social Security Undertakings Development,* 2008.

7. Announcement by the National Auditing Bureau at the Third National Forum on Social Security, November 6, 2007. See the website "People" (in Chinese): http://politics.people.com.cn/GB/1027/8299118.html.

8. At least initially, the balance of the reserves of the NDC would be far greater than the required minimum level of funding of the individual accounts.

9. The rate 5.8 percent is a benchmark set up for a research project sponsored by China's ministry of Human Resources and Social Security about 10 years ago.

References

China, MHRSS (Ministry of Human Resources and Social Security). Annual. *Statistical Bulletin of Human Resources and Social Security Undertakings Development.* Beijing: MHRSS.

China, Ministry of Finance. Annual. *Final Financial Statement of National Expenditure.* Beijing: Ministry of Finance.

China, Ministry of Labor and Social Security. Annual. *Statistical Bulletin of Labor and Social Security Undertakings Development.* Beijing: Ministry of Labor and Social Security.

China Statistics Press. Annual. *China Statistical Yearbook.* Beijing: China Statistics Press.

NBS (National Bureau of Statistics of China). 2007. *2005 China 1% Population Sample Survey.* Beijing: China Statistics Press.

———. Annual. *National Economic and Social Development Statistics Bulletin.* Beijing: National Statistics Press.

United Nations, Population Division. 2007. *World Population Prospects: The 2006 Revision.* New York: United Nations.

Zheng Bingwen. 2009a. "Harm and Damage of the Fragmented Social Security System in China and the Study of the Impulse for the Fragmentation of Social Security System." [In Chinese.] *Social Science of Gansu Province* (October 5).

———. 2009b. "60 Years of Social Security in China: Achievements and Lessons." [In Chinese.] *Chinese Journal of Population Science* (October 5).

CHAPTER 6
COMMENT

Agnieszka Chłoń-Domińczak

In chapter 6 in this volume, Zheng Bingwen provides an interesting proposal for reform of the Chinese pension system based on a hybrid design that incorporates the nonfinancial (notional) defined contribution (NDC) approach. The application of the NDC-based solution seems to present an opportunity to solve the problems of China's current pension system that are associated with ongoing demographic processes such as population aging and migration.

As indicated in the literature, well-designed NDC systems allow a good diversification of demographic risks (see, e.g., Góra and Palmer 2004). The introduction of an NDC formula enables the system to adjust to increasing life expectancies, and properly designed indexation of NDC accounts allows for sharing of the risk of changes in the age structure and in the relative sizes of the working and retired generations.

NDC systems also provide a good basis for facilitating transferability of pension rights and the migration of workers. Given the fragmentation of pension systems in China and the high mobility of workers, a defined contribution platform could support better recognition of pension rights acquired throughout the working career.

Finally, an NDC-based scheme can help meet the challenge of expanding the currently low coverage of China's pension systems. The defined contribution scheme both creates incentives to contribute and allows for recognition of pension rights even for short periods of contribution payments. As a result, it may make possible better old-age protection for workers in the future.

The combination of the above-mentioned factors—demographic change, a highly mobile workforce, and low coverage—is unique for China and is not observed in any other country implementing or considering NDC schemes. The author identifies and describes the challenges, indicating a deep understanding of emerging issues and problems. The chapter's insider view of the pension reform discussion in China is complemented by chapter 7, by Heikki Oksanen, who presents an external assessment of the challenges facing pension systems in China.

Zheng's proposal for a hybrid NDC design, as described in chapter 6, provides a good starting point for a discussion of a potential framework for an NDC pension system in China. The chapter outlines major elements of the proposed system, including the level of contribution rates, the split of contributions between employees and employers, and the indexation of NDC accounts, and examines options for extending coverage to farmers. It also discusses the introduction of a social pension as a means of protecting against poverty those who have little (or no) pension rights. Given other countries' experience with NDC pension design, as discussed by Chłoń-Domińczak, Franco, and Palmer in chapter 2 in this volume, some elements of the proposal require further elaboration.

Agnieszka Chłoń-Domińczak is an assistant professor at the Warsaw School of Economics and is at the Educational Research Institute, Warsaw.

First, the determination of the contribution rate for the new system should take into account not only the current financial situation of the Chinese pension system but also its future outlook—both the financial sustainability of the pension scheme and the adequacy of pension benefits. As the experience of other countries shows, an old-age contribution rate of about 20 percent of wages affords a basis for achieving a replacement rate of about 60–70 percent, depending on the given country's economic and demographic situation. Lower contribution levels may lead to relatively low benefit levels in the future, a fact that should be taken into account when designing the pension system.

Another important element of the proposed pension system is the rate of return earned on both NDC and financial defined contribution (FDC) accounts. The author proposes that the rate of return for the NDC component be set administratively at the level of the expected growth of the wage bill in China. Predefining rates of return may lead to inefficiencies in the pension system. In the NDC system, the rate of return should be linked to the growth of the covered wage bill, which takes into account both changes in the average covered wage and changes in the number of workers participating in the pension system. If the administratively set rate of return is lower, the future level of pensions will be less than the pension that could be offered without compromising the financial sustainability of the pension system. If it is higher, the result could be loss of financial stability. In such a case, additional safeguards—for example, a balancing mechanism, as in the Swedish pension system—would be needed (see chapter 2 in this volume).

Turning to recognition of accrued pension rights, the proposed solution is to reconstruct the individual's contribution history so that the value of the NDC account can be calculated. Such a solution was implemented in Sweden. It should be noted, however, that this option requires high-quality records of past earnings and employee contributions. In the absence of such information, other, simplified solutions can be applied, using the approach of the prereform pension systems.

The author proposes mixed financing for the hybrid system, with a portion of the old-age contribution diverted to the FDC component. The central government would manage the assets. In further elaborating the system design, care should be taken with the design of the rules for management and investment of the assets. Design issues include, among other things, the development of benchmarks, the determination of the asset classes in which the contribution will be invested, and the degree of international exposure of such investments. Finally, the institutional setting of the investments requires attention. Investment policies should take into account international standards, such as the guidelines issued by the Organisation for Economic Co-operation and Development (OECD)—"OECD Guidelines for Pension Fund Governance" (OECD 2005) and "OECD Guidelines on Pension Fund Asset Management" (OECD 2006)—and the "Guidelines for the Investment of Social Security Funds" developed by the International Social Security Association (ISSA 2005), which cover both governance and investment management issues.

The chapter also touches on future extension of coverage by the pension systems. Of particular concern are self-employed persons and farmers. The author rightly indicates that owing to the low income of these groups, there is likely to be a problem with the future adequacy of their pension benefits. A potential solution offered by the author is to subsidize contributions for selected groups of workers who are responsible for financing their own contributions. Although such a suggestion seems to solve some of the potential problems, it may create others, such as contribution evasion. Control mechanisms would be needed to support such a redistribution mechanism. It should also be noted that contribution subsidies and redistribution should not only be linked to specific worker categories but also be provided for selected periods of inactivity such as maternity and paternity leave and periods of unemployment.

A complementary part of the redistribution mechanism would be a proposed social pension that guarantees a minimum income for those who have not accumulated sufficient pension rights. The author indicates that, depending on the financial condition of the pension system, the social pension could be universal or could be tested against pension income. The existence of such a mechanism means a reduction in other social safety net mechanisms for older people, as is rightly noted in the chapter.

The chapter includes projections of the potential outcomes of the proposed changes, focusing mainly on financial sustainability and overall expenditure levels. Although the projections presented support some of the recommendations, further work should include a set of sensitivity tests that would allow for ex ante evaluation of the proposed solutions.

The author does not discuss the important issue of the administration of the system and of individual accounts, which is one of the most challenging aspects of implementation of NDC systems. This challenge is particularly significant in China because of the size of the population and the difficulty of securing portability of pension rights for migrant workers.

To summarize, the hybrid NDC proposal elaborated in the chapter addresses most of the challenges faced by China's pension systems. The proposal covers all the constituent elements of the pension system, but in many cases, these are still on a very general level. As the experience of other countries shows, the details of system design and good administrative preparation matter in further implementation.

References

Góra, Marek, and Edward Palmer. 2004. "Shifting Perspectives in Pensions." IZA Discussion Paper 1369, Institute for the Study of Labor, Bonn.

ISSA (International Social Security Association). 2005. "Guidelines for the Investment of Social Security Funds." Technical Report 13, ISSA, Geneva. http://www.issa.int/pdf/GA2004/2guidelines.pdf.

OECD (Organisation for Economic Co-operation and Development). 2005. "OECD Guidelines for Pension Fund Governance: Recommendation of the Council." OECD, Paris. http://www.oecd.org/dataoecd/18/52/34799965.pdf.

———. 2006. "OECD Guidelines on Pension Fund Asset Management: Recommendation of the Council." OECD, Paris. http://www.oecd.org/dataoecd/59/53/36316399.pdf.

Ribe, Helena, David Robalino, and lan Walker. 2012. *From Right to Reality: Incentives, Labor Markets, and the Challenge of Universal Social Protection in Latin America and the Caribbean.* Washington, DC: World Bank.

CHAPTER 7

China: Pension Reform for an Aging Economy

Heikki Oksanen

This chapter analyzes options for reforming the fragmented Chinese pension system, which now covers only 55 percent of urban employees and a very small part of the rural population. After a brief survey of the history of pensions in China, we present recent reform proposals and discuss principles of pension reform, with particular attention to the need to reduce pension contribution rates in order to improve compliance and increase coverage. In view of the rapid aging of the Chinese population, we propose a transition to a nonfinancial (notional) defined contribution (NDC) scheme as a model for adjusting the pension rules to take account of increasing longevity.

The move toward transforming the accrued pension rights into NDC accounts and beginning to apply new NDC-inspired rules on indexation is not necessarily a jump into the unknown for the Chinese pension system. Rather, it could be a useful and long-awaited clarification of the rules and a way of moving toward a more uniform system nationwide. With the help of a simulation model based on Chinese data, we construct scenarios for a range of pension reforms and assess their properties.

Overview and Background of China's Pension System

Pensions in China face a dual challenge: the current system covers only a small fraction of the population and does not function as intended, and population aging is progressing rapidly.

Under the basic pension scheme for urban employees, pension expenditure was 2.5 percent of gross domestic product (GDP) in 2008, and revenue from contributions was 2.7 percent. Revenues have constantly exceeded expenditures, and so reserves have accumulated, amounting to 3.3 percent of GDP in 2008.[1] These figures are relatively small, and the pensions of the rural population added hardly anything to them. The main reason for the surplus is that coverage has increased slowly from a low base: less than 30 percent of all employees had coverage, and most of the rural elderly received no pension.

The current multipillar pension system for urban employees, which was established in the 1990s, was supposed to introduce individual fully funded accounts to top up the

Heikki Oksanen was a research adviser in the Directorate General for Economic and Financial Affairs of the European Commission, Brussels, until early 2012. The views expressed in this paper are those of the author and do not necessarily reflect the views of the European Commission.

basic pension of 20 percent of the average urban wage. Owing to implementation problems (including fraud), these accounts are virtually empty; contributions were used to pay the pensions of current pensioners, or perhaps other expenditures. The question is how to cope with the accrued pension rights—whether to replenish the individual accounts, or to accept that the system has de facto come to resemble an unfunded pay-as-you-go (PAYG) system and set up modified rules to be applied from now on.

LOW COVERAGE

The current system is supposed to cover all 302 million (in 2008) urban employees, but in fact, contributions are paid by or on behalf of 55 percent of them. The rules regarding mandating are not clear-cut, and compliance is imperfect. An obvious reason for evasion and avoidance is the relatively high contribution rate; employer and employee contributions together typically amount to 28 percent of the wage. Furthermore, people do not trust the system because rules are unclear and there is suspicion that the system is not sustainable and that contributions might be used for expenditures for other than their declared purpose.

The urban scheme covers some public service units, mainly in the education and health sectors. The rest of these entities, as well as government civil servants, have their own pension systems financed from government budgets. These systems' expenditure is estimated at roughly 1 percent of GDP.

As for the 473 million employees in rural areas, in 2008, only 56 million, or 12 percent, were covered by the public pension system. The 5.1 million rural retirees received quite low pensions, amounting in 2005 to 58 yuan a month (Birmingham and Cui 2006).[2] The extension of coverage to the rural population is a challenge that is clearly recognized by the Chinese authorities, as demonstrated by the government plan issued in August 2009 (China 2009) and described below.

RAPIDLY AGING POPULATION

The Chinese population, totaling 1.3 billion, is aging rapidly, at a rate that ranks the fastest in the world. As of 2010, the population over age 65 numbers 111 million and is expected to grow to 331 million by 2050. Life expectancy at birth is projected to increase from 73 years at present to 80 years by 2050. The ratio of those age 65 and older to those ages 15–64 is currently 11 percent and will increase to 38 percent by 2050, as is shown in figure 7.1. According to the medium variant of the United Nations (UN) demographic projections, the old-age dependency ratio for 2050 is higher only in Western Europe and other high-income economies, where it is currently about 25 percent. Figure 7.1 also depicts the projection from the simulation model used here, which roughly follows the UN projection. The slower pace in the UN projection for 2045 and 2050 can be doubted; our projection, based on the same fertility and longevity assumptions, shows a more pronounced rise, heading toward the same level as in the most affluent welfare states.

IMPORTANCE OF A SYSTEMIC PENSION REFORM

In as much as previous pension reforms have not succeeded in creating a stable and financially sustainable pension system, Chinese authorities and experts have been considering proposals to reform the structure and expand the scope of the system. In the past few

FIGURE 7.1 **Old-age dependency ratio in China and in the rest of the world, actual and projected to 2080**
percent

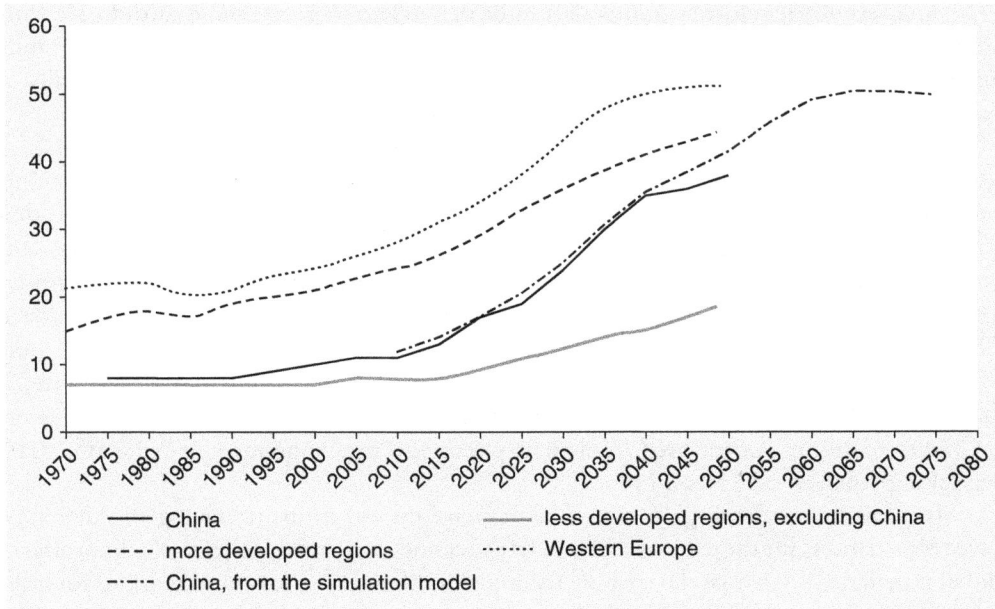

SOURCE: For China and world regions to 2050, United Nations 2009. For the model result, author's calculations using the China Pension-System Simulation Model.

NOTE: The old-age dependency ratio is the ratio of the population age 65 or older to the population ages 15–64, expressed as a percentage. For regions, the United Nations definitions are used; see http://www.un.org/en/development /progareas/population.shtml.

years, a number of proposals have been put forward jointly by Chinese and non-Chinese experts (e.g., CERAP 2005a, 2005b). Some of these proposals recommend accepting that the system has become virtually a pure PAYG one and moving on to an NDC scheme inspired by reforms in Latvia, Poland, and Sweden. In an NDC system, the contribution rate is fixed, and the contributions accumulate in a notional capital account that earns a return in accordance with the rules (e.g., using the rate of increase in the wage bill) set by the authorities to ensure financial balance. At retirement, the pension is determined by an annuity factor based on the estimated remaining life expectancy at the retirement age, with the latter possibly chosen by the beneficiary under flexible but financially sustainable rules. An NDC system can be unfunded or partly funded. In cases of partial funding, there is no strict link between individual pension rights and assets held by the system, and the return on the assets is distributed across generations under separately designed rules reflecting, especially, transitional arrangements.

In this chapter, we will examine the various reform proposals and present model simulations to analyze the implications of the proposals. We offer alternative reform options and, perhaps most important, a template for designing new reform options and expressing them in terms of the key pension system variables. The general thrust will be to move from the fragmented system to more coherent rules following NDC principles, bearing in mind that NDC is not a panacea or a blueprint and that it leaves scope for variance in design and implementation. A fully funded, private sector–managed, defined contribution (DC) second pillar is a possible complement to the NDC pillar.

Analysis of the reform options should be of interest to government authorities who bear the responsibility for the functioning of the system. Announcing reforms convincingly and early enough is important for citizens, who need to be able to form realistic expectations regarding retirement age and pensions.

There are, however, wider reasons for studying pensions in China. Low-cost unskilled labor from rural areas is an abundant source of labor supply. Pensions and their financing will affect its cost. Furthermore, the labor supply is affected by the retirement age, and it is obvious that the retirement age will have to be raised sooner or later in order to alleviate the pension burden. The supply of labor and its cost, including pension contributions, will have an effect on the production of goods and services. Therefore, pensions affect China as a whole—and China affects the global economy because of its size. Measured by purchasing power standards, it is currently second only to the United States; it is more than double the size of Japan's economy, and more than three times that of Germany. Even if China's economy is measured in current prices and exchange rates, it is (as of 2010) overtaking Japan to take second place.[3]

In addition to affecting the cost of labor, pensions also influence saving and therefore have repercussions for the external balance of the economy.[4] Owing to its size, China affects global imbalances—that is, the current accounts of other countries—and world economic conditions, in general. In the current discussion of remedies for the global economic crisis, the view that China could and should boost domestic consumption is constantly repeated both by Chinese authorities and by others. Chinese pensions are increasingly a critical factor for domestic consumption.

Pensions in China: A Brief History

Soon after the founding of the People's Republic of China in 1949, a centralized pension system was established, under which 3 percent of wages was collected for revenue. The system was mainly administered at the local level by the trade unions. In 1969, during the Cultural Revolution, the trade unions were dismantled, and state-owned enterprises (SOEs) were made responsible for pensions. This was the origin of the very fragmented system that still prevails today.

In the late 1970s, under Deng Xiaoping, economic reforms were initiated that included looser pension eligibility criteria. This resulted in a dramatic increase in the number of pensioners. The one-child policy was also instituted in this period, leading to a drop in the fertility rate to well below the replacement rate of roughly 2.1 children per woman. According to a recent Chinese census, fertility is currently 1.3. (The UN estimate is 1.77.) Pensions became an increasing burden for SOEs, which were under pressure in many other ways because of having to adjust to a more market-oriented economy, and the various levels of government were called on to take over pension obligations. This led to an attempt in the mid-1980s to establish nationwide municipal pooling of pensions, which again became very fragmented owing to disparities across regions and sectors (Williamson and Deitelbaum 2005).

In the early years of the 1990s, it was recognized not only that the system was fragmented, giving rise to problems of portability and the like, but also that its financial sustainability was seriously jeopardized by the expected demographic developments. This realization led to an attempt to build a multipillar system in which basic pensions were topped up by mandatory individual accounts and augmented by voluntary pension savings supported by tax concessions. The process of introducing these principles was initiated in 1991 and was followed by several directives that struggled with the balance between establishing unified rules for the whole country and leaving choice to the provinces. This process coincided with the publication of a 1994 World Bank report that prompted the move toward a significant, fully funded, individual-based second pillar (World Bank 1994). Subsequently, in 1997, the World Bank published a report recommending a multipillar system for China, with 9 percent of wages going to the first pillar and 8 percent to individual accounts in the second pillar (Agarwala 1997; see also Piggott and Lu Bei 2007). The first pillar was supposed to deliver a 24 percent replacement rate and the second, a 35 replacement rate. The report identified some problems with the financial sustainability of the first pillar and also recognized that to realize the projected yield from the second pillar, the rate of return on assets had to be higher than the rate of growth of the economy—which was and still is a far from obvious outcome.

In July 1997, State Council Document 26 (China 1997) laid down broad principles for pensions and left scope for differing implementation by the provinces. Broadly, the document specified both a first pillar—a pure defined benefit (DB) PAYG scheme aimed at delivering, on the basis of contributions paid over 15 years, a pension of 20 percent of average urban pay—and a second pillar of individual accounts. The retirement age was set at 60 for men, 55 for women in management cadres, and 50 for women workers. The main deviation from the World Bank recommendations was that the contribution rates were set considerably higher (see the commentary cited in "Recent Proposals," below). Employers and employees were originally supposed to contribute 28 percent of wages, of which a 20 percentage point (pp) portion was paid by the employers. Of this contribution, a share of 7 pp, gradually decreasing to 3 pp, was to go to individual accounts. Half of the 8 pp of contributions from employees was initially supposed to go to individual accounts, and this share was to be gradually increased to the full 8 pp by 2005.

These parameter values were supposed to lead to a 58.5 percent replacement rate, of which 20.0 pp, on average, came from the defined benefit PAYG pillar and 38.5 pp from individual accounts. The formula applied was as follows: a contribution of 11 percent of wages over 35 years, placed in individual accounts with a rate of return equal to the average wage increase, generates capital equal to 3.85 times the annual wage at retirement, which is then divided by 120 to derive the monthly pension, assuming 10 years of remaining life expectancy. This computation yields a pension equal to 38.5 percent of the wage (Leckie and Pai 2005). On the death of the employee or retiree, the balance in the account was to be inheritable. Because of this and the fact that remaining average life expectancy at retirement was then already more than 10 years and would go on increasing, the system was never financially sustainable.

The rules were supposed to be introduced gradually so that employees who started working after 1996 would be covered only by the new system, whereas pensioners who had retired before the end of 1996 would receive pensions from the old system at the municipal level, and those in between would be covered by the old and new systems on a pro rata basis.[5]

The system did not work as intended. In particular, with large-scale SOE restructuring, many laid-off workers were given immediate pensions at quite young ages—as young as age 40. The individual accounts became empty for the most part, as the administration used the revenues to pay the pensions of current retirees. In 2001, in pursuance of State Council Document 42 (China 2000), a pilot program was launched in Liaoning Province that, among other things, separated the defined benefit PAYG pillar from the individual accounts. Twenty percentage points of the wage contribution from employers went to the defined benefit PAYG pillar, and the employee contribution was raised to 8 percent. In addition, employers were encouraged in various ways to make contributions to the voluntary pillar. For the first pillar, the new rules provided an incentive to make contributions beyond 15 years by raising the maximum pension to 30 percent of average urban pay.

As mentioned above, the balance on individual accounts at retirement is converted into monthly payments by dividing it by 120, if one assumes an annuity factor of 10. State Council Document 42 reconfirmed this factor and stated explicitly that "when the accumulation in the individual account runs out, the individual account pension will then be paid from the social pooling fund." The authorities thereby became liable for the deficit. In late 2000, the central government, aware of financing difficulties at the provincial level, established the National Social Security Fund (NSSF) as "a strategic reserve fund." The deficits were to be met partly by transferring part of the SOE wealth to the NSSF: 10 percent of the proceeds raised from initial public offerings (IPOs) was supposed to be remitted to the national fund. However, the Chinese equity market did not perform well, and the "IPO tax" took part of the blame. Transfers from domestic offerings to the NSSF were suspended (Leckie and Pan 2007). Furthermore, pension fund losses owing to corruption were encountered in several provinces, including a major fraud case in Shanghai in 2006.[6] At the end of 2009, the NSSF was reported to have assets equal to 2.4 percent of GDP.

In 2004–06, the Liaoning pilot was extended to 10 other provinces (out of 31). The 11 participating provinces account for 39 percent of the Chinese population (Salditt, Whiteford, and Adema 2007). The contribution shares of the central and local governments depend on the fiscal position of the pilot provinces. In 2008, the total transfer from various levels of the government was 0.5 percent of GDP. One of the symptoms of the fundamental problems is that government financing has become permanent and indispensable.

These factors and others meant that the effort to establish a financially sustainable pension system met with only limited success. For further details of the current system and its problems, the reader is invited to consult, for example, Dunaway and Arora (2007), Leckie and Pan (2007), Clarke (2008, 2009), Sin (2008), and the references given above.

The bottom line is that the 1997 reform for urban areas did not establish a coherent nationwide system but, rather, something very patchy. There was supposed to be a significant funded pillar, but at the end of 2008, the estimated reserves were about 5 percent of GDP—a fraction of the original blueprint. Today, only 55 percent of employees in urban areas are covered, and most of the rural population is not covered at all. The aim of the pilot programs mentioned above is to gain more experience with the revised and refined rules in order to set up a more comprehensive reform plan. We next describe some of the new proposals and initiatives and the thinking behind them.

RECENT PROPOSALS

Chinese pension reform has attracted considerable attention internationally since the 1990s, and for good reason: it concerns a major economy that is already a key player in international trade and finance. Perhaps even more important, the range of reform options was and still is very wide, and thus China's course will have an impact on the world economy. It is hardly surprising that the Chinese pension system has been one of the arenas in the controversy between those advocating a large role for mandatory fully funded personal accounts and those favoring (mostly) PAYG government-managed defined benefit public pensions.[7]

Early expressions of this controversy can be found in Yin, Lin, and Gates (2000), a collection of papers by Chinese and non-Chinese experts. Martin Feldstein represents the first school described above, and Henry Aaron, the second. In a recent World Bank volume, Feldstein and Liebman (2008) reiterate their support for moving to a fully funded DC system while proposing to cope with the transition costs by swapping the implicit pension debt for explicit public debt.[8] In the same volume, Li, Dorfman, and Wang (2008) advocate a shift to an NDC system that combines some features of both funded DC systems and unfunded PAYG systems. A forthcoming World Bank think piece on pension reform commissioned by the Chinese Ministry of Finance makes the NDC scheme the centerpiece of the reform proposal to which urban and rural pension schemes should converge (World Bank forthcoming).

Meanwhile, a joint study by Chinese and non-Chinese experts, published under the China Economic Research and Advisory Programme (CERAP 2005a, 2005b), makes extensive recommendations concerning policies and system design. Two members of the team, Nicholas Barr and Peter Diamond, published the same views in Barr and Diamond (2008) and developed them further in Barr and Diamond (2010). The team forcefully recommends a reform whereby individual pension accounts are organized on an NDC basis. In their opinion, it should be accepted that individual accounts have de facto become only very partially funded and that filling the empty accounts should not be attempted, as this would place an undue burden on current workers.

This same view is taken by Zhang (2007) and, as stated above, by Li, Dorfman, and Wang (2008), and it is endorsed by Williamson and Deitelbaum (2005). Zheng (2007) recommends that pension contributions to the "social pool" of defined benefit PAYG pensions be reduced to 8 pp of wages and that 16 pp should go to individual accounts, which should be partly funded and should operate (at least in part) on the basis of NDC. The remaining 4 pp of the total contribution of 28 percent of wages would be placed in the second-pillar fully funded DC scheme. Zheng, in chapter 6 in this volume, presents new NDC-based proposals.

Feldstein and Liebman (2008) effectively reproduce the World Bank recommendations of 1997 and argue that an 8 percent payroll tax should be levied on the newly established fully funded individual accounts. They repeat, without much caution, that this would produce a 35 percent replacement rate, which, together with (reduced and better targeted) social pool pensions, would—in their view—be a reasonable and sufficient level of pensions. They would eliminate the pension contributions paid to the first pillar, cover accrued pension rights by issuing public debt, and service the debt and the basic social pool pensions from broadly based taxes such as a value added tax (VAT).

Under certain simplifying assumptions, the maintenance of an unfunded pension system and a transition to fully funded individual accounts, combined with the financing of accrued pension rights by issuing public debt (thus swapping implicit debt for explicit public debt), would produce an equivalent outcome for pension benefits and total financing costs. The proponents of a move to full funding emphasize the benefits of alleviating the distortions to labor supply as a result of the transfer of part of the financing burden to taxes other than the payroll tax. They also see significant positive effects from giving a boost to financial market institutions.

The proponents of maintaining the broadly unfunded system see a danger in increasing public debt by, say, 100 percent of annual GDP and having the corresponding amount of assets managed by the private (mandatory) pension funds. For them, to make this major shift in financial markets in which institutions and their supervision are not fully developed (as in China) is a potentially dangerous gamble. Also, if pensions were mainly on a DC basis, which (under the fully funded arrangement) would mean making workers' pensions dependent on the rate of return on the financial market, ordinary people would be at excessive risk. These authors argue that maintaining risk sharing under a defined benefit system is more reasonable for mandatory social insurance.

Quite a few of the proponents of the PAYG system find the NDC-based PAYG to be the most promising for China, where pension rights need to be adjusted to demographic aging. According to them, an advantage of the NDC system is that the pensions are not at risk in the financial market; rather, an administratively set rate of return is applied to the individual accounts. (Under the conditions in China, most authors prefer to use the increase in average wages as the most appropriate rate of return.) Seen in this light, the NDC system is a modified DB system in which benefits are based on individual contributions and are indexed to average wages, retirement age, and expected longevity. It thus significantly helps avoid the problems of sustainability that traditional DB systems with fixed replacement rates and retirement ages encounter under conditions of reduced fertility and increasing longevity. Because of population aging, the parameters of standard DB systems need to be revised, but this is always a difficult process, politically and otherwise. The NDC rules make these required adjustments automatic (or, to be more precise, quasi-automatic, since full autopilot is not feasible, as is explained below). This feature is considered especially useful for China because of the rapid demographic change that will take place in the next 20 to 30 years and beyond.[9]

The controversy between, on the one hand, the proponents of fully funded DC, and therefore of financial market–based, pensions (resembling voluntary saving instruments) and, on the other hand, those who see public pensions as social insurance whereby the government acts as a broker for intergenerational solidarity and corrects market failure by providing DB pensions (or NDC as their variant) will not go away easily, in China or anywhere else. This controversy is at the same time economic, social, and ideological, and the adversaries attach different weights to the various issues involved. Whatever differences they otherwise have, there is one common worry that is shared by experts from both schools of thought: a significant increase in retirement age is badly needed in China because otherwise the pension system will become unsustainable (or at least difficult to manage), whatever basic financing mode is applied. This will have important repercussions for the whole economy via the supply of labor. A higher retirement age will mean an increased labor supply in urban areas because the existing urban labor force will remain active for more working years and there will still be a large pool of excess labor in rural areas. The latter workforce is mainly unskilled, but with compulsory free education being established in rural areas, larger pools of increasingly skilled labor will become available in due course. These large sources of an expanding effective labor supply (despite low fertility) will mean that the transition process of the Chinese economy will continue for many decades. This will, for the most part, happen regardless of the pension system reforms, but it will have a significant effect on pension financing, especially if the growing labor force is successfully made to contribute to pension financing.

SIMULATIONS WITH THE WORLD BANK PROST MODEL

The literature cited above discusses most of the pertinent issues in the design of pension reform in China and gives at least preliminary projections for key variables. However, the authors do not convert their recommendations into scenarios that would systematically and transparently illustrate the reform options.

A notable exception is Sin (2005), who presents a set of simulation results for the urban pension system from the World Bank PROST pension projection model.[10] Three measures emerge as the most critical for establishing a financially sustainable system that would provide at least a minimum socially acceptable level of pension (about a 40 percent replacement rate): correcting the annuity factor from 120 to correspond to realistic life expectancy at retirement; gradually raising the retirement age to 65; and significantly increasing the coverage of the urban population from the current 50 percent.

Sin's scenarios show a wide range of options, starting from the baseline without reforms. That scenario would require a 37 percent contribution rate to be technically sustainable. Because a contribution rate of that order is not feasible in reality, the system would soon collapse. Sin's various reform scenarios then show that changing the benefit rules and retirement age can help greatly and that the required contribution rate could fall to below 20 percent. Stronger reforms would reduce the contribution rate even further, and pension fund reserves would still increase to close to the relative figures seen in the wealthiest industrial countries. Thus, Sin provides a wide range of options that inspire further analysis.

Toward a New Pension System: Principles and Issues

There is broad agreement that, despite the efforts over the past 15 years, the Chinese pension system is still very limited and fragmented and that its future direction is unclear. This section looks at basic principles for establishing an integrated system and at the considerations that need to be kept in mind in designing a pension system for China.

NEW VERSUS MATURE PENSION SYSTEMS

China only began adopting market economy principles three decades ago, and it was confronted with the need to establish nationwide social policy institutions when SOEs were relieved of their pension liabilities. Because of the relative newness of the institutions, the design of scenarios for establishing a proper public pension system has to be based on broader issues than the internal rules of the pension system. Any analysis geared to assessing the current problems in industrial welfare states by looking at a systemic transition that starts with a mature (or close to mature) PAYG system is not a suitable approach for China.

For example, Beetsma and Oksanen (2008), in presenting a framework for analyzing the consequences of population aging and pension reforms for explicit and implicit public debt, use the basic concept of "actuarial neutrality across generations" as a benchmark for setting pension system rules for the demographic transition. This neutrality rule may provide some guidance for dealing with intergenerational fairness in industrial welfare states with mature pension systems that are hit by population aging. For China, however, deviations from actuarial neutrality by expanding the public unfunded pension system may well be justified.

VICIOUS CIRCLE OF HIGH CONTRIBUTION RATES AND LOW COVERAGE

One of the most pertinent issues is low coverage in the urban system. This is probably partly caused by the vicious circle of a high contribution rate (about 28 percent of wages) that leads to low compliance—and therefore to the need to maintain the high contribution rate. What are the possibilities for breaking this circle by reducing the contribution rate?

For a simple calculation, assume a normal working life of 35 years and note that life expectancy at age 60 is currently 19 years for men and 22 for women. If a person retires at age 60 with a pension of 50 percent of the unit wage, the contribution rate in the public unfunded system should be about 28 percent (taking roughly into account mortality below age 60). So, the 28 percent is justified.

But it is quite likely that the wage tax of about 28 percent is prohibitive if the goal is to expand coverage. Note that other taxes on wages are also quite high, amounting to 12–16 percent of the wage, for a total of more than 40 percent, and on top of this is a 16 percent contribution to funds for housing purchase (see Clarke 2009; Hu and Davis 2009). It is plausible that wage tax rates as a whole are too high, so that cutting them could bring more revenue to the coffers of the state because of increased compliance. If this move can be combined with an increase in the retirement age, even more leeway is available for a transitional period of a couple of decades. Because this respite is only transitory, not all of the improved financial balance should be used for reducing current contribution rates.

For wider options for breaking the vicious circle, we should look more broadly at what has happened in the Chinese economy over the past 30 years. GDP has been growing, on average, at 10 percent a year. Per capita income has risen by 9 percent and, correspondingly, private consumption per capita has expanded by 8 percent, making the current level of per capita income 11 times the 1980 level in 1980 and per capita consumption, 9 times higher. Does this give pension policy some room for maneuver?

PUBLIC PENSIONS AS A REWARD FOR EFFORTS BY OLDER GENERATIONS

In Western Europe in the 1950s and 1960s, public pension systems became broadly unfunded because the first generation of retirees was accorded benefits that clearly exceeded the value of the contributions they had paid into the system. However, we can consider this imbalance justified because that generation had worked hard rebuilding the economies ruined by World War II. Furthermore, government finances were strong, and saving in the public sector was high and had been used partly to build public infrastructure. In other words, the generation working from 1950 until the early 1970s did not formally cover through their contributions to the public pension system the value of the pensions they subsequently received, but they had worked hard and saved collectively, laying the basis for more wealth for themselves and for future generations.[11] Similarly, in the case of China, one could argue that the generations that suffered during the Cultural Revolution and were able to start the economic and social transition only three decades ago have already made a huge contribution to building a wealthier society for themselves and coming generations.

Reform of the public pension system in China can be justifiably based on the real assets of the government—not least, infrastructure and SOEs, which are adjusting to market economy principles—and on its financial assets (foreign assets holdings through its sovereign wealth funds and central bank), which grossly outweigh the relatively small public debt. The government's strong financial position can be used to reduce the contribution rates and so promote compliance and expanded coverage. Solid finances will help meet the costs of honoring accrued rights (under reasonably generous indexation rules, to share the fruits of growth more broadly); of establishing pension rights for the elderly who did not fully contribute; and of refilling the accounts from which funds disappeared as a result of inadequate rules, mismanagement, corruption, or fraud.

HIGHER RETIREMENT AGE FOR LONG-TERM SUSTAINABILITY

The above arguments are based on the past and current features of the pension system. It is important to design the rules in such a way that they take into account the projected demographic change early enough so that expenditures do not explode with the change in the age structure. Crucially, this will require that the retirement age be raised. The rules for pensions need to include proper incentives for people to work considerably longer than the current retirement age. This should be relatively clear from a long-term perspective, but it has to be recognized that in the case of China, the need to raise the retirement age significantly will not be self-evident because the pool of underutilized labor in rural areas seeking employment will remain large for quite a long time.

GAP BETWEEN THE INTEREST RATE AND THE GROWTH RATE

The large supply of labor will mean that the economy can still grow relatively rapidly for two to three decades. This prospect has consequences for a key variable related to pensions: the difference between the interest rate and the growth rate. We tend to take for granted that in the industrial welfare states, the long-term interest rate has been somewhat higher than the rate of growth. In China, it has been grossly the other way round. This was the case also in Western industrial countries in the golden age of growth between the late 1940s and the early 1970s, when public pension systems were established. In China, the relatively low interest rate does not necessarily mean that the economy is dynamically inefficient and that the capital stock should be (quickly) reduced. On the contrary, a high rate of growth, consistently higher than interest rates, can continue while the excess labor is being gradually utilized and the continuous flow of technological and institutional innovation, including reorganization of SOEs enterprises, drives the process. This description of an economy cannot be valid "forever," but in China, this kind of growth process could last for several decades, as it did in the Western world until the early 1970s. The future of the public pension system should be analyzed in the light of this outlook.

One consequence is that, with regard to the rate of return on pension contributions, a fully funded pension system with its assets in financial market instruments is not necessarily superior to a public scheme in which the expansion of the economy is shared among the members by linking the internal rate of return of the system (to be obtained in the form of pensions) to the general rate of growth. Yet, as will be argued below, the level of pensions that can be reasonably expected from the public pillar in China will clearly be lower than that currently prevailing in Western Europe. Additional pension saving in a fully funded mandatory or voluntary pension scheme and various other forms of private saving will have their roles. There is thus no reason to take an extreme view and totally exclude financial market–based pension saving.

NEED FOR EXPANDED COVERAGE OF THE RURAL POPULATION

Soon after 1949, the Chinese population was divided by the *hukou* registration system into urban and rural citizens. The system regulates citizens' rights and, in particular, limits the rights of rural people working in the cities. Pension systems, among many other government policies, follow this segregation.

Most of the reform proposals referred to above are restricted to discussing the options for pensions for the urban population, although quite a few at least mention that old-age security of the Chinese rural population is also an issue. The 1991 decisions also covered pensions for rural employees, to be financed by a contribution rate of 3 percent. Coverage remained low, and changes in organizations and policies since the late 1990s have led to shrinkage of the system (Birmingham and Cui 2006). In 2008, only 12 percent of rural employees were covered, and the average pension was very low. The majority of the population still lives in rural areas, and the age structure there is changing even faster than in the cities (see figure 7.2, below).

The issue with rural pensions is recognized, for example, by Barr and Diamond (2008, 2010), Clarke (2008), Sin (2008), and the World Bank (forthcoming). Herd, Hu, and Koen (2010) and OECD (2010) provide useful insights into the complex relationships between old-age support and land ownership, especially with regard to changes in property rights in rural areas and the conversion of land to nonagricultural use, under, for example, the new property laws issued in 2002 and 2007. The problems with rural pensions have been recognized by Chinese authorities, and a response came in August 2009, when a plan was issued that would establish a new system with a goal of universal pension coverage by 2020, to be achieved gradually. The benefits from this plan will be relatively modest. Financing will come mostly from the central government, but the effort will be shared with the governments of high-income provinces. Although there are many links between the urban and rural social security systems, especially through workers from rural areas who are employed in the cities, and discontinuation of the hukou system is currently under discussion, the two systems will probably coexist for quite some time. Therefore, it is advisable to keep them apart for analysis, as we do here, while our model also allows us to run scenarios where they converge.

FIGURE 7.2 **Old-age dependency ratio in China, urban and rural areas, 2008–2120**
percent

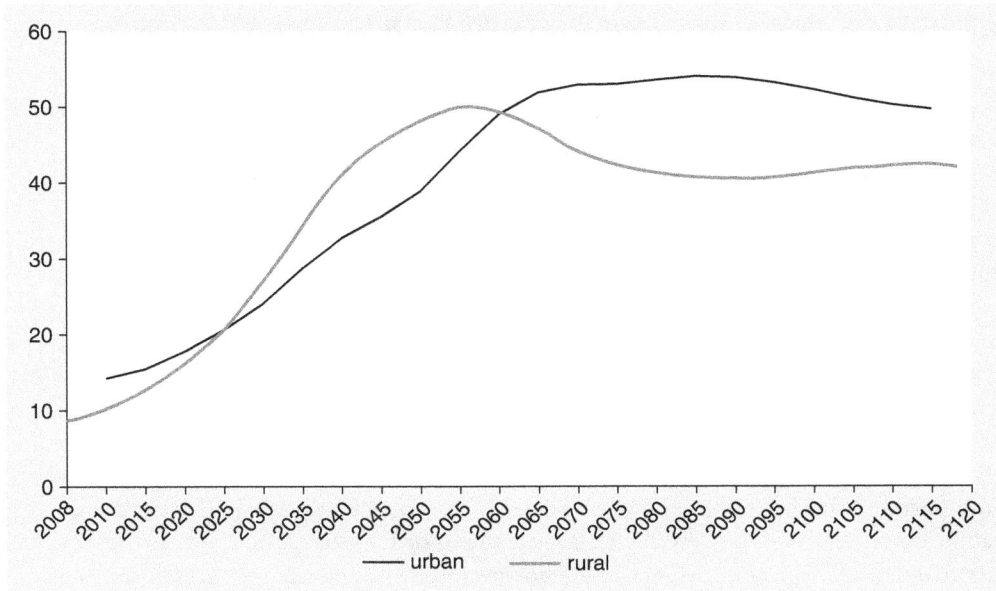

SOURCE: Author's calculations based on the China Pension-System Simulation Model, described in the text.

NOTE: The old-age dependency ratio is the ratio of the population age 65 years or older to the population ages 15–64, as a percentage.

IMPLICATIONS OF THE ONE-CHILD POLICY FOR OLD-AGE SECURITY

China's one-child policy has effectively meant that the fertility rate is below 2, even though not as low as 1. Here, fundamental analytical and normative issues regarding the responsibility of the state are triggered. One line of research has given rise to the hypothesis that public pensions cause a reduction in fertility (Cigno and Werding 2007). We may doubt whether the expansion of public pension systems in Western Europe since the mid-1970s had this effect, as many other societal factors may have contributed to the decline in fertility. However, it is probably plausible that in developing countries, fertility is high because there is no pension system and also because well-developed financial markets that could offer instruments for private pension saving are lacking. People accordingly have many children to guarantee sufficient support when they are older. If so, it also follows that the establishment of a public pension system in developing countries should help reduce population growth—something that is probably desirable in view of limited global resources.

Although the one-child policy has been more relaxed in rural areas, the migration of descendants to cities has meant that many elderly people in rural areas are left without sufficient family support. Remittances from children who have moved to a city and visit occasionally help to a certain degree, but this support might not be sufficient, and its continuation might be uncertain. This turns around the argument regarding the link between public pensions and fertility decline; the state induced the decline in fertility by regulation, and so the state must take the responsibility, financial and otherwise, for support for the elderly who are left with narrow or no family-based security. Thus, public pensions for the large rural population should be expanded considerably.

BENEFITS OF AN NDC SYSTEM AND ISSUES WITH ITS INTRODUCTION

The advantage of an NDC system is that it can help secure the financial sustainability of the pension system in a situation of population aging. Under an NDC approach, the scheme can adjust to increasing longevity because benefits are calculated using the latest available projection for the life expectancy of the beneficiary at the moment of retirement. (This same effect can be achieved by modifying the rules of a more traditional DB system to introduce a longevity factor into the determination of the benefits, as has been recently done in some countries, such as Finland and Germany.)

An NDC system consists of notional accounts to register individual contributions and of rules for determining annuity payments (pension benefits); the rate of return on individual accounts; and the indexation of pensions in payment. An NDC system can operate without (significant) reserves, like a pure defined benefit PAYG system, but it may have significant reserves, similar to a DB scheme (see Holzmann, Palmer, and Robalino 2012 for a discussion of the role of a reserve fund in NDC schemes). A key feature of both only partially funded schemes is that benefits are not directly affected by the assets (or liabilities) of the system, or by the return on them, or by interest on debt, as they are in a fully funded DC system. Indirect links, however, may operate as interest on assets brings resources to the system.

It should be noted that an NDC system without assets is fully in financial balance in a steady state, provided that the rate of return on the notional accounts is sustainable (i.e., equal to the rate of growth of the covered wage bill) and that this same rate is used for determining annuity payments. If these conditions are not fulfilled, the system deviates from equilibrium and explodes or implodes. This could also happen if and when the system is out of equilibrium at its start or is hit by an unexpected change in its key factors, such as a change in longevity that is not offset by adjustment of pensions in payment.[12]

The NDC system thus cannot work under full autopilot; it needs additional rules for adjustment, or discrete decisions. For example, the Swedish NDC system was not implemented according to the predetermined rules. Greater leeway for determining the pensions was considered more appropriate at times of financial crisis, and policy discretion supplanted the supposed autopilot. Perhaps more important, the transition from a traditional DB system to NDC always requires specific rules, which do not directly follow from the basic NDC rules.

If the transition starts from a mature DB system, there is normally a deficit because contribution payments are frozen but expenditures to honor accrued rights continue rising. Application of NDC rules to China, or to any country that does not yet have a full-fledged public pension system, encounters the opposite situation.

To make the point in a simple way, consider a country without any public pension system that establishes a system emulating the NDC rules. It then, in fact, establishes a funded system because pensions are paid out only when the participants retire and start claiming their pensions on the basis of their individual account balances. The main difference between this and a fully funded DC system is the interest rate: in an NDC scheme, it is determined by a rule referring to wage statistics, whereas in a fully funded DC system, it is the rate of return on assets as they accrue de facto.

As noted, coverage in the Chinese pension system for urban employees is only about 55 percent. If and when coverage increases, the revenue from the new participants will bring in a significant accumulation of reserves. For this reason, the transition to an NDC system does not necessarily cause a deficit (as it did in European countries) but, rather, a surplus.

The main reason for China to shift to an NDC-type scheme is that the country is going to have to deal with rapid population aging. It is probably wise to do so now, when the process is only starting and there is still time to establish new pension system rules.

OPTIONS FOR CHINA

The deadlock of the poorly functioning Chinese urban pension system (low coverage and high contribution rates) can be tackled using basic concepts of pension economics. The options are as follows:

1. Move to fully funded individual accounts. Current employees should bear a double burden, or accrued rights should be covered by issuing debt. Both options may be unfeasible—the former because of unacceptably high contribution rates and the latter, because it could lead to unacceptably high public debt.

2. Accept that the system is virtually PAYG and follow the principle of actuarial neutrality, meaning that the implicit pension debt is carried over to the next generation and each working generation pays for its share of servicing that debt and for its own future pensions (Beetsma and Oksanen 2008). In this case, the additional revenues from possible expansion of coverage and from a growing labor force resulting from migration to urban areas should not be extracted only for current employees but should be put into a reserve fund for the benefit of future generations, as well.

3. Recognize that at least the older members of the current working generation and current retirees have already contributed significantly to the wealth of the nation and can therefore justifiably be provided with pension benefits that exceed the level that they have paid in the form of pension contributions. In pension economics, this is called an introductory gain—a gain that is received by the first generation when a PAYG public pension system is established. In China, this view can justify cutting contribution rates to a level that would improve compliance. Eventually, the rules should take into account the increase in longevity so that the retirement age will rise. NDC-type rules are consistent with both actions if accompanied by appropriate transitional arrangements for the first phase of two to three decades.

4. Acknowledge that the level of generosity currently prevailing in more affluent welfare states is probably not viable for earnings-related public pensions in China. There will, accordingly, be a need for both basic social pensions for the low-income elderly and additional pension savings managed by various types of financial institutions operating in gradually opening and more efficient markets.

China Pension-System Simulation Model and Reform Options

To illustrate a wide range of pension reform options, we employ the China Pension-System Simulation Model, which is calibrated for the Chinese public pension system, demographics, and economy in 2008. Because the Chinese pension system is so patchy, and because comprehensive data are not available, we have to accept that the baseline simulation gives only a grossly stylized picture of reality. This, however, is not a serious drawback because the main purpose here is to present various options for reform—in particular, for transition to an NDC system and the accompanying DC and flat-rate pensions—and to allow for any changes in the retirement age.

A great advantage of this model, compared with previous exercises, is that urban and rural sectors have separate demographics and separate pension system rules. The model can be used flexibly with regard to the assumptions concerning various exogenous variables related to the economy, such as wage growth (presented separately for urban and rural areas), interest rates, and inflation.

The model is simple in that the agents within it (workers and pensioners) are representative individuals for each group, classified by gender, urban or rural residence, and birth cohort. The model is partial equilibrium, as it covers only the financial situation of the pension system (and its reform options). It is constructed to calculate pensions for each set of policy parameters or rules under a set of assumptions concerning exogenously determined demographic and economic variables. For example, labor supply is determined by the demographic variables, and employment rates for each group are determined by gender and age. In the baseline scenario, employment rates are assumed to stay at their initial levels, and in the reform option scenarios, they are assumed to increase, especially for older workers, as a function of an increase in retirement age. We can combine the various parameters freely with the pension policy parameters set as we deem plausible in each case. Note also that working with a partial equilibrium model does not significantly affect most of our results because we concentrate on cases in which pensions are indexed to the unit urban wage and we express the main results as percentages of GDP. Furthermore, even in the absence of an endogenous link from pensions (and their financing from contributions based on wages) to the supply of labor (the employment rate in each group) or to the interest rate, we can run the model for any combinations of these variables we deem reasonable and interesting.

We offer here several alternative pension scenarios. We begin with a demonstration that population aging requires significant changes in the Chinese pension system because otherwise the system is not viable. We then present reform options that are financially sustainable and that can serve as blueprints for possible reform. As with almost all the assumptions on demographics, the economy and the pension system can be easily modified in the model, and a wide range of reform options can be investigated and sensitivity tests performed. Such flexibility could enrich further discussion beyond the scope of this study.

The time horizon for exogenously determined variables stretches to 2060. This (nearly) covers the expected lifetime of those now entering the labor force. It is also adequate for analyzing intergenerational distribution because it covers two to three consecutive generations. (The average age of mothers giving birth is 20–30 years and is increasing.) The assumption that changes in exogenous variables cease by 2060 is merely technical; we make it to be able to verify whether the model (and especially the pension system), under each set of assumptions, implies a steady and sustainable path over an infinite future. This is done by running the model and showing the results up to 2120 to see whether each set of rules is inherently sustainable. If it is not, the rules will need to be changed sooner or later. Technically, the model does not prevent us from assuming further changes in exogenous variables after 2060, but because the future becomes become more uncertain the further we look out, the relevance of the results diminishes. Covering the key issues for the next 50 years is sufficient for our purposes here.

We now explain the main structure of the model and the most important assumptions.

DEMOGRAPHICS

The demographics block is based on the most recent data on China's age structure by gender. To construct the projection, we use the UN population projection medium variant to 2050 as a source of key data and as a reference. This variant is used for longevity and fertility in China and we add a further one-year increase in longevity for 2060. We use the current figures for mortality by age and gender from the UN *Demographic Yearbook 2007* (United Nations 2010). The model rescales these numbers according to the projected changes in longevity and produces a full age-gender matrix for each year in the future.

In addition, because it is essential that our exercise look into urban and rural pension systems separately, we constructed the demographic scenario separately for urban and rural areas on the basis of indicative data from various sources. We assume that the difference in longevity between urban and rural areas is now five years, narrowing to four years by 2060. The model rescales the age-gender mortality figures accordingly. Nationwide fertility is currently, according to the UN projection, 1.77 per woman of fertile age and converges to 1.85 by 2050. We assume that it is currently 1.30 in urban areas and 1.95 in rural areas, and we set these rates to converge so that the country average follows the UN projection. We set our fertility estimates for 2060 so that the shares of urban and rural population remain constant in the ultimate steady state. (Fertility in rural areas has to be a little higher to compensate for higher female mortality rates at all ages.) This way, the model can produce a fully stable structure of the economy in a steady state, albeit with an ever-shrinking population because the ultimate fertility rate is assumed to be below the reproduction level of about 2.1.

A key advantage of our model is that it takes into account the migration flow from rural to urban areas. We shall see below that in the next few decades, migration will be in some respects even more important for the urban pension system than population aging alone. We have to accept that we can make only very rough assumptions because migration is a mixture of official and unofficial movements and the data are therefore not accurate; in any case, migration is difficult to project. Currently, 46 percent of the population is urban, and Chinese authorities have mentioned 70 percent as a target by 2050 (OECD 2010). We assume simple numbers for the migration flow by age (converging to zero by 2060), which leads to the target of 70 percent in 2050. For simplicity, we assume that people acquire urban demographic characteristics when they move and that they are fully integrated into the urban system. This is currently not the case, and how to treat the migrants is indeed one of the key issues faced by the authorities. Thus, the findings discussed below offer baseline results for immediate integration; deviations from this assumption would require a separate investigation.[13]

The implications of the demographic projection for the old-age dependency ratio, defined as the ratio of the number of people age 65 and older to the number of people ages 15–64, both nationwide and separately in urban and rural areas, are illustrated in figure 7.2. The increase is relatively faster in rural areas, partly because we assume that the migrants are to a great degree working-age people. The rural old-age dependency ratio exceeds the urban ratio by 2025 and reaches a peak of more than 50 percent in 2055. The steady-state level of the ratio is lower than in urban areas because of our assumption that longevity in rural areas will remain lower than in urban areas even after 2060—an assumption that does not affect our main results.

ECONOMY

Technically, our reference unit is the urban real wage (henceforth, the contributory wage), which is used for determining pension contributions. It is calibrated at two-thirds of the urban average wage reported in official statistics because this, together with other assumptions made, yields in the model the reported total contribution revenue of the urban pension system in 2008 (2.7 percent of GDP). The contributory wage is assumed to increase by 8 percent in 2010 and then to decline gradually to a growth rate of 2 percent by 2060. [14] This may be simple, but it is justified by the initial results. The same holds for inflation. We set it at 3 percent per year, which we understand to be a conventional assumption. Other assumptions, on wages, prices, and indexation, are technically possible in our model, and a large number of their combinations could be explored.

The model is specified for wages and employment and thus for the wage bill, while the other components of GDP remain outside the model. For convenience, we express the results as percentages of GDP, and we therefore need an assumption concerning the relation between the wage bill growth and GDP growth. In China, the share of the wage bill in GDP is currently quite low, around 40 percent, while the share of the return on capital is large. Correspondingly, private consumption is only 36 percent of GDP, whereas investment and net exports are large. We simply assume that the wage bill will at first, in 2010, grow 1 pp faster than GDP and that this difference gradually declines to zero by 2060, so that the share of the wage bill in GDP increases by 7 pp by 2030 and by 11 pp by 2060. This may still imply a relatively low wage share internationally, but it could be justified by the need for infrastructure investment (including investment to reduce air pollution) and, in general, by relatively high investment and growth in China over many decades to come.

The rural wage rate is initially set at 33 percent of the urban wage rate, based on rough figures on income differences between urban and rural areas (from China Statistics Press 2009). This ratio is assumed to increase smoothly, to 70 percent by 2060. Obviously, this is again a very rough assumption, and it affects the results to some extent. Alternative numbers could be used in further testing.

The model technically allows many variants in setting the interest rate, which can be linked to inflation, the urban wage, the total wage bill, or GDP growth. Separate interest rates can be entered for the rate of return on DC pension fund assets, the liabilities or assets of the public pension system, and the calculation of implicit pension debt (equal to the present value of accrued rights). We could take GDP or wage bill growth or inflation as the reference and add or subtract any freely chosen margin, which can vary over time. For the scenarios reported, we choose the same uniform figure for all these interest rates, using GDP growth as the reference. Over the past decade, the interest rate on government bonds has been mostly about 5 to 6 percent, except for 2008, during the first phase of the global financial crisis, when it was higher. Referring to GDP growth at about 9 percent and inflation of about 2 percent, we set the interest rate at 5 percent below GDP growth in 2010 and assume that it declines to zero by 2040 and that a positive margin of

1 percent emerges by 2060. Separately, we set the administratively controlled interest rate on NDC accounts equal to total wage bill growth. (Note that for the assets or debts of the NDC scheme, the interest rate proper is assumed.)

EMPLOYMENT

The model uses separate age- and gender-specific data on employment rates for urban and rural areas, based on the Chinese census of 2005. Broadly speaking, in 2008 in our model, 72 percent of persons ages 18–59 in urban areas are employed; for those ages 60–69, the figure is 21 percent. In rural areas, practically everyone in the 18–59 age group is working, as is 65 percent of those in the 60–69 age group and a declining proportion of those age 70 and older. In the model, receiving a pension does not mean that one stops working. Especially in rural areas, almost everyone is working because other subsistence options are meager.

CALIBRATION OF PENSIONS FOR THE INITIAL YEAR 2008

Our main target here is the urban basic pension system, leaving out government civil servants and those in public service units (mainly in the education and health sectors) that are covered directly from government budgets.

The very scattered urban pension system cannot be easily captured. In brief, we first observe that in 2008, the average pension is 48 percent of the statistical average wage, or 71 percent of the assumed contributory wage. We then calibrate the baseline for the continuation of the initial rules as a simplified DB system, inferring that a 2 percent per year accrual starting at age 20 produces a scenario in which the average pension for an urban-born representative employee is maintained.

The contribution rate is set at 28 percent of the (contributory) wage. Coverage in the urban system is calibrated to conform to the reported 55 percent of those employed. We also have in the model a variable for the percentage of those covered who contribute each year. Without much insight into this, we put it at 90 percent, making allowance for various reasons for not contributing, such as unemployment or temporary work in the informal sector. For the retirement age in 2008, we assume age 60 for urban men and age 55 for women.

These assumptions, including that on the contributory wage rate, yield the reported total contribution revenue and pension expenditure in 2008. We leave out the transfer of 0.5 percent of GDP from the government because the idea is to present scenarios for a self-sufficient earnings-related system. The possible transfer from the government and its use can then be discussed separately. For the reserves of the system in 2008, we assume a round figure of 5 percent of GDP.

For rural areas, the initial system is quite small, and we have used simple numbers that replicate the recorded expenditures. The assumption on retirement age means hardly anything for our initial year 2008 because coverage is so low, so we already set it at age 60 for both genders for 2008, as that is the retirement age to be implemented in the new rural pension system.

BASELINE SCENARIO FOR THE URBAN SYSTEM

The baseline is constructed to show the implications of the initial assumptions combined with the aging process. For urban employees, the current employment and coverage rates are maintained, as are the assumed 2 percent per year pension accrual and indexation to urban wages. Men's retirement age is maintained at age 60, and for women, it is assumed to increase from 55 in 2008 to 58 by 2020 and then to 60 by 2030. (There is no firm basis for this assumption, and it can be recalibrated.) The contribution rate of 28 percent of wages is maintained. The 2008 employment rate for persons ages 60–69 is assumed to increase a little, from 21 to 25 percent, by 2020, reflecting the view that the rate may rise slightly owing to improving health status even if the pension system rules do not change.

As is easily understandable, the urban pension system is not sustainable under the assumptions made. Contributions exceed expenditures until 2025, but then the system goes into deficit, and its debt explodes, as shown in figures 7.3 and 7.4. (Henceforth, for shortness, contributions minus expenditures, omitting interest, is termed the deficit.)

The pensions of new retirees fall from the initial 71 percent of the contributory wage to less than 60 percent by 2045 (figure 7.5). This follows from the lower-than-average pensions of the migrants, who will have a shorter contribution history than the urban-born representative employee in our model. We see from figure 7.5 that our model is technically consistent in the sense that when migration has ceased, the average pension returns to its initial level. However, the main implication is that the system is not financially sustainable on its own but requires either a significantly increased contribution rate or a government subsidy of 4 percent of GDP (see figure 7.3).

FIGURE 7.3 **Chinese urban pension system, projected contributions minus expenditures, 2008–20** percentage of GDP

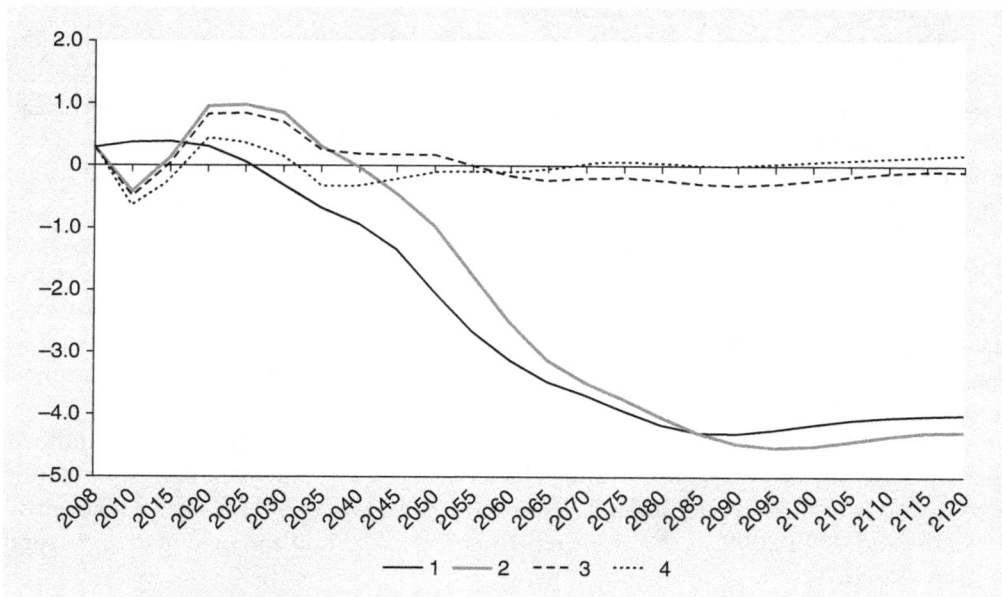

SOURCE: Author's calculations based on the China Pension-System Simulation Model, described in the text.

NOTE: DB = defined benefit; GDP = gross domestic product; NDC = nonfinancial defined contribution. Contributions and expenditures do not include interest on assets or debt. The scenarios are as follows: 1, baseline; 2, reformed DB scheme; 3, NDC reform with 20.0 percent contribution and 2.4 percent flat-rate pension; 4, NDC reform with 16.0 percent pension contribution and 0.3 percent flat-rate pension. For details, see the text.

FIGURE 7.4 **Chinese urban pension system, projected accumulated assets, 2008–20**
percentage of GDP

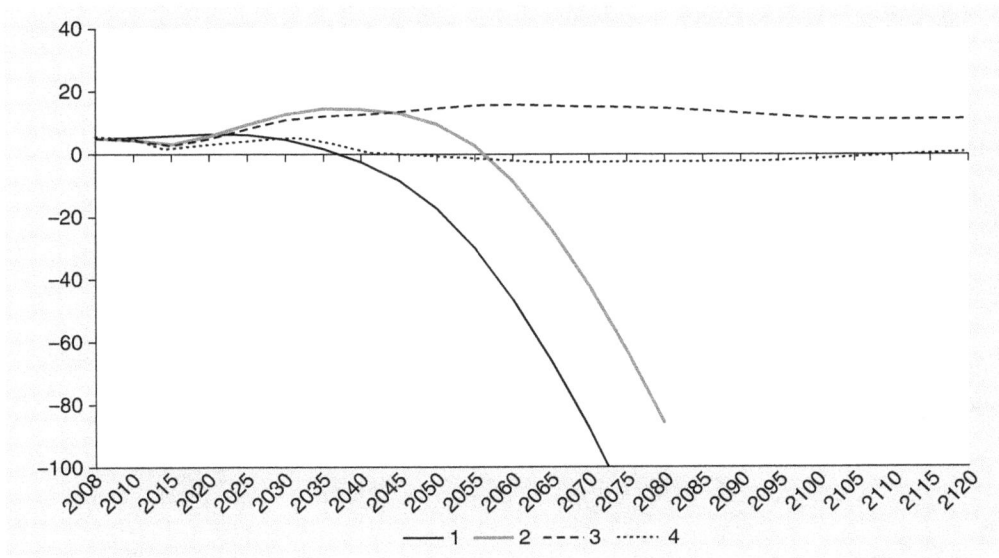

SOURCE: Author's calculations based on the China Pension-System Simulation Model, described in the text.

NOTE: DB = defined benefit; GDP = gross domestic product; NDC = nonfinancial defined contribution. Contributions and expenditures, including interest, are cumulative over time. The scenarios are as follows: 1, baseline; 2, reformed DB scheme; 3, NDC reform with 20.0 percent contribution and 2.4 percent flat-rate pension; 4, NDC reform with 16.0 percent pension contribution and 0.3 percent flat-rate pension. For details, see the text.

REFORMED DEFINED BENEFIT SYSTEM SCENARIO FOR URBAN AREAS

In the UN population projection that we follow here, life expectancy is projected to increase by 6.3 years from the present until 2050 (and we assume that it will increase by one more year by 2060). As a response, we assume for urban males a five-year increase in the retirement age by 2020, a further two years' increase by 2030, and an increase of one more year for women by 2040. For women, we assume an even faster increase in retirement age by nine years: five years by 2040 in the benchmark and an additional four years in the reformed DB scenario. This brings the ultimate retirement age to 67 for males and 64 for females. Front-loading the increase, as compared with the more gradual increase in life expectancy, reflects the idea that the necessity of making a significant change is recognized and accepted. The retirement age is defined in the model such that it triggers the pension, but the person may continue working, although he or she no longer pays pension contributions.

The employment rate in urban areas for persons ages 60–69 is initially 21 percent in 2008. With the increasing retirement age, we assume that the employment rate rises to 40 percent by 2020 and gradually increases to 65 percent by 2060. Note that these figures include those working after having become eligible for a pension. We are here not assuming a larger increase in the employment rate of the urban elderly, as they have to compete for jobs with the still ample source of labor in rural areas.

In the reformed DB scenario, accrued rights are maintained, but new accrual from 2010 onward is reduced to 1.78 percent per year. This is based on a hypothetical case in

FIGURE 7.5 **Chinese urban pension system, projected entry pensions, total, 2008–20**
percentage of contributory wage

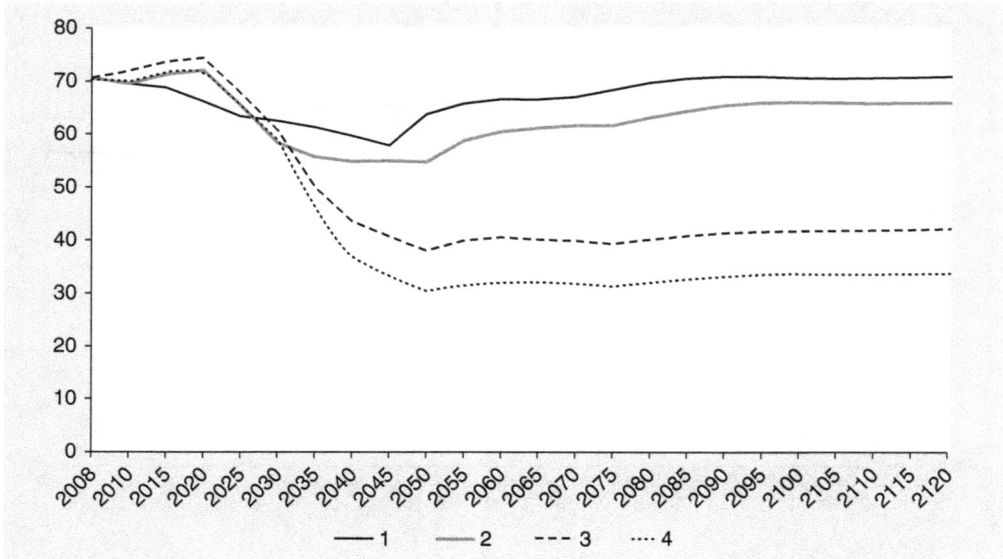

SOURCE: Author's calculations based on the China Pension-System Simulation Model, described in the text.

NOTE: DB = defined benefit; DC = defined contribution; NDC = nonfinancial defined contribution. Sum of DB, NDC, flat-rate, and DC pensions, average for both genders. The scenarios are as follows: 1, baseline; 2, reformed DB scheme; 3, NDC reform with 20.0 percent contribution and 2.4 percent flat-rate pension; 4, NDC reform with 16.0 percent pension contribution and 0.3 percent flat-rate pension. For details, see the text.

which the reference person, who previously worked for 40 years, will work 5 years more and will attain the same replacement rate as before. Over the transition, the replacement rates will be higher because accrued rights are maintained and additional rights will be acquired by working longer.

We now also assume a reduction in the pension contribution rate from 28 to 20 percent in 2010. As stated above, the 20 percent would not be sufficient to finance the current pension expenditure, much less the increase in expenditure as a result of increasing longevity. However, the reduced contribution level could be justified by two considerations: current workers have already contributed significantly to national wealth, and the reduced contribution level would lead to an increase in coverage and bring more revenue to the system. We assume that owing to increasing confidence, the coverage of the pension system will increase by 2020 to more than 90 percent of those employed. Remember that of those covered, 90 percent are assumed to contribute each year.

With these assumptions, as the contribution rate is reduced to 20.0 percent, the system initially runs a deficit of 0.4 percent of GDP for two years, but as increased coverage brings additional revenue, it again records a surplus, peaking at 1.0 percent of GDP and remaining in surplus until 2040. However, as the aging process continues, a deficit emerges, and debt explodes (see figures 7.3 and 7.4). The pensions of new retirees first increase because additional rights accumulate owing to the rising retirement age and then decrease, as in the baseline (see figure 7.5).

This scenario shows that the assumed increase in the retirement age, combined with maintenance of the initial level of pensions, is far from sufficient for sustainable financing.

NEW PLAN FOR RURAL AREAS

The current expenditure on rural pensions is so small that it is not worthwhile to present a separate projection replicating the current data. Instead, we model the new rural pensions on the plan issued by the Chinese government in August 2009. According to the information presented (and interpreted) by Herd, Hu, and Koen (2010), the new plan will expand gradually so that by 2020, the rural population over age 60 will be fully covered. A flat-rate pension of 55 yuan per month, or about 25 euros purchasing power in the 15-member European Union as of 2004 (EU-15), is paid, which is estimated to make up 15 percent of rural per capita household income.

In addition, contributory pensions are set up with individual choice with regard to contributions. As an indirect incentive, participation is required to be eligible for the flat-rate pension. As a rule, a minimum of 15 years of contribution history is required, and persons older than age 45 are required to make an additional contribution to compensate for the missing years. Those older than age 60 receive the flat-rate pension if their adult children join the scheme.

According to Herd, Hu, and Koen (2010), the plan is that coverage is to be 10 percent at the end of 2009, 50 percent in 2012, 80 percent in 2017, and 100 percent in 2020. The authors cite an estimate for average rural household income and wages and suggest that the 25 percent target is the equivalent of 15 percent of the rural average wage. Using these figures, we simply assume that the basic flat-rate pension is 9 percent of the rural wage, to be paid beginning in 2010 to all those covered, and that the second component gradually increases from zero in 2009 to 6 percent by 2025 (that is, over 15 years). Technically, these two components together are inserted as a flat-rate pension into the model and are expressed as a percentage of urban wages according to our assumption about the rural-urban wage ratio.

With regard to financing, the plan allows participants to choose the level of their payments to the contributory pillar, at between 100 yuan and 500 yuan per year. We use 3 percent of the wage, which is a rough average figure in this range. For the rest, we simply record the balance of expenditures and contributions to be covered by the central government, which shares the burden with local governments in the higher-income eastern provinces.

The rural pension system is set up as being sponsored by the government, and so the essential information is the deficit that needs to be covered by the government. The deficit increases to 0.5 percent of GDP by 2025, when full coverage and the target pension level are supposed to be reached. As aging continues, the financing need exceeds 1 percent of GDP by 2040, which is roughly its level in the (hypothetical) ultimate steady state; see figure 7.6. (For GDP, the figures from the previous scenario with increased employment are used.)

SCENARIOS FOR TRANSITION TO NDC IN THE URBAN SYSTEM

The problem with our reformed DB scenario for the urban system is clearly that pensions are not duly adjusted to increasing longevity. In general, a DB system can be adjusted for longevity, as has been done in some European countries, and financial sustainability can be secured. However, as explained above, the main advantage of an NDC reform is that longevity enters into the calculation of the annuity when the balance in the notional account is transformed into a pension at retirement age. Therefore, an NDC blueprint can set a useful reference for a parametric reform of a DB system and can possibly trigger more comprehensive reform proposals. For China, we now also look at transition to an

FIGURE 7.6 **Chinese rural pension system, projected expenditures, contributions, and deficits, 2008–20**
percentage of GDP

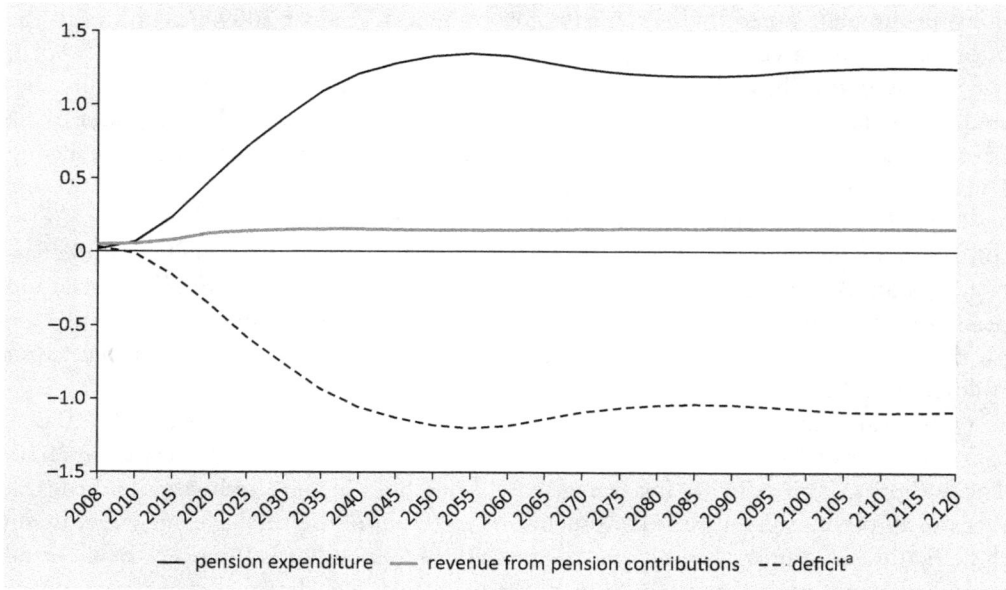

SOURCE: Author's calculations based on the China Pension-System Simulation Model, described in the text.
NOTE: GDP = gross domestic product.
a. The deficit is defined as pension expenditures minus contribution revenue; interest is not included.

NDC system because individual accounts have been part of the reforms and they resemble notional accounts—not by deliberate planning but, rather, as a consequence of problems in implementation.

First NDC scenario: 20 percent contribution. For a blueprint for China, we now assume that in addition to raising the retirement age, the system moves to NDC from 2010 onward so that the 20 percent contributions from all participants age 40 or younger in 2010 are registered in the NDC accounts. All previously accumulated pension rights are respected, and starting from 2010, the accrual rate for participants above age 40 is reduced to 1.78 percent, as in the preceding scenario.

We now turn to a number of specific rules of the NDC system, going into greater detail than in the very basic system without assets that is often presented in the literature. (See, for example, Palmer 2006, 2012; Gronchi and Nisticò 2008.)

The rule for the rate of return on the balance in the notional account during the accumulation phase has to be established. Setting the rate at the growth rate of the covered wage bill, which is required for satisfactory steady-state results, is not justifiable in the Chinese case—why should incumbent workers benefit from the expansion of coverage and the increasing number of participants flowing from rural areas to the cities? Although other options are technically possible in our model, we set the rate of return to equal the growth rate of the total wage bill. Note that in the ultimate steady state, the latter is equal to the rate of growth of the covered wage bill because the transitional factors have disappeared.

The indexation of pensions in payment also needs to be determined. We set it at the urban wage rate, being aware that this does not take into account the constantly decreasing labor force in the new steady state. We know that our assumption is not consistent with full balance in the very long run, but for the same reason as given above, we do not want to use the rate of growth of the covered wage bill here.

Next, we need to specify the rule for calculating the annuity. A simple method is to divide the account balance by expected remaining life years at retirement. This is done in real-world applications because it is easily understandable. It has to be decided, however, whether to apply static mortality figures for the year of retirement or to take into account their expected change over the projected retirement period. We use the latter here because it is more correct. Another question is whether the expected change in the interest rate is taken into account in determining the annuity. We will use a calculation in which it is not.

We use gender-specific annuity factors, meaning that for a given NDC balance at retirement, men have higher pensions. With unisex annuity factors, the results for financial balance and average pensions would be roughly the same as here.

The annuity calculation determines the entry pension, and it has to be decided which index it follows. We assume that pensions in payment follow the unit wage, although we recognize that future changes in employment (which affect the contribution base) also affect the balance of the system, and therefore, in a mature system, indexing to the wage bill can be more correct.

One more issue is what happens to the NDC balance of a participant who dies before reaching retirement age. In some real-world applications, the balance goes to the heirs. We exclude this outcome here and assume that the account balances of those who die before retirement remain in the system. This corresponds to the normal DB pension rule.

The possible inheritance of the account balance is linked to survivors' pensions. These, as well as disability pensions, are left outside our simple model of representative agents. We could add a roughly estimated additional burden from these pensions, but we prefer to omit it here and wait for an extension of the analysis to cover these pensions more properly.

These various issues, albeit not an exhaustive list, show that there are quite a few questions to be answered when setting up an NDC system. We know that the answer to each of them affects the financial sustainability of the system, at least in principle. We also know that an NDC application starting from a state that is out of equilibrium in general never automatically settles down to a perfect long-term balance; as noted above, some additional adjustment is always needed. This does not mean that the NDC blueprint should be rejected. Its advantage is that its basic rules respond to increasing longevity by reducing pensions at any given retirement age, thereby significantly easing, if not solving, the issues with the long-term financial sustainability of public pensions. If employees have a choice as to when they claim their pension and cease to make contributions, the NDC rules provide close to actuarially fair incentives to postpone that date.

Because we can already envisage that these rules will lead in the long run to a significant decline in the replacement rate, we add a 4 pp contribution to a newly established fully funded mandatory pillar (which could also be interpreted as an amount of voluntary pension saving). The outcomes of the two pillars are reported separately.

As in the previous scenario, the public system first goes into deficit as a result of the reduction in the contribution rate to 20 percent, but expanded coverage then creates a surplus that rises to 1 percent of GDP over 2020–30. The assets of the system reach

16 percent of GDP by 2040, and because contribution revenue still exceeds expenditure and the interest rate is assumed to exceed the growth rate, their amount expands without limit. This illustrates the general point that with a somewhat richer structure than the very basic steady-state NDC model, some kind of additional balancing mechanism or fine-tuning is needed. In this case, the system can be modified to be more generous, and there are countless ways to do so by changing one or another parameter.

To illustrate the order of magnitude of the leeway, we present a scenario in which an additional flat-rate pension is paid to all urban pensioners after the same retirement age as for the NDC pensions. We find that if a 2.4 pp flat-rate pension can be paid starting from 2010, the system is still sustainable: its assets reach 15 percent of GDP by 2050 and stabilize at about 11 percent (see figure 7.4). Expenditure for this additional flat-rate pension reaches 0.2 percent of GDP by 2040 and stabilizes at 0.3 percent of GDP in the steady state. Thus, we have identified an expenditure flow that is not large but could alternatively be used for other purposes, such as survivors' pensions.

When the youngest male entrants to the system in 2010 retire in 2057, the average NDC entry pension is 32 percent of the contributory wage (figure 7.7). At the same time, the funded DC pension based on the 4 percent contribution reaches 6 percent of the wage, increasing to 8 percent in the steady state, as we assume that the rate of return on its assets relative to GDP growth rises. The total pension decreases to about 40 percent of the wage. This scenario for the urban system is financially stable, and expenditure from the first pillar (NDC plus flat-rate pensions) stabilizes at 4.3 percent of GDP and in the second pillar, at 1.0 percent.

FIGURE 7.7 **Chinese urban pensions, projected entry pensions under first NDC scenario, 2008–20**
percentage of wage

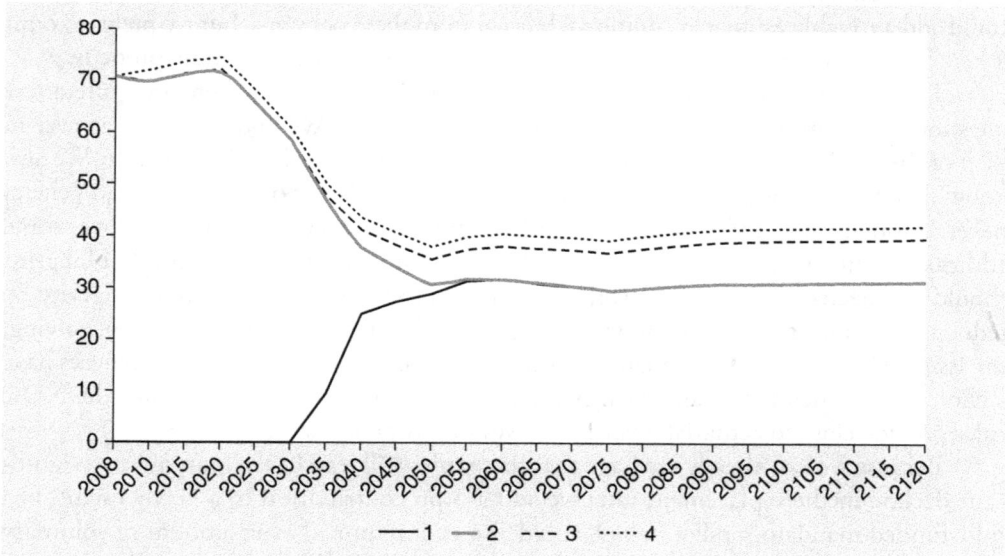

SOURCE: Author's calculations based on the China Pension-System Simulation Model, described in the text.

NOTE: DB = defined benefit; DC = defined contribution; NDC = nonfinancial defined contribution. 1, NDC entry pension; 2, sum of old-system DB and NDC entry pensions; 3, (2) plus DC entry pension; 4, total entry pension, including flat-rate pension (2.4 percent). For details, see the text.

FIGURE 7.8 **Chinese urban pensions, projected entry pensions under second NDC scenario, 2008–20**
percentage of wage

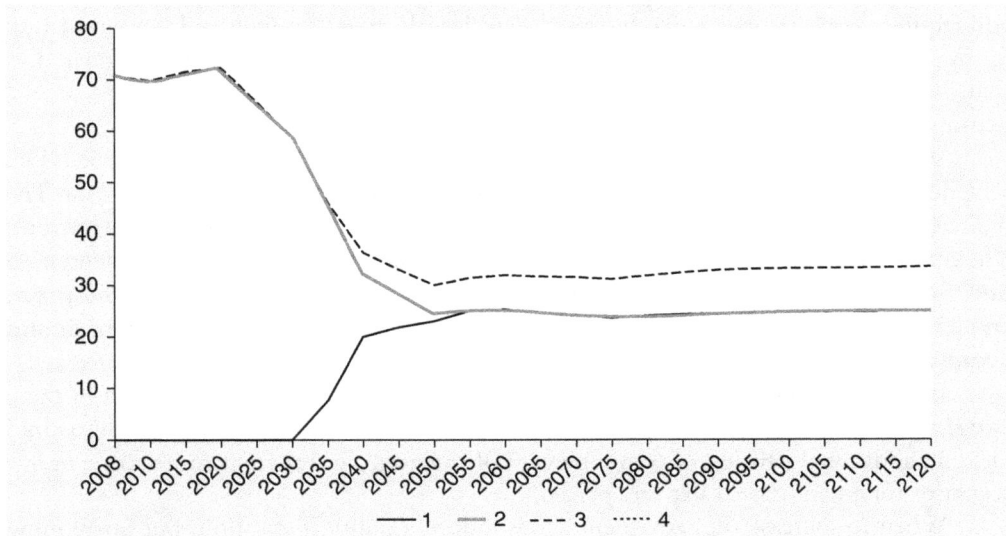

SOURCE: Author's calculations based on the China Pension-System Simulation Model, described in the text.

NOTE: DB = defined benefit; DC = defined contribution; NDC = nonfinancial defined contribution. 1, NDC entry pension; 2, sum of old-system DB and NDC entry pensions; 3, (2) plus DC entry pension; 4, total entry pension, including flat-rate pension (0.3 percent). For details, see the text.

Second NDC scenario: 16 percent contribution. The total contribution rate in the first scenario two-pillar system is 24 percent. That may be considered to be too high, and possibly so high as to jeopardize the assumed improvement in compliance and coverage. Therefore, we present an alternative scenario in which the contribution rate to the NDC pillar is set at 16 percent and combine it with the same 4 percent contribution to the second pillar as above. It turns out that this scheme can afford to pay only a tiny 0.3 pp of the wage in flat-rate pensions. The assets of the system fall below the initial 5 percent of GDP and stabilize at zero (see figure 7.4). The NDC pensions reach 25 percent of the wage, and the total pension, together with the DC pension, is 33 percent of the wage (figure 7.8).

The assets of the second pillar reach 23 percent of GDP in 2057, when the first full-career members retire. Their amount then increases marginally toward the steady state as the assumed rate of return on assets gradually increases from below the rate of GDP growth until 2040 to 1 percentage point above GDP growth.

Other possible fully balanced NDC scenarios could include a further increase in the retirement age. Such scenarios could also be interpreted to calculate the retirement age an individual should choose for obtaining any given targeted replacement rate.

Assessment and Discussion of the Results

In this section, we examine the implications of the simulations for the retirement age, savings, and other aspects of the economy, and we look more closely at the issues involved in the transition to a reformed system.

INCREASE IN THE RETIREMENT AGE

Our simulations for the urban system show that for public pensions, reducing the contribution rate to 20 percent of wage, which is deemed to be necessary to increase coverage, will require the retirement age to be raised significantly, to 67 for men and, for women, to 63 by 2030 and thereafter to 64. The rules for pension benefits will have to be revised so that the replacement rate reflects remaining life expectancy at retirement. Otherwise, the pension system is not financially sustainable.

We should note that under these policy assumptions, pensions from the public NDC scheme are not generous, and they are even less so if the contribution rate is 16 percent. The main reason is the rapidly changing population age structure, which leaves no easy way out. The cost of pensions is high because the number of remaining life years on retirement, even under our assumption of a significant increase in the retirement age, is about 18 for men and 23 for women. Note also that the pension is one-tenth below the theoretical maximum because we assume that those covered do not contribute for 10 percent of their careers.

If it is considered that additional contributions can be accepted, we have in these two simulations an additional 4 pp contribution to a fully funded DC scheme. This would yield an additional pension of 6 to 8 percent of the wage, and there is some scope in our scenarios for an additional flat-rate pension.

When to increase the retirement age is indeed a political question, but postponing an increase for too long may itself jeopardize the sustainability of the system politically. Essentially, the population projection over the next three to four decades drives the above result, and it is therefore not affected by uncertainty over the more distant future. It can thus be considered as nearly a hard fact that to have more generous pensions requires a higher retirement age or a higher contribution rate, or both. Recognizing this, even a further increase in retirement age may have to be considered.

In all discussions on raising the retirement age, the question arises as to whether it unduly harms the job opportunities of the younger cohorts. Economists normally dismiss this worry and label it as a fallacy of a fixed number of jobs. We do not attempt to invent any new arguments about this, but it might be interesting to see the numbers of employed in our scenarios, as shown in figure 7.9. They clearly indicate that the assumed migration from rural to urban areas is far more important for the supply of labor in urban areas than the assumed increase in the retirement age. For example, over the next 20 years, migration contributes more than a 50 percent addition to urban employment, and after that, it still produces an increase, both absolutely and relatively. The incremental effect of the increase in the retirement age is only 6.7 percent by 2030, and the full effect is not more than 16.0 percent. With regard to nationwide employment figures, the increment brought about by the retirement age increase practically coincides with the decrease in the number of employed as a result of the lagged effect of lower fertility. So, in the dynamic Chinese labor markets, the increase in retirement age hardly poses a serious problem for the broad picture. This is not to say that there are no issues involved—examples include the health status of older workers, their training, and the determination of their wages.

EFFECTS ON SAVINGS

The model in the present study does not cover the effects of the pension reforms on savings and growth or on, for example, the external balance of the Chinese economy. Here,

FIGURE 7.9 **Number of employed persons under various scenarios, China, 2008–20**
millions

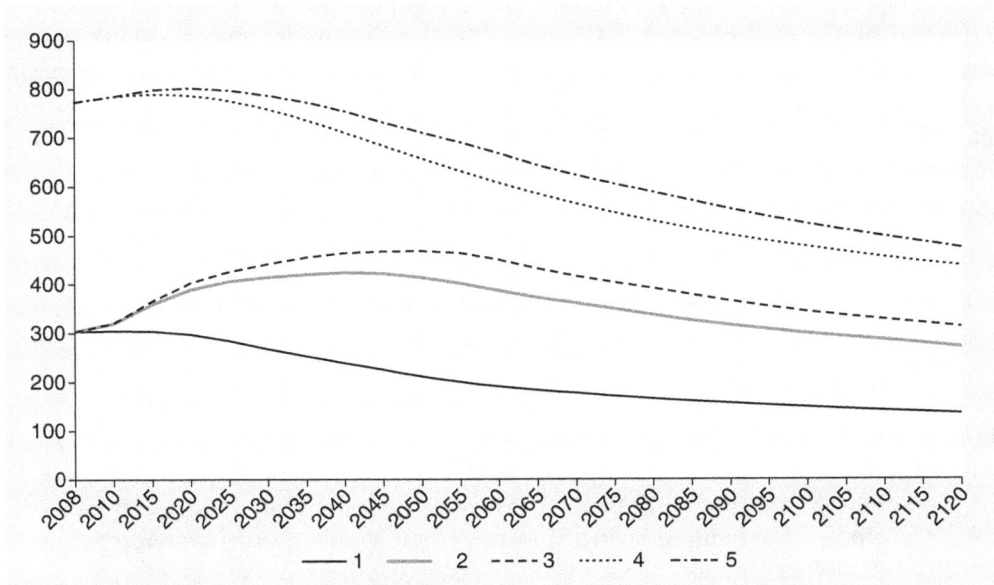

SOURCE: Author's calculations based on the China Pension-System Simulation Model, described in the text.

NOTE: 1, urban employment without migration; 2, urban employment baseline (with migration); 3, urban employment with higher retirement age; 4, total employment baseline; 5, total employment with higher retirement age (in urban areas).

too, the problem can be the opposite of that described for the European welfare states and the United States, where the conventional wisdom is that public pensions have led to too low aggregate savings and that saving for future pensions should therefore be increased. By contrast, the conventional wisdom for China is that saving is too high, contributing to global imbalances.

Note that in our two NDC scenarios, the contribution of the pension system to government saving, under conventional national accounting, is at first negative but then increases to 0.5–1.0 percent of GDP for the 2020s. The system is supposed to be in surplus without reforms, and our baseline indicates a surplus of 0.4 percent of GDP over the period 2010–20. However, in the baseline, the surplus is based on the 28 percent contribution rate, whereas in the NDC scenarios, the contribution rate is 20 percent, and the surplus is mainly provided by the coverage increase, which is meant to steer the pension system toward long-term stability, both financially and socially. Note also that during its accumulation phase, the modest second pillar, with a 4 pp contribution rate, contributes about 0.5 pp of GDP to saving over a few decades.

Here, we should emphasize that assessment of the effect of pension reform on total saving (and via that, on the rest of the economy) has to be linked to government finances as a whole, that is, to its real and financial assets and debt. We can and should make this link, for example, when analyzing the option of filling the empty individual accounts with assets, which is one of the reform options, or in any case, a possible element. If this is done from additional contributions, or if the government transfers to these accounts money collected from other taxes, the current generation bears a double burden. If this is not considered fair or feasible and the government fills the accounts by issuing debt (or selling assets), the outcome is roughly neutral for burden sharing and saving. This is the debt-financing strategy advocated by Feldstein and Liebman (2008), and it could, if applied to the entire system, lead to an increase of public debt by 100 percent of GDP or to the depletion of state-owned assets. This is just to state the relatively obvious main effect. The desirability of this refilling-cum-financing strategy should be assessed on the basis of a full analysis of the capacity of financial and other institutions to absorb such a large structural change.

For a full picture, it is also useful to note the empirical result reported by Feng, He, and Sato (2009), that the reduction of pensions as a result of the pension reforms of the 1990s indeed led to an increase in household savings. Thus, further reductions in pension benefits that are deemed to be necessary for sustainability, as exemplified by our NDC scenarios, may lead to higher private savings, and this could possibly be fostered by people's understanding that their time in retirement will be long even if the retirement age is raised.

As a caveat on this conclusion, we should note that the sheer projections for the cuts in future benefits do not necessarily by themselves determine saving for old age. It can also be that lack of confidence in future pensions currently keeps saving high. If confidence in future pensions improves, even if the level of pensions is lower than the current uncertain level, this could lead to reduced saving. It is too early to judge this matter, but these complex issues should be carefully considered in assessing the macroeconomic impacts.

RELATIVE MERITS OF A FULLY FUNDED DC SCHEME VERSUS NDC

Under our assumptions, the 4 percent contribution to a DC pillar yields a 6–8 pp addition to the replacement rate and results in pension fund assets of around 25 percent of GDP. In our straightforward setting, we can simply multiply all these numbers by 2 and obtain the results for the 8 percent contribution rate that we find both in the 1997 World Bank recommendations and in policy actually implemented. An interesting outcome is that the projection made in 1997, and repeated by Feldstein and Liebman (2008)—that the 8 percent DC contribution would yield a 35 percent replacement rate—requires, in our model, that the rate of return on DC assets exceed the GDP growth rate by 3 pp. No one knew the future in 1997, but in retrospect, we can note that the annual rate of real GDP growth for the period 1997–2009 was, on average, 9.7 percent. How realistic would it have been to assume a 13 percent rate of real return under whatever structural reforms were to take place in the Chinese capital market? It seems that reality would probably not have reproduced the 1997 World Bank projections for the 8 pp DC contribution rates. We have to repeat that the much higher contribution rates set by the Chinese authorities in 1997 did not produce a well-functioning system either, as compliance and coverage remained low.

In our scenarios for the future, we have assumed a prudent rate of return on assets that is, in fact, below the rate of GDP growth to 2040. The outcome for the replacement rate supported by an 8 pp DC contribution is then less than half the 35 percent cited above. This is to draw attention to this significant driver of all pension system scenarios. Under the assumption of relatively rapid growth in China for a few decades more, we fail to see how the rate of return on financial instruments available for pension saving could considerably exceed GDP growth. We could argue that there is, rather, a downside risk because, with gradually opening capital markets and expectations of appreciation of the yuan, interest rates in China could persistently remain at a relatively low level as a result of market factors, even if the authorities were to lift their policy of keeping them low by administrative means.

If this is plausible, then it also follows that the practical arguments for reviving and expanding the fully funded individual accounts over the next few decades are overshadowed by the NDC option. In an NDC scheme, the natural choice for the administratively determined rate of return is the increase in wages. No relatively safe assets can easily outperform that rate in China. So, a given addition to the contribution rate yields a higher prospective addition to pensions in an NDC system than in a funded DC scheme! Admittedly, setting up an NDC system so that it does not accumulate any significant amount of reserves means that future generations will carry the burden of the implicit pension debt. But as argued above, this can be justified by other contributions that the current generations have made to national wealth.

TRANSFORMING EXISTING ACCOUNTS INTO NDC ACCOUNTS

Because the current system of basic pensions and individual accounts is fragmented and is not uniform across provinces, there is no way to capture here all the initial institutional details and practical problems that will be encountered in transforming the existing accounts into NDC accounts. In broad terms, however, the existing individual accounts, which are expressed as the capital value of the accrued pension right, regardless of the amount of financial assets backing them, could be transformed into NDC accounts by declaring a guaranteed rate of return equal to the rate of increase of average wages in the particular region. As long as this guaranteed minimum is higher than the interest rate on (relatively secure) assets, the system would work like an NDC scheme from the point of view of the participant. The accrued rights that are not expressed as an account balance, such as a basic pension linked to the local average wage, could also be transformed into an NDC balance and possibly kept as a separate account, if there are practical reasons to do so.

Seen this way, the transformation from the current fragmented system to NDC rules need not be a jump into the unknown but, rather, a process of clarifying various issues—notably, the accrued rights—and linking them to objectively observed economic variables. Clarification of the accrued rights is surely needed under any reform option. Expressing pension rights as an account balance instead of as a proportion of the wage, and replacing an indexation rule by a rate of return calculated from a wage index, should not be seen as a replacement of the old system by something totally new. Rather, the NDC system can be a more easily understandable pension contract for employees and also a useful way for the pension authorities to work out their own role and commitments.

Above, we simply assumed that those older than age 40 at the time of the reform would remain under the old defined benefit rules, but one could also consider setting a higher or lower age for the move to the new system, with good arguments for both. The question is merely about the way their accrued rights are expressed.

MANAGING ASSETS

The second main issue, after the establishment of the NDC accounts, is management of the assets held by the system, which currently stand at about 5 percent of GDP, including those held by the NSSF, and which increase in our first NDC scenario to 25 percent of GDP. In an NDC system, management of assets is separate from the management of pensions. This feature is probably an advantage of the NDC system over the option of refilling individual accounts with assets and moving to fully funded accounts.

To assess the refilling strategy, one can distinguish between two alternatives: (a) refilling by a one-off capital transfer operation, and (b) moving gradually toward fully funded individual accounts by ensuring that new contributions to them do not flow out to current pension expenditures but that the government provides the required additional financing for these expenditures. The first option would require a multitude of capital transfers from the government to individual accounts (managed by provincial or local pension authorities). Estimating the amounts of missing assets would be a complicated task, both politically and financially. By way of comparison, estimation of the implicit pension debt of the European Union (EU) governments is only just starting, now that those estimates will be required for the supplementary accounts under the revised national accounting rules. This work will take several years (ECB 2010). Estimation of the missing assets in China is even more demanding because pension rights have not been fully clarified and, to name just one issue, determining the interest rate to be used in the calculations is even more controversial than in mature welfare states with much deeper (although at times turbulent) financial markets. Such an estimation exercise would not be feasible and practical because it could disrupt the work of the different actors (including various ministries) for years, and it is therefore probably not being seriously considered.

The second option is not necessarily infeasible, and it is understood to be part of the ongoing pilot schemes in Liaoning and other provinces. It requires a subsidy from the government over several decades—part of the current transfer from the government of 0.5 percent of GDP. It also requires that management of the assets on behalf of the participants be improved by clarifying principles and practices, possibly introducing more competition and strengthening regulation.

The NDC blueprint avoids many of these requirements because the NDC accounts are merely employed for bookkeeping and determination of pension rights, and management of the true assets can be entrusted to a central body. The purpose of the accounts is to smooth the pension burden across generations, with no direct effect on individual accounts and pensions.

In addition, our two NDC blueprints show that the pension system would not necessarily require a capital transfer or permanent financial subsidy from the rest of the government. The crux of the matter is that the assumed coverage expansion helps provide the resources to cover the cost of reducing the contribution rate while respecting the accrued rights. (See Holzmann and Jousten 2012, who see this way of meeting the legacy costs especially relevant for developing counties that start from low coverage.) Avoiding a permanent subsidy from the government can be viewed as an advantage because it highlights the link between individual contributions and benefits and passes on the message that, ultimately, higher pensions require either higher contribution payments or an increase in the retirement age.

If the government wanted to support the pension system financially through a capital transfer or permanent subsidy—motivated, for example, by the desire to transfer the proceeds from privatizing state-owned enterprises to the population at large in order to boost private consumption—filling the empty individual accounts with assets is not the only option. This can also be done under a partially funded pension system with NDC accounts and central management of assets. Another relevant use for a permanent subsidy from the government could be a basic social pension scheme, since, according to our scenarios, the level of the financially sustainable earnings-related pensions seems to be relatively low.

RURAL SYSTEM

The scenario we have presented for the rural pension system attempts to emulate the plan issued by the Chinese government in August 2009, targeting full coverage by 2020. The flat-rate pension, to which is added the individual accounts based on contributions estimated at 3 percent of rural wages, would yield a pension of only 15 percent of rural wages. If this were financed from the budgets of the central government and, in part, from those of the higher-income provinces, it would reach 0.5 percent of GDP in the early 2020s, increasing to 1.2 percent by 2050.

There could be social and political reasons for further increasing rural pensions. Setting up the new pension system with full coverage as announced helps in establishing the necessary administration so that it is ready for possible further changes in generosity. Our model could also be used for other scenarios incorporating NDC and DC accounts and possible convergence toward the urban system.

OVERALL IMPROVEMENTS

Our results are driven by the assumption that the reduction of pension contributions from the current level of about 28 percent of wages would lead to a significant improvement in compliance and in the coverage of the system. Other reforms and improvements in the system may help achieve the goal, or may even be required for achieving it. One task is to deal with the portability of pension rights, which is hampered by the fragmentation of the current system. Another situation calling for improvement is that at least 15 years of contributions is required to receive a pension; otherwise a lump sum is paid. Setting sufficiently similar rules across provinces would improve portability and contribute to making the vesting rules less binding. All this, together with financial sustainability, could enhance confidence and compliance and thereby coverage.[15]

Regarding the overall size of the public pension system, in our first NDC scenario based on a 20 percent contribution rate to the first pillar, the total expenditure of the urban system in 2060 is 4.4 percent of GDP, and in the rural system, it is 1.3 percent of GDP.[16] Adding the cost of pensions of civil servants and public service unit personnel, which is currently 1 percent of GDP and is obviously increasing, the overall expenditure after the foreseeable aging would be perhaps 7 percent of GDP. By comparison, in the EU-15, the expenditure of the public pension systems currently accounts for 10 percent of GDP and is projected to increase to 13 percent of GDP by 2060 (EPC–DG ECFIN 2009). The relative numbers for the United States are roughly half of these. Given that per capita GDP in China is currently 20 percent that of the EU-15, and given that collecting pension contributions and taxes is generally more difficult in a low-income country, our scenarios for China may come close to the size that can be managed credibly.

This raises the question of how to assess adequacy of income support for the less-well-off elderly—something not addressed in our model, in which we assume a representative individual for each cohort, with only gender and urban-rural distinctions and with average contribution histories. Tackling this issue would require the abolition of the current rule that participants receive a basic pension equal to 20 percent of the local average wage after a relatively short contribution period of 15 years. In China, as elsewhere, one purpose of public pensions is the elimination of poverty among the elderly, and a basic flat-rate pension scheme is probably an indispensable part of the system. If, as is currently the case, everybody received a flat-rate pension, and if it were financed from pension contributions and subtracted from contributions put into the NDC accounts, the link between the contributions and the benefits for the individual would become weaker than in a strict earnings-related system such as the NDC. This would impair compliance and might give rise to evasion and lower coverage.

Furthermore, a basic flat-rate pension for everybody is always costly. For example, from our model we can calculate that an additional pension equal to 10 percent of average wage for all urban retirees (even with the assumed higher retirement age) would cost 1.3 percent of GDP in 2040 and 2.0 percent in 2060.

There is no general solution to the problem of providing adequate pensions at a reasonable cost, but the authorities must face the trade-off between competing goals and strike a compromise. One solution is to pension-test basic income support; that is, to make it negatively dependent on the earnings-related pension so that it is reduced to zero at a given level of the latter. The disadvantage is that the implicit tax on the earnings-related pension is high for those who face the partial reduction. The advantage is that for those above the earnings level at which the basic pension is zero, the link between their own contributions and benefits is strong.

Combining basic and earnings-related pensions is not new to the Chinese system; it has been a central feature since the reforms that began in the 1990s. Furthermore, part of the means-tested cash transfer program, popularly referred to as *dibao*, which currently amounts to 0.2 percent of GDP, goes to the elderly. For the functioning of the earnings-related pension system, it is generally favorable if the flat-rate pension can be financed from sources other than taxes on wages. In China, the proceeds from state-owned enterprises constitute a possible source. Other options could emerge from a more general review of tax collection from different sources (various incomes, consumption, and so on) and different levels of government (Hussain and Stern 2008).

HEALTH CARE EXPENDITURE

Public health care expenditure is as big an issue as pensions in China, as in other countries. In 2008, expenditure on basic medical care insurance for urban employees was 0.7 percent of GDP, with reserves amounting to about 1.5 years of expenditure. Recently, schemes have been set up for the rural population and for the unemployed urban population. Even though the level of such expenditure is initially lower than that on pensions, increasing it might be even more difficult to manage because it is affected by many factors that are hard to control and predict—for example, changes in medical technology, involvement of both the public and private sectors, and risk and uncertainty at the individual and aggregate levels. The consequences for public finances are significant. The same type of relatively simple scenarios as for pensions could be useful for estimating the rough magnitudes and discussing the sharing of both benefits and costs across generations.

The consequences of public health care programs for the quality and quantity of labor and so for the economy as a whole can be huge. There is also a link to the acceptability of pension system reforms, since healthier people can and probably will accept a higher retirement age.

EDUCATION

Public expenditure on education is also affected by demographic variables, not least fertility. Especially in China, assessing intergenerational burden sharing, including contributions to pensions, should take into account not only the number of children but also parents' expenditure in educating them. This expense represents an investment in the human capital of the younger generation that increases their capacity to pay for their parents' pensions. Both private and collective investment in education should be taken into consideration here.

We argued above that the efforts of current old-age pensioners and employees can justify a pension reform that does not require a significant accumulation of reserves in the system because the prefunding has already been achieved in various other forms in the past. The current level of education for the young that has been financed or supported by today's working generation can be seen as an additional justification. The principle should be relatively clear, although there are other pertinent considerations.

Conclusion

Pensions in China face a dual challenge: the current system covers only a fraction of the population, and population aging is progressing more rapidly than anywhere else in the world. The ratio of people age 65 and older to those ages 15–64 years, currently at 11 percent, is projected to increase to 38 percent by 2050.

The current multipillar pension system for urban employees is fragmented; it does not work as intended; and compliance with the rules is low. The system, established in the 1990s, was supposed to introduce individual fully funded accounts to top up the basic pension (20 percent of the average urban wage), but the accounts are virtually empty because contributions were used to pay current pensioners.

As for rural employees, who still constitute the majority of workers, the pension system covers only a very small fraction of the population and provides very low pensions. Extending the coverage of the system is a challenge that is clearly recognized by the Chinese authorities, as demonstrated by the government plan issued in August 2009.

There are many links between the urban and rural social security systems, especially through migrants from rural areas who work in the cities, and coverage can be enhanced through such policies as changes to the registration system. This process will, however, be gradual, and it is therefore advisable to keep the urban and rural pension systems separate for analysis, as we have done in this chapter, while looking at scenarios where they may converge.

URBAN SYSTEM

Numerous and diverse reform options have been advanced by both Chinese and non-Chinese experts. It is broadly agreed that the contribution rate of about 28 percent is an obstacle to increasing coverage, and even this contribution level would be insufficient to support the current level of pensions as population aging progresses. To solve the dilemma of high contributions and low coverage is not easy. Our analysis is based on the view that coverage cannot be increased without reducing the pension contribution rate significantly and adjusting the benefits so that the system becomes credible for coping with the rapid aging of the Chinese population.

The proposal for paying for the pension rights already accrued by issuing government debt and establishing a truly fully funded pension system, to take effect from now on, is one option, but the capacity of the financial markets and institutions to absorb the amount of debt is not self-evident. Furthermore, the rate of return on the assets in fully funded accounts will, in the medium term, probably be less than the rate of growth of wages. Therefore, the conventional view that a fully funded system yields a higher return than a public PAYG system is not valid for China.

In this chapter, we have discussed the argument that at least the older members of the current working generation and current retirees have already contributed significantly to the wealth of the nation and can justifiably be provided with pension benefits that exceed the level that they have paid for in the form of pension contributions. This principle, and the acceptance that the current system is virtually PAYG, can lead to an option that does not aim to accumulate significant reserves. It is important to design the new rules so that the projected increase in longevity is taken into account early enough, and this primarily means that the retirement age should rise significantly.

These principles can be implemented under the NDC system, which is, according to many experts, the most promising option for China, or at least one that provides useful guidance for a comprehensive reform. It is seen as an advantage of the NDC system that pensions are not at risk in the financial market. The NDC system does not necessarily require large reserves—which can be an advantage in the case of China, where the saving rate is already very high and is possibly excessive. Under NDC, benefits are adjusted according to retirement age and expected longevity, and financial sustainability is thereby secured quasi-automatically.

In the discussion of the NDC model, we have shown that beyond the elementary principles, there is scope for choice in a number of areas (indexing rules, longevity tables, and so on). In any case, the first phase of the transition to an NDC system, lasting two to three decades, always requires tailor-made rules.

Using the China Pension-System Simulation Model, we have presented several NDC reform scenarios. All previously accumulated pension rights are respected. However, the implicit pension debt does not become an explicit debt of the government, nor is the current working generation required to pay a "double burden," as is the case when moving to a fully funded system. Instead, under an unfunded (or partially funded) public pension system, the burden is shared by all current and future generations.

Because longevity is increasing, we have assumed a gradual but significant increase in retirement age, to 67 for males and 64 for females. In the first scenario, the contribution to the NDC pillar is 20 percent of the wage and in the second, 16 percent. We have also assumed a moderate DC pillar with a 4 percent contribution.

Given these assumptions, as a result of the increase in coverage, under both contribution rate options the pension system would accumulate reserves without limit. Therefore, an additional (small) flat-rate pension can be paid on top of the NDC and DC components. With a 20 percent contribution rate, the total pension, including all three components, decreases to 40 percent of the contributory wage. With a contribution rate of 16 percent, it declines to a little more than 30 percent.

Thus, the unfortunate conclusion is that the projected pensions are not generous. This outcome mainly follows from the population projections over the next three to four decades and is not affected by uncertainty over the more distant future. Higher pensions will require higher pension contributions or a higher retirement age. Accepting this choice is not easy. The high cost of pensions primarily stems from the high expected number of years in retirement—about 18 for men and 23 for women in our scenarios, even though we assume a significant increase in retirement age. The implication is that a higher retirement age than is assumed in our scenarios should be considered.

RURAL SYSTEM

In August 2009, the Chinese government issued a new plan calling for full coverage of the rural elderly by 2020. The flat-rate pension, to which is added the individual accounts based on contributions of 3 percent of rural wages, would yield a pension of 15 percent of rural wages. According to our scenario, financing the deficit from the budgets of the central government and, in part, those of the higher-income provinces would involve a cost of 0.5 percent of GDP in the early 2020s, increasing to 1.2 percent by 2050. There could be social and political reasons for increasing rural pensions further. However, even a continuous expenditure flow of 0.5–1.2 percent of GDP cannot be persistently financed by issuing debt. The difference between expenditure and contributions has to be covered in an orderly manner from other government revenue sources because otherwise the credibility of the system will be undermined.

IMPLEMENTATION ISSUES

In our model, we cannot capture all the initial institutional details and practical problems to be encountered in reforming the Chinese pension system, but our NDC reform still provides some guidance. One question is how to transform the existing individual accounts that are only partially filled with real assets into the new NDC accounts. An option could be for the government to guarantee a rate of return that is at least equal to the rate of increase of average wages in the particular region. As long as this guaranteed minimum is higher than the interest rate on (relatively secure) assets, the system would work like an NDC scheme from the point of view of the participant. The management of the assets, which are currently about 5 percent of GDP and increase in our NDC scenarios, can in this way be separated from the management of pensions. Similarly, possible transfers of assets from other government bodies to the pension system could be dealt with as a separate question, without a direct link to the definition of pension rights.

The move toward transforming the accrued pension rights into NDC accounts and starting to apply the new NDC-inspired rules on indexation is not necessarily a jump into the unknown for the Chinese pension system. Rather, it could be a useful and long-awaited clarification of the rules and a way to leave fragmentation behind and move toward a more uniform system nationwide. It would enhance the portability of pensions and thereby improve the functioning of the labor market, including migration from rural areas, and it would facilitate the integration of migrants and their families into a nationwide system. Nationwide harmonization could also be gradually extended to the pensions of government officials and civil servants. All this would help improve the functioning of the labor market and would serve both economic efficiency and social fairness.

The level of public pensions is relatively modest, both in our NDC scenarios for the urban system and in the scenario depicting the new system for the rural population. Two additional schemes will therefore be needed: basic social income support for the elderly, financed from government budgets, and additional individual pension savings managed by various types of financial institutions. Financing requirements for the basic pensions will compete for government funds to replenish the empty individual accounts of the current system. Increased coverage under an NDC scheme would leave more scope for government support for basic pensions.

Since part of the additional individual savings can go into mandatory fully funded DC accounts, an essential question is how the compulsory pension contributions should be shared between these accounts and the NDC accounts. There is no general guidance for this allocation, especially over the two to three decades when the new schemes are being established and the institutional structure of the economy is undergoing fundamental transition. Note that the contribution rate to the NDC system can be increased or decreased later without compromising its principles. The desired relative sizes of the public pension system and the private sector–managed pension funds will also depend on how financial markets develop and on the targeted total savings in the economy.

We emphasize in the present study that savings in the economy as a whole, including government-owned assets and public debt, should be taken into account when setting the targeted degree of funding in the public pension system. The NDC blueprint accepts that the public pension system can be only partially funded—or not funded at all. The argument that the current working generation and current retirees, because of their contributions to the wealth of the nation, can justifiably be provided with pension benefits that exceed what they have paid for in the form of contributions would justify a modest degree of funding and reduction of contribution rates to a level that would improve compliance. In addition, an NDC scheme outperforms the traditional defined benefit schemes because it provides a firm link between individual contributions and future pensions and because it takes the increase in longevity into account, so that the retirement age will rise.

The simulations in this chapter, which demonstrate the feasibility and advantages of a financially sustainable NDC pillar combined with basic social income support for the elderly and with moderate DC pensions, could be used as a framework for drawing up pension reform proposals that cover a wider range of options. Designing coherent reform options and explaining their characteristics will, it is hoped, facilitate political decision making.

Notes

Without holding them responsible for any errors, the author thanks Grayson Clarke, Jin Feng, Leila Fernandez Stembridge, Tarhan Feyzioglu, Shuyan Geng, Almas Heshmati, Yu-Wei Hu, Athar Hussain, Stuart Leckie, Mihai Macovei, András Simonovits, and two anonymous referees for their useful comments on earlier drafts. The author benefited greatly from the opportunity to discuss his work with numerous people in Beijing, from March 28 to April 2, 2010, and at the Asia Research Centre at the London School of Economics on May 5, 2010. The author is deeply grateful to Patrick Wiese, who developed and programmed the China Pension-System Simulation Model.

1.   Unless otherwise indicated, the source of the data is the *China Statistical Yearbook 2009* (China Statistics Press 2009). We refer here to revenue from contributions. Total revenue, according to the yearbook, was 3.2 percent of GDP. Of this, 0.5 percent was a transfer from the government, according to China's Ministry of Human Resources and Social Security (MHRSS). The assets are managed at the provincial, city, or county level (Impavido, Hu, and Li 2009). The

assets managed by the National Social Security Fund (NSSF), amounting to 2.4 percent of GDP at the end of 2009, are additional.

2. For comparison, 58 yuan is equivalent to 6–7 euros, according to 2010 nominal exchange rates. However, according to *World Economic Outlook 2010,* published by the International Monetary Fund (IMF), the purchasing power of the euro in China is 4.5 times its value in the 15 countries that made up the European Union before the 2004 enlargement (EU-15). Thus, in terms of purchasing power, 58 yuan is about 30 euros in the EU-15.

3. If the comparison is between currency areas, China's GDP in purchasing power terms took second place, having overtaken the euro area in 2011 (according to the IMF World Economic Outlook Database).

4. Although saving in China is obviously influenced by pensions, it may have also been affected by other factors such as housing policies (see Chamon and Prasad 2008).

5. Leckie and Pai (2005); Williamson and Deitelbaum (2005); Drouin and Thompson (2006); Zhang (2007); Li, Dorfman, and Wang (2008); Hu and Davis (2009); Impavido, Hu, and Li (2009); Herd, Hu, and Koen (2010); World Bank and OECD (2008).

6. Chen Liangyu, then Shanghai secretary of the Communist Party of China and head of Shanghai's NSSF, was dismissed in 2006 for alleged corruption and "misuse of Shanghai's social security funds."

7. For the main arguments, see Orszag and Stiglitz (2001); Feldstein and Liebman (2002); and Oksanen (2004, 2010).

8. Feldstein and Liebman (2008) claim that an 8 percent contribution rate would produce a 35 percent replacement rate in a fully funded system. Given our demographic assumptions and a significantly increased retirement age, as advocated here, this would require that the rate of return on assets exceed the rate of GDP growth by 3 percentage points. In our scenarios (see "China Pension-System Simulation Model and Reform Options"), we cautiously assume that the interest rate (and the rate of return on DC system assets) is less than the growth rate for the next 30 years.

9. Clarke (2008) explicitly argues that a defined benefit system offers advantages over NDC, but he also recognizes that such a system needs to be adjusted for affordability through conditional indexation. Therefore, for the urban population, his DB and NDC schemes are not necessarily that far apart, depending on the detail. With regard to pensions for rural areas, he might be right in proposing a primarily tax-financed system in which contributions would merely be for recording entitlements rather than for providing the bulk of the financing.

10. *Pensions at a Glance: Asia/Pacific Edition* (World Bank and OECD 2008) contains simulations for replacement rates.

11. This justification for establishing an unfunded public pension system is somewhat broader than that discussed by Schokkaert and Van Parijs (2003) for Europe and by Barr and Diamond (2008) for the United States. Those authors refer to compensation for the suffering imposed by the two world wars and the Great Depression. We emphasize the contribution that the elderly made to collective well-being from the late 1940s to the mid-1970s, in various ways.

12. Valdés-Prieto (2005) constructs an NDC model in which the pension debt of an initially solvent plan is securitized using bonds indexed to the covered wage bill. This makes the system financially sustainable under autopilot. However, in a case in which coverage is supposed to increase significantly, one may ask whether such a system is fair across generations, since the incumbent contributors would benefit from the injection of new entrants. Because it is difficult to see that this would always be the case, we do not consider this option here.

13. The model does not incorporate the flow back to rural areas, when people return after having retired from urban employment. This omission does not disturb our pension calculations if and when the returned migrants still receive the urban pension. However, the indicator of urbanization should be recalibrated to take their numbers into account.

14. The latter assumption, especially the increase in the real wage 50 years from now, is not crucial for our results because for the scenarios reported here, we assume that pensions—both in their accumulation phase and in payment—are indexed to the urban wage rate.

15. Increasing coverage would also even out the labor costs of the SOEs and the private sector. In the former, coverage is currently 90 percent, whereas in the latter it is well below 50 percent

16. The implicit pension debt (urban and rural schemes) declines from the current 300 percent of GDP (as calculated by our model for the baseline) to 160 percent by 2060.

References

Agarwala, Ramgopal. 1997. *Old Age Security: Pension Reform in China*. China 2020 Series. Washington, DC: World Bank.

Barr, Nicholas, and Peter Diamond. 2008. *Reforming Pensions: Principles and Policy Choices*. Oxford: Oxford University Press.

———. 2010. "Pension Reform in China: Issues, Options and Recommendations." Massachusetts Institute of Technology, Cambridge, MA.

Beetsma, Roel, and Heikki Oksanen. 2008. "Pensions under Ageing Populations and the EU Stability and Growth Pact." *CESifo Economic Studies* 54 (4): 563–92. "Appendix" to article available at http://www1.fee.uva.nl/toe/content/people/content/beetsma/downloadablepapers.htm (accessed January 30, 2012).

Birmingham, Bill, and Shaomin Cui. 2006. "An Introduction to Pension Schemes in China." ASIE/2004/3252, EU–China Social Security (EUCSS) Reform Co-operation Project, Beijing. http://www.eucss.org.cn/fileadmin/research_papers/policy/Pension/PensionschemesChina .pdf (accessed January 30, 2012).

CERAP (China Economic Research and Advisory Programme). 2005a. *Social Security Reform in China: Issues and Options*. Beijing: CERAP.

———. 2005b. *Social Security Reform in China: Further Notes on Issues and Options*. Beijing: CERAP.

Chamon, Marcos, and Eswar Prasad. 2008. "Why Are Saving Rates of Urban Households in China Rising?" IMF Working Paper WP/08/145, International Monetary Fund, Washington, DC.

China. 1997. "The Unified Basic Old-Age Insurance System." State Council Document 26, Government of China, Beijing.

———. 2000. "The Pilot Programme for Improving the Urban Social Security System in China (Liaoning Pilot)." State Council Document 42, Government of China, Beijing.

———. 2009. "Pilot Guidance for the New Rural Pension System." State Council Document 32, Government of China, Beijing.

China Statistics Press. 2009. *China Statistical Yearbook 2009*. Beijing: China Statistics Press.

Cigno, Alessandro, and Martin Werding. 2007. *Children and Pensions*. CESifo Book Series. Cambridge, MA: MIT Press.

Clarke, Grayson. 2008. "Redesigning Chinese Pensions—A Financial Perspective." EU–China Social Security (EUCSS) Reform Co-operation Project, ASIE/2004/3252, Beijing.

———. 2009. "The Financial Control of Social Insurance in China." EU-China Social Security (EUCSS) Reform Co-operation Project, Beijing.

Drouin, Anne, and Lawrence H. Thompson. 2006. "Perspectives on the Social Security System of China." Extension of Social Security (ESS) Paper 25, International Labour Organization, Geneva.

Dunaway, Steven, and Vivek Arora. 2007. "Pension Reform in China: The Need for a New Approach." IMF Working Paper WP/07/109, International Monetary Fund, Washington, DC.

ECB (European Central Bank). 2010. "Entitlements of Households under Government Pension Schemes in the Euro Area: Results on the Basis of the New System of National Accounts." *ECB Monthly Bulletin* (January): 85–101.

EPC–DG ECFIN (Economic Policy Committee and Directorate-General for Economic and Financial Affairs). 2009. *Pension Schemes and Pension Projections in the EU-27 Member States—2008–2060.* Vol. 1 of *European Economy,* Occasional Papers 56. Brussels: European Commission.

Feldstein, Martin, and Jeffrey Liebman. 2002. "Social Security." In *Handbook of Public Economics,* vol. 4, ed. Alan J. Auerbach and Martin S. Feldstein, 2245–141. Amsterdam: North-Holland.

———. 2008. "Realizing the Potential of China's Social Security Pension System." In *Public Finance in China: Reform and Growth for a Harmonious Society*, ed. Jiwei Lou and Shuilin Wang, 309–16. Washington, DC: World Bank.

Feng, Jin, Lixin He, and Hiroshi Sato. 2009. "Public Pensions and Household Saving: Evidence from China." BOFIT Discussion Paper 2/2009, Bank of Finland Institute for Economies in Transition, Helsinki.

Gronchi, Sandro, and Sergio Nisticò. 2008. "Theoretical Foundations of Pay-as-You-Go Defined-Contribution Pension Schemes." *Metroeconomica* 50: 2: 131–59.

Herd, Richard, Yu-Wei Hu, and Vincent Koen. 2010. "Providing Greater Old-Age Security in China." OECD Working Paper, Organisation for Economic Co-operation and Development, Paris.

Holzmann, Robert, and Alain Jousten. 2012. "Addressing the Legacy Costs in an NDC Reform: Conceptualization, Measurement, Financing." In *Gender, Politics, and Financial Stability,* chap. 18, vol. 2 of *Nonfinancial Defined Contribution Pension Schemes in a Changing Pension World,* ed. Robert Holzmann, Edward Palmer, and David A. Robalino. Washington, DC: World Bank and Swedish Social Insurance Agency.

Holzmann, Robert, Edward Palmer, and David A. Robalino. 2012. "The Economics of Reserve Funds in NDC Schemes: Role, Means, and Size to Manage Shocks." In *Gender, Politics, and Financial Stability,* chap. 20, vol. 2 of *Nonfinancial Defined Contribution Pension Schemes in a Changing Pension World,* ed. Robert Holzmann, Edward Palmer, and David A. Robalino. Washington, DC: World Bank and Swedish Social Insurance Agency.

Hu, Yu-Wei, and E. Philip Davis. 2009. "Pension Reform in China: A Simulation Study and Some Policy Recommendations." Economics and Finance Section, School of Social Sciences, Universiti Brunei Darussalam.

Hussain, Athar, and Nicholas Stern. 2008. "Public Finances, the Role of the State, and Economic Transformation, 1978–2020." In *Public Finance in China, Reform and Growth for a Harmonious Society*, ed. Jiwei Lou and Shuilin Wang, 13–38. Washington, DC: World Bank.

IMF (International Monetary Fund). Annual. *World Economic Outlook.* Washington, DC: IMF.

Impavido, Gregorio, Yu-Wei Hu, and Xiaohomg Li. 2009. "Governance and Fund Management in the Chinese Pension System." IMF Working Paper WP/09/246, International Monetary Fund, Washington, DC.

Leckie, Stuart, and Yasue Pai. 2005. *Pension Funds in China—A New Look.* Toronto: ISI Publications.

Leckie, Stuart, and Ning Pan. 2007. "A Review of the National Social Security Fund in China." *Pensions: An International Journal* 12 (2): 88–97.

Li, Jiange, Mark Dorfman, and Yan Wang. 2008. "Notional Defined Contribution Accounts: A Pension Reform Model Worth Considering." In *Public Finance in China: Reform and Growth for a Harmonious Society,* ed. Jiwei Lou and Shuilin Wang, 289–308. Washington, DC: World Bank.

OECD (Organisation for Economic Co-operation and Development). 2010. *OECD Economic Surveys, China 2010,* vol. 2010/6 (February). Paris: OECD.

Oksanen, Heikki. 2004. "Pension Reforms: An Illustrated Basic Analysis." In *CESifo Economic Studies* 3/2004. Also published in *European Economy, Economic Papers* 201 (Brussels: Directorate General for Economic and Financial Affairs, European Commission, 2004).

———. 2010. "Setting Targets for Government Budgets under the EU Stability and Growth Pact and Ageing Populations." *International Journal of Economics and Business Research* 2 (1/2): 87–111.

Orszag, Peter E., and Joseph E. Stiglitz. 2001. "Rethinking Pension Reform: Ten Myths About Social Security Systems." In *New Ideas about Old Age Security,* ed. Robert Holzmann and Joseph E. Stiglitz, 17–56. Washington, DC: World Bank.

Palmer, Edward. 2006. "What Is NDC?" In *Pension Reform: Issues and Prospects for Non-Financial Defined Contribution (NDC) Schemes,* ed. Robert Holzmann and Edward Palmer, 17–34. Washington, DC: World Bank.

———. 2012. "Generic NDC: Equilibrium, Valuation, and Risk Sharing with and without NDC Bonds." In *Gender, Politics, and Financial Stability,* chap. 19, vol. 2 of *Nonfinancial Defined Contribution Pension Schemes in a Changing Pension World,* ed. Robert Holzmann, Edward Palmer, and David A. Robalino. Washington, DC: World Bank and Swedish Social Insurance Agency.

Piggott, John, and Lu Bei. 2007. "Pension Reform and the Development of Pension Systems: An Evaluation of World Bank Assistance." Background paper, China Country Study, World Bank, Washington, DC.

Salditt, Felix, Peter Whiteford, and Willem Adema. 2007. "Pension Reform in China: Progress and Prospects." OECD Social, Employment and Migration Working Papers, DELSA/ELSA/WD/SEM(2007)8, Organisation for Economic Co-operation and Development, Paris.

Schokkaert, Erik, and Philippe Van Parijs. 2003. "Social Justice and the Reform of Europe's Pension Systems." *Journal of European Social Policy* 13 (3): 245–63.

Sin, Yvonne. 2005. "China Pension Liabilities and Reform Options for Old Age Insurance." Working Paper 2005-1, World Bank, Washington, DC.

———. 2008. "Understanding China's Pension System—Yesterday, Today and Tomorrow." Watson Wyatt, New York.

United Nations. 2009. *World Population Prospects: The 2008 Revision.* New York: United Nations.

———. 2010. *Demographic Yearbook 2007.* New York: United Nations.

Valdés-Prieto, Salvador. 2005. "Securitization of Taxes Implicit in PAYG Pensions." *Economic Policy* (April): 215–65.

Williamson, John B., and Catherine Deitelbaum. 2005. "Social Security Reform: Does Partial Privatization Make Sense for China?" *Journal of Aging Studies* 19: 257–71.

World Bank. 1994. *Averting the Old-Age Crisis: Policies to Protect the Old and Promote Growth.* World Bank Policy Research Report. New York: Oxford University Press.

————. Forthcoming. *China—A Vision for Pension Policy Reform.* Washington, DC: World Bank.

World Bank and OECD (Organisation for Economic Co-operation and Development). 2008. *Pensions at a Glance: Asia/Pacific Edition.* Paris: World Bank and OECD.

Yin, Jason Z., Shuanglin Lin, and David F. Gates, eds. 2000. *Social Security Reform: Options for China.* Singapore: World Scientific.

Zhang, Wei. 2007. "Further Reform of China's Pension System: A Realistic Alternative Option to Fully Funded Individual Accounts." *Asian Economic Papers* 6 (2): 112–35.

Zheng, Bingwen. 2007. "The Origin of China's Partially Funded Social Security Scheme and Its Future Direction." *Chinese Economy* 40 (4): 6–28.

The Rationale behind an NDC Approach to China's Urban Pension Insurance

Mark C. Dorfman

Reforms to strengthen the design and implementation of China's pension insurance are needed to address current and future trends in Chinese society. These trends include rapid aging of the population; labor mobility, migration, and volatility; and changes in family income support systems. An objective of reform should be to improve social protection so as to encourage risk taking and consumption-led growth. Reforms of the urban old-age insurance system in the 1990s and, more recently, of rural pensions are important steps forward, but additional measures are needed in view of the rapid changes in China's economy and society.

We suggest a holistic multipillar approach for addressing these challenges and objectives. We believe that a nonfinancial (notional) defined contribution (NDC) framework is particularly well-suited for addressing the reform needs of China's urban old-age insurance system of social pooling and individual accounts and dealing with the conditions that face it. These conditions include the following:

- *Aging.* China is one of the most rapidly aging societies in the world. It needs pension provisions that can automatically adjust to dramatic demographic shifts resulting from substantial changes in fertility rates and increasing longevity. The NDC framework, with a well-designed balancing mechanism and buffer fund, offers a design that can accommodate such demographic shifts and unforeseen adjustments in the years ahead. The direct link between contributions and benefits and the automatic adjustment features of NDC design can address China's aging challenges sustainably. The current defined benefit pay-as-you-go social pooling scheme, by contrast, would require almost continuous parametric adjustments to accommodate rapid aging.

- *Labor diversity and mobility.* China exhibits highly diverse economic conditions and increasing labor mobility between regions and professions. The NDC framework provides a common basis by which accrued entitlements can be calculated and made portable. Moreover, by directly linking notional balances to wages and contributions, the NDC framework can accommodate varying economic circumstances and the associated differing wage and contribution rates. Finally, the NDC framework is well suited to dealing with increasing labor volatility because only periods of contribution increase notional balances.

Mark Dorfman is a senior economist with the Pensions Team in the Social Protection and Labor Group of the World Bank.

- *Financial market conditions and transition cost financing.* In contrast to funded schemes, an NDC framework would eliminate the need for government debt issuance for transition costs while minimizing the risks of reserves invested in China's immature financial markets. As a short-term issue, the country's economic policies seek to increase current consumption by reducing the high personal and household saving rates. The NDC approach would be more consistent with such objectives than funded schemes would be.

Additional advantages of a defined contribution (DC) approach, including NDC, are that DC architecture (a) provides the basis for separately financing legacy costs, resulting in a material reduction in the contribution rate; (b) provides a unifying basis for conveniently adding up prior entitlements in spite of fragmented benefit formulas, contribution rates, and qualifying conditions; and (c) enables benefit calculation based on life expectancy and prevailing conditions at the retirement age.

Technical Design Considerations

The following NDC design considerations should be considered in the Chinese context:

- Establishment of the basis for calculating the notional interest rate should reflect anticipated future changes and needs. Although disparities in circumstances may support the use of locally or provincially based notional interest rates, adoption of a national index would reduce the geographic variation in benefits rather than contribute to it. Furthermore, how the notional interest rate is determined will profoundly affect the evolution of pension assets and liabilities. In an effort to reduce geographic disparities, national gross domestic product growth could be considered as the basis for the notional interest rate.

- Establishment of a buffer fund is essential given the dramatic medium-term projections of cash flows in China's pension system under an NDC arrangement. A buffer fund also serves an important purpose by insulating against future shocks,

- Recognition and financing of legacy costs will materially affect pension incentives, including NDC provisions.

- The minimum retirement age established will have a profound impact on benefit levels, as well as affecting the labor force. We have suggested a gradual increase in the retirement age to 65 for men and women as essential for both system sustainability and reasonable income replacement in retirement.

Institutional Challenges

Most of the institutional challenges in reforming China's pension provision are common to whatever policy design is chosen. Key institutional challenges include (a) establishing a common data platform nationwide during the accumulation and decumulation phases; (b) developing a policy design for consolidating notional account balances across jurisdictions; (c) creating the institutional basis for recognition of prior rights; and (d) strengthening the framework for annuitized benefit determination and adjustment during retirement.

A Holistic View

Achieving China's core objectives of strengthening its old-age income protection while also addressing the challenges of aging and a dynamic labor market will require reforms not only of the urban old-age insurance system but also of other pension and contractual savings provisions. These reforms should include (a) a stronger and more uniform framework for rural and urban social pensions for those individuals who have inadequate pension provisions or who find themselves vulnerable in old age; (b) provisions for saving by rural and informal sector workers, which is best done through matching subsidies much along the lines of those that have been recently introduced in China; (c) substantially strengthened enterprise and individual voluntary saving arrangements to supplement mandated pensions; and (d) continued improvements in the health insurance system to mitigate the risk of health care costs that cannot be supported.

CHAPTER 8

Greece: The NDC Paradigm as a Framework for a Sustainable Pension System

Milton Nektarios

Until 2010, Greece was one of the few countries in the European Union (EU) that had not yet undertaken a full and effective pension reform. The country's pension system was a representative case of the "Mediterranean welfare state," characterized as it was by extensive segmentation, very high payroll tax rates, and—despite the high contribution rates—inadequate pension benefits.

As early as the 1980s, even before the emergence of demographic tensions, the Greek pension system encountered financial difficulties caused by excessive fragmentation, contribution evasion, and a very low formal participation rate. The state began contributing one-third of the cost of the system annually.

The pension structure suffered from multiple major problems:

- The rules of the system did not facilitate long-term financial planning by citizens, who were not given a clear picture of their current and future entitlements to pension benefits. In most cases, they had to reach the day of retirement before they found out what they would receive.

- Considerable intragenerational unfairness was built into the system, which redistributed lifetime income from persons with long, but relatively flat, earnings profiles over their working careers to persons with shorter and steeper lifetime earnings profiles. (This is a characteristic shared by most defined benefit systems.)

- The defined benefit (DB) pay-as-you-go (PAYG) construction of the system, with no mechanism for changing the retirement age or making actuarial adjustments of newly granted benefits to allow for increasing longevity, meant that it could not deliver intergenerational fairness. Without a change in the design of the system, the share of earnings needed to finance the PAYG pensions would continue to increase for future generations of workers. If one assumes that the future growth rates of the Greek economy are lower than the current rates (which is the most likely scenario), the share of future worker earnings that would have to be transferred to cover pension commitments would rise. This feature of the old pension system created an unacceptable downside risk.

Milton Nektarios is associate professor of insurance at the University of Piraeus, Greece. From 1999 to 2004, he was governor of the Social Insurance Organization (IKA) of Greece.

- The construction of the pension system, as is often the case with defined benefit PAYG systems, exercised a negative influence on labor markets by promoting early retirement, and on economic growth by lowering saving rates.

- Finally, the biggest problem of the Greek pension system was its expected financial instability in the period 2015–50. Reliable actuarial assessments (GAD 2001a, 2001b) demonstrated that if the Greek pension system did not undertake a major reform, its future costs would be the highest among the 15 members of the European Union at the time of the studies (the EU-15). Such a prospect would require an ever-increasing amount of government budget financing to support pension commitments, and the outlay would undermine the country's public finances.

In 2010, Greece undertook a drastic and hasty pension reform to comply with the Economic Adjustment Program for Greece (European Commission 2010) that had been agreed between Greece and the joint negotiators of the European Commission (EC), the International Monetary Fund (IMF), and the European Central Bank (ECB). The reform of the pension system that was imposed had the aim of improving the long-run sustainability of the pension system, simplifying its operations, and increasing covered participation in the system. This reform was rapidly implemented by the Greek government in the first half of 2010, reversing the political inertia of the preceding 35 years.

At the Stockholm Conference in December 2009, we argued that time was running out for the Greek pension system, as a consequence of the political impotence of successive governments since 1975. We proposed then, and reiterate here, that a Greek pension reform should be based on the ready-made architecture of the nonfinancial (notional) defined contribution (NDC) paradigm—the so-called Swedish model. A properly designed NDC scheme neutralizes the impact of economic and demographic factors on the financial stability of the pension system.

By contrast, economically, under the current system, pension costs, as a percentage of gross domestic product (GDP) and of the nation's wage base, are greater when growth is low and lower when growth is higher. Demographically, with a fixed pension age and increasing longevity, costs increase with each new generation of pensioners. The introduction of an NDC scheme brings with it an automatic adjustment mechanism to offset declining economic and labor force growth. Furthermore, the Swedish model takes into consideration the individual's life expectancy when the pension benefit is calculated, and life expectancy adjustments are made continuously as longevity increases.

NDC brings financial stability to PAYG pensions, but introduction of a prefunded supplementary pension would also promote saving. In 2000, we had suggested the full funding of supplementary pension schemes, which, in our proposal, would eventually cover half of the total pension benefit (Nektarios 2000). This combination was seen as the only means of controlling the long-term total costs of the pension system in the period up to 2050, if the goal was to guarantee the payment of promised benefits in the long run. Such a scheme would require substantial additional resources, and setting up full funding would necessitate the application of transition rules over a decade or more. Taking into consideration that the combination of lower fertility rates in the past two decades and increasing longevity of pensioners will gradually start affecting the pension system adversely after 2015, we concluded that time was running out for an effective pension reform in Greece.

Now, even without the 2010 reform, the full funding of supplementary pensions is no longer feasible because there is not enough time for it and the country's public finances do not permit such an option. In the aftermath of the 2010 reform, the important issue now is to consider a rebalancing of primary and supplementary pensions in order to examine the prospects for reducing total insurance contributions, which were left unchanged by the new reform even though they are the highest in the EU.

The next two sections describe the Greek pension system as it existed up to 2010 and outline the successive attempts that were made to reform the system, mainly through inadequate parametric measures. The third section (which updates the original Stockholm Conference presentation) describes the pension reform that Greece undertook in the first half of 2010. In the fourth section, we argue that the expedited reform of 2010 is incomplete and that the primary public scheme should be transformed into an NDC scheme to reap all the technical attributes of a good NDC design. In addition, a new balance should be established between the primary and the supplementary pension systems with the aim of reducing total insurance contributions. The fifth section sums up the discussion.

The Greek Pension System before the 2010 Reform

Greece's public pension system has been highly segmented and complex, comprising 24 primary pension funds and more than 120 (public) supplementary funds, with many different regulations on pension rights. The fragmentation of the system opens numerous ways to take early retirement, facilitates contribution evasion, creates extensive intragenerational and intergenerational inequity, and gives rise to high administrative costs. Accrual rates are more than 3.00 percent for the employees of certain public organizations, about 2.86 percent for public servants, and 2.00 percent for salaried employees. In 2008, the numerous funds were legally (but not operationally) merged into five primary pension funds, and eight supplementary pension funds. The primary pension funds can be classified by employment category into five groups (table 8.1). The supplementary funds cover much smaller groups of workers than primary funds and are often based on enterprise agreements.

The standard contribution rates for primary pensions (old-age, survivors', and disability benefits) are 6.67 percent for the employee, 13.33 percent for the employer, and 10.00 percent for the government. For supplementary pensions, the standard rates are 3 percent for the employee and 3 percent for the employer. It is important to note that the supplementary funds are unfunded and effectively operate as PAYG schemes.

In spite of these relatively high contribution rates, the contribution income from employers and employees is insufficient to cover the current

TABLE 8.1 **Coverage of primary pension funds in Greece, 2008**

Employment group	Number of insured	Number of pensioners
Private sector wage earners	2,425,000	955,000
Farmers	661,000	837,000
Nonagricultural self-employed workers	576,000	280,000
Civil servants	549,000	345,000
All others	398,000	135,000

SOURCE: Greece, National Actuarial Authority, 2008.

NOTE: The data are based on the most recent study by the National Actuarial Authority.

level of pensions. The state, in effect, finances the deficits through the budget process. In 2008, the required government financing of current pensions amounted to 6 percent of GDP.

Replacement rates are quite high, on average, for most pension funds, and they are expected to rise further in the future. Table 8.2 shows that the average replacement rate (the average of new pensions divided by average salary) was 60.6 percent in 2007, and it is projected to increase to 70.0 percent by 2050. There are significant differences in replacement rates among the primary pension funds, ranging from 10.6 percent for farmers to 149.8 percent for public servants. In fact, there are significant differences within the same fund, especially between persons insured before and after 1992, with the former enjoying more privileges with respect to retirement ages, replacement rates, and the like.

The relative generosity of pensions in Greece is a matter of concern in most comparative studies of EU pension systems. The average nominal replacement rate for Greece is among the highest among the Organisation for Economic Co-operation and Development members (OECD; see OECD 2005). In figure 8.1, replacement rates (for men) are the highest among the sample countries, and they are the same across all income groups, in contrast to what happens in most other countries.

The relative generosity of the Greek pension system is also evidenced by the estimates in table 8.3, which shows the average pension as a percentage of GDP per worker. (For Greece, it is assumed that the average pension increases annually at 1 percent above inflation.) For the period 2000–50, Greece has the highest average pension in the EU-15.

The complexity and segmentation of the Greek pension system obscures the factors that are straining its finances. The common theme in all the groups of funds is the generosity of nominal individual payments relative to contributions—yet pensioners complain about low primary pensions. This paradox is partly explained by the fact that contributions were quite low in the past (corresponding to the low declared payroll) and were paid for relatively short periods of time. Despite the low declared payrolls and the short contribution periods, most salaried employees were entitled to relatively generous minimum pensions; almost 60 percent of salaried employees received minimum pensions. In addition, before the new legislation of 2010, pensions were paid out at an early age, usually before age 55 in the public sector and close to age 60 in the private sector; the shorter contribution period also resulted in the awarding of low pensions. Another extensive group that has, in particular, received

TABLE 8.2 **Replacement rates for pension funds, Greece, 2007–60**
percent

	2007	2020	2030	2040	2050	2060
All funds	60.6	67.9	70.7	67.8	70.0	66.5
IKA (salaried employees)	84.2	87.1	81.6	76.4	73.7	70.0
OAEE (nonfarm self-employed)	79.8	108.5	123.2	92.0	84.6	85.1
Public servants	149.8	130.5	116.0	103.6	112.3	111.2
OGA (farmers)	10.6	11.5	23.4	22.4	19.6	21.0
Other funds	48.2	45.0	38.8	38.2	45.9	44.0

SOURCE: Greece, National Actuarial Authority, 2008.

NOTE: IKA = Social Insurance Organization; OAEE = Insurance Organization for the Self-Employed; OGA = Farmers' Insurance Organization.

FIGURE 8.1 **Replacement rates in selected countries, primary and supplementary pensions, for men and by income group, 2010, before reform**
percent

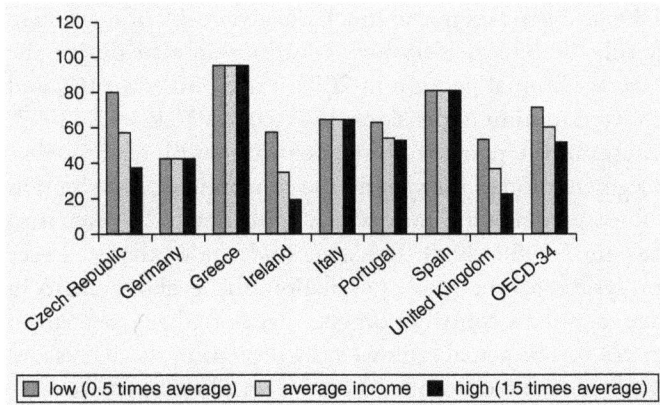

low (0.5 times average)   average income   high (1.5 times average)

SOURCE: OECD 2011.

NOTE: OECD-34 refers to the 34 member countries of the Organisation for Economic Co-operation and Development (OECD).

TABLE 8.3 **Average pension as a share of GDP per worker, selected countries, 2000 and 2050**
percent

Country	2000	2050	Change
Austria	22	19	16
Belgium	16	14	−16
Denmark	23	21	−12
Finland	22	22	−1
France	24	16	−34
Germany	19	15	−20
Greece	25	32	29
Ireland	20	19	−4
Italy	16	12	−27
Netherlands	17	18	3
Portugal	17	18	7
Spain	17	16	−5
Sweden	24	19	−21
United Kingdom	14	7	−49
EU-15	19	15	−21

SOURCE: European Commission and Economic Policy Committee 2001.

NOTE: GDP = gross domestic product. EU-15 refers to the 15 member countries of the European Union before the 2004 expansion.

little from the system is farmers, for whom a primary fund was established in 1998. Their pensions are essentially a flat welfare benefit that is less than 30 percent of the minimum pension for wage earners.

Complexity and segmentation, in conjunction with poor administration, have led to a lack of transparency and to inadequate monitoring. As a result, pension fraud is difficult to detect. Contribution evasion is sizable and is estimated at about 20–30 percent of current revenue (Tatsos 2001). Many studies have demonstrated the inadequate organization of the system and the inequity of the insurance conditions and pension rights involved in the intragenerational and intergenerational transfers.[1]

Major studies of the Greek pension system (OECD 1997; Mylonas and de la Maisonneuve 1999) have identified as the main shortcomings of the current public pension system loose eligibility conditions and perverse incentives that foster early retirement and contribution evasion. These country-specific problems are additional to a low fertility rate and population aging, giving rise to a high and increasing old-age dependency ratio. Long-term projections indicate that the unfunded liabilities of the PAYG system are among the highest among OECD countries. The present value of future pension liabilities, net only of employer and employee contributions, was estimated to be of the order of 200 percent of GDP (Roseveare et al. 1996; Mylonas and de la Maisonneuve 1999).

Most diagnostic studies have failed to distinguish between the symptoms and the causes of the system's past and prospective problems. It is true that in the future, the inherent generosity of the Greek pension system, along with evolving demographic factors, will result in the largest increase in pension costs of any EU-15 country (IMF 2006). In the past, however, the essence of the problem was not so much the generosity of the system as the inadequacy of the revenue side, despite the very high contribution rates during the period 1980–2000. In fact, the average annual pension in 2004 was 6,380 euros (€), and about 65 percent of pensioners received minimum pensions (IMF 2006). Nektarios (2007) has demonstrated that the real causes of the paradox of low pensions and high contribution rates have been the extreme segmentation of the system, the concomitant contribution evasion, and the very low labor force participation rate, which contributed 26 percent to the increase in payroll taxes in the period 1980–2000. The same study shows that if Greece had had a single, uniform pension system for the whole population, the level of benefits in the period 1980–2000 would have required a contribution rate that started at 7 percent in 1980, increasing to 16 percent in 2000. The actual rates were 14 percent in the 1980s and about 25–30 percent after 1993, which resulted from far too low contribution payments.

In 2001, the Greek government employed the U.K. Government Actuary's Department (GAD) to undertake a thorough actuarial analysis of the pension system and make estimates of the required financing by the government budget in the period 2000–50 (GAD 2001a, 2001b). The projected deficits of the pension system that would have to be financed by general revenues are shown in table 8.4. Pension deficits during the period up to 2050 will, in the best scenario, double in size and, in the worst scenario, triple. That is, the required financing of the pension system by the government budget will have to increase from current levels (4.8 percent of GDP in 2000 and 5.5 percent of GDP in 2009) to about 8.00–12.00 percent of GDP in future decades.

TABLE 8.4 **Estimates of the deficits of the Greek pension system, 2000–50**

	Deficit (% of GDP)				Change, 2000–50 (%)	Difference from central scenario (%)
	2000	2020	2030	2050		
Scenario						
Central scenario[a]	4.8	6.9	11.1	16.8	12.0	n.a.
Pessimistic scenario	4.8	8.7	13.4	23.0	15.6	3.6
Optimistic scenario	4.8	4.7	8.2	9.3	4.5	−7.5
Parametric reforms						
Indexing of pensions to inflation only	4.8	5.4	8.8	12.8	8.0	−4.0
Retirement age at 67 (if applicant was below age 50 in 2001)	4.8	5.0	8.6	13.2	8.4	−3.6
Application of the 1992 provisions	4.8	6.6	10.3	16.2	11.4	−0.6
Calculation of pension benefits on the basis of all years of contributions	4.8	6.8	9.5	14.6	9.8	−2.2

SOURCE: GAD 2001a.

NOTE: GDP = gross domestic product; n.a. = not applicable.

a. The assumptions of the central scenario are as follows: inflation, 2.50 percent per year; increase in real wages, 1.75 percent per year; increase in real pensions, 1.00 percent per year; increase in GDP, 2.00 percent per year.

It is not logical to assume that in the future the government budget will have a greater capacity to finance pension deficits of such magnitudes (higher than in any other EU-15 country) than it has now. It is expected that the growth rate of the economy will decrease from the average of 3.5 percent in the decade 2010–20 to 2.5 percent in the 2020s, 2.0 percent in the 2030s, 1.3 percent in the 2040s, and 0.9 percent in the 2050s. Growth will be sustained mainly by productivity growth (2.5 percent currently, and 1.9 percent in 2050). The labor force will reach its peak in 2020 and will then decline as a result of the past two decades of low birth rates (IMF 2006).

The European Commission has undertaken a series of comparative studies of pension costs for all European countries. Table 8.5 shows that pension cost increases for

TABLE 8.5 **Public pension expenditure, European Union countries, 2007–60**
percentage of GDP

Country	2007	2010	2020	2030	2040	2050	2060	Change, 2007–60 (%)
Austria	12.8	12.7	13.0	13.8	13.9	14.0	13.6	0.9
Belgium	10.0	10.3	11.8	13.9	14.6	14.7	14.7	4.8
Bulgaria	8.3	9.1	8.4	8.6	9.5	10.8	11.3	3.0
Cyprus	6.3	6.9	8.9	10.8	12.8	15.5	17.7	11.4
Czech Republic	7.8	7.1	6.9	7.1	8.4	10.2	11.0	3.3
Denmark	9.1	9.4	10.6	10.6	10.4	9.6	9.2	0.1
Estonia	5.6	6.4	5.9	5.6	5.4	5.3	4.9	−0.7
Finland	10.0	10.7	12.6	13.9	13.6	13.3	13.4	3.3
France	13.0	13.5	13.6	14.2	14.4	14.2	14.0	1.0
Germany	10.4	10.2	10.5	11.5	12.1	12.3	12.8	2.3
Greece	11.7	11.6	13.2	17.1	21.4	24.0	24.1	12.4
Hungary	10.9	11.3	11.0	11.0	12.2	13.2	13.8	3.0
Ireland	5.2	5.5	6.4	7.5	8.7	10.5	11.3	6.1
Italy	14.0	14.0	14.1	14.8	15.6	14.7	13.6	−0.4
Latvia	5.4	5.1	5.2	5.9	6.1	5.8	5.1	−0.4
Lithuania	6.8	6.5	6.9	8.2	9.1	10.4	11.4	4.6
Luxembourg	8.7	8.6	9.9	14.2	18.4	22.1	23.9	15.2
Malta	7.2	8.3	9.3	9.3	10.5	12.0	13.4	6.2
Netherlands	6.6	6.5	7.8	9.3	10.3	10.3	10.5	4.0
Norway	8.9	9.6	11.5	12.7	13.4	13.3	13.6	4.7
Poland	11.6	10.8	9.7	9.4	9.2	9.1	8.8	−2.8
Portugal	11.4	11.9	12.4	12.6	12.5	13.3	13.4	2.1
Romania	6.6	8.4	8.8	10.4	12.6	14.8	15.8	9.2
Slovak Republic	6.8	6.6	6.3	7.3	8.3	9.4	10.2	3.4
Slovenia	9.9	10.1	11.1	13.3	16.1	18.2	18.6	8.8
Spain	8.4	8.9	9.5	10.8	13.2	15.5	15.1	6.7
Sweden	9.5	9.6	9.4	9.5	9.4	9.0	9.4	−0.1
United Kingdom	6.6	6.7	6.9	7.6	8.0	8.1	9.3	2.7
EU-27	10.2	10.2	10.5	11.4	12.1	12.4	12.6	2.4
EU-12	11.1	11.2	11.6	12.7	13.6	14.0	13.9	2.8
EU-15	10.2	10.3	10.7	11.6	12.3	12.5	12.7	2.4
EU-10	9.7	9.3	8.8	9.0	9.6	10.4	10.7	1.0
EU-25	10.2	10.3	10.6	11.4	12.1	12.4	12.5	2.3

SOURCE: European Commission and Economic Policy Committee 2008.

NOTE: GDP = gross domestic product. EU-27 refers to the 27 current members of the European Union. EU-12 refers to the original 12 European Union states in 1986; EU-15, EU-25, and EU-27 refer to the European Union after the enlargements in 1995, 2004, and 2007, respectively. EU-10 refers to the group of 10 countries that joined the European Union in 2004.

Greece in the period 2007–60 will be the highest in the EU if the current pension system is not restructured. Pension expenditures for Greece exhibit the highest increase among all EU-15 countries, which without reform would have increased to 24.0 percent of GDP; the average for the EU-25 (the 25 member countries of the EU before the 2007 expansion) is about 12.4 percent.

Successive Parametric Reforms up to 2010

The welfare state in Greece was established in 1934, when the Social Insurance Organization (IKA) was assigned the primary responsibility of gradually absorbing all existing social insurance funds and becoming the only social insurance organization for pensions and health care. Unfortunately, a chain of adverse historical events (World War II, a civil war, and dictatorship) led to outcomes different from those planned. Most professional groups, depending on their political power, succeeded in establishing their own pension funds, both primary and supplementary, as well as health insurance funds. By 1997, the total number of social insurance funds was 325. All of them have the legal status of public funds, and the state is therefore ultimately responsible for guaranteeing the payment of the promised benefits.

After the collapse of the dictatorship in 1974, Greece entered an era of political stability and extensive economic growth. Even during this period, however, it proved impossible to form a political consensus for undertaking major reforms in public administration, education, and the pension system. Since 1974, almost every new government has passed some type of legislation to remedy the pension system; but all those interventions were piecemeal attempts to satisfy current political needs and lacked an overriding strategy.

In 1981, minimum pensions were increased by 50 percent, and in 1983, the system of supplementary pensions was expanded to cover all citizens. In 1992, a major reform led to the harmonization of insurance, contribution, and benefit provisions across all pension funds and introduced a government subsidy amounting to 10 percent of taxable earnings. The reform had two serious shortcomings: it reduced future minimum pensions by half, and it ignored the issue of the unfunded liabilities of the supplementary pensions. In 1996, a system of minimum pensions was established and was financed by general revenues on the basis of the negative income tax methodology. In 1997, a primary pension fund was established for farmers, who had been receiving minimum welfare payments after age 65. In 2002, the year that Greece adopted the euro, the IKA started using modern electronic systems. In 2008, the primary pension funds were merged into five funds, and the supplementary pension funds were consolidated into eight.

Undoubtedly, the parametric reforms of the past 35 years have been useful and have improved the operation of the pension system in Greece, but they have not resolved the main problem—the long-run financial instability of the pension system. This instability is the result of the inherent generosity of the benefit structure, the increasing dependency ratio, and the informality of the labor force. As was shown in the preceding section, Greece has had the most serious problems with the financial instability of its pension system among the EU-15 group of countries.

If we assume that the objective was for the pension system to be able to deliver the promised benefits in the long run, the developments of the past 35 years, and especially the lack of political consensus for a major pension reform, represented a great missed opportunity for the country, in the sense that very few options remained. In 2010, the

Greek state had essentially three choices: (a) to legislate substantial reductions in the promised pension benefits, (b) to fund the financial deficit of the pension system with ever-increasing amounts of general revenues, or (c) to undertake a major reform of the pension system along the lines described later in this chapter.

We shall argue in the next section that the lack of political consensus for a pension reform in the period 1980–2010 resulted in the pension reform imposed on Greece in 2010, which is essentially an adoption of option (a) to avoid option (b). The new pension reform, however, does not constitute an efficient reform; rather, it represents yet another lost opportunity to improve the country's social insurance infrastructure.

The Pension Reform of 2010

Since this paper was first presented at the Stockholm Conference in December 2009, many things have changed dramatically in Greece's pension landscape.

The politics of irresponsibility practiced by successive governments since 1975 resulted in the effective bankruptcy of the country and led to a request for international financial assistance. The joint EC/IMF/ECB financing package that was offered included requirements for supporting economic policies—among them, the drastic pension reform described below. Undoubtedly, the reform was necessary, as this study in fact shows. But the Ministry for Labor and Social Insurance, without any serious preparation, started producing successive drafts of legislation that attempted both to appease the citizens and the labor unions and to satisfy the demands of the EC/IMF/ECB mission regarding pension reform. Eventually, the final legislation had to follow the terms of the Economic Adjustment Program, the main direction of which was to reduce the incremental financing of pension costs over the period 2010–60 by 10.0 percentage points of GDP—from the projected cost increase of 12.5 percentage points of GDP (see table 8.5) down to 2.5 percentage points, the average rate of increase for the EU-15 countries.

PRINCIPAL PROVISIONS OF THE 2010 PENSION LEGISLATION

The main reform elements of the new pension legislation are as follows.

Benefit reductions for current pensioners. Two monthly pensions (out of 14 annually) are abolished (for monthly pensions of less than €2,500 gross), and a flat bonus is provided in their place. The highest pensions, representing about 10 percent of pensioners and exceeding €1,400 per month gross, are reduced by an average of 8 percent, starting in July 2010.

Uniform and lower accrual rates. The old system had different accrual rates for various pension plans. The new law proposes one profile of accrual rates for all workers and reduces these from 2.0–3.0 percent per year to 0.8–1.5 percent per year, depending on years of service. This measure simplifies the pension system, reduces costs, and creates incentives to participate longer in the workforce because the accrual rate is progressive with the number of years spent working.

Increased retirement age and years of contributions. The old system often allowed workers to claim benefits before age 60. For example, in 1997, in the salaried employees fund (IKA), special provisions allowed about 80 percent of new retirees (85 percent for men and 70 percent for women) to retire and obtain old-age benefits before age 60; only

20 percent of new retirees opted to retire at the normal age of 65 (Börsch-Supan and Tinios 2001). The new system sets the minimum age of retirement at 60 for all workers (both men and women); requires 40 years of contributions to qualify for full benefits; and reduces benefits by 6 percent per year for those who claim benefits before age 65 without 40 years of contributions. In addition, the two anchors (ages 60 and 65) will now be indexed to life expectancy.

Revision of list of arduous professions. The reform requires a revision of the list of strenuous and hazardous occupations to reduce claims in these categories.

Calculation of pensionable earnings. The old system used the "best" 5 years of the last 10 years of earnings as the pensionable base. The new law uses the full earnings history to calculate pensionable earnings. Annual pensionable earnings are to be adjusted by the consumer price index (CPI), plus an index of maturation that has so far not been specified.

Indexation of pensions. The old system tended to adjust pensions with wage growth. The new system caps indexation at inflation.

Simplification. The new law proposes to merge all funds into three funds, roughly corresponding to those for private sector workers, the self-employed, and the remaining categories of workers. New public servants will be insured through the IKA, the salaried employees' fund. Employees of the Bank of Greece, however, will retain their own pension fund, and "third-party" (social) contributions will be maintained for the funds covering engineers, lawyers, and journalists.

Financial impact. Initial estimates show that the proposed changes will substantially slow the rise in pension spending through 2060; the *increase* over costs in 2010, expressed as a percentage of GDP, could drop from a projected 12.5 percentage points of GDP to about 4.0–6.0 percentage points of GDP as a result of the new legislation (still above the target of 2.5 percentage points of GDP). The main area of uncertainty has to do with the costs of supplementary pensions, which require further analysis.

Safeguard clause. If actuarial analysis suggests that the reform is falling short of the final objective of reducing increases in future pension costs to 2.5 percentage points of GDP, a ministerial decision can lower costs further through a combination of adjustments in the parameters of the system, the basic pension, and the supplementary pensions.

ASSESSMENT

Some comments are in order concerning the 2010 pension reform. First, the general opinion is that the reform does not create a new system with a well-designed architecture that gives the sense of a new start; it is, rather, a hasty restructuring of the old system. Major issues such as the more exact details of the new reform and the structure of the system of supplementary pensions are left for future consideration. This is not a bad prospect, provided that decisions are made in a quieter and less urgent setting.

Second, the new system separates the insurance and welfare elements in the overall pension benefit. Starting in 2015, the new monthly pension will consist of a basic pension of €360 and a primary (proportional) pension calculated from career pensionable earnings. The basic pension will be financed by public revenues, and the primary pension will be financed by a total contribution of 20 percent, paid by employers and employees.

The accrual rate for the primary pension will gradually increase from 0.8 to 1.5 percent, depending on length of employment. In comparison with the old system, the new pension will be higher for those with low incomes and long periods of employment. It should be noted that the basic pension will be awarded even if the insurance period is less than 15 years; in the old system, there was no benefit for insurance periods of less than 15 years. It is not clear whether short-career pensioners will be entitled to a proportional pension, as well.

Third, the new system retains the provision of a minimum pension (about €495 in 2010). However, the role of this benefit should have been assigned to the basic pension. As it now stands, this feature of the reform violates the principle of separation of insurance and welfare elements. In addition, it is not clear how the minimum pension will be financed. Moreover, a provision of this kind in the new system will create negative employment incentives.

Fourth, the new system abolishes all special provisions for early retirement; after 2011, all the insured will have to reach age 65 and have had 40 years of employment to receive a full pension and will have to be age 60 to qualify for an early, reduced pension. The financial impact of this provision is very strong in reducing pension expenditures up to 2020 through postponed retirement.

Fifth, the new system provides that up to 2015, new pensioners will have their pensions calculated on the basis of past provisions. For those who retire after 2015, pensions will be calculated in part according to the old system and in part under the new one, depending on the year of retirement and the length of employment. This provision implies that the first serious reductions in pension benefits will not occur until after 2018.

UNRESOLVED ISSUES

Certain serious issues were not considered in the new pension reform. First, and most important, the very high insurance contribution rates were not dealt with, and these might create adverse incentives against participating fully in the formal economy for future generations of young workers. Second, the new legislation did not deal at all with the system of supplementary pensions, its financial stability, and possible rebalancing with the system of primary pensions. Third, the new pension reform does not consider issues of distributional equity during the transition period. And finally, the new reform does not provide a solid foundation that would create a long-term financial contract through a constant contribution rate, which would facilitate economic planning for the new generations.

The conclusion is that Greece eventually had its own pension reform, but one of the worst kind for those in retirement or nearing retirement, in the sense that these people are faced with an abrupt disruption in their economic and financial planning without being given the time or the means to adjust to the new situation. The inertia and the lack of political consensus for an orderly pension reform during the past 30 years were reversed in the first half of 2010, when, in a panic situation, legislation had to be drafted and passed through the parliament. The Greek government adopted, without comprehensive deliberation, the main guidelines of the pension experts of the EC/IMF/ECB team. The ultimate goal will probably be attained; that is, the growth of pension expenditure over the period 2010–60 will be kept under 2.5 percentage points of GDP.

There is no doubt that the new pension reform was necessary to accomplish some of the principal goals of a modern pension system—issues that successive Greek governments had not had the strength or courage to address. Specifically, the new reform attempts to simplify the organization of the pension system; to establish intragenerational (but not intergenerational) equity in the treatment of successive generations of workers; to abolish many unfair differences in insurance and retirement provisions among the various professional groups; and to reduce drastically the growth trend of future pension expenditures to relieve the burden on the public budget.

The NDC Paradigm as a Framework for a Complete Pension Reform

At first glance, one could say that the mission of pension reform in Greece was accomplished in 2010. We argue, however, that the 2010 legislation represented another missed opportunity for an orderly reform of the pension system. There is no doubt that the pension guidelines imposed by the EC/IMF/ECB project team were necessary and that they pointed in the right direction for relieving the government budget of the current and future burdens of the pension system. (Most of the features of the reform undertaken were, indeed, suggested in the initial version of this study.) But the sufficient condition for an effective reform would be to place those changes in the framework of a "new paradigm"—the ready-made architecture of the NDC model that would signal a new beginning for a modern and sustainable pension system for Greece. Then Greece would have achieved the best outcome in pension reform: it would have established a modern, flexible, and transparent pension system, and, at the same time, it could have reduced the excessive contribution rates, which remain unchanged under the new reform plan and represent one of its principal shortcomings. In such a case, the Greek people would have been offered a systematic framework to plan effectively for their future pensions.

In 2000, when the socialist government was contemplating reform, we proposed that the long-term financial stability of the pension system could be ensured by prefunding the supplementary pensions and rebalancing the relative weights of the primary and supplementary pension benefits (Nektarios 2000). This chapter suggests, as a way of reducing the sharp rise in contributions that is needed in the medium- and longer-term future to finance pensions, that lower pensions be paid from the current PAYG system but that this reduction be offset by the introduction of a new, prefunded supplement.

Table 8.6 presents the expected costs of the existing pension system, in terms of current earnings, with no reform, and the effects of the introduction of the proposed new system, which includes the prefunded system, assuming retirement ages of 60 and 65. It can be seen that the total pension cost of the new system is initially higher, reflecting the need to pay for current pensions and, at the same time, to finance future pensions. Following a transition period, however, the total costs are significantly lower than if the present system had continued. In effect, the income received on the investments built up from the funded system would meet the extra costs of actually paying the current pensions. (The assumed rate of investment return in the table is 2 percent higher than wage growth, which is a rather conservative assumption in the long run.)

The costs of the new system, including the funded system, are reduced considerably if the retirement age is 65 (the age established by the 2010 reform). In this case, additional financing of the funded system is needed, in the order of 3.1 percent of GDP annually for the first decade; it subsequently falls to 0.4 percent of GDP. The transition period for the full financing of the funded system is about 10 years. With such a financial rearrangement, the total cost of the new national pension system would have been reduced substantially in comparison with the costs of the old system without reform. In effect, after the 10-year transitional financing period, the total costs of the new system would return to the 2000 level, which would be even below the average level of pension expenditures of the EU-15 countries.

The findings in table 8.6 show that this solution to the Greek pension problem was quite feasible, if only a political consensus had been attained in time. The people would have received their promised benefits, and the long-term financial stability of the pension system would have been even better than under the 2010 reform.

In 2008, when the conservative government was contemplating yet another pension reform, we made the additional suggestion that the system of primary pensions be restructured on the basis of the NDC model (Nektarios 2008). The NDC model is considered the new paradigm for pension reform in the EU, and such an evolution could facilitate the process of harmonization of pension systems within the EU (Holzmann 2006). The argument here is that the NDC model may still be employed as the appropriate architecture for completing pension reform in Greece, but the original proposal now has to be modified to take into consideration the legislation of 2010. The main elements of the proposed reform are briefly described below.

OBJECTIVES OF THE REFORM

The primary aim of a reform of the Greek pension system is to facilitate effective long-term financial planning by all generations of citizens. This is accomplished, first, by selecting the most efficient combination of compulsory and (public and private) voluntary pension plans. The second objective is to ensure intragenerational and intergenerational equity and to make the system fully transparent. To this end, the conditions of the intergenerational contract have to be clearly laid out, including the social commitment of the government in the form of noncontributory components and a minimum guarantee. This commitment is confirmed through the creation of individual accounts and individual account statements that are sent out annually to all the insured. However, the fulfillment of this objective requires the long-term financial stability of the pension system. The pension system should have a positive or neutral influence on employment and economic

TABLE 8.6 **Preliminary cost estimates for the proposed pension reform in Greece, in current earnings, 2000–50**

Year	Current system without reform		New system, retirement age 60		New system, retirement age 65	
	€ (billion)	% of GDP	€ (billion)	% of GDP	€ (billion)	% of GDP
2000	12.9	11.3	18.2	15.9	16.5	14.4
2010	15.3	13.2	20.0	17.2	15.8	13.6
2020	17.9	15.9	20.3	18.0	15.6	13.8
2030	20.8	18.8	16.2	14.6	12.3	11.1
2040	22.3	21.5	16.2	15.6	12.3	11.8
2050	22.3	21.8	15.9	15.5	12.0	11.7

SOURCE: Nektarios 2000.

NOTE: GDP = gross domestic product, 1 billion is 1,000 million.

growth. Both of these features are provided by a well-designed combination of NDC and prefunded financial defined contribution supplementary schemes.

An additional goal of the proposed reform is to suggest alternative financial structures to ensure that total insurance contributions are reduced from their current level of 26 percent of the payroll, which is one of the highest in the EU.

BASIC STRUCTURE OF THE PROPOSED PENSION SYSTEM

The proposed pension system has four pillars:

- Social (minimum) pensions, financed by general revenues
- The compulsory primary pension system (NDC model)
- The universal and compulsory supplementary pension system, which is fully prefunded
- Voluntary occupational prefunded pensions

The primary pension system, which is based on the NDC model, is financed by employers and employees and operates on a PAYG basis. The supplementary pension system provides defined contribution benefits; it is financed by employers and employees and operates on the basis of full prefunding. The new system covers those people who were insured for the first time after 1992.

It is proposed that the current system of multiple funds be completely reorganized to satisfy the main objectives stated above. The principal changes would be, first, the establishment of a single, uniform national organization for basic pensions that will absorb all the primary pension funds and will also include public servants, and, second, the establishment of a single, uniform national organization for supplementary pensions that will absorb all supplementary pension schemes. There will be a common information platform for both schemes. An agreement should be reached between the pension schemes and the tax authorities for permanent cooperation in the collection of contributions and for the creation of a single tax collection service, to reduce contribution evasion and make collection more efficient from the point of view of both the government and employees. Finally, the management of the accumulated reserves of pension funds is to be assigned to the existing Asset Management Company of Pension Funds.

To satisfy the additional goal of reducing total insurance contributions, we suggest, as the most effective method, rebalancing the primary and supplementary systems. We propose to reduce the relative weight of the primary system by decreasing contributions from 20 percent to 16 percent and to enhance the role of the supplementary system by keeping contributions at 6 percent and capitalizing the system. In this way, the total replacement rate will be in the range of 60 to 70 percent for a 40-year employment period, and total insurance contributions will decrease from 26 percent to 22 percent. The transition process for the rebalancing of the two systems should provide for mandatory participation of the insured after a certain age, but participation should be voluntary for older persons.

THE PRIMARY PENSION SYSTEM AND THE NDC MODEL

The principal proposal is to employ the NDC model to construct and operate the system for the primary pensions. A PAYG NDC system would operate on the basis of individual notional accounts, with a contribution rate of 16 percent of the payroll. A special project is required to transform current insurance records into the initial capital of the individual notional accounts. Adequate international know-how to assist with the effective implementation of this project is available. In NDC, the notional capital of the individual account is transformed into a life annuity based on the individual birth cohort's life expectancy at the time of retirement. Both the accounts and the annuities are adjusted annually on the basis of average covered earnings or the growth of covered wages. The minimum age of retirement is set at 62 for both men and women, but the relevant provisions are flexible enough to encourage continued work during retirement. Careful attention should be given to the different alternatives available for establishing a transparent rule to accommodate residual economic and demographic risk (Palmer 2012) and to the possibility of creating NDC reserves (Holzmann, Palmer, and Robalino 2012). The primary pension benefit is gradually reduced and is matched by the gradually increasing supplementary pension benefit.

Most special privileges were eliminated in the 2010 reform. A completed reform should abolish any remaining privileges for special interest groups, including the possibility of early retirement before age 62. Even here, there are international precedents for how rights already acquired can be transformed into rights in the new system (see Chłoń-Domińczak, Franco, and Palmer, chapter 2 in this volume, and the references provided therein).

The proposed NDC model is flexible enough to accommodate distributional considerations. It is proposed that the new system contain provisions for noncontributory periods for reasons such as higher education, military service, child care by either parent, sickness, unemployment, and disability. In all such cases, either the state or the respective authority (the health fund or the unemployment fund) contributes the employer's part of the total contribution to the individual account of the insured person. In addition, it is proposed that the new system provide survivors' pensions, as well as joint annuities for spouses.

THE SUPPLEMENTARY PENSION SYSTEM

Supplementary pensions should be universal, compulsory, and fully prefunded. Regular contributions are 6 percent of the payroll, and pension benefits are of the defined contribution type. Every insured person has an individual account, which, at a freely chosen time after reaching age 62, can be converted into an insurance product, to be selected from alternatives specified in the law.

The introduction of the prefunded scheme would require the mandatory participation of the insured after a certain age. Participation would be voluntary for older cohorts.

The accumulated funds and their effective investment play a crucial role in the reduction of the long-term overall cost of the national pension system. The structure and operation of the supplementary pension system are also crucial for the satisfaction of the stated goal of reducing total insurance contributions. This part of the total pension system will provide an increasing part of the final pension benefit. Therefore, the management of the accumulated funds should be assigned exclusively to the existing Asset Management Company of Pension Funds, which, since its inception in 2001, has proved the most effective mechanism for investing the assets of pension funds in Greece.

There should be a special provision for contracting out. That is, the existing supplementary pension funds (with a public status) that decide not to join the national scheme will be transformed into occupational pension funds without any further social subsidies to their revenues or their benefit guarantees.

OCCUPATIONAL PENSION SCHEMES

Occupational pension schemes are voluntary and are organized and financed by the interested parties. There is no state guarantee of these pension benefits. The state supervises the establishment and operation of occupational plans according to the relevant EC directive.

SOCIAL PENSIONS

The current (well-functioning) social pension system is extended to cover all persons with inadequate or no insurance history. Whenever the sum of the compulsory pensions (primary and supplementary) is below the poverty line, the social pension is paid to bring the retiree to a level close to the poverty line. Social pensions are awarded after verification of a residency requirement and a means test. They are financed from general revenues.

EXPECTED RESULTS OF THE REFORM

The benefits of the adoption of the NDC model transcend the usual objectives of a pension reform. Additional positive externalities will be created and diffused in the broader social and political environment. It is suggested that the adoption of the NDC model as a new paradigm for pension reform would lead to a considerable limitation of the state's role in providing future pensions and would establish a transparent foundation for individual long-term planning for all the Greek people. Furthermore, a political strategy aimed at winning broader popular support for the proposed reform would emphasize the comparative advantages and political assets of the NDC model (as stressed by Marin 2006):

- *NDC as a fairness standard, anticorruption device, and promoter of pension literacy.* An NDC scheme sets broadly shared standards of fairness, with actuarial fairness as the minimum common denominator. NDC exposes explicit hidden or perverse redistributions. It makes people think in terms of lifetime contributions, lifetime incomes, annuities, and lifetime pension entitlements and of choices, trade-offs, and budget constraints.

- *NDC as a trigger for the functional differentiation of welfare.* Functional differentiation of social insurance risk management measures and correspondingly separate flows of resources permit transparent and politically defensible forms of redistribution. In an NDC scheme, this is done by creating a guarantee and noncontributory rights for specific social political purposes such as child-care rights, with earmarked financial sources.

- *NDC as better risk management.* NDC is superior to other PAYG pension paradigms in management of economic and demographic risks. It is also much less exposed to political manipulation. It does not create excessive expectations, and no promises will ever be broken.

- *NDC as a core component of any pension constitution.* The NDC corpus, as a PAYG lifetime saving scheme for life-cycle smoothing of consumption, could help turn an implicit and frequently heavily distorted generational compact into an explicit contract that ensures fairness and equity within and between generations. In preventing the emergence of future excess liabilities, NDC can help overcome system imbalances that so far have been the major obstacles to pension reform in Greece, as in many other countries.

It follows from the arguments above that the value added in the adoption of the NDC model, vis-à-vis the 2010 reform package, would soon surpass the logical expectations for a substantial improvement in the current pension problem and would create positive side effects in the form of political assets for Greek society.

Conclusion

Greece has passed up many opportunities to reform its pension system during the past 30 years. The drastic reduction in promised rights and benefits that took place in 2010 could have been accomplished simultaneously with the adoption of the ready-made pension architecture of the NDC model, along the lines analyzed in this chapter. We would argue that in such a case, the relief of public finances could have been accomplished with broad popular support.

The aim of the initial version of this article, presented at the Stockholm Conference in December 2009, was to outline an overall pension reform that would guarantee the pension promises of the current system. The proposal was originally made in 2000, when there was adequate time to divert substantial general revenues to start up the prefunded component of the pension system. It was proposed that the pension reform in Greece should be based, in equal weights, on a mix of the NDC model and the supplementary funded pension. Such a pension system would guarantee the payment of the promised pension benefits in the long term. In addition, it would treat everyone equally, within and between generations—at least, those insured for the first time after 1992. Furthermore, the operation of the pension system would not have adverse effects on the labor market and economic growth. A comprehensive reform would require the consolidation of all pension schemes into a universal fund, putting an end to the problems of segmentation and contribution evasion.

When considering a major reform, the most important issue is the political feasibility of the project. In such a framework, economic reasoning and efficiency arguments are necessary, but not sufficient, whereas fairness and equity issues building on optimal efficiency are crucial. In the case of Greek pension reform, the political impotence of successive governments since 1975 resulted in a hasty reform imposed under the joint EC/IMF/ECB scheme. The lack of an orderly process of studying and evaluating the alternative options has deprived the country and its people of the opportunity to benefit from a modern pension architecture that would satisfy all stated objectives. Instead, the government invoked the urgency of the crisis and instituted policies that will lead to the drastic reduction of current and future pension rights and benefits, without considering the option of placing those reforms in the framework of the logic of the NDC structure. There is still time to correct this error before 2014. If this is done, and if the logic of the new construction is communicated clearly to the public, it is very likely that most people would consent to a reduction in benefit provisions, accompanied by the generally accepted principles of a modern pension system. Let us hope that this task will be taken on.

Notes

The original article presented at the Stockholm Conference in December 2009 has been modified in light of the pension reform of 2010, described in the text.

1. CEPR (1976); Greece, Ministry of Social Services (1981); Provopoulos (1987); Nektarios (1996); Commission for Long-Run Economic Policy (1997); OECD (1997).

References

Börsch-Supan, Axel H., and Platon Tinios. 2001. "The Greek Pension System: Strategic Framework for Reform." In *Greece's Economic Performance and Prospects,* ed. Ralph C. Bryant, Nicholas C. Garganas, and George S. Tavlas, 435–533. Athens: Bank of Greece; Washington, DC: Brookings Institution.

CEPR (Center for Economic Planning and Research). 1976. "Social Insurance: Development Program 1976–1980." CEPR, Athens.

Commission for Long-Run Economic Policy. 1997. *Economy and Pensions.* Athens: National Bank of Greece.

European Commission. 2010. "The Economic Adjustment Program for Greece." Occasional Paper 61, Directorate General for Economic and Financial Affairs, European Commission, Brussels.

European Commission and Economic Policy Committee. 2001. "Budgetary Challenges Posed by Ageing Populations." EPC/PCFIN/655/01-EN Final, European Commission, Brussels.

———. 2008. "The 2009 Ageing Report: Underlying Assumptions and Projection Methodologies for EU-27 Member States (2007–2060)." *European Economy* (European Commission) 7.

GAD (U.K. Government Actuary's Department). 2001a. "Review of the Retirement Pension System: Financial Estimates." Ministry of National Economy, Athens.

———. 2001b. "Review of the Retirement Pension System: Report by the Government Actuary's Department, United Kingdom." Ministry of National Economy, Athens.

Greece, Ministry of National Economy. 2001. "Basic National Accounts." Athens.

Greece, Ministry of Social Services. 1981. "Social Insurance in Greece." Athens.

Greece, National Actuarial Authority. 2008. "National Bulletin for Pension Expenditures: 2008" (November). Athens.

Holzmann, Robert. 2006. "Toward a Coordinated Pension System in Europe: Rationale and Potential Structure." In *Pension Reform: Issues and Prospects for Non-Financial Defined Contribution (NDC) Schemes,* ed. Robert Holzmann and Edward Palmer, 225–65. Washington, DC: World Bank.

Holzmann, Robert, Edward Palmer, and David A. Robalino. 2012. "The Economics of Reserve Funds in NDC Schemes: Role, Means, and Size to Manage Shocks." In *Gender, Politics, and Financial Stability,* chap. 20, vol. 2 of *Nonfinancial Defined Contribution Pension Schemes in a Changing Pension World,* ed. Robert Holzmann, Edward Palmer, and David A. Robalino. Washington, DC: World Bank and Swedish Social Insurance Agency.

IMF (International Monetary Fund). 2006. "Greece: Issues in Pension Reform." Country Report 06/5, IMF, Washington, DC.

Marin, Bernd. 2006. "A Magic All-European Pension Reform Formula: Selective Comments." In *Pension Reform: Issues and Prospects for Non-Financial Defined Contribution (NDC) Schemes,* ed. Robert Holzmann and Edward Palmer, 266–92. Washington, DC: World Bank.

Mylonas, Paul, and Christine de la Maisonneuve. 1999. "The Problems and Prospects Faced by PAYG Pension Systems: A Case Study of Greece." Economics Department Working Paper 215, Organisation for Economic Co-operation and Development, Paris.

Nektarios, Milton. 1996. *Social Insurance in Greece.* [In Greek.] Athens: Forum Publishers.

———. 2000. "Financing Public Pensions in Greece." *Spoudai* 50 (3–4): 125–39.

———. 2007. "Public Pensions and Labor Force Participation: The Case of Greece." *Geneva Papers on Risk and Insurance* 32: 553–69.

———. 2008. *Pension Reform with Consensus and Transparency.* [In Greek.] Athens: Papazisis.

OECD (Organisation for Economic Co-operation and Development). 1997. "Annual Review—Greece." OECD, Paris.

———. 2005. *Pensions at a Glance.* Paris: OECD.

———. 2011. *Pensions at a Glance: Retirement-Income Systems in OECD and G20 Countries.* Paris: OECD.

Palmer, Edward. 2012. "Generic NDC: Equilibrium, Valuation, and Risk Sharing with and without NDC Bonds." In *Gender, Politics, and Financial Stability,* chap. 19, vol. 2 of *Nonfinancial Defined Contribution Pension Schemes in a Changing Pension World,* ed. Robert Holzmann, Edward Palmer, and David A. Robalino. Washington, DC: World Bank and Swedish Social Insurance Agency.

Provopoulos, George. 1987. *Social Insurance.* [In Greek.] Athens: Foundation for Economic and Industrial Research (IOBE).

Roseveare, Deborah, Willi Leibfritz, Douglas Fore, and Eckhard Wurzel. 1996. "Ageing Populations, Pension Systems and Government Budgets: Simulations for 20 OECD Countries." Economics Department Working Paper 168, Organisation for Economic Cooperation and Development, Paris.

Tatsos, Nikolaos. 2001. *Underground Economy and Tax Evasion in Greece.* [In Greek.] Athens: Papazisis.

Noriyuki Takayama

Until mid-2010, Greece's pension system was a typical example of the Mediterranean welfare state, with extensive segmentation, concomitant contribution evasion, and a very low labor force participation rate. The system also had serious problems with regard to equity and long-term financial sustainability. Greece has missed many opportunities to reform its pension system over the past 30 years, largely because of a lack of political consensus.

Political Risks in Pension Reform

The basic aim of recent pension reforms in developed countries has been to provide a specific solution to the problem of sharing the increasing cost of pensions among various groups and setting a limit for what is acceptable. This is the point at which many countries have turned to nonfinancial (notional) defined contribution (NDC) schemes. Whatever the solution adopted, there will inevitably be winners and losers. Usually, it is very difficult for losers to accept any disadvantages arising from the reforms proposed by policy makers. The painstaking process of pension reform may thereby be delayed or even blocked. Strong leadership is required to deal with this kind of political risk.

Another driving force for pension reform has been growing pressure from outside. The 2010 pension reform of Greece is an example. Greece's sovereign debt got out of hand, and the Greeks were forced to adopt a hasty and drastic reform that substantially reduced promised pension benefits to secure the country's long-term borrowing requirements on the international financial market. The most significant measure mandated in 2010 was the abolition of all special provisions for early retirement before age 60, while the standard pensionable age was raised to 65. As Milton Nektarios explains in chapter 8, people in Greece were subjected to a sudden disruption of their economic and financial life planning without being given enough time or appropriate means to adjust to the new situation.

Greece needed a pension system that was under financial control, and so the reform imposed in 2010 was necessary—but it was not sufficient; it was only step one in the reform process. The country still does not seem to have given clear enough thought to the basic structure of a pension system that would be equitable, adequate, and financially sustainable. Generally speaking, a national pension system should have an NDC scheme as a core component. Nektarios argues that Greece needs to move on to step two of the reform process by replacing the present earnings-related scheme with NDC and financial defined contribution (FDC) schemes. This, however, is easier said than done.

One difficulty with this shift to a new paradigm is that it is expensive in the short run. The transfer from general revenues would have to increase in the short run if the contribution rate for the main earnings-related system were reduced from 20 percent to 16 percent, with the remainder going to the financial scheme, in accordance with the

---

Noriyuki Takayama is the JRI Pension Research Chair Professor at the Institute of Economic Research, Hitotsubashi University, Tokyo.

proposal put forward by Nektarios. Another difficulty could arise from the possibility that potential losers under the paradigm shift might persistently oppose step two.

If one takes a broader perspective, if Greece opted out of the euro area, the country could alter its exchange rate and follow more decisive fiscal policies. As a consequence, the fiscal strain could be reduced, and the country might have more time to implement the step two reform. This in itself can be viewed as a potential lesson from the Greek experience.

The Plight of Greece Viewed from the Japanese Perspective

Politicians in Japan have also been reluctant to propose thoroughgoing pension reform. In 2004, however, they succeeded in making a paradigm shift virtually to NDC by fixing the contribution rate of the principal pension system at 18.3 percent from 2017 on. At the same time, they introduced an automatic balancing mechanism that was free from political risk. This mechanism is a new formula for indexation of pension benefits that takes demographic factors into account (see Takayama 2004).

Japan still has many challenges in pension management:

- The automatic balancing mechanism has not yet been activated because it was legislatively designed not to apply during deflation, from which Japan has been suffering for more than 10 years. The new balancing formula, by contrast, must be followed irrespective of inflation or deflation.

- The proportion of atypical employees has been increasing, reaching 40 percent in 2010. Growing numbers of young employees are forced to enter the job market as irregulars and are given few opportunities thereafter to be upgraded to regular status, with higher and more stable salaries. In addition, Japan is seriously affected by the "bad start, bad finish" problem described by Italian and other experts (Franco and Sartor 2006; Gronchi and Nisticò 2006; Boeri and Galasso 2012; Chłoń-Domińczak, Franco, and Palmer, chapter 2 in this volume).

- The normal pensionable age in Japan is still 65. Automatic indexation to longevity is essential to the long-term financial sustainability of the pension system.

- Current provisions for full-time housewives are under severe attack from dual-income couples and single women (Takayama 2009). An income split between an income-earning husband and his dependent wife could be a solution to this problem.

- Employees working less than 30 hours a week are currently not covered by the earnings-related component of the pension system. The issue of extending coverage to employees working at least 20 hours a week is currently under heated discussion.

Because new measures like those mentioned above involve winners and losers, Japan will be taking a political risk if it seeks to implement another pension reform in the near future. In this sense, Japan has put itself into much the same position as Greece. The answer is to take a more definitive step forward, after having built a political consensus. Whether Japan is capable of doing this remains to be seen.

References

Boeri, Tito, and Vincenzo Galasso. 2012. "Is Social Security Secure with NDC?" In *Gender, Politics, and Financial Stability,* chap. 15, vol. 2 of *Nonfinancial Defined Contribution Pension Schemes in a Changing Pension World,* ed. Robert Holzmann, Edward Palmer, and David A. Robalino. Washington, DC: World Bank and Swedish Social Insurance Agency.

Franco, Daniele, and Nicola Sartor. 2006. "NDCs in Italy: Unsatisfactory Present, Uncertain Future." In *Pension Reform: Issues and Prospects for Non-Financial Defined Contribution (NDC) Schemes,* ed. Robert Holzmann and Edward Palmer, 467–92. Washington, DC: World Bank.

Gronchi, Sandro, and Sergio Nisticò. 2006. "Implementing the NDC Theoretical Model: A Comparison of Italy and Sweden." In *Pension Reform: Issues and Prospects for Non-Financial Defined Contribution (NDC) Schemes,* ed. Robert Holzmann and Edward Palmer, 493–516. Washington, DC: World Bank.

Takayama, Noriyuki. 2004. "Changes in the Pension System." *Japan Echo* (October): 9–12.

———. 2009. "Pension Coverage in Japan." In *Closing the Coverage Gap: The Role of Social Pensions and Other Retirement Income Transfers,* ed. Robert Holzmann, David A. Robalino, and Noriyuki Takayama, 111–18. Washington, DC: World Bank.

CHAPTER 9

Assessing Fiscal Costs and Pension Distribution in Transitions to Defined Contribution Systems: A Retrospective Analysis for Chile

Eduardo Fajnzylber and David A. Robalino

Countries that are considering structural pension reforms to address problems of financial sustainability and improve economic incentives face the choice between moving to a financial defined contribution (FDC) system, to a nonfinancial (notional) defined contribution (NDC) system, or to one of its variants. Unfortunately, comparisons of the performance of the two systems, in terms of the pensions provided and the transition costs, are normally based on prospective actuarial estimations. By contrast, in this chapter, we take a retrospective approach by simulating what would have happened in Chile if, instead of the original FDC system introduced in 1981, the country had implemented an NDC scheme.

We find that transition costs under an FDC system can be considerably higher than under an NDC system. In the case of Chile, other things being equal, introducing an NDC system would have generated fiscal savings during the first 45 years after the reform equivalent to 50 percent of initial gross domestic product (GDP). The cost of the minimum pension guarantee would have been higher under an NDC system that pays the growth rate of the covered wage bill. This is because during the first 20 years after the reform, the rate of return on financial assets was higher than the growth rate of wages. Our analysis suggests, however, that this need not be always the case. Depending on the assumptions regarding the stochastic process driving the dynamics of the rate of return paid by the FDC system, expected replacement rates under the NDC are not necessarily lower.

NDC and FDC Models Compared

During the past decade, NDC schemes have been introduced as a promising alternative for addressing the problems of financial insolvency, nontransparent redistribution, and

Eduardo Fajnzylber is an assistant professor at the School of Government, Universidad Adolfo Ibáñez, Chile. This chapter was prepared while he was head of the Research Department at the Chilean Pension Supervising Authority. David A. Robalino is lead economist in the Human Development Department of the World Bank and codirector of the Employment and Development Program at the Institute for the Study of Labor, Bonn. Under no circumstances should the estimates presented in this chapter be considered official projections.

weak incentives that pervade traditional defined benefit (DB) pay-as-you-go (PAYG) pension systems. NDCs are financed on a PAYG basis, but the benefit formula is modified to establish a transparent and actuarially fair link between contributions and benefits. If well designed, the system can be solvent at all times and will not accumulate the unfunded liabilities that are common in defined benefit schemes. Thus, the main difference between the NDC and FDC models is that in the latter, contributions from active workers are invested in financial instruments, whereas in the former, contributions are used to pay for current pensions. As a result, in an FDC system, contributions earn the rate of return on investments in financial assets, while in the "pure" NDC system, the rate of return is equal to the growth rate of the PAYG asset—the present value of future contributions net of the value of pension rights accruing from those contributions (see Robalino and Bodor 2009).[1] Because the growth rate of the PAYG asset is not readily observable, several proxies are used in practice.

One of the benefits of an NDC scheme is that it can facilitate the financing of the implicit pension debt of the "old" system and thus reduce the need to increase taxes or reduce expenditures over the short term. This is because the system remains PAYG, and therefore, new contributions can be used to finance current pensions. In a transition to an FDC scheme, new contributions go to the financial market, but the system needs to keep paying pensions to retirees from the previous system and acknowledging the past contributions of workers who switch to the new one. These two factors can induce considerable transition costs.[2] In the case of an NDC system, by contrast, the government can continue to borrow contributions to finance the liabilities of the old system. What remains to be financed under an NDC reform—through current fiscal revenues—is the difference between the implicit liabilities of the old system and the current PAYG asset, which will depend on the value of the new contribution rate (Holzmann and Jousten 2012).

On the down side, in a dynamically efficient economy, the growth rate of the PAYG asset (or its proxies) is expected to be below the rate of return on financial assets. The empirical evidence on the issue is mixed (see Holzmann and Hinz 2005), but it could be that an NDC system, on average, pays a lower pension than the FDC system for the same contribution rate, albeit presumably with less risk. This characteristic could give rise to higher fiscal costs because the expected value of minimum pension guarantees by the government increases.

Understanding these trade-offs between short-term and long-term transition costs is fundamental for guiding policy choices regarding the implementation of one system over another or, more likely, the degree of diversification of savings between the two. To our knowledge, however, these trade-offs have not undergone a rigorous assessment. The studies that exist (see for instance, World Bank 2004, 2006, forthcoming) are normally based on prospective actuarial estimations, which usually involve nontrivial assumptions about the evolution of the most relevant parameters: growth of GDP and wages, interest rates, and coverage and contribution densities. And not enough attention has been given to the question of whether the rate of return of FDCs is consistently above the rate of return of NDCs or to differences in the distribution of initial pensions.[3]

This chapter compares fiscal costs and the distribution of pensions under an FDC and NDC reform in Chile.

This chapter sheds lights on these two questions. To address the limitations of prospective studies, we follow a retrospective approach by simulating what would have happened in Chile between 1981 and 2026 if, instead of the FDC reform introduced in 1981, an NDC scheme had been implemented. We use actual contribution histories from individuals who switched to the reformed system to compare the relative performance of the FDC and NDC schemes in terms of fiscal costs and the distribution of replacement rates at the aggregate and individual levels. Clearly, this approach is subject to the criticism that the general equilibrium effects of an alternative reform are not taken into account. If an NDC had been introduced in 1981, individual incentives, and therefore labor supply and saving decisions, may have been different. The accumulation of capital in individual accounts certainly had important macroeconomic effects, as well (see Holzmann 1997; Schmidt-Hebbel 2000). As a result, the dynamics of all prices, including interest rates and wages, may have been different. That stated, we are not attempting in this chapter to estimate the welfare impact of an alternative reform. Our more modest goal is to inform policy makers about (a) the order of magnitude of the potential fiscal savings from lower transition costs under NDCs, (b) the difference in the levels of pensions and replacement rates under the two reforms and the potential extra costs related to the provision of minimum pension guarantees, and (c) the level of plan members' exposure to risk under the two systems.[4]

The next section briefly describes the main features of the 1981 Chilean reform and explains the assumptions made regarding the implementation of the hypothetical NDC system. There follows a description of the data and methods used to compare fiscal costs and the distribution of pensions at the aggregate and individual levels. The principal results from the analysis and the general conclusions are the subjects of the final two sections.

The Original FDC Reform and the Hypothetical NDC Reform

In 1980, the Chilean government introduced a major reform of the country's pension systems, replacing traditional PAYG arrangements with a unique national scheme based on individual accounts, market capitalization, and private management.[5] The main motive was to address problems of fragmentation and fiscal sustainability (see annex A).

Under the new system, all civilian dependent workers were required to contribute 10 percent of their covered income to the pension fund administrator (*administradora de fondos de pensiones,* AFP) of their choice, which charged an additional administration fee and an insurance premium for disability and survivorship insurance (DSI).[6] AFPs are private firms created for the sole purpose of administering the benefits set by law; their duties include collecting contributions, managing individual accounts, investing the funds accumulated, managing DSI policies, providing customer service, and paying old-age, disability, and survivorship benefits under a programmed withdrawal schedule or transferring the accumulated resources to a life insurance company, should the beneficiary choose to buy an annuity. Most of these requirements are strictly regulated by law and by secondary regulations generated by the Pensions Supervisor (*Superintendencia de Pensiones,* SP), the institution created in 1980 to regulate and supervise the AFPs.[7] In particular, investment options are closely regulated by a complex structure of eligible instruments, quantitative limits, and minimum return requirements.[8]

The key aspects of the FDC system are summarized below. For our hypothetical NDC system, we keep as many of the original features as possible. The main differences concern the calculation of the rate of return on contributions, the design of the payout phase, and the role of the minimum pension guarantee.

OLD AND NEW ENROLLEES

Under the 1980 reform, individuals who made contributions to one of the old PAYG systems were allowed to choose whether to stay in their existing regime or transfer to the new one. Individuals who switched to the new system were not allowed to return to their previous regime. Persons who entered the labor market for the first time after the reform were automatically enrolled in the new system. For the hypothetical NDC reform, we will maintain these rules.

CONTRIBUTION RATE

The contribution rate in the new system was significantly reduced, from about 23 percent for the PAYG regimes to approximately 14 percent (10 percent plus the administrative fee charged by the AFPs, which averaged 4 percent for the average worker in the first 10 years).[9] This decrease could explain the massive transfers that occurred in the initial years of the Chilean reform. To maintain consistency with the observed switching behavior, we assume a 10 percent contribution rate to the notional account for the base scenario of the hypothetical reform. Later in our analysis, we take into account differences in administrative costs between the two systems under alternative scenarios. The total contribution rate flowing to the NDC could be lower, but our focus is only on the effective amount that is deposited in the individual accounts in the two systems.

ACKNOWLEDGMENT OF PAST CONTRIBUTIONS

Past contributions from individuals who switched to the new system were generally acknowledged in the form of a recognition bond—a promise made by the state to deposit a certain amount in the individual account once the person reached legal retirement age. The recognition bond was issued on request of the individual and earned a fixed 4 percent real interest rate from the moment the person joined the new system until the legal retirement age.

For the hypothetical NDC reform, a similar procedure would apply. A notional recognition bond would be issued on request of the affiliate, using the same formulas as for the current recognition bonds. The recognized balance would be automatically credited to the individual account at retirement age and would earn the same notional interest rate as current contributions from that moment on.[10]

RATE OF RETURN ON CONTRIBUTIONS

Current contributions to the AFP system (not including the administrative fee) are saved in the individual's account and are automatically invested in a diversified portfolio of financial instruments. Balances are recalculated on a daily basis, as contributions or withdrawals from the fund and the daily return on the pension fund chosen by the participant are posted.

Under the hypothetical NDC reform, the procedure would be the same, except that the daily interest rate earned by the notional funds would be based not on financial returns but on a notional return calculated from the growth rate of wages or the growth rate of the wage bill of formal dependent workers.

RETIREMENT OPTIONS

In general, individuals cannot retire until they reach the legal retirement age (age 60 for women and age 65 for men). When a person decides to retire—which does not imply that he or she has to stop working—the accumulated balance in the individual account (including the recognition bond and the voluntary savings of the individual, if any) can be returned to the participant in the form of a programmed withdrawal paid by an AFP or can be used to purchase an annuity from a life insurance company.[11] In the first case, that of withdrawal, the pension is recalculated every year on the basis of the current balance and age- and sex-specific life expectancy. On the death of the participant, the remaining balance can be transferred to legal beneficiaries or to the heirs of the deceased. The schedule of payment generally decreases over time, and if the person lives long enough, the balance might be exhausted. In the second case, the entire balance is transferred to the insurance company in exchange for a fixed real annuity until the death of the pensioner and, after that, a survivorship annuity for legal beneficiaries. No inheritance is paid in the absence of beneficiaries, and survivorship benefits are a fixed fraction of the original pension, independent of the timing of death. Individuals with low balances are not allowed to buy annuities and may only receive programmed withdrawals.

Under the hypothetical NDC reform, notional balances are always transformed into a fixed annuity paid by the state, the amount of which depends on the balance, the age-specific (but not gender-specific) life expectancies of the participant and potential beneficiaries, and a fixed interest rate corresponding to the average notional rate of the year prior to retirement. Survivorship benefits are paid on death, but no inheritance is paid in the absence of beneficiaries.

POVERTY PREVENTION PROGRAMS

Until 2008, the government offered two publicly funded programs for individuals with low pensions or no pension at all: the minimum pension guarantee (MPG) and assistance pensions (*pensiones asistenciales,* PASIS).[12] An individual who had contributed for at least 20 years (including the time contributing to the old system) was entitled to an MPG, which was a fixed pension paid by the state when the individual balance was exhausted or when the annuity was below the minimum pension level. PASIS benefits were paid to poor individuals over age 65 who did not receive pensions or other forms of income.

The hypothetical NDC simulated in this chapter includes an MPG for individuals with calculated pensions below the minimum pension. PASIS benefits are not required for affiliates of the system, who receive lifetime annuities. We focus on estimating and projecting the fiscal costs of the provisions associated with the population affiliated with the pension system. In other words, we do not attempt to estimate the cost of PASIS for the nonaffiliated population, on the assumption that this cost would be the same under both the FDC and the NDC regimes.

Data and Methods

Account balances can be constructed both for the new system and for the hypothetical NDC scheme, using data from a representative sample of AFP affiliates for whom the entire (administrative) contribution history has been collected by the SP.

The affiliates' pension histories (*historias previsionales administrativas,* HPA) include basic demographic information (gender and date of birth) and monthly details of all the contributions that were made, the fees charged, the pensions paid, and the financial rates of return earned from the investments made by the pension fund administrators (the AFPs). The histories also include information on the recognition bonds issued by the government, representing the accrued rights earned by workers who contributed to the PAYG system before switching to the new one. (For further details concerning this dataset, see Berstein, Larrain, and Pino 2006.)

The methodology has two parts: the estimation of pensions and the fiscal burden under the current FDC system, and an equivalent analysis for the hypothetical NDC regime. In both cases, the analysis covers the period 1981–2025.

In the first part, actual contribution histories between 1981 and 2006 are completed for the period 2007–25, using an imputation method similar to that of Berstein, Larrain, and Pino (2006). For a given history of rates of return, pensions are calculated for cohorts of workers, assuming that all individuals retire at the minimum retirement age (60 for women, 65 for men) and that they use the balance in their accounts, including recognition bonds, to buy fixed annuities from that point on. (Actual mortality tables and a given interest rate are applied.)[13] The transition cost generated by this reform has been estimated for the period 1981–2010 in a number of publications, and this estimation is extended to the period 2010–25 using the information on recognition bonds from the HPA individuals and aggregate data on active affiliates and pensioners from the closed PAYG system operational deficit.[14]

In the second part, pensions and fiscal costs are estimated under the hypothetical NDC reform. The calculation of pensions follows a procedure similar to that of the first step, with the exception that contributions are credited to a notional account, where they earn a notional rate of return. On retirement, the notional balance is converted into a fixed annuity. The key element in this estimation is the calculation procedure for the notional interest rate. In this application, we limit ourselves to the growth rate of the wage bill.[15]

THE AFFILIATES' PENSION HISTORIES DATASET AND PROJECTED CONTRIBUTION HISTORIES

The HPA dataset includes the complete contribution histories, from the moment of joining the system until December 2006, for a sample of approximately 24,000 individuals who are representative of the stock of affiliates of the AFP system in July 2002. In addition, the dataset includes information on the recognition bonds held by the sampled individuals. For our purposes, we concentrate on the 4,869 individuals who would attain legal retirement age before 2026 (women born before 1966, and men born before 1961).[16] Figure 9.1 shows the projected number of individuals who would retire each year (those who reach the legal retirement age).[17]

Our interest is in comparing pensions received by these individuals when they reach the legal retirement age, and so we need to project contributions from 2007 until the individuals retire. Following a method similar to that employed by Berstein, Larrain, and Pino (2006), we use a simple fixed-effect procedure to predict the probability of making contributions at any point in time and the expected covered wage (conditional

FIGURE 9.1 **Projected number of individuals retiring each year from the AFP system, Chile, 1982–2025**

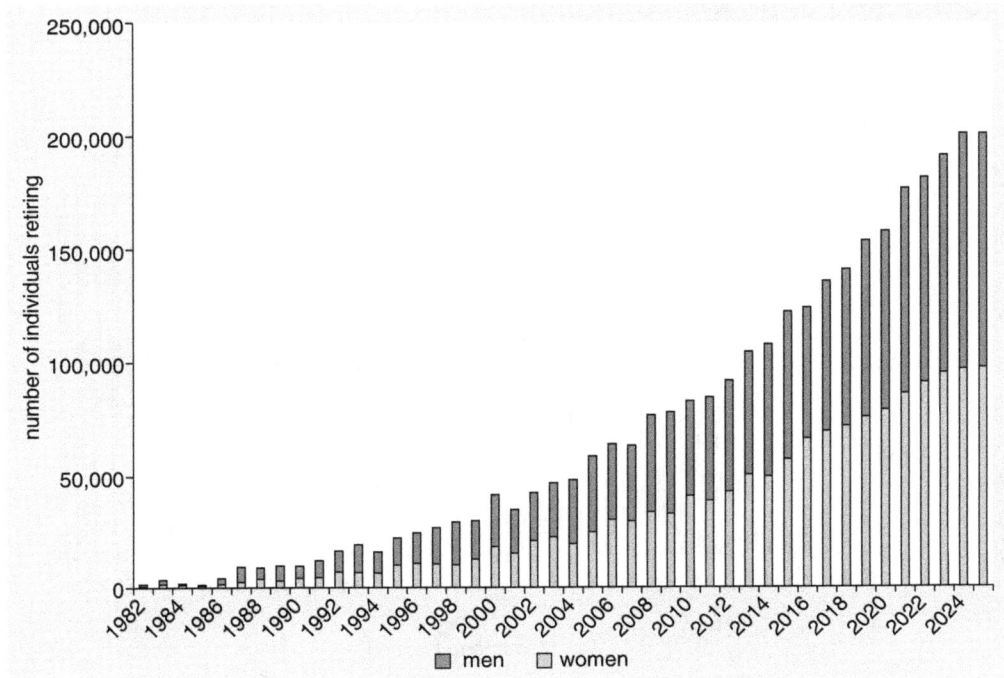

SOURCE: Authors' calculations based on the HPA dataset.

NOTE: AFP = pension fund administrator (*administradora de fondos de pensiones*); HPA = affiliates' pension histories (*historias previsionales administrativas*).

on contributions having been made). Specifically, we separately estimate the following equations, using standard fixed-effect procedures with a linear probability model:[18]

$$Contributes_{it} = \alpha + \beta_1 Age_{it} + \beta_2 Age_{it}^2 + \chi_1 \left(Female_i \cdot Age_{it} \right)$$
$$+ \chi_2 \left(Female_i \cdot Age_{it}^2 \right) + \eta_i + \varepsilon_{it}$$
$$LogEarnings_{it} = \alpha + \phi_1 Age_{it} + \phi_2 Age_{it}^2 + \varphi_1 \left(Female_i \cdot Age_{it} \right)$$
$$+ \varphi_2 \left(Female_i \cdot Age_{it}^2 \right) + \gamma + \varepsilon_{it}. \tag{9.1}$$

In these specifications, $Contributes_{it}$ is a dummy variable equal to 1 if individual i makes a contribution in month t, and $LogEarnings_{it}$ is the log of earnings of individual i in month t. The independent variables are Age_{it} (in months); the interaction between $Female_i$ (a dummy variable equal to 1 if person i is a woman); and Age_{it}, the same interaction, with Age_{it} squared and an individual-level fixed effect.

The results of the estimation are summarized in annex B. We use the estimators (including the individual fixed effects) to predict contribution probabilities and expected earnings by age and gender. Expected contributions are then obtained by multiplying, for each month, the predicted probability by the predicted covered wage (see figure 9.2).

FIGURE 9.2 **Predicted expected contribution, by age and gender, Chile**

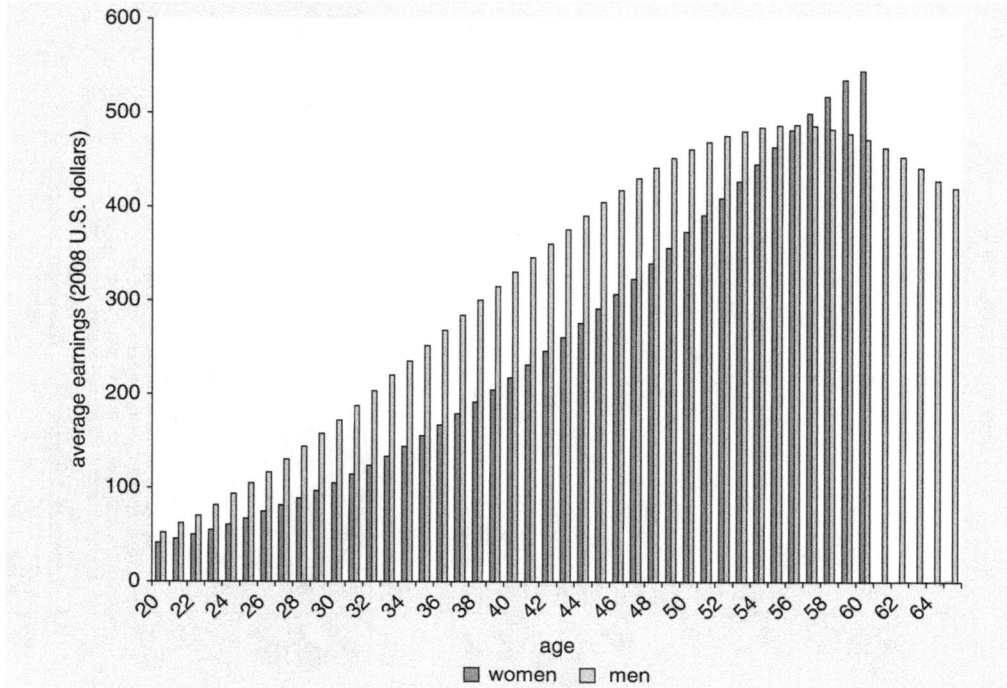

SOURCE: Authors' calculations based on the HPA dataset.

NOTE: HPA = affiliates' pension histories (*historias previsionales administrativas*).The expected contribution is calculated by multiplying the probability of contributing at a given age (for a given gender) by the conditional income if contributing. The figure presents the average expected contribution for the individuals in the sample. Predictions for each individual also include the individual fixed-effect components.

MONTHLY RATES OF RETURN

Under both the FDC and NDC systems, balances are constructed as the sum of contributions made during the participant's lifetime, plus the returns earned over time.[19] We then have

$$Balance_i = Recognition\ Bond_i + \sum_{age\ t=15}^{lra}\left[10\% \cdot Wage_{it} * \prod_{s=1}^{lra}(1+r_s)\right], \qquad (9.2)$$

where r_s is the real rate of return and *lra* is legal retirement age.

The difference between the two systems is that under the FDC scheme, r_s corresponds to the financial return of the instruments in which the pension funds are invested; whereas in the NDC scheme, the notional return is set by the pension authority according to a predetermined rule—usually, a proxy for the PAYG asset.

In this chapter, the rate of return that we use for the FDC scheme is the historical rate of return earned by the AFP system between 1981 and 2007.[20] For the years after 2007, we assume a fixed rate of return, set at a level of 4 percent per year.[21] In the case of the NDC system, we use demographic data on the growth rate of the real wage bill (the number of covered dependent workers multiplied by their average wage).[22] After 2007, we also assume a constant growth rate of the wage bill equivalent to 4 percent per year. The annualized value of these two rates is graphed in figure 9.3.

PENSION CALCULATION

To calculate pensions under both schemes, we make use of the actuarial formulas currently applied under the AFP scheme. For simplicity, we assume that all individuals are single and that they use their current balances to buy a fixed annuity. In this case, pensions can be obtained using the formula

$$Annual\ Pension_t = \frac{Balance_i}{Unitary\ Necessary\ Capital_t} = \frac{Balance_i}{\sum_{s=0}^{110-t} \frac{\Pr(Alive\ at\ age\ s | Alive\ at\ age\ t)}{(1+R)^s}}, \quad (9.3)$$

where the probabilities are obtained from gender-specific dynamic mortality tables and R represents the discount rate used by insurance companies to estimate the rate of return earned by the funds during the payment period for the annuity.

In the case of the FDC system, R is obtained from market data as the average implicit rate of return on all annuities sold during the previous six months. In periods for which no market data are available for the implicit rate on annuities (before 1989 and after 2007), a fixed 3.5 percent is assumed. For simplicity, we use the same rates to calculate pensions from the NDC scheme.[23] These rates are presented in figure 9.4.

Since pensions are calculated for all individuals in the sample, it is possible to construct different statistics for the distribution of pensions over time (e.g., average pension, median pension by distribution quintile, or average pension per quintile).

FIGURE 9.3 **Annualized real rates of return under the FDC and NDC systems, Chile, 1982–2025**
percent

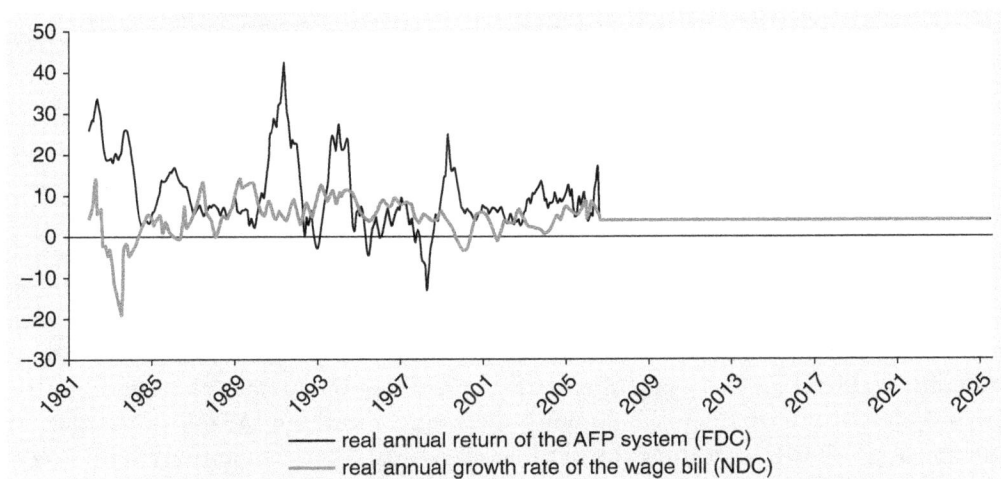

SOURCE: Authors based on the historical returns of the AFP system and on labor data from the Instituto Nacional de Estadisticas.

NOTE: AFP = pension fund administrator (*administradora de fondos de pensiones*); FDC = financial defined contribution; NDC = nonfinancial defined contribution.

FIGURE 9.4 **Discount rates for annuity calculations, six-month average, Chile, 1981–2025**
percent

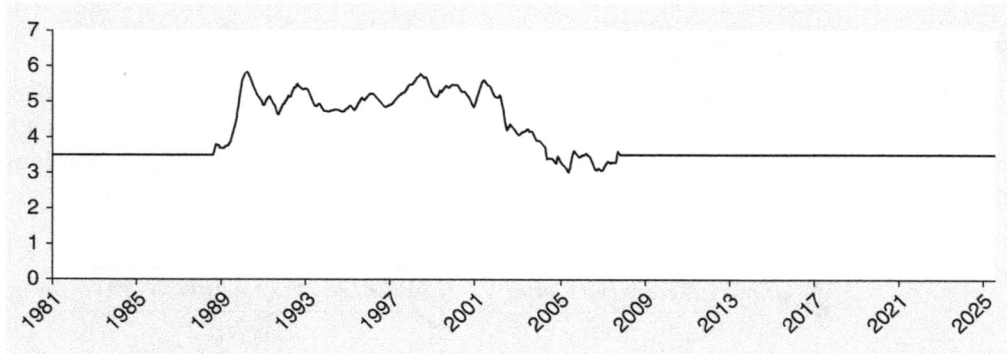

SOURCE: Authors based on historical implicit rates on annuities.

FISCAL COST CALCULATIONS

The fiscal burden associated with the civil pension system can be decomposed into four components:[24]

- The operational deficit from the PAYG system managed by the Instituto de Normal-ización Previsional (INP), the agency in charge of administering the previous PAYG regimes. This is the difference between pensions paid to individuals who stayed in the old system and contributions from active workers affiliated with that system

- The cost of recognition bonds awarded to individuals who switched to the new system

- The cost of MPGs to retirees with pensions below a guaranteed level who have at least 20 years of contributions

- The cost of financing PASIS to the fraction of retirees (those in the poorest quintile of the earnings distribution) who did not participate in the formal schemes or who have exhausted their funds and do not have the 20 years of contributions required for the MPG

Projections for the first three components are presented in the next subsection. The first two projections come directly from the individual pension projections under both systems. Minimum pension guarantees are calculated for each individual when the contributory pension is below the minimum and the individual has contributed for at least 20 years. As discussed above, the state finances the difference between the pension and the guaranteed minimum.[25] The cost of the minimum pension is thus projected at the individual level for every year after retirement, taking into account age- and gender-specific survival probabilities. We do not project expenditures in the fourth component (assistance pensions); we assume instead that all retirees receive an annuity until death. Moreover, performing an accurate estimation of nonaffiliated individuals is beyond the scope of this chapter.

It is important to note that the present value of the accumulated deficits in the old system and the value of the recognition bonds are exactly the same under both schemes.

The differences we care about have to do with the present value of the minimum pension guarantee and, more important, cash flows. Under the NDC scheme, government transfers to pay pensions in the old system are lower because excess contributions are used to pay these pensions. Repayments of recognition bonds could also be initially lower because, in contrast to the FDC case, under the NDC scheme the government would not need to transfer the total value of the bond to an AFP when the individual retires, but only what is needed to cover any deficit that may appear between pensions in payment and contributions.[26] In our analysis, we will assume, for the sake of transparency, that cash flows related to the repayment of recognition bonds in the NDC are the same as in the FDC.

ESTIMATING THE DISTRIBUTION OF BENEFITS AND THE PER CAPITA COST OF GUARANTEES

So far, we have discussed the assessment of the fiscal costs and the distribution of pensions under the FDC and NDC schemes from a prospective approach. These calculations, however, reflect one particular realization of the stochastic process driving the evolution of the interest rate and wages. We are interested in characterizing the *distribution* of pensions (at the individual level) under the FDC and NDC schemes. In other words, for individuals entering the pension system today, what would be the expected value of their pensions at retirement if the system were an FDC scheme or if it were an NDC one?

Clearly, several factors determine the dynamics of interest rates and wages, from changing conditions in financial and labor markets to technological progress and foreign direct investment. Trying to capture these, however, would be a futile exercise. Instead, we focus on approximating the statistical process that best replicates current dynamics. We do this by using a very general time-series model in which the value of the interest rate (or of wages) at time t is a function of past values and past and current random shocks; this is termed an autoregressive moving average (ARMA) process. In addition, we allow the variance of the random shocks to move over time as a function of past shocks and past variances; that is, we allow generalized autoregressive conditional heteroskedasticity (GARCH) in the error term. These models are commonly used in the study of the dynamics of asset prices. The ARMA component implies that there can be sequences of growing prices alternating with sequences of falling prices. The GARCH element implies that periods of high volatility in prices can be followed by periods of low volatility. The random shocks that generate these changes in regime can be the result of policies or of fluctuations in "animal spirits." For the purpose of our analysis, we do not need to know; we simply seek the model structure (the set of model parameters) that best replicates the data.

In its general form, the model can be described by the following equation:

$$r_t = \gamma_0 + \sum_m \gamma_m r_{t-m} + \sum_i \varphi_i \varepsilon_{t-i} + \varepsilon_t; \ i > 0, \tag{9.4}$$

where $\varepsilon_t \sim N\left(0, \sigma_t^2\right)$ and σ_t^2, the variance, evolves over time according to

$$\sigma_t^2 = \sum_j \alpha_j \varepsilon_{t-j}^2 + \beta_0 + \sum_k \beta_k \sigma_{t-k}^2; \ j > 0, \ k > 0, \ \alpha_j > 0. \tag{9.5}$$

Combined with model (9.1), which gives the probabilities of contributing and the conditional covered earnings for a given age and gender, model (9.4 and 9.5) can be used to simulate forward career histories for individuals at different income levels. Using Monte Carlo simulations, we can then derive both the distribution of pensions (replacement rates) at retirement and the distribution of expected fiscal costs related to the financing of the minimum pension guarantee.

Results

In this section, we examine the way pensions are distributed under the FDC and NDC schemes, the fiscal costs of the two schemes, and the comparative individual distributions and per capita fiscal costs.

PENSION COMPARISONS

We first look at the complete distribution of pensions under the two schemes. Figure 9.5 presents the scatter plot of pensions under the FDC and NDC regimes. Clearly, the systematically higher historical returns under the FDC scheme imply higher pensions for all individuals (24 percent higher, on average). We then look at the level of coverage obtained by the system under the two alternative reforms, measured by the fraction of individuals who are able to self-finance a pension at least equivalent to the guaranteed minimum

FIGURE 9.5 **Distribution of monthly pension under FDC and NDC reforms, given past rates of return, Chile**
U.S. dollars

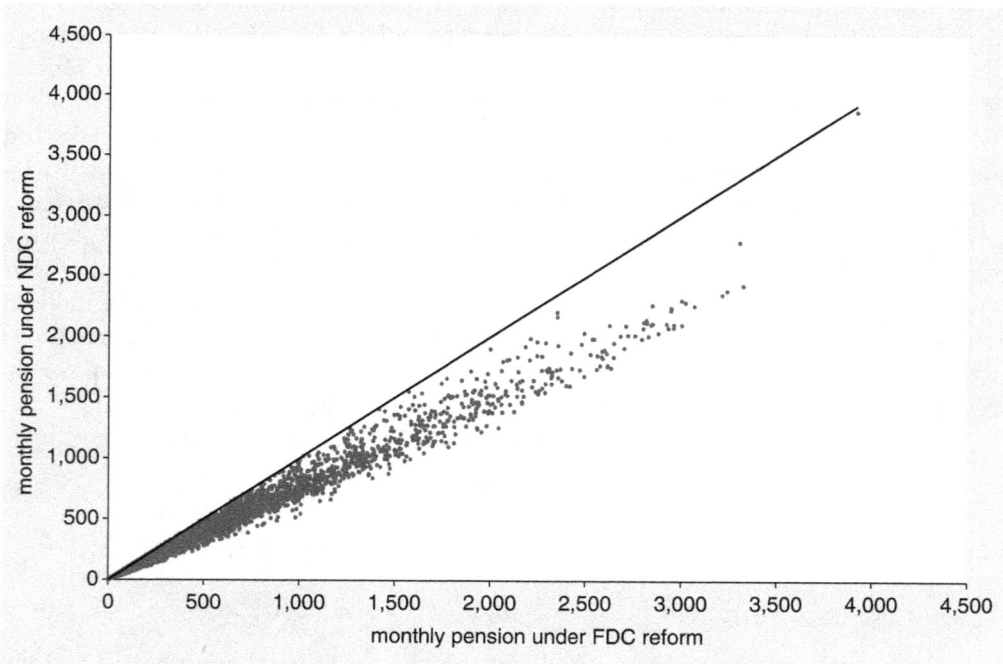

SOURCE: Authors' calculations based on the HPA dataset.

NOTE: FDC = financial defined contribution; HPA = affiliates' pension histories (*historias previsionales administrativas*); NDC = nonfinancial defined contribution.

pension; the fraction of individuals who are not able to finance this amount but who are covered by the MPG; and the proportion of retirees who neither finance a minimum pension nor are covered by the MPG program (see figure 9.6).[27]

Overall, 51 percent of retirees would be unable to finance a minimum pension and would not be eligible for the MPG program under the FDC scheme.[28] Under the NDC reform, the proportion would be only slightly higher (52 percent). The main difference arises between the other groups of individuals: under the FDC reform, 39 percent of all retirees would be able to self-finance a minimum pension and the remaining 10 percent would require the state MPG program in order to reach that level, whereas with the NDC reform, accumulated balances would be smaller, and a larger fraction of retirees (14 percent) would require a top-up from the state.

To interpret these results, we must keep in mind that no behavioral changes were assumed, so that MPG eligibility (given by the number of contributions) would be the same in both cases. In other words, differences only originate in the different rates of returns of the systems and the resulting balances. In this case, notional returns for the past have been generally smaller than financial returns, and the accumulated balances are therefore also smaller. Yet this difference in rates of return seems to mostly affect individuals who fulfilled the 20-year requirement, causing some of them to fall below the minimum pension threshold.

To take a closer look at the effect on the income distribution, we calculate average pensions by quintile of the pension distribution, for both types of reform (see figure 9.7). The main conclusion is that the difference in outcomes between the two types of reform is more important in the higher range of the pension distribution, especially for the cohorts retiring in the intermediate periods, between 2006 and 2015. This phenomenon could be explained by the timing of the highest financial returns, which were strongly concentrated in the first 15 years, with a number of periods having rates over 20 percent, and by the fact that we assume, for both the FDC and NDC schemes, a constant 4 percent rate for contributions after 2007. In addition, low-income workers have contribution densities that are shorter and tend to be concentrated later in life and are therefore less affected by differences between the rates of return on contributions between the FDC and NDC systems.

COMPARISONS OF FISCAL COSTS

As discussed above, in our setting, differences in the fiscal impact of the two types of reform stem from two elements: (a) differences in the costs of the MPG program, originating in the higher past returns generated by the FDC regime, and (b) differences in the value of government transfers to cover the deficit of the old system, given that the initial fiscal surplus generated by the NDC regime can be used to cover this deficit, at least in part.

Regarding the first component, our prospective simulations show that the lower returns earned by contributions to the NDC scheme translate into higher MPG costs. Over the long term, minimum pensions would cost 44 percent more under the NDC than under the FDC reform (see figure 9.8). The magnitude of the MPG cost under both reforms, however, is relatively small compared with the other components of fiscal cost. As explained above, only a few individuals would be eligible for the state guarantee, and the cost associated with these individuals is relatively low because the state is responsible only

FIGURE 9.6 **Coverage of the minimum pension guarantee over time under FDC and NDC reforms, Chile**

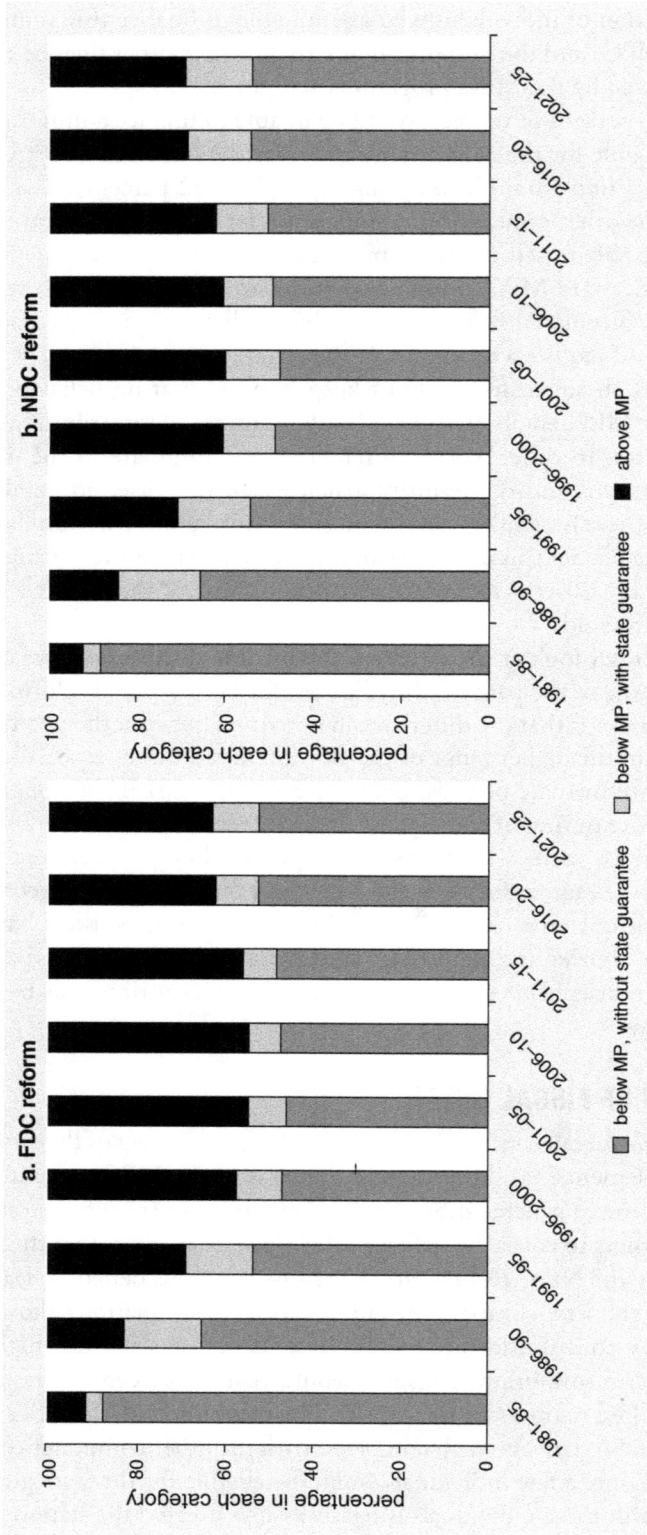

SOURCE: Authors' calculations based on the HPA dataset.

NOTE: FDC = financial defined contribution; HPA = affiliates' pension histories (*historias previsionales administrativas*); MP = minimum pension; NDC = nonfinancial defined contribution.

FIGURE 9.7 **Average self-financed pensions, by quintile, under the FDC and NDC reforms, Chile, 1981–2025**
2008 U.S. dollars

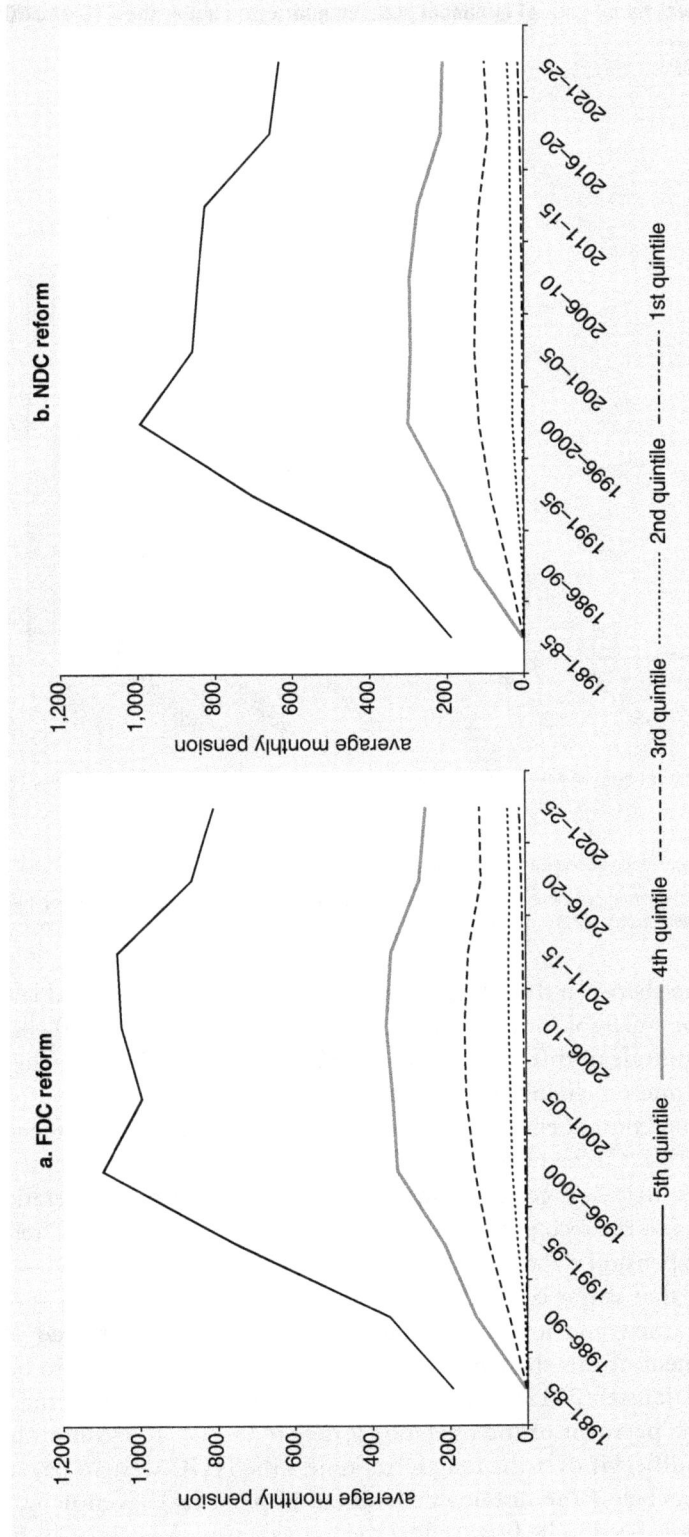

SOURCE: Authors' calculations based on the HPA dataset.

NOTE: FDC = financial defined contribution; HPA = affiliates' pension histories (*historias previsionales administrativas*); NDC = nonfinancial defined contribution.

FIGURE 9.8 **Annual fiscal cost of minimum pension guarantee under the FDC and NDC reforms, Chile, 1981–2025**
percentage of GDP

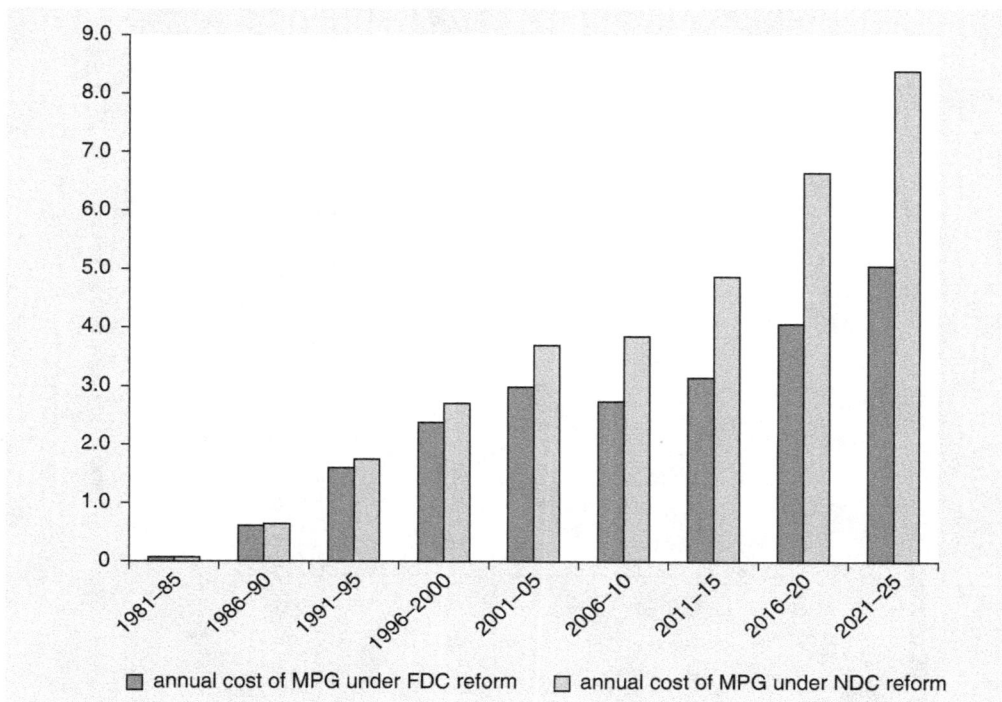

SOURCE: Authors' calculations based on the HPA dataset.

NOTE: FDC = financial defined contribution; GDP = gross domestic product; HPA = affiliates' pension histories (*historias previsionales administrativas*); MPG = minimum pension guarantee; NDC = nonfinancial defined contribution.

for the difference between the self-financed pension and the guaranteed level. This difference tends to be small for individuals who fulfill the requirement of 20 years of contributions. The magnitude of this effect could be different in other contexts, depending on the guarantee level and on eligibility requirements.

The second component of the fiscal difference between the two regimes arises from the fact that the NDC scheme remains PAYG. The FDC reform makes most of the implicit pension debt explicit, and general revenues need to cover both the operational deficits of the old system and the recognition bonds that mature. Under an NDC reform, only part of the implicit pension debt needs to be financed by general revenues—the liability of the old system that is not covered by financial and PAYG assets. But the NDC reform also moves to a new and lower contribution rate (10 percent, instead of 23 percent), and the repayment of this share of the implicit pension debt also has to be financed (see Holzmann and Jousten 2012). The new NDC scheme creates transitional surpluses that help finance the payment of the operational deficit and the recognition bonds, but this surplus is not sufficient over the long term, unless the NDC were to pay a rate of return on contributions below the sustainable level (an implicit tax). Eventually, the rest of the NDC legacy costs need to be financed by the budget, as in the case of an FDC reform.

In our simulations, figure 9.9 shows the annual contributions paid into the NDC scheme and the annual pensions paid to NDC participants, excluding the portion financed by the recognition bonds paid to individuals who switched to the new system. During the first 45 years, the flow of contributions exceeds the flow of new obligations acquired by the NDC scheme; the government borrows this surplus to finance part of the operational deficit of the INP. In the long run (and assuming that the selected wage growth is a good proxy for the sustainable notional interest rate), the surplus would disappear, and no deficit should emerge that is not covered by the repayments that the government needs to make to finance the unfunded liabilities of the old scheme. It is important to note that if the government only repaid recognition bonds when the NDC system generated a deficit, the surplus of the NDC system would be smaller (and could even be zero in some cases), but the fiscal costs to the government would also be lower.

To construct the evolution of total government expenditures on pensions, we also need the transition costs generated from the commitments made to individuals who had contributed to the previous defined benefit scheme. These commitments take the form of (a) recognition bonds to be paid to individuals who switched to the new system, whether

FIGURE 9.9 **Fiscal surplus of the NDC regime, Chile, 1981–2025**
percentage of GDP

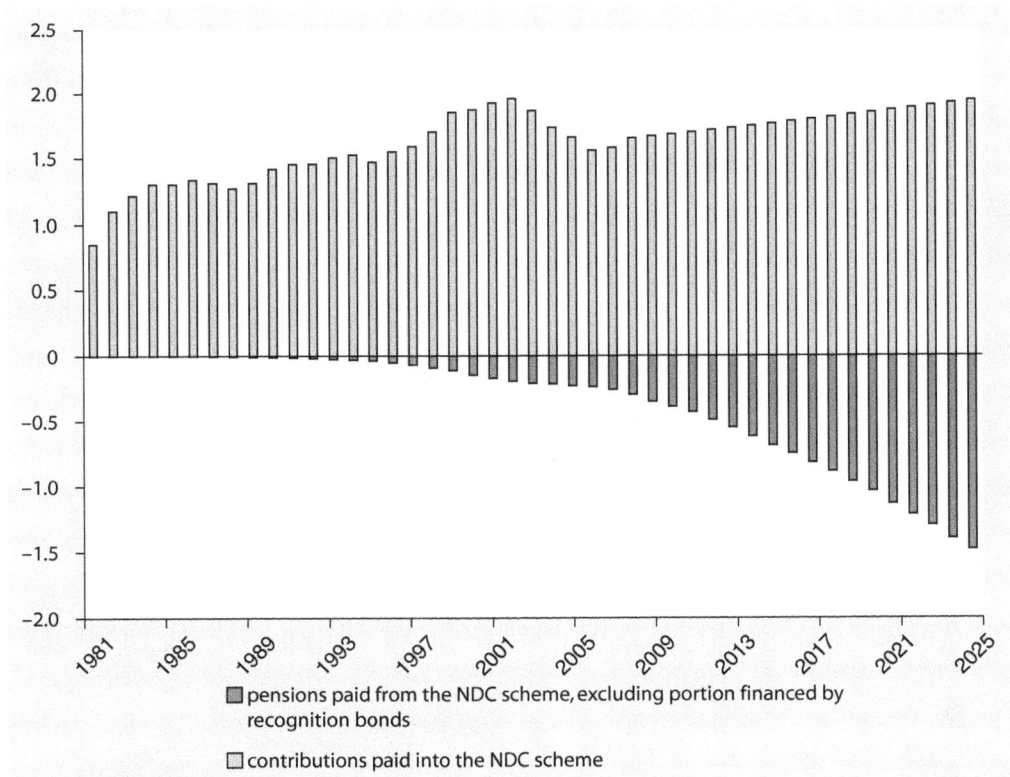

- pensions paid from the NDC scheme, excluding portion financed by recognition bonds
- contributions paid into the NDC scheme

SOURCE: Authors' calculations based on the HPA dataset.

NOTE: GDP = gross domestic product; HPA = affiliates' pension histories (*historias previsionales administrativas*); NDC = nonfinancial defined contribution.

the FDC or the NDC, and (b) the operational deficit of the INP, originating in the difference between the contributions paid by workers who chose to stay in the previous scheme and the pensions paid from this program.

Based on a study by Arenas de Mesa, Llanes, and Miranda Bravo (2005), ECLAC (2006) presents projections to 2010 for the various components of Chilean fiscal expenditures. Because we are particularly interested in the level and timing of government transfers under both types of reform, we extend the projections of the transition costs to the entire period. To this end, we employ current aggregate data on contributors and pensioners from the INP.[29] Using recognition bonds data from the HPA sample, we also estimate the cost paid each year on this item throughout the projection horizon (figure 9.10).

We see that because large numbers of participants change schemes early in the reform, the operational deficit of the old system increases rapidly at first, reflecting the drop in revenues from contributions. Then, as the number of pensions paid declines, the deficit of the old system falls over time. The cost associated with recognition bonds, by contrast, picks up slowly. This is because these obligations are paid when individuals reach legal retirement age and only begin to decline as the number of active contributors who participated in the previous scheme diminishes.

FIGURE 9.10 **Projected fiscal cost from INP operational deficit and recognition bonds, Chile, 1981–2025**
percentage of GDP

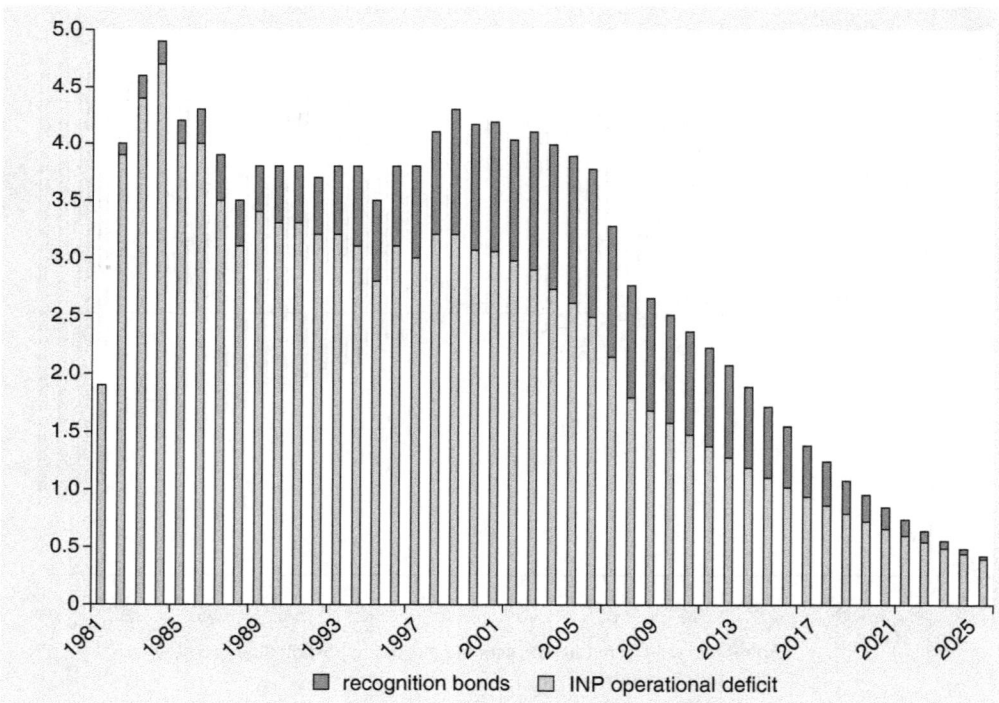

SOURCE: For the 1981–2006 period, ECLAC (2006); for the 2007–25 period, authors' calculations based on INP statistics on current contributors and pensioners and HPA data on recognition bonds.

NOTE: GDP = gross domestic product; HPA = affiliates' pension histories (*historias previsionales administrativas*); INP = Instituto de Normalización Previsional.

Finally, we are able to compute the total fiscal expenditure under both reforms. The net present value (for the first 45 years) of the fiscal cost under the FDC reform represents 133.7 percent of initial GDP, compared with 78.1 percent under the NDC reform.[30] As expected, there is a significant difference in the level and timing of the fiscal impacts of the FDC and NDC reforms. The NDC scheme implies lower fiscal pressures from the pension system during the entire 45-year period (the average difference is 1.24 percent of GDP between 1981 and 2025), but the difference is reduced over time (see figure 9.11).

Table 9.1 presents the net present value, for the first 45 years, of the various components of fiscal expenditure under a number of different scenarios. Notice that in all scenarios, the transition cost components (INP operational deficit and recognition bonds) are kept constant. The first row corresponds to the FDC reform, which implies not only a lower fiscal cost associated with the minimum pension guarantee (MPG) but also the highest fiscal cost in net present value. The reason for this outcome is that the transition cost is paid entirely by the state during the first few years, whereas under the NDC scenarios, the surplus generated by the NDC scheme helps finance the initial transition cost.

The second row corresponds to the base NDC case described in the earlier sections, under which the notional interest rate is set equal to the growth rate of the wage bill, which is usually lower than the financial interest rate borne by the FDC scheme. For this

FIGURE 9.11 **Total fiscal expenditures under the FDC and NDC reforms, Chile, 1981–2025**
percentage of GDP

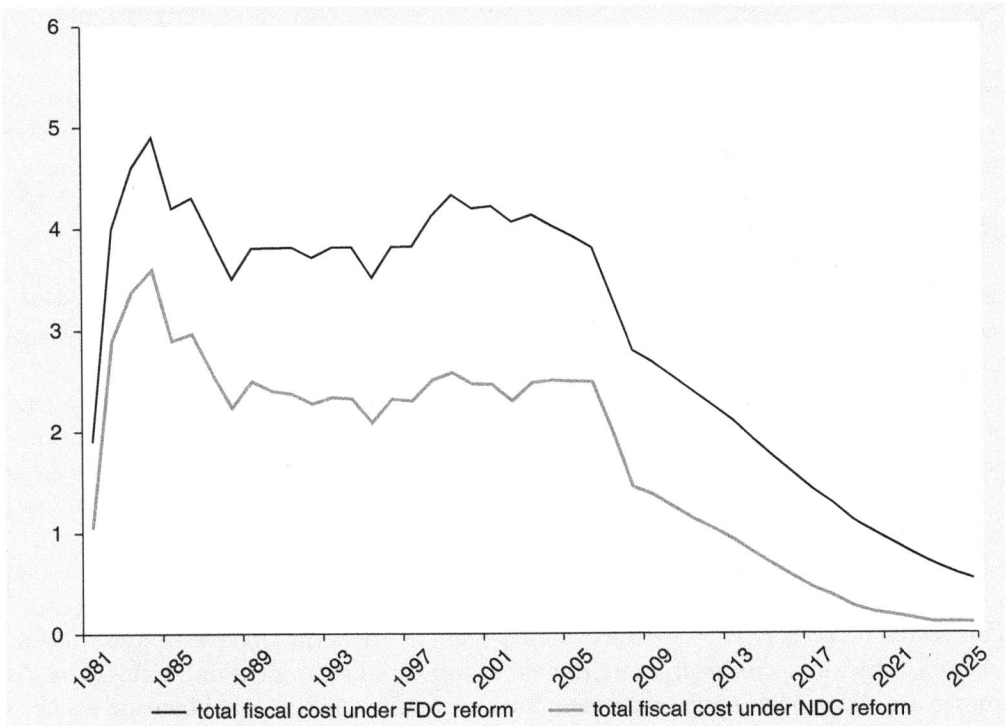

SOURCE: Authors based on results of the simulations.

NOTE: FDC = financial defined contribution; GDP = gross domestic product; NDC = nonfinancial defined contribution.

TABLE 9.1 **Net present value of selected components of fiscal expenditure under alternative scenarios, Chile**
percentage of 1980 GDP

Scenario	INP operational deficit	Recognition bonds	Minimum pension guarantee	NDC surplus	Total fiscal expenditure
FDC reform	104.87	27.73	1.13	0.00	133.73
NDC base scenario: notional rate = base wage growth	104.87	27.73	1.62	56.17	78.06
NDC scenario 1: notional rate = 1.5%	104.87	27.73	2.43	62.98	72.06
NDC scenario 2: notional rate = 3.0%	104.87	27.73	2.08	60.64	74.05
NDC scenario 3: notional rate = 4.5%	104.87	27.73	1.73	57.53	76.81
NDC scenario 4: notional rate = base wage growth; 10.5% contribution rate	104.87	27.73	1.55	58.98	75.18
NDC scenario 5: notional rate = base wage growth; unisex mortality tables	104.87	27.73	1.70	56.86	77.44

SOURCE: Authors based on results of the simulations.

NOTE: FDC = financial defined contribution; GDP = gross domestic product; INP = Instituto de Normalización Previsional; NDC = nonfinancial defined contribution.

reason, pensions are lower, implying that a higher percentage of the population qualifies for the MPG, thus generating a higher fiscal cost. The fact that workers keep contributing to the common pool from which pensions are paid produces an important fiscal surplus during the whole period, equivalent to 56.2 percent of 1980 GDP.[31] Overall, the NDC reform implies a 42 percent lower fiscal cost than the FDC reform.

Scenarios 1, 2, and 3 were constructed using a fixed annual notional rate, set at 1.5, 3.0, and 4.5 percent, respectively. With the lower notional rate, NDC pensions are lower, which translates into not only a higher MPG cost but also a much higher NDC surplus. The fixed 4.5 percent interest rate yields results very similar to those of the NDC base scenario.

Scenario 4 is the same as the base NDC scenario, but we assume that because operational costs are usually lower under a centralized PAYG scheme than under the FDC competitive system, the contribution rate could be set at 10.5 percent of covered wages instead of the actual 10.0 percent. This higher contribution rate translates into higher pensions, lower MPG costs, and a higher NDC surplus.

Finally, pensions under scenario 5 were calculated using unisex mortality tables instead of the gender-differentiated tables that are currently in use in the FDC program.[32] This scenario was suggested by the experience of countries that have introduced NDC schemes, which tend to incorporate the use of unisex tables in pension calculations. As women are likely to live longer than men, the use of unisex tables should increase women's pensions and reduce men's. The results suggest that the net effect is an increase in the fiscal cost of the MPG (relative to the base scenario) and an increase in the surplus of the NDC.

The explanation behind these results is that there are slightly more men than women in the sample (52.6 percent against 47.4 percent), and the unisex tables were constructed assuming a 50-50 split.

In summary, the NDC reform implies significantly lower fiscal expenditures over a long period of time, which is only partially offset by the increased cost of the MPG program. As explained earlier, this small MPG effect is an effect of the limited coverage of the program. Under a more generous scheme, such as the new solidarity pillar that was introduced in Chile in 2008, the effect of lower pensions on costs related to poverty prevention could be significantly higher.

EXPECTED DISTRIBUTION OF PENSIONS AND FISCAL COSTS AT THE INDIVIDUAL LEVEL

As discussed above, the calculations in the previous section take into account a given realization of the stochastic process driving the dynamics of the rates of return in the two systems. In the past, rates of return on the FDC scheme (i.e., rates of return on financial assets) have generally been above the rates of return of the NDC system, proxied in this chapter by the growth rate of the covered wage bill. Our estimates for scenarios 4 and 5, however, suggest that this does not always have to be the case. The best fit of the data for both rates of return (for the FDC and NDC schemes) involves setting $i = 0$ and $j = k = 1$ in equations (9.4) and (9.5); see also annex C. Depending on the assumptions regarding m (the number of past values of the rates of return that influence current values), the FDC and NDC systems could pay similar rates of return on contributions, assuming that the sustainable rate of return for the NDC system is the wage bill.

When the rate of return on financial assets is assumed to evolve around a constant mean ($m = 0$), which in the estimation converges to the mean observed between 1981 and 2006, or about 0.7 percent per month, the FDC system could pay very high returns on contributions. The annualized average rate of return is close to 9 percent per year, similar to the level observed during the past two decades. However, when the rate of return depends on its past realizations ($m = 3$), which is a model that provides a better fit to the data, the mean converges to a lower level, closer to 5 percent real per year (see figure 9.12).

Simulations of the rates of return on financial assets resulting from the two models are presented in figure 9.13. Clearly, adopting one over the other has very important effects on the distribution of pensions. With the high rate of return, for instance, the average replacement rate for the average worker would be equal to or above 100 percent and for many individuals even higher, as is seen in panel b of figure 9.13. The second model, however, generates a more realistic distribution for the replacement rate which would average 50 percent (see panel a of figure 9.13). In what follows, therefore, we work with the latter.

Using the estimated time-series models, we look at the impact of FDCs and NDCs on the distribution of replacement rates at the individual level and the distribution of the per capita fiscal costs of offering a minimum pension guarantee. In both cases, we report the mean and the variance of the distribution. As a reference, we also look at three other systems. Two are mixed systems in which 70 and 40 percent of the contribution rate, respectively, is allocated to an FDC scheme and the remainder to an NDC plan. The third is a pure NDC system that pays a constant 3 percent real annual rate of return on contributions.[33]

FIGURE 9.12 **Simulated annualized rates of return on financial assets, Chile**
percentage points

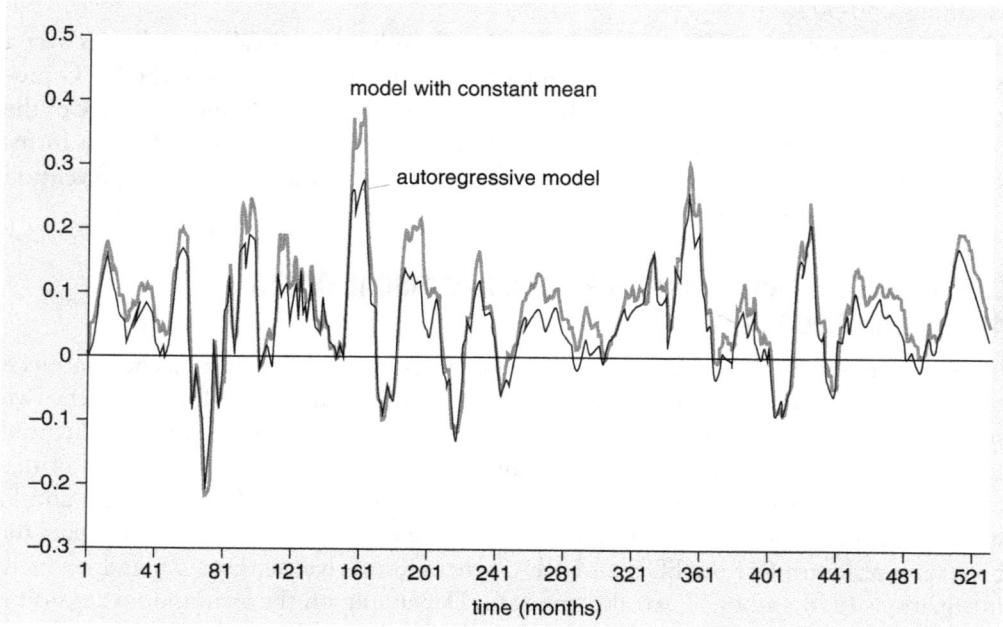

SOURCE: Authors based on results of the simulations.

FIGURE 9.13 **Distribution of replacement rates for the average worker, Chile**
percent

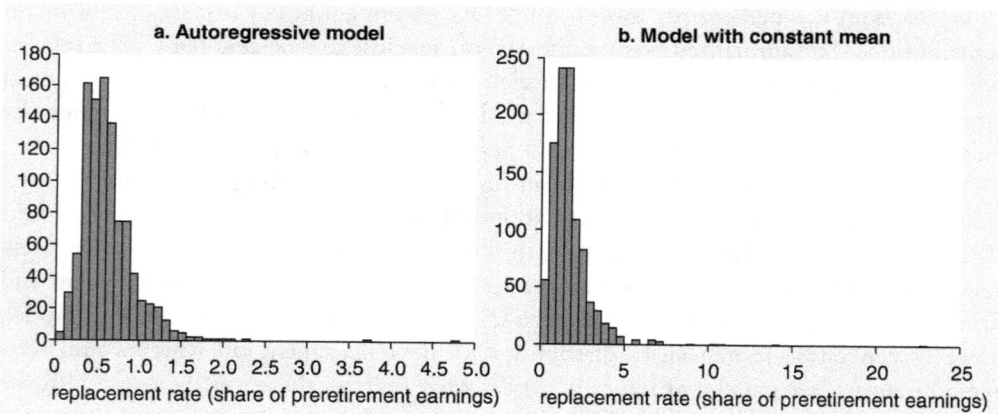

SOURCE: Authors based on results of the simulations.

We work with an average worker and a low-income worker belonging to the 25th percentile of the income distribution. Regarding the minimum pension, we consider four scenarios: no minimum pension, a minimum pension indexed with inflation, a minimum pension growing at 1.5 percent real per year, and a minimum pension growing at 2.5 percent real per year—which could be observed, for instance, if pensions were indexed by the growth rate of the average covered wage.

The results are presented in table 9.2. Within each minimum pension scenario, each row refers to one of the FDC–NDC combinations.

A first observation about the results, which can be seen in the case of a pension system without a minimum pension guarantee, is that the differences in the rates of return paid by the two systems do not generate a large difference in the distribution of

TABLE 9.2 **Impacts of alternative combinations of FDCs and NDCs on the distribution of replacement rates and fiscal costs related to the minimum pension, Chile**

Scenario and FDC share (%)	Workers with average earnings				Workers with low earnings (25th percentile)			
	E(RR)[a]	V(RR)[a]	E(cost)[b]	V(cost)[b]	E(RR)[a]	V(RR)[a]	E(cost)[b]	V(cost)[b]
No minimum pension								
100	0.610	0.145	0.000	0.000	0.082	0.002	0.000	0.000
70	0.627	0.084	0.000	0.000	0.085	0.004	0.000	0.000
40	0.638	0.069	0.000	0.000	0.082	0.001	0.000	0.000
0	0.640	0.048	0.000	0.000	0.084	0.001	0.000	0.000
NDC, 3% rate of return	0.284	0.000			0.043	0.000		
Minimum pension, 0% real growth								
100	0.637	0.130	0.055	0.206	0.457	0.000	5.385	0.399
70	0.637	0.097	0.002	0.002	0.457	0.000	5.363	0.224
40	0.635	0.045	0.000	0.000	0.457	0.000	5.384	0.195
0	0.638	0.054	0.002	0.002	0.457	0.000	5.379	0.186
NDC, 3% rate of return	0.284	0.000	10.795	21.537	0.457	0.000	6.528	0.075
Minimum pension, 1.5% real growth								
100	0.624	0.099	1.200	4.918	0.895	0.000	13.953	0.344
70	0.632	0.070	0.507	1.457	0.895	0.000	13.915	0.308
40	0.632	0.040	0.308	0.834	0.895	0.000	13.920	0.135
0	0.645	0.048	0.383	1.145	0.895	0.000	13.898	0.196
NDC, 3% rate of return	0.374	0.000	15.933	18.213	0.895	0.000	15.031	0.049
Minimum pension, 2.5% real growth								
100	0.915	8.581	15.024	58.978	1.736	0.000	33.436	1.055
70	0.797	0.128	13.919	38.410	1.736	0.000	33.458	0.327
40	0.787	0.074	13.228	32.374	1.736	0.000	33.408	0.161
0	0.771	0.015	13.201	31.614	1.736	0.000	33.404	0.217

SOURCE: Authors based on results of the simulations.

NOTE: E( ) and V( ) give, respectively, the mean and variance of the distributions.
a. RR is the replacement rate (the pension at retirement divided by the last salary).
b. Cost refers to fiscal costs expressed in thousands of U.S. dollars per capita.

replacement rates. For the average worker, the average replacement rate under the FDC system would be 61 percent, whereas in the pure NDC system it would be 64 percent, and with a lower variance. In essence, over the medium term, the average rate of return on financial assets does not differ systematically from the growth rate of the covered wage bill. If the latter is used as the notional interest rate, the NDC system offers similar pension benefits. Benefits would be considerably higher than those paid by a system in which contributions are remunerated at a 3 percent real rate of return. For an average worker, for instance, such a system would generate an average replacement rate of only 28 percent.[34]

We also observe that low-income individuals would end up with very low replacement rates of close to 8 percent. This is mainly explained by shorter contribution densities. Hence, whereas model 1 predicts that the average worker would contribute around 50 percent of the time while active, workers in the 25th percentile would contribute less than 20 percent of the time. As a result, the minimum pension guarantee plays an important role. However, contrary to what would have been observed to date (and particularly during the early times of the Chilean reform), the cost of financing the minimum pension does not have to be higher under the NDC unless the rate of return that the system can finance is in the order of 3 percent per year. This can be seen in the second section of table 9.2, in which the minimum pension is supposed to be indexed with inflation. The average worker would not need access to the minimum pension. The large majority of low-income workers, however, would, and the average cost would be about US$5,300 per capita, regardless of the combination of FDC and NDC.

Clearly, if the minimum pension grows faster than inflation, more individuals, including average earners, would become eligible, and costs would increase sharply. For instance, if the minimum pension grew at 2.5 percent real per year, the cost of the guarantee for an average worker would be close to US$15,000 in the FDC case and about US$13,000 in the NDC case. For the low-income worker these costs would be more than US$33,000.

Conclusion

In this chapter, we have analyzed the relative impacts that the introduction of FDC and NDC schemes can have on fiscal expenditures and the distribution of pensions, using Chile as the reference country. The methodological innovation in the analysis is the use of long-term retrospective simulations that look at what would have happened in Chile if, instead of the original FDC system introduced in 1981, the country had implemented an NDC system. This method offers a large advantage over prospective simulations that depend strongly on nontrivial assumptions about the evolution of the most relevant parameters (growth of GDP and wages, interest rates, and coverage and contribution densities). We are able to use actual contribution histories from individuals who switched to the FDC system, as well as monthly time-series of rates of return on savings and the growth rate of the wage bill, to compare the fiscal impacts of the reforms and the distribution of pensions and replacement rates at the aggregate and individual levels.

The main finding is that transition costs under an FDC system are considerably higher than under an NDC system. In the case of Chile, other things being equal, introducing an NDC system in 1981 instead of an FDC system would have generated fiscal savings, during the first 45 years after the reform, equivalent to 50 percent of initial GDP. The fiscal costs of a hypothetical NDC reform are not linked to the NDC design per se but are specific to Chile: (a) the inherited costs stemming from the financial unsustainability of the old scheme (under the old 23 percent contribution rate), which would have had to be paid in any case, and (b) the reform-induced legacy costs resulting from the move toward a much lower contribution rate of 10 percent.

The lower fiscal costs of an NDC reform are the product of the continued PAYG character of the scheme, in which liabilities can be financed by PAYG assets. As a result, under an NDC scheme (or a sustainable nonfinancial defined benefit, or NDB, scheme), a sustainable implicit pension debt need never be repaid because it can be rolled over from generation to generation. Savings over the short term could have been even larger if, under the NDC scheme, the government had not paid in full the recognition bonds when individuals retired. The unfunded liabilities of the old system do not disappear when there is an NDC reform, and the part not covered by PAYG assets would need to be repaid eventually through general revenues. But an NDC system can allow governments to better spread costs over time.

Clearly, if the rate of return of an FDC scheme is, on average, above the rate of an NDC scheme, the ability of the government to roll over the debt would be based on an implicit tax on plan members. Our analysis suggests, however, that an NDC does not necessarily have to pay a lower rate of return on contributions. Historically, in the case of Chile, rates of return under the FDC system were much higher during the first 20 years of the reform. As a result, pensions under the FDC system were higher than under the NDC system, and thus the minimum pension guarantee cost less. Consequently, an NDC reform would have imposed an implicit tax on the contributors and taxpayers. But depending on the assumptions regarding the stochastic process driving the dynamics of the rate of return paid by the FDC system, expected replacement rates under the NDC are not necessarily lower, and no implicit tax may emerge.

A few caveats are worth noting. The results presented in this chapter are representative of the case of a middle-income country, with an intermediate degree of coverage of dependent workers and in the middle of its demographic transition. The transition cost of the FDC-type reform undertaken by Chile would be much larger in countries with a larger formal sector or an older population but smaller for young, low-income countries with large informal sectors. In addition, the Chilean experience was effective in successfully introducing a market-based system, but the high financial returns were the result of a number of economic and financial market reforms, including privatization of public enterprises, capital market reforms, the development of a housing mortgage market, and infrastructure concession projects that provided a steady supply of long-term investment vehicles.

Finally, the trade-offs presented here are not the only elements to be taken into consideration when planning a reform of this nature.[35] Reliance on financial capitalization can imply higher returns than notional schemes, but with higher volatility. Administrative costs should also be considered; these are likely to be considerably higher in FDC than in

NDC schemes, particularly in the absence of centralized schemes for fund management. In addition, public schemes are often subject to political pressures to increase benefits without the necessary compensation in the form of higher contribution rates. This compromises the financial sustainability of the system and exposes plan members to an additional source of uncertainty.

Annex A. Background to the Chilean Pension Reform

By 1980, Chile's pension system was no different than the systems of many other countries that had based their social protection for old age on compulsory contributions by dependent workers to defined benefit PAYG schemes.[36] After the original Social Security Service was created in 1924, a number of additional schemes were introduced to cover different types of workers, the main ones being the Private Employees' Fund (*Caja de Empleados Particulares*, EMPART) and the Public Employees' and Journalists' Fund (*Caja National de Empleados Públicos y Periodistas*, CANAEMPU). By 1979, there were 32 social security institutions (*cajas de previsión*), giving rise to over 100 different social security schemes, with considerable inequality between the benefits offered by the various institutions providing the service. There were different requirements for receiving a pension (in terms of age, years of service, or gender), different contribution rates, and different benefit structures.

Although the funds were originally created as partial capitalization systems and the reserve funds accumulated excess contributions during the early period, by the end of the 1970s, and despite contribution rates of more than 30 percent of covered wages, benefit payments largely exceeded contributions to the system. Approximately 40 percent of the system's income came from the state, amounting to 3.11 percent of 1980 GDP (SAFP 2003). These strong financial imbalances stemmed from demographic, economic, and administrative factors.

As a result of the demographic transition and generous provisions to pensioners, the ratio of number of contributors to pensioners fell from 10.8 in 1960 to 2.2 in 1980. Despite sizable increases in real wages (128.9 percent between 1965 and 1972) and reductions in unemployment (from 5.4 percent to 3.0 percent), there were substantial increases in average pensions and in a number of other benefits—for family allowances, sickness, industrial accidents, unemployment, and the like. After 1973, during the early years of the military regime, real wages dropped dramatically; unemployment rose, together with social security evasion; and the lack of indexation mechanisms significantly eroded the real level of average pensions. Finally, accumulated reserves had been invested in public and private financial instruments (including loans to participants for a variety of purposes) without explicit inflation adjustments. These factors translated into a gradual reduction in the real value of reserves, and by the end of the 1970s, there was a substantial financial imbalance.

A number of measures were introduced between 1974 and 1979 to improve the fiscal situation. These measures included a fiscal tightening program initiated in 1977; the introduction of uniform indexing rules for all pensions; and uniform retirement ages (60 for women, 65 for men) for all schemes, independent of the number of years contributed (Diamond and Valdés 1993). In 1981, the new system was introduced.

Annex B. Results of the Estimation of the Fixed-Effect Models

TABLE 9B.1 **Contribution equation: Fixed-effects (within) regression**
dependent variable = 1, if individual is contributing; = 0, otherwise

Variable	Coefficient	Standard error	t-statistic	P > |t|	95% confidence interval	
Age in months	0.0041767	0.0000123	339.7200000	0.000	0.0041526	0.0042008
Age >2	−0.0000038	0.0000000	−285.9300000	0.000	−0.0000038	−0.0000037
Female	−0.0020546	0.0000210	−97.7000000	0.000	−0.0020958	−0.0020134
Female*age >2	0.0000023	0.0000000	96.6300000	0.000	0.0000022	0.0000023
Constant	−0.4343761	0.0022074	−196.7800000	0.000	−0.4387024	−0.4300497
σ^u	0.34410044					
σ^e	0.38421923					
ρ	0.44508258					

SOURCE: Authors' estimations.

NOTE:
Number of observations = 5,715,884
Number of groups = 24,172
Observations per group: minimum = 1; average = 236.5; maximum = 324
R^2: within = 0.0394; between = 0.0345; overall = 0.0276
$F_{(4,5691708)}$ = 58,421.81
Prob > F = 0.0000
corr(u_i, Xb) = −0.4631
F-test that all u_i = 0: $F_{(24171, 5691708)}$ = 143.42
Prob > F = 0.0000

TABLE 9B.2 **Log (earnings) equation: Fixed-effects (within) regression**
dependent variable = contributes as in table 9B.1

Variable	Coefficient	Standard error	t-statistic	P > |t|	95% confidence interval	
Age in months	0.0092647	0.0000383	241.9100000	0.000	0.0091897	0.0093398
Age >2	−0.0000059	0.0000000	−144.8600000	0.000	−0.0000059	−0.0000058
Female	−0.0026423	0.0000725	−36.4700000	0.000	−0.0027843	−0.0025003
Female*age >2	0.0000034	0.0000001	43.3500000	0.000	0.0000032	0.0000035
Constant	−0.4084472	0.0074511	−54.8200000	0.000	−0.4230511	−0.3938433
σ^u	0.83107918					
σ^e	0.655581					
ρ	0.61642616					

SOURCE: Authors' estimations.

NOTE:
Number of observations = 2,439,073
Number of groups = 23,663
Observations per group: minimum = 1; average = 103.1; maximum = 321
R^2: within = 0.1431; between = 0.0409; overall = 0.0472
$F_{(4,2415406)}$ = 100,805.01
Corr(u_i, Xb) = −0.4204
Prob > F = 0.0000.
F-test that all u_i = 0: $F_{(23662, 2415406)}$ = 117.20
Prob > F = 0.0000

Annex C. Results of the Estimation of the ARMA-GARCH Models

TABLE 9C.1 **Model growth rate of covered wage bill**

xW	Coefficient	OPG standard error	z	P> |z|	95% confidence interval	
xW						
_cons	0.004759	0.0013145	3.62	0.000	0.0021827	0.0073354
ARMA						
ma						
L1.	0.4208174	0.0646961	6.50	0.000	0.2940153	0.5476195
L2.	0.3254827	0.0656815	4.96	0.000	0.1967494	0.4542161
L3.	0.2065236	0.0687021	3.01	0.003	0.0718699	0.3411772
GARCH						
arch						
L1.	0.0620752	0.0127976	4.85	0.000	0.0369923	0.0871581
garch						
L1.	0.933307	0.0117302	79.56	0.000	0.9103163	0.9562978
_cons	6.94e-07	8.56e-07	0.81	0.418	−9.85e-07	2.37e-06
Log likelihood	858.4386					
Wald $\chi^2(3)$	49.62					
Prob > χ^2	0.0000					

SOURCE: Authors' estimations.

NOTE: ARMA = autoregressive moving average; GARCH = generalized autoregressive conditional heteroskedasticity; OPG = outer product of gradients.

TABLE 9C.2 **Model A for rate of return on financial assets**

xI	Coefficient	OPG standard error	z	P> |z|	95% confidence interval	
xI						
_cons	0.0072569	0.0010867	6.68	0.000	0.0051269	0.0093868
ARMA						
ma						
L1.	0.3651807	0.0647395	5.64	0.000	0.2382936	0.4920678
L2.	0.1364818	0.065762	2.08	0.038	0.0075906	0.2653731
L3.	0.0841355	0.0695468	1,21	0.226	−0.0521738	0.2204448

(continued next page)

TABLE 9C.2 **Model A for rate of return on financial assets (continued)**

xl	Coefficient	OPG standard error	z	P > |z|	95% confidence interval	
GARCH						
arch						
L1.	0.2190412	0.0605914	3.62	0.000	0.1002842	0.3377982
garch						
L1.	0.7753848	0.0560713	13.83	0.000	0.6654871	0.8852825
_cons	7.31e-06	4.18e-06	1.75	0.080	−8.72e-07	0.0000155
Log likelihood	888.1482					
Wald $\chi^2(3)$	32.08					
Prob > χ^2	0.0000					

SOURCE: Authors' estimations.

NOTE: ARMA = autoregressive moving average; GARCH = generalized autoregressive conditional heteroskedasticity; OPG = outer product of gradients.

FIGURE 9C.1 **Observed and predicted growth rate of the rate of return on financial assets**
percent

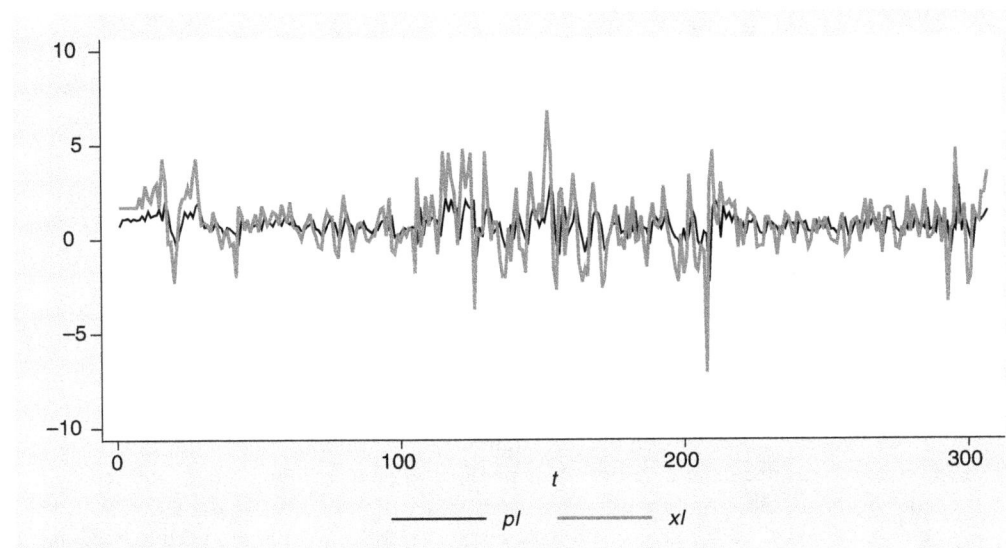

SOURCE: Authors' estimations.

NOTE: t = time; pl = predicted observations; xl = observed.

FIGURE 9C.2 **Observed and predicted growth rate of the covered wage bill**
percent

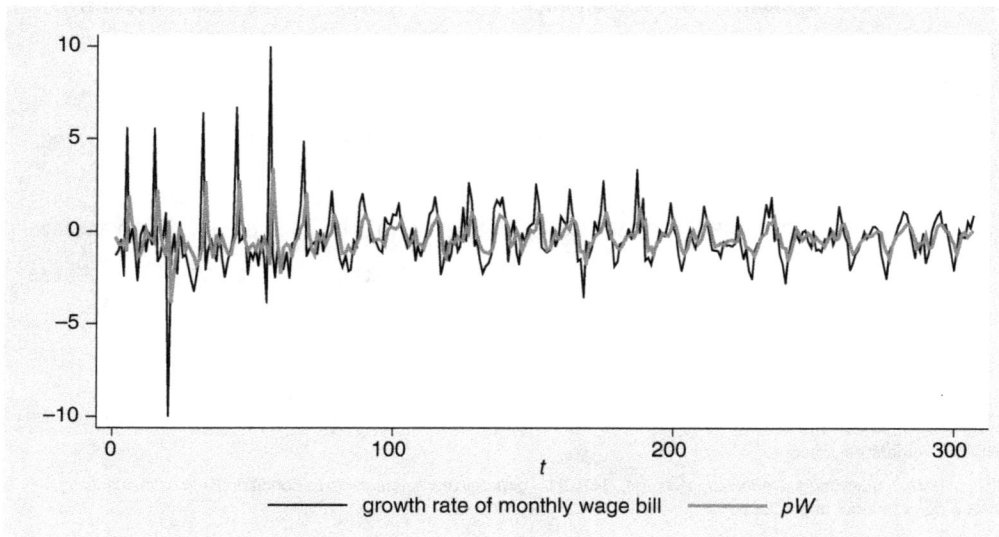

SOURCE: Authors' estimations.

NOTE: Values are as follows: t = time; pW = predicted wage growth.

Notes

1. For a discussion of the differences between contributions, PAYG systems, and hidden assets and the conditions under which they coincide, see Vidal-Meliá and Boado-Penas (2010); Boado-Penas and Vidal-Meliá (2012).

2. Transition costs appear to the extent that contributions are redirected from the PAYG to the FDC scheme. If the FDC scheme is introduced on top of the previous plan, without changing the contribution rate to the defined benefit scheme, there is no associated transition cost.

3. Dimson, Marsh, and Staunton (2002) report that, for the period 1900–2000, the average real return on equity for 16 developed countries was 5.1 percent, whereas Maddison (2003) suggests that the equivalent growth rate of real GDP per capita was 2.0 percent. Risk considerations are taken into account in Dutta, Kapur, and Orszag (2000); Matsen and Thøgersen (2004); and De Menil, Murten, and Sheshinski (2006), which tend to suggest that the optimal combination of funded and unfunded systems is not at either of the two extremes. Knell (2008) incorporates the effect of preferences for relative consumption (with respect to a reference group), giving further support for the inclusion of an unfunded component in the optimal pension mix.

4. In this chapter, we concentrate on the risk originating from the variability of the rates of return and on how this affects the distribution of pensions. The latter outcome is captured by the variance of the distribution of replacement rates under both systems (and a series of alternative combinations of both). There are other sources of risk that are not modeled here. Some of these affect both schemes in a similar way (e.g., economic risks affect the likelihood of making contributions), and some have differential impacts on the two systems. For example, under an FDC scheme, the government can influence, through regulation, the type of instruments eligible for investment by fund managers or could even choose to reverse the FDC reform. Under an NDC scheme, the government could directly influence the notional rate of return or could refuse to disburse the promised benefits in times of fiscal stress.

5. The systems for the armed forces (army, navy, air force, and police) were not included in this reform and are still in place.

6. As of May 2011, the administrative fee is equivalent to approximately 1.49 percent of covered wages, and the DSI premium corresponds to an additional 1.49 percent, amounting to a total contribution rate equivalent to 12.98 percent of covered wages.

7. The SP was formerly known as the Superintendency of Pension Fund Administrators (*Superintendencia de Administradora de Fondos de Pensiones*).

8. AFPs are currently allowed to invest the funds in fixed and variable income instruments, both in Chile and abroad. Starting in 2002, they have been required to offer at least four different funds (with an optional fifth possibility), which are differentiated by the proportion of the assets that are allowed to be invested in variable income instruments (multifunds). Some of the investment regulations were modified by the 2008 reform (see Rofman, Fajnzylber, and Herrera 2008); only the main quantitative limits were retained in the law, while the more detailed investment regime was left for secondary regulation.

9. In 1980, global contribution rates were 33.20, 41.04, and 32.50 percent for the Social Security Service, the Private Employees' Fund (EMPART), and the Public Employees' and Journalists' Fund (CANAEMPU), respectively (SAFP 2003). These rates, however, included benefits for old age, sickness, and industrial accidents, among other contingencies. Official contribution rates for pensions were lower (22.95, 24.91, and 15.75 percent, respectively, for the three cases) but were not representative of the real financing needs because resources were pooled to finance all types of benefits.

10. An alternative procedure might be to credit the recognized balance from the moment of calculation. In this case, the bond would earn the notional rate from the beginning, instead of the exogenous 4 percent rate.

11. In the simulation part, we will assume that everybody chooses to annuitize, using the required gender-differentiated mortality tables.

12. This scheme was modified by the 2008 reform, which replaced the MPG and PASIS programs with the new solidarity pillar. The latter provides a basic solidarity pension for uncovered individuals in the poorest 60 percent of the population and a solidarity complement for individuals in the same group with low pension rights. (See Rofman, Fajnzylber, and Herrera 2008 for further details on this program.) In this chapter, we do not consider the new benefits introduced by this reform because the MPG represents the most common form of protection introduced by countries that have followed a Chilean-style reform.

13. We implicitly assume that individuals do not become disabled or die before retirement age. Survivors' and disability pensions, even if potentially important in terms of cost, require a more complex treatment that is beyond the scope of this chapter, which seeks to compare two systems rather than to achieve a precise projection of the Chilean pension system. Furthermore, mortality, at least, should not play an important role because approximately 97 percent of men and 98 percent of women age 20 will reach age 65, according to demographic mortality tables by gender, age group, and marital status from the Instituto Nacional de Estadísticas (INE 2006).

14. We use the fiscal expenditure estimations presented in ECLAC (2006), based on a publication by Arenas de Mesa, Llanes, and Miranda Bravo (2005).

15. The growth rate of the wage bill is a commonly used proxy that may not be fully sustainable in the long run. Poland, for instance, adopted this type of rule for the notional rate of return. In "Results," we perform sensitivity analyses for a range of alternative notional rates of return.

16. Under the AFP system, individuals can start withdrawing funds at any time after the legal retirement age, or, if they have accumulated sufficient funds to finance a reasonable pension

and a reasonable replacement rate, they can retire earlier. In practice, a large fraction of individuals retire at the legal retirement age, and for this study, we assume that all individuals do so. This simplifying assumption should not affect the main results here because (a) early retirement would affect both the FDC and the NDC schemes in a similar way (as pensions are actuarially calculated) and the relation between them would be maintained, and (b) the fiscal cost should not be affected because recognition bonds are paid at the legal retirement age.

17. Figure 9.1 was constructed using the 24,000 individuals included in the sample and applying expansion factors that were developed by the Chilean Pensions Supervisor. It assumes that all individuals reach the legal retirement age and retire at that point. In practice, some of these individuals may have died prior to the legal retirement age, and some of them may have retired before or after the legal retirement age.

18. The choice of a linear model allows us to estimate the fixed effect for each individual and to use it to predict their future contributions. This is particularly important because in this case, given the administrative nature of the data, we do not have measures of education or ability.

19. Equation (9.2) represents a slight simplification of the actual calculation because, during some periods, AFPs were allowed to charge additional fees that were withdrawn directly from the balance in the account. These charges were historically low, and not all APFs actually applied them. They were eliminated during the 2008 reform.

20. In every period, the rate of return is constructed as the monthly weighted average return of the system, where the weights are given by the funds administered by each AFP and by each type of fund. (After 2002, each AFP started offering five different funds.)

21. The historical annual rate of return for the system between 1981 and 2007 was 10.1 percent. During the same period, the real wage bill experienced an average 4.9 percent growth rate per year. Both employment and wage data were obtained from the INE.

22. By assuming the same rate of return for the FDC and NDC schemes in nonobserved periods, we avoid having the results being determined by explicit differences in return assumptions. In "Results," as a sensitivity analysis, we make alternative assumptions about the notional rate of return.

23. A potential difference between the FDC and the counterfactual NDC scheme is the cost associated with commissions for annuity intermediation. These commissions reached a maximum at the end of 1999, representing 6 percent of balances (Reyes and Stewart 2008). Since then, additional regulations have reduced the commissions drastically, to an effective maximum of 2.5 percent. Under an NDC scheme, annuities are implicitly provided by the state, arguably at a lower intermediation cost. These differences are implicitly captured in the sensitivity analysis, in which alternative rates for the NDC scheme are used.

24. The fiscal burden stemming from the armed forces pension schemes (which were not reformed in 1980) are not included in this study, as it should be the same under either reformed system. It is important to note that the projections do not necessarily apply to the system currently in place, which was reformed in 2008, when the MPG and assistance pension programs were replaced with a new solidarity pillar. This development is not included here.

25. The guaranteed levels are currently set at US$209 for individuals between ages 65 and 70, US$228 for individuals between ages 70 and 75, and US$244 for qualifying workers over age 75.

26. A deficit has to appear eventually unless the rate of return in the NDC is set "low enough." But in that case, plan members would be implicitly taxed to cover the liabilities of the old system.

27. In the calculations, we use the minimum pension amount that was in effect in 2007; it is equivalent to approximately 25 percent of the average covered wage of participants in the system, as of December 2007.

28. This result is similar to that of Berstein, Larrain, and Pino (2006). This was one of the main elements of the diagnostic presented to the Reform Committee created by President Michelle Bachelet in March 2006. Ultimately, the outcome was the introduction, in July 2008, of a new solidarity pillar that will cover all individuals above age 65 in the bottom three quartiles. See Rofman, Fajnzylber, and Herrera (2008) for a description of this reform and the diagnostic that led to it.

29. We draw on the INP's annual summary of pensioners (average pension) and contributors (average earnings) by age and gender. We assume that current contributors continue to participate in the system until they reach the legal retirement age, at which point they retire and begin receiving 70 percent of their last income (with a floor set at today's minimum pension) until they die. Using current mortality tables, pension expenditure is projected for current and future pensioners. The 70 percent replacement rate is the maximum replacement rate under the main programs, so these estimates should be considered an upper bound on future operational deficits.

30. The net present value calculations are made by simply adding up the annual ratios of deficit to GDP. This is equivalent to the sum of discounted expenditure (using the GDP growth rates as discount rates), divided by the initial GDP. The magnitude using the same discount rate assumption is broadly in line with estimates based on Schmidt-Hebbel (1995) that arrive at 126 percent of GDP (see Holzmann 1999).

31. Under the FDC scheme, the equivalent of the NDC surplus corresponds to the rapid accumulation of assets owned by participants in the system, which are invested in financial instruments by the pension fund managers. As of December 2009, these funds were equivalent to 64 percent of 2009 GDP.

32. More precisely, pensions were calculated using the current tables for the sex of each individual in the sample and using the opposite sex. Both pensions were then averaged using the inverses of the alternative pensions: unisex pension = $1/(0.5/\text{pension\_man} + 0.5/\text{pension\_woman})$. This is equivalent to constructing mortality tables by averaging mortalities using a 50-50 proportion between men and women.

33. The 3 percent real annual rate of return is an arbitrary reference considered to be a lower bound of the long-term growth rate of the economy.

34. Clearly, the growth rate of the wage bill is not necessarily sustainable (see Robalino and Bodor 2009). A more robust proxy for the sustainable rate could be the growth rate of the average covered wage, which tends to be lower and would therefore generate lower pensions.

35. See Holzmann and Hinz (2005, 73–140) for a detailed discussion of pension reform options and enabling conditions.

36. For a detailed description of the old system, see SAFP (2003, chap. 2).

References

Arenas de Mesa, Alberto, Maria Claudia Llanes, and Fidel Miranda Bravo. 2005. "Protección social efectiva, calidad de la cobertura y efectos distributivos del sistema de pensiones en Chile." Comisión Económica para América Latina y el Caribe (CEPAL), Santiago de Chile.

Berstein, Solange, Guillermo Larrain, and Francisco Pino. 2006. "Chilean Pension Reform: Coverage Facts and Policy Alternatives." *Economia* 6 (2): 227–79.

Boado-Penas, María del Carmen, and Carlos Vidal-Meliá. 2012. "The Actuarial Balance of the PAYG Pension System: The Swedish NDC Model versus the U.S. DB Model." In *Gender, Politics, and Financial Stability*, chap. 23, vol. 2 of *Nonfinancial Defined Contribution Pension Schemes in a Changing Pension World*, ed. Robert Holzmann, Edward Palmer, and David A. Robalino. Washington, DC: World Bank and Swedish Social Insurance Agency.

De Menil, Georges, Fabrice Murten, and Eytan Sheshinski. 2006, "Planning for the Optimal Mix of PAYGO Tax and Funded Savings." *Journal of Pension Economics and Finance* 5 (1, March): 1–25.

Diamond, Peter, and Salvador Valdés. 1993. "Social Security Reforms in Chile." Documento de Trabajo 161, Instituto de Economía, Pontificia Universidad Católica de Chile. http://www.economia.puc.cl/docs/dt_161.pdf.

Dimson, Elroy, Paul Marsh, and Mike Staunton. 2002. *Triumph of the Optimists: 101 Years of Global Investment Returns*. Princeton, NJ: Princeton University Press.

Dutta, Jayasri, Sandeep Kapur, and J. Michael Orszag. 2000. "A Portfolio Approach to the Optimal Funding of Pensions." *Economics Letters* 69 (2, November): 201–6.

ECLAC (Economic Commission for Latin America and the Caribbean). 2006. "Shaping the Future of Social Protection: Access, Financing and Solidarity." Thirty-First Session of ECLAC, Montevideo, Uruguay.

Holzmann, Robert. 1997. "Pension Reform, Financial Market Development, and Economic Growth: Preliminary Evidence from Chile." *IMF Staff Papers* 44 (2, June): 149–78.

———. 1999. "On the Economic Benefits and Fiscal Requirements of Moving from Unfunded to Funded Pensions." In *The Welfare State in Europe: Challenges and Reforms*, ed. Marco Buti, Daniele Franco, and Lucio R. Pench, 139–96. Cheltenham, U.K.: Edward Elgar.

Holzmann, Robert, and Richard Hinz, eds. 2005. *Old Age Income Support in the 21st Century: An International Perspective on Pension Systems and Reform*. Washington, DC: World Bank.

Holzmann, Robert, and Alain Jousten. 2012. "Addressing the Legacy Costs in an NDC Reform: Conceptualization, Measurement, Financing." In *Gender, Politics, and Financial Stability*, chap. 18, vol. 2 of *Nonfinancial Defined Contribution Pension Schemes in a Changing Pension World*, ed. Robert Holzmann, Edward Palmer, and David A. Robalino. Washington, DC: World Bank and Swedish Social Insurance Agency.

Holzmann, Robert, and Edward Palmer, eds. 2006. *Pension Reform: Issues and Prospects for Non-Financial Defined Contribution (NDC) Schemes*. Washington, DC: World Bank.

INE (Instituto Nacional de Estadísticas). 2006. "Mortalidad. Tablas abreviadas por estado civil y sexo. País 2001–2002." INE, Santiago.

Knell, Markus. 2008. "The Optimal Mix between Funded and Unfunded Pensions Systems When People Care about Relative Consumption." Working Paper 146, Österreichische National-bank (Austrian Central Bank), Vienna.

Maddison, Angus. 2003. "The World Economy: Historical Statistics." Organisation for Economic Co-operation and Development, Development Centre, Paris.

Matsen, Egil, and Øystein Thøgersen. 2004. "Designing Social Security: A Portfolio Choice Approach." *European Economic Review* 48 (4, August): 883–904.

Reyes, Gonzalo, and Fiona Stewart. 2008. "Transparency and Competition in the Choice of Pension Products: The Chilean and UK Experience." Working Paper 7, International Organisation of Pension Supervisors, Geneva.

Robalino, David A., and András Bodor. 2009. "On the Financial Sustainability of Earnings-Related Pension Schemes with Pay-as-You-Go Financing and the Role of Government-Indexed Bonds." *Journal of Pension Economics and Finance* 8 (2): 153–87.

Rofman, Rafael, Eduardo Fajnzylber, and German Herrera. 2008. "Reforming the Pension Reforms: The Recent Initiatives and Actions on Pensions in Argentina and Chile." Social Protection Discussion Paper 083, World Bank, Washington, DC. http://siteresources.worldbank.org/SOCIALPROTECTION/Resources/SP-Discussion-papers/Pensions-DP/0831.pdf.

SAFP (Superintendency of Pension Fund Administrators). 2003. "The Chilean Pension System," 4th ed. SAFP, Santiago. http://www.safp.cl/573/article-3523.html.

Schmidt-Hebbel, Klaus. 1995. *Colombia's Pension Reform: Fiscal and Macroeconomic Implications.* World Bank Discussion Paper 314. Washington, DC: World Bank.

———. 2000. "La contribución de la reforma de pensiones al desarrollo económico." In *AFP 18 Años: Logros y Desafíos*, ed. Corporación de Investigación, Estudio y Desarrollo de la Seguridad Social (CIEDESS). Santiago: Asociación de Administradoras de Fondos de Pensiones.

Vidal-Meliá, Carlos, and María del Carmen Boado-Penas. 2010. "Notes on Using the Hidden Asset or Contribution Asset to Compile the Actuarial Balance for Pay-As-You-Go Pension Systems." Working Paper WP-571, Fundación de las Cajas de Ahorros (FUNCAS), Madrid.

World Bank. 2004. "Egypt: Improving the Welfare of Future Generations through Pension Reform." Human Development Department, Middle East and North Africa Region, World Bank, Washington, DC.

———. 2006. "Morocco: Skills Development and Social Protection within an Integrated Strategy for Employment Creation." World Bank, Washington, DC.

———. Forthcoming. "Morocco: Skills, Social Insurance and Employment." Human Development Department, Middle East and North Africa Region, World Bank, Washington, DC.

María del Carmen Boado-Penas and Carlos Vidal-Meliá

In chapter 9 of this volume, Eduardo Fajnzylber and David A. Robalino deal with an issue of great interest not only to researchers on public pensions (public finance economists, social security actuaries) but also to policy makers. The authors investigate what would have happened in Chile if, instead of the original financial defined contribution (FDC) system introduced in 1981, the country had implemented a nonfinancial (notional) defined contribution (NDC) scheme. With this aim in mind, they construct the account balances for the hypothetical NDC scenario, using actual contribution data from a representative sample of affiliates between 1981 and 2006 and projecting the balances for 2007–26, applying a method similar to that of Berstein, Larrain, and Pino (2006).

Pay-as-you-go (PAYG) systems in Latin American countries collapsed for various reasons—serious economic problems, obvious design flaws, a general lack of trust in politicians, the inability of the state to administer the public systems, the low level of coverage, unfair differences among beneficiaries, regressivity in the distribution of income, high administrative costs, and bad management of existing funds (Schulthess 1999). Reforms in some of these Latin American countries partially or completely transformed their pension systems into individual capitalization systems in which individual responsibility and freedom of choice were accorded greater importance. These systems were installed with the goals of consolidating investment markets, reducing the charge on the state, bringing about greater participation by private management and individuals in providing for personal risk, increasing fairness, diversifying the risks associated with pure PAYG systems, and, above all, increasing the clarity and transparency of the system by making it more independent of political factors. Chile pioneered the reforms in 1981 and was perhaps the country that put them into practice in the most drastic way, owing to its own particular political situation.

According to Edwards (1996), in 1980 the Chilean pension system was in crisis. It was paying more in benefits than it was receiving in contributions, and the projected actuarial imbalance was greater than the country's gross domestic product (GDP). The traditional Chilean system was chaotic and vulnerable to political pressures, as Soto (2005) has pointed out. The "system" was nothing more than a collection of more than 100 separate pension regimes. Each regime had its own rules, demanded different levels of contributions, and promised different benefits, tailored to satisfy special interest groups. In some cases, white-collar workers could comfortably retire in their 40s, whereas blue-collar workers had to wait until their 60s to qualify for minimum retirement benefits. The contribution rate reached levels that discouraged participation and compliance. In the

María del Carmen Boado-Penas is a lecturer in economics at the Keele Management School, Keele University, United Kingdom. Carlos Vidal-Meliá is associate professor of social security and actuarial science at Valencia University, Spain, and is an independent consultant-actuary.

·1970s, for example, average contribution rates exceeded 20 percent of taxable wages. ña and Iglesias (2001) describe the system as poorly administered and inefficient.

The main conclusion reached by Fajnzylber and Robalino is that the transition costs ler an FDC system are considerably higher than they would have been if an NDC tem had been implemented. In particular, introducing an NDC system would have produced fiscal savings during the first 45 years after the reform equivalent to 50 percent of the initial GDP.

Our first comment is that the authors should give special attention to the transition costs of two alternatives:

- A shift from a defined benefit PAYG scheme to an FDC scheme, which in principle generates fiscal costs by diverting PAYG contributions to the funding or capitalization system
- A shift from a defined benefit PAYG scheme to an NDC scheme, which in theory does not generate fiscal costs because there is no diversion of contributions. What happens, basically, is a change in the way the benefits—specifically, retirement pensions—are calculated.

The authors should have stressed more strongly the fact that the fiscal cost of the second alternative really emerges because there was an appreciable decrease in the contribution rate when the system was reformed in 1981, as Valdés-Prieto (2006) points out. If the reform had not brought with it this decrease in contributions, the second alternative would not have incurred a fiscal cost deriving from the diversion of contributions. If, instead of introducing the FDC system in 1981, an NDC system had been implemented without reductions in contributions and with additional financing for the redistributive component deriving from minimum pensions and the real increases in benefits, the fiscal cost would have been nil. Indeed, in the proposal by Boado-Penas et al. (2007) that recommended the introduction of an NDC system in Spain, the fiscal impact of the reform was forecast as positive because the income from contributions would have been maintained and the amount of new retirement pensions awarded would have been lower as a result of the effect of actuarial rebalancing under the NDC system.

With regard to the comparison between pension distributions and replacement rates at the aggregate and individual levels, anyone familiar with the Chilean system would know the result beforehand, given that the real returns achieved by the capitalization system have been extremely high. It would be difficult for any notional formula to do it better. The questions are whether the result is the same when the risk involved, or the degree of risk aversion, is taken into account, and whether this extremely high return could reasonably be maintained in the future. According to Vidal-Meliá, Boado-Penas, and Settergren (2010), the Swedish experience shows that during the period 1995–2007, the average rate of return in the notional-type (Inkomstpension) system, measured as the capital-weighted rate of return, was 3.1 percent. The average annual variation in the rate of return, as measured by the standard deviation, was 1.1 percentage points. Since the first payments into the funded pension system in 1995, the average return of this system, after deduction of fund management fees, has been 5.8 percent. The annual variation in this rate of return, as measured by the standard deviation, was 14.3 percentage points. The risk-adjusted return for the Inkomstpension system would be 2.81 percent, but it is barely

0.41 percent for the premium pension system. If the return were measured by methods that took into account the degree of risk aversion, the comparison would still be more favorable for the notional account system.

If we consider the period 1995–2008, the average rates of return in Sweden's notional-type and premium pension systems were 3.1 and –0.8 percent, respectively. The 2008 annual report does not provide information about the annual variation in this rate of return.

As Fajnzylber and Robalino acknowledge, the results reported in chapter 9 depend strongly on nontrivial assumptions about the evolution of the most relevant parameters (growth of GDP and wages, interest rates, and coverage and contribution densities). The authors therefore carried out sensitivity analyses in order to study different scenarios over the long term. What struck us is that the authors assume, as a baseline scenario, a fixed rate of return, set at a level of 4 percent per year, when the historical annual rate for the system between 1981 and 2007 was 10.1 percent. The same rate is used for both schemes in spite of their very different natures. In an FDC scheme, the contributions are indexed in line with the rate of interest in the financial markets, whereas the notional rate for contributions under an NDC scheme is meant to reflect the financial health of the system and, accordingly, is usually linked to some macroeconomic index such as GDP growth.

Finally, in our estimation, what these calculations really show is that the Chilean system has two serious problems. The first problem, which the authors have rightly stressed, concerns coverage and the density of contributions. The authors show that more than 50 percent of contributors will be unable to finance a minimum pension even though, during the first 26 years of operation, the annual rate of return was extremely high in real terms—a feat which will be difficult to maintain in the future. The second is a design problem: with contributions set at 10 percent of taxable salary and a scenario in which longevity continues to increase, it is difficult to see how worthwhile pensions can be achieved. The contribution rate should be higher, or contributions should be paid over a longer period of time, or both.

It is worth mentioning two examples in order to address the problem of the very low contribution rate in Chile. In Sweden, the contribution rate for the retirement contingency is 18.5 percent (16.0 percent plus 2.5 percent). In the base scenario (SSIA 2008, 34), the average pension level for the year when the individual turns age 65 drops from 66 percent for birth cohort 1944 to approximately 53 percent for birth cohort 1990. For Spain— assuming a 15 percent contribution rate for the retirement contingency and following several macroeconomic projections—Boado-Penas, Domínguez-Fabián, and Vidal-Meliá (2007) analyze the impact on the initial amount of retirement pension and the internal rate of return of applying 10 different formulas for the calculation of the retirement pension based on notional accounts. For a retiree age 65, after 50 years of contributions, the average replacement rate as a function of the average wage would be about 62 percent. If, however, the increase in longevity observed over the past 50 years in Spain continues into the next 50 years, and the aim was to preserve the financial equilibrium of the system, the replacement rate should be set at 51 percent of the average wage after 40 years of contributions.

Overall, the chapter attempts to shed some light on the consequences for the Chilean pension system of a hypothetical NDC reform in 1981. Special attention is paid to the fiscal impact and the distribution of the pensions. The authors have put considerable effort into working with a large database and applying a sophisticated methodology to project some of the variables. However, as mentioned above, the results are quite dependent on the assumptions used. We encourage the authors to produce further studies under different and more realistic assumptions or to apply their model to other countries. It would also be interesting to consider different retirement ages (replicating the current retirement age distribution), to model married individuals and study their pension distribution, or to take account of survivorship pensions.

References

Acuña R., Rodrigo, and Augusto Iglesias P. 2001. "Chile's Pension Reform after 20 Years." Social Protection Discussion Paper 0129, World Bank, Washington, DC.

Berstein, Solange, Guillermo Larrain, and Francisco Pino. 2006. "Chilean Pension Reform: Coverage Facts and Policy Alternatives." *Economia* 6 (2): 227–79.

Boado-Penas, María del Carmen, Immaculada Domínguez-Fabián, and Carlos Vidal-Meliá. 2007. "Notional Defined Contribution Accounts (NDCs): Solvency and Risk; Application to the Case of Spain." *International Social Security Review* 60: 105–27.

Boado-Penas, María del Carmen, Immaculada Domínguez-Fabián, Salvador Valdés-Prieto, and Carlos Vidal-Meliá. 2007. "Mejora de la equidad y sostenibilidad financiera del sistema público español de pensiones de jubilación mediante el empleo de cuentas nocionales de aportación definida (NDCs)." Ministerio de Trabajo y Asuntos Sociales, FIPROS (2005-138), Madrid.

Edwards, Sebastian. 1996. "The Chilean Pension Reform: A Pioneering Program." NBER Working Paper 5811, National Bureau of Economic Research, Cambridge, MA.

Schulthess, Walter E. 1999. "América Latina—Una visión de conjunto." In *El futuro de la Seguridad Social: Conferencia de Estocolmo, 29 de junio–1 de julio de 1998*, ed. Federación de Oficinas del Seguro Social. Stockholm: Federación de Oficinas del Seguro Social. http://intranet.oit .org.pe/WDMS/bib/virtual/coleccion_tem/seg_soc/futuro_sesoc%5Baiss%5D.pdf.

Soto, Mauricio. 2005. "Chilean Pension Reform: The Good, the Bad and the In Between." Issue in Brief 31, Center for Retirement Research, Boston College, Newton, MA.

SSIA (Swedish Social Insurance Agency). 2008. *Orange Report: Annual Report of the Swedish Pension System 2007*. Stockholm: SSIA.

Vidal-Meliá, Carlos, María del Carmen Boado-Penas, and Ole Settergren. 2010. "Instruments for Improving the Equity, Transparency and Solvency of Pay-as-You-Go Pension Systems: NDCs, ABs and ABMs." In *Pension Fund Risk Management: Financial and Actuarial Modeling*, ed. Marco Micocci, Greg N. Gregoriou, and Giovanni Batista Masala, chap. 18, 419–72. New York: Chapman & Hall/CRC Finance Series.

Valdés-Prieto, Salvador. 2006. "Política fiscal y gasto en pensiones mínimas y asistenciales." *Estudios Públicos* 103: 43–110.

www.ingramcontent.com/pod-product-compliance
Lightning Source LLC
Chambersburg PA
CBHW082138210326
41599CB00031B/6018